"This book provides a welcome introduction to a memorable Christian statesman who also happened to be a formidable theologian, a pious devotional writer, an ever-active journalist, and an important theoretician concerning Christian life in the world. Those who do not yet know Abraham Kuyper will find Craig Bartholomew a reliable guide, while those who have already encountered this 'flying Dutchman' will be pleased with the range and depth of Bartholomew's insights."

Mark Noll, author of *The Scandal of the Evangelical Mind*

"Abraham Kuyper's life and work merit close attention in our times, and *Contours of the Kuyperian Tradition* is an indispensable guide to this rich tradition and its contemporary relevance. Kuyper's labors ranged far and wide, and it can be easy to get lost in the complexity of this dynamic legacy. This volume provides a valuable introduction to these diverse efforts, clarifying and distilling Kuyper's wisdom for today."

Jordan J. Ballor, senior research fellow, Acton Institute for the Study of Religion & Liberty, general editor of *Abraham Kuyper Collected Works in Public Theology*

"Abraham Kuyper began the neo-Calvinist movement in the Netherlands in the late 1800s as a way to make classic Christianity speak with fresh relevance to the modern world. Now, over a century later, Craig Bartholomew has given us this clear, thorough overview of Kuyper's original insights, their further development, and their relevance in the postmodern world. Both veterans of the movement and those new to it will find here a concise presentation of the distinctive Kuyperian themes—creation, worldview, and sphere sovereignty—as they characteristically unfolded in Christian education, philosophy, and political and cultural engagement. Best of all, Bartholomew lays out where Kuyperians can learn from others—and how they might (and must) recover the spirituality and saturation in Scripture that animated Kuyper in the first place. Agree with Kuyper or not, this is the place to go to learn, in brief, what he said, did, and wrought."

James D. Bratt, author of *Abraham Kuyper: Modern Calvinist, Christian Democrat*

"Craig Bartholomew numbers among the consummate insiders of the Kuyperian tradition, but he has written an accessible guide for the new and curious. Bartholomew presents the distinctive features of neo-Calvinism, such as its emphasis on worldview, sphere sovereignty, and structural pluralism, while also highlighting neglected dimensions such as its spirituality, concern for the poor, and focus on mission. Writing from a South African perspective, Bartholomew also does not shy away from criticizing the tradition when necessary. We've needed a contemporary theological introduction to neo-Calvinism for a long time, and *Contours of the Kuyperian Tradition* will undoubtedly become a standard textbook in this burgeoning field."

Clifford B. Anderson, associate university librarian for research and learning, Vanderbilt University, Nashville, Tennessee

"What do you get when one of the world's most masterful contemporary theologians engages in constructive and critical dialogue with one of history's most powerful and relevant theological traditions? You get Craig Bartholomew's *Contours of the Kuyperian Tradition*. Bartholomew's interaction with Kuyper, Bavinck, Prinsterer, Plantinga, and others is smart, accessible, and relevant to a broad range of interests, including public theology, systematic theology, philosophy, political science, education, and biblical theology. Highly recommended."

Bruce Riley Ashford, provost and professor of theology and culture, Southeastern Baptist Theological Seminary

"Craig Bartholomew's study offers one of the best English-language interactions with Abraham Kuyper and neo-Calvinism that I know of. He transcends the often repeated and stereotyped key slogans and concepts. As he often relies on his personal fresh and independent observations, he addresses the reader with the persuasiveness of the established theologian. He succeeds in really connecting this tradition, which already existed in the nineteenth century, with today's world and problems, proving neo-Calvinism to be still very much alive. Everywhere the reader tastes Bartholomew's lively and appealing enthusiasm for the Kuyperian tradition, which he discovered already some time ago. At the same time, however, his book offers much more than just an overview or summary of that tradition. On the contrary, we receive an independent contemporary engagement with it that does not hesitate to generously use related accents from other traditions. Bartholomew's book illustrates the importance of Kuyper and neo-Calvinism but also offers an important and creative continuation of that tradition."

A. L. Th. de Bruijne, professor of ethics and spirituality, Theological University Kampen

CONTOURS

of the

KUYPERIAN TRADITION

A SYSTEMATIC INTRODUCTION

CRAIG G. BARTHOLOMEW

IVP Academic

An imprint of InterVarsity Press
Downers Grove, Illinois

InterVarsity Press
P.O. Box 1400, Downers Grove, IL 60515-1426
ivpress.com
email@ivpress.com

InterVarsity Press® is the book-publishing division of InterVarsity Christian Fellowship/USA®, a movement of students and faculty active on campus at hundreds of universities, colleges, and schools of nursing in the United States of America, and a member movement of the International Fellowship of Evangelical Students. For information about local and regional activities, visit intervarsity.org.

Cover design: David Fassett
Interior design: Dan van Loon
Images: Red Vineyards at Arles: Red Vineyards at Arles by Vincent van Gogh at Pushkin Museum, Moscow, Russia/
    Bridgeman Images
    graphic globe: © Ani_ka/iStockphoto

ISBN 978-0-8308-5158-4 (print)
ISBN 978-0-8308-9160-3 (digital)

Printed in the United States of America ∞

g green press INITIATIVE *As a member of the Green Press Initiative, InterVarsity Press is committed to protecting the environment and to the responsible use of natural resources. To learn more, visit greenpressinitiative.org.*

Library of Congress Cataloging-in-Publication Data
A catalog record for this book is available from the Library of Congress.

P 25 24 23 22 21 20 19 18 17 16 15 14 13 12 11 10 9 8 7 6 5 4 3 2 1
Y 38 37 36 35 34 33 32 31 30 29 28 27 26 25 24 23 22 21 20 19 18 17

To Gert and Istine Swart,

sculptor and mathematician,

good friends,

and fellow pilgrims on that long

obedience in the same direction.

CONTENTS

PREFACE

John Bolt rightly asserts that "Kuyper cannot be presented dispassionately; his spirit forbids it!"[1] Certainly this book is not a dispassionate presentation of Kuyper's thought. Writing it has given me a unique opportunity to immerse myself in Kuyper himself, and I have emerged wildly passionate about his thought and its profound relevance for today. This is not to suggest that we should absolutize Kuyper—he would be the first to protest against such a move—but it is to argue that it would be greatly to our benefit to retrieve his thought for today.

George Marsden wrote some years ago about the relative triumph of Kuyperianism in North American evangelicalism.[2] While this is true, I suspect that it is often a general view of Kuyper reduced to some of his influential insights.

In this book I aim to introduce readers in some depth to the contours of the Kuyperian tradition and their contemporary relevance. This is not an historical work, though some history is essential if we are to understand Kuyper in his context. The aim is rather to flesh out the great landmarks of his thought and that of his immediate colleagues. As I have worked away at this, I have been struck again and again by the genius of Kuyper, and this book will achieve its goal if readers are pushed to read Kuyper himself.

Richard Mouw commented to me that "this is a Kuyperian moment" in which we are living. This is true in more ways than one. At about the same time

---

[1]John Bolt, *A Free Church, A Holy Nation: Abraham Kuyper's American Public Theology* (Grand Rapids: Eerdmans, 2001), xix.
[2]George Marsden, "The State of Evangelical Christian Scholarship," *Reformed Journal* 37 (1987): 14, speaks of "The triumph—or nearly so—of what may be loosely called Kuyperian presuppositionalism in the evangelical (academic) community."

as this book is published, Lexham Press will be releasing what is close to the complete, major works of Kuyper in English. Acton Institute houses the Kuyper translation project, and I am deeply in debt to them, and to Mel Flikkema in particular, for making available to me via Dropbox translations while they were being done. Although I read Dutch, this made my task immeasurably easier. It also means that if this book excites you about Kuyper and his colleagues, as I hope it will, you have no excuse for not diving into Kuyper himself. *Ad fontes* is what I would strongly recommend!

Brannon Ellis of Lexham said to me that one wonders what Kuyper's influence might have been if he had been English and had published all his vast corpus in English! Of course, we do not know. What is clear to me is that Kuyper's *time has come*. Kuyper lived when the Enlightenment vision was taking hold all around him in Europe and in the Netherlands. We live at a time when that same project is unraveling, and religion is making a major comeback globally. I propose that in our fragile time the Kuyperian tradition holds resources for finding constructive ways forward that can defuse some of the major threats we face, renew the life of the church, and promote human flourishing.

In his remarkable book *The Stillborn God: Religion, Politics, and the Modern West*, Mark Lilla articulates the effect of the Enlightenment with a clarity with which Kuyper would concur:

> By attacking Christian political theology and denying its legitimacy, the new philosophy simultaneously challenged the basic principles on which authority had been justified in most societies in history. That was the decisive break. The ambition of the new philosophy was to develop habits of thinking and talking about politics exclusively in human terms, without appeal to divine revelation or cosmological speculation. The hope was to wean Western societies from all political theology and cross to the other shore. What began as a thought-experiment became an experiment in living that we inherited. Now the long tradition of Christian political theology is forgotten, and with it memory of the age-old quest to bring the whole of human life under God's authority.[3]

Now, however, we are in an unforeseen situation in which "the twilight of the idols has been postponed."[4] During the twentieth and twenty-first centuries,

---

[3]Mark Lilla, *The Stillborn God: Religion, Politics, and the Modern West* (New York: Vintage, 2007, 2008), 5.
[4]Ibid., 3.

religion has made a major comeback, and the West is badly unprepared to cope with such a situation. Groen van Prinsterer, Kuyper's mentor, and Kuyper himself confront us again and again with the choice between "the revolution" (the Enlightenment tradition) and Christ. Comparably, Lilla says in *The Stillborn God,*

> The story reconstructed here should remind us that the actual choice contemporary societies face is not between past and present, or between the West and "the rest." It is between two grand traditions of thought, two ways of envisaging the human condition. We must be clear about those alternatives, choose between them, and live with the consequences of our choice. That *is* the human condition.[5]

Kuyper could hardly have said it better!

Lilla notes that for most moderns, "To think that the West could produce its own political theology, in a thoroughly modern vein, is surprising and unsettling. More unsettling still is the fact that these new political theologians produced original and challenging works not to be dismissed lightly."[6] Kuyper was far more than a political theologian, but politics was central to his thought and life. And he embodied what Lilla refers to. Kuyper clung tenaciously to the heart of the Christian faith, but he was no antimodern. As much as he despised "the revolution," he acknowledged the gifts it brought and the new historical situation it introduced. He was not reactive but proactive in seeking to contextualize the Christian tradition for the new situation in which it found itself. And his work is original and challenging, certainly not to be dismissed lightly.

Doubtless, staunch defenders of the Enlightenment tradition will find Lilla's comments, let alone Kuyper's thought, disturbing. At one level there is little to be done about that. However, Kuyper was also an apologist and sought to show again and again, in all spheres of life, how the Christian tradition offers a better way for all of us in all the dimensions of our lives. He was no theocrat but advocated a genuine pluralism within modern societies in which the state is responsible for creating the conditions for all to be free and to flourish. I often wonder what Kuyper would have thought of John Paul II. One thinks

---

[5]Ibid., 13.
[6]Ibid., 11.

back to John Paul's becoming pope and to his early exhortation to his audience of thousands, indeed millions, to have no fear but to open our hearts wide to Christ. I hear Kuyper nodding "Amen."

It remains to thank IVP Academic for publishing this work. It is a delight to work with them, and in particular I thank my editor David Congdon. Rimmer de Vries first approached me about writing this book and then wonderfully provided funding to carve the time out to write it. I am grateful to Redeemer University College for allowing that time, Keegan Lodder for his work as my research assistant, and to my students for their warm engagement with a first draft of the book. Also to Jennifer Jones, who did sterling work in producing the thorough indexes in the short time available. And finally to the Jesuit Fathers, priests, and nuns of the Pontifical Biblical Institute in Jerusalem, for their gracious hospitality during which time I read the proofs of this book. Harry van Dyke, Ad de Bruijne, and George Harinck read the manuscript closely and helped make it a far better book. Of course, the deficiencies remain my own!

It is a pleasure to dedicate this book to my good friends Istine and Gert Swart. They have been on the Kuyperian journey with me for many years and continue to taste the cost and exhilaration of that journey.

ABBREVIATIONS

AK   James D. Bratt. *Abraham Kuyper: Modern Calvinist, Christian Democrat*. Grand Rapids: Eerdmans, 2013

AK:CR   James D. Bratt, ed. *Abraham Kuyper: A Centennial Reader*. Grand Rapids: Eerdmans, 1998

CD   Karl Barth. *Church Dogmatics*. Edited by G. W. Bromiley and T. F. Torrance. 14 vols. Edinburgh: T&T Clark, 1957–1975

CG   Abraham Kuyper. *Common Grace: God's Gifts for a Fallen World: The Historical Section*. Translated by N. D. Kloosterman and E. M. van der Maas. Bellingham, WA: Lexham Press, 2015

CTJ   *Calvin Theological Journal*

LC   Abraham Kuyper. *Lectures on Calvinism*. Peabody, MA: Hendrickson, 2008

PR   Herman Bavinck. *The Philosophy of Revelation*. Grand Rapids: Baker, 1909

PST   Abraham Kuyper. *Principles of Sacred Theology*. Translated by J. Hendrik de Vries. Grand Rapids: Baker, 1980

RD   Herman Bavinck. *Reformed Dogmatics*. 4 vols. Grand Rapids: Baker Academic, 2008

R&G   Abraham Kuyper. *Rooted and Grounded: The Church as Organism and Institution*. Grand Rapids: Christian's Library Press, 2013

INTRODUCTION

Seeking the Welfare of the City

A DISCIPLE IS A FOLLOWER OF JESUS. This is true of any Christian who has lived or will live. However, discipleship is always lived in particular historical and cultural contexts, and in these contexts particular challenges are faced. When I pastored and then taught at a seminary during racist, apartheid South Africa, I would tell students that if they were preaching the gospel in predominantly white churches they would inevitably need to call for deep repentance from racism. To my students who were preaching in predominantly black churches I suggested that they would need to deal with issues such as hatred and the temptation to resort to violence. Both groups would encounter resistance.

We are always called to follow Christ together amid our particular cultures and historical contexts, and in these contexts to "seek the welfare of the city" (Jer 29:7).[1] George Weigel said of Pope John Paul II that he scouted the future in order to discern how best to direct the church in the present.[2] Of course, we do not know the future, and history is inevitably full of surprises. The future, however, always proceeds from the present and, while we need to follow Christ fully aware that many surprises might lie ahead, we do have a responsibility to become as conscious as we can of the spirits of our age and where they appear to be taking us. We are called and we desire to follow Christ; we can only do that *today*, in our present context and circumstances.

---

[1]"Welfare," translated as "peace and prosperity" by the NIV, is a rich Hebrew word, namely *shalom*. *Shalom* refers to the rich well-being of creation when ordered correctly.

[2]Weigel makes this point in more than one place. Cf. George Weigel, *The End and the Beginning: Pope John Paul II—The Victory of Freedom, The Last Years, The Legacy* (New York: Image, 2010), 195.

John Stott expressed this clearly in his call for *double listening*: disciples need to have one ear to the Bible and one to the culture. In Scripture we hear the authoritative word of God addressed to us, but we need to embody that word, and we can only do so *in our contexts*.[3] Immersion in Scripture is utterly indispensable for discipleship, but so too is cultural analysis. We need to know the challenges of our age so that we can scout *our* age and work out how to embody the gospel together in *our context*.

Of course, our contexts vary. I am particularly aware that the global centers of Christianity have shifted so that the secular West is no longer the center of world Christianity. While we are witnessing a revival of Christianity around the world, including in parts of the West, the new centers of Christianity are located in Asia, Latin America, and Africa. Much of the West is governed by a virulent secular elite, whereas in much of the developing world and in some of the most advanced countries of our day, such as South Korea, the church is alive and thriving.

Thus, it is important to note that we will need to assess the challenges we face in our particular contexts and cultures. At the same time there is truth to what is called *globalization,* in which a Western-style consumer culture is being spread across the globe.[4] In the West it has, however, been common to call the spirit of our age *postmodernism,* the word for the widespread reaction to modernity that gathered force in the West in the latter half of the twentieth century, a century in which the hubris with which the century opened was dealt devastating blow after blow: World War I, the war to end all wars; the rise of Communism; the Great Depression; World War II; the nuclear threat; the ecological threat; and so the list continues. Indeed, it is argued that the twentieth century was the most brutal in history. Intriguingly, it was during the years of relative stability and affluence in the West following World War II that the postmodern reaction set in, ruthlessly questioning the foundations of modernity and its trust in science and reason. Postmodernism has indeed savaged much of the belief structure of modernity, but what the very name *post*modernism conceals is the triumph of modernity economically and technologically

---

[3]John Stott, *The Contemporary Christian: An Urgent Plea for Double Listening* (Leicester, UK: Inter-Varsity Press, 1992).

[4]See Michael W. Goheen and Erin G. Glanville, eds., *The Gospel and Globalization: Exploring the Religious Roots of a Globalized World* (Vancouver: Regent, 2009); Craig G. Bartholomew and Thorsten Moritz, eds., *Christ and Consumerism: A Critical Analysis of the Spirit of the Age* (Carlisle, UK: Paternoster, 2000).

in globalization. Consumer capitalism is quintessentially a modern phenomenon.[5] Postmodernism is largely deconstructive rather than constructive, and useful as its critique of modernity is, the failure to provide alternative, constructive theories has meant that there is no longer any commonly held modern ideology or worldview to restrain the excesses of consumer capitalism. We are left with a free-floating consumerism that is its own justification.

The effects are faced across the world. An economic apartheid has opened up between north and south,[6] and intriguingly, in the north leadership is moving to nations such as China, Singapore, South Korea, India, and others. No matter where we are in the world, these forces of globalization affect us in some way on a day-to-day basis, as they interact with the particular challenges of our contexts.

Take South Africa, for example, the country where I grew up and where I started writing this book. My family home, where I am based when I am in South Africa, is close to where Alan Paton lived, the author of the acclaimed novel *Cry, the Beloved Country*. South Africa is exceptionally beautiful, and some ten minutes' drive from where I live in KwaZulu Natal one enters the valley of a thousand hills, exquisite beauty symbolic of the diverse landscapes found in South Africa. Not too far north of the valley of a thousand hills is Ixopo, where Paton begins his novel:

> There is a lovely road that runs from Ixopo into the hills. These hills are grass-covered and rolling, and they are lovely beyond any singing of it. The road climbs seven miles into them, to Carisbrooke; and from there, if there is no mist, you look down on one of the fairest valleys of Africa. About you there is grass and bracken and you may hear the forlorn crying of the titihoya, one of the birds of the veld. Below you is the valley of the Umzimkulu, on its journey from the Drakensberg to the sea; and beyond and behind the river, great hill after great hill; and beyond and behind them, the mountains of Ingeli and East Griqualand.[7]

Paton wrote most of *Cry, the Beloved Country* while on a trip to reformatories in Scandinavian countries. In his autobiography *Towards the Mountain* he

---

[5]See the important work by Dutch economist Bob Goudzwaard, *Capitalism and Progress: A Diagnosis of Western Society* (Carlisle, UK: Paternoster, 1997).

[6]See Harm de Blij, *The Power of Place: Geography, Destiny, and Globalization's Rough Landscape* (Oxford: Oxford University Press, 2009).

[7]Alan Paton, *Cry, the Beloved Country* (New York: Scribner, 1948, 2003), 7.

describes how he was feeling homesick, and after spending time in a cathedral, he went back to his hotel room and the novel started to pour out of him.[8] As only narrative can, the book evokes the pathos of apartheid South Africa.

Cry, the Beloved Country has as a central character, a black priest, whose son goes off to Johannesburg. The son gets into trouble and ends up murdering a young white lawyer. The novel ends with the execution of the priest's son. The priest wakes early to spend time meditating and praying while his son is executed. The book ends: "For it is the dawn that has come, as it has come for a thousand centuries, never failing. But when that dawn will come, of our emancipation, from the fear of bondage and the bondage of fear, why, that is a secret."[9]

In many ways the emancipation of South Africa did come in 1994, the year of the first democratic election. On the night when Nelson Mandela and F. W. de Klerk were awarded the Nobel Peace Prize in 1993, Archbishop Desmond Tutu declared, "Once we have got it right South Africa will be the paradigm for the rest of the world."[10] In 2014 South Africa celebrated twenty years of democracy. Alas, it is widely apparent that we have not got it right. Recent years have seen the publication of books such as *A Rumour of Spring: South Africa After 20 Years of Democracy*, by well-known journalist Max du Preez (2013); *A Nation in Crisis: An Appeal for Morality*, by Catholic academic Paulus Zulu (2013); *What's Gone Wrong? On the Brink of a Failed State*, by Methodist minister and politician Alex Boraine (2014); and *How Long Will South Africa Survive? The Looming Crisis* (2015), by Oxford and South African historian R. W. Johnson.[11]

All these books make worrying reading, written as they are by strong critics of apartheid South Africa and great supporters of and contributors to the new South Africa. Du Preez and Boraine both put the years the African National Congress spent in exile under the microscope to see whether the disturbing patterns we see now have their roots there.[12] Both find that they do. A tendency

---

[8]Alan Paton, *Towards the Mountain: An Autobiography* (London: Penguin, 1986).

[9]Paton, *Cry, the Beloved Country*, 251.

[10]Reported in Allister Sparks, *Tomorrow Is Another Country: The Inside Story of South Africa's Negotiated Revolution* (Wynberg, Cape Town: Struik, 1994), 10.

[11]Max du Preez, *A Rumour of Spring: South Africa After 20 Years of Democracy* (Cape Town: Zebra Press, 2013); Paulus Zulu, *A Nation in Crisis: An Appeal for Morality* (Cape Town: Tafelberg, 2013); Alex Boraine, *What's Gone Wrong? On the Brink of a Failed State* (Johannesburg: Jonathan Ball, 2014); R. W. Johnson, *How Long Will South Africa Survive? The Looming Crisis* (Johannesburg: Jonathan Ball, 2015).

[12]See the important book by Stephen Ellis, *External Mission: The ANC in Exile, 1960–1990* (Oxford: Oxford University Press, 2013).

in the years in exile was to absolutize the authority of the party, and this continues into the present, except that the party is now governing. Ethically, a political party is simply inadequate as the final authority, and yet when under pressure it is appeal to the party that we hear again and again. It was not always so with the African National Congress. Some of its founders, such as Albert Luthuli and its leader in exile, Oliver Tambo, were committed Christians, and Luthuli in particular stands out as someone whose primary allegiance was to the God who has shown himself in Christ.

Such a transcendent point of authority is essential for healthy politics. In this sense politics and the nation need religion. However, as is well-known, the relationship between Christianity and politics in the history of South Africa has been anything but straightforward. Christianity did produce such luminaries as Archbishop Desmond Tutu, but a great many Christians, and Reformed ones in particular, used Christianity to justify their support of apartheid. The result is that Christianity, and especially Reformed Christianity, lacks credibility in South Africa.

Clearly South Africa has its *particular demons* to exorcize. Christians seeking to follow Jesus in *this* context will need to be deeply aware of South Africa's troubled history and how that translates into the present. However, in combination with this, one needs to explore critically the interface between South Africa and globalization. Veteran South African journalist Allister Sparks took on a job as a political analyst in semiretirement, a job in which he found himself

> covering not only the fast-moving events in South Africa but in the world as a whole, because it soon became apparent that my own country was no longer an isolated entity. This was the age of globalization, and any major event anywhere impacted on everyone. We were all living in Marshall McLuhan's global village, where an airplane flying into a skyscraper in New York could cause economic shudders in Johannesburg, a war in the Middle East could send oil prices and thus living costs rocketing world-wide. Even the political ideologies being cooked up by the neo-conservatives in Washington could impose constraints on the policy choices faced by President Mbeki in Pretoria.[13]

---

[13]Allister Sparks, *First Drafts: South African History in the Making* (Johannesburg and Cape Town: Jonathan Ball, 2009), xiv.

Johnson asserts, "The key to understanding South Africa's development lies in its integration into a world capitalist political economy."[14] Undoubtedly many of the problems of South Africa are internal to the country, but these are inseparable from the opportunities and problems represented by global consumerism and their impact on South Africa.

Ironically, prior to the release of Nelson Mandela and the first democratic election in 1994, South Africa was somewhat protected from global forces because of its political isolation. In 1994 the gates were opened and not just to democracy but to the vortex of globalization, the drug trade, pornography, and so on. The Eastern Bloc lay in tatters so that the socialism of the African National Congress had little traction. Our second president, Thabo Mbeki, made the momentous decision to follow the Washington consensus economically, and while this has provided for a relatively stable economy, a great frustration in South Africa is the continuing large-scale unemployment while an elite—now black and white—appropriate enormous wealth, and the poor get poorer.

Clearly the challenges of development for South Africa are immense. There are *particular* challenges of its history, and there are the *global* challenges as they affect South Africa on a daily basis. To give one example: South African shops are awash with Chinese goods. In 2010, when the country proudly hosted the soccer World Cup, the all-pervasive flags of participating countries were . . . made in China. It would be one thing if one could easily tease out the local from the global challenges but, of course, they coalesce into a cauldron that threatens to blow up in one's face. Something that helped me a great deal as a South African to understand this context was the point that many of the problems facing the "new" South Africa are faced by all developing nations, and a major reason for this is that any developing nation today is seeking to mature and come of age amid globalization.

How, then, do we *seek the welfare of the city* at such a time? For Christians and those of other faiths, and Islam in particular, this is a crucial question, for the developing nations are the countries in which religion is exploding, as Philip Jenkins has shown.[15] We live amid *desecularization* globally and not

---

[14]Johnson, *How Long*, 15.

[15]Philip Jenkins, *The Next Christendom: The Coming of Global Christianity*, 3rd ed. (Oxford: Oxford University Press, 2011); *The New Faces of Christianity: Believing the Bible in the Global South* (Oxford: Oxford University Press, 2006); *God's Continent: Christianity, Islam, and Europe's Religious Crisis* (Oxford: Oxford University Press, 2007).

increasing secularization. Can religion, and Christianity in particular, be part of the solution rather than, alas, is often the case, part of the problem? The history of South Africa is eloquent testimony to the way in which Christians can become captive to and even proponents of the worst ideologies of the day, in this case racism. At the same time South Africa's history is alive with examples of Christians who resisted apartheid because they understood that their neighbor, be he or she whatever color, is made in the image of God and therefore worthy of respect and equality. And the "new" South Africa is desperately in need of a vital church that can help it find paths of *shalom* into the future. Alas, there is little sign of this. Johnson writes, "After 1990 the churches fell into a deep somnolence from which they could not be awakened. It was as if the anti-apartheid struggle had exhausted them and they simply had no energy or appetite for a new struggle against corruption, inequality and illiberality."[16]

If the resurgent Christianity across the globe is to be healthy and to contribute to the flourishing of humanity in our challenging contexts, what ought its priorities to be? Perhaps we can all agree that we ought to be *missional*. But what exactly does this mean? *Mission* is easily reduced to evangelism and church activities, and indispensable as these indeed are, mission is much broader. As David Bosch points out, "Mission is more than and different from recruitment to our brand of religion; it is alerting people to the universal reign of God."[17] Bosch goes on to say that what we need to pursue is

> how to express, ethically, the coming of God's reign, how to help people respond to the real questions of their context, how to break with the paradigm according to which religion has to do only with the private sphere. . . . This is not to suggest that we will build God's kingdom on earth. It is not ours to inaugurate, but we can help make it more visible, more tangible; we can initiate approximations of God's coming reign.[18]

Bosch rightly picks up on the kingdom of God as the central theme of Jesus' ministry (cf. Mk 1:14-15), as we will see in chapter three. Indeed, a strong case can be made for the kingdom or reign of God as the main theme of the Bible.[19]

---

[16]Johnson, *How Long*, 128.

[17]This and other references to David Bosch are from his last, posthumous publication, *Believing in the Future: Towards a Missiology of Western Culture* (Valley Forge, PA: Trinity Press International, 1995), 33.

[18]Ibid., 35.

[19]See Craig G. Bartholomew and Michael W. Goheen, *The Drama of Scripture: Finding Our Place in the Biblical Story*, 2nd ed. (Grand Rapids: Baker Academic, 2014).

If, as Bosch says, the church's role in mission is to point to and to embody the reign/kingdom of God, what are the particular challenges of this for us at our time and place? "What is it," asks David Bosch, "that we have to communicate to the Western 'post-Christian' public? It seems to me that we must demonstrate the role that plausibility structures, or rather, worldviews, play in people's lives."[20] Similarly, Andrew Walker, in the concluding chapter of his *Telling the Story: Gospel, Mission and Culture*, focuses on three missional imperatives for the church in our day, and the first is building new plausibility structures. "If," writes Walker, "the world staggers onwards with more consumption, wrapped up in mass culture yet splitting at the seams, we will still need to create sectarian plausibility structures in order for our story to take hold of our congregations and root them in the gospel handed down by our forebears."[21]

Bosch addresses primarily Western, irreligious cultures, whereas we have noted the importance of developing countries in which religion is resurgent. Developing countries are at a major advantage in this regard; the churches are full and the faith vital and alive. However, Bosch's priorities remain relevant in such contexts, billowed as they are by the global forces issuing forth from the secular West, and often led by a secular elite trained in the best secular Western universities. Numbers alone will not avail in developing countries if Christians do not attend to (1) plausibility structures and (2) worldviews. In one sense the rest of this book will be about these two issues. For now, let me elaborate on them briefly.

The best way for me to illustrate plausibility is to use the example of one of my heroes, Mother Teresa. She once went to address the White House under President Clinton and berated her audience over the issue of abortion. How was she able to do this, and why did they have to take her seriously? Because her life among the poor in Calcutta spoke so loudly that she had to be listened to! She was *inherently plausible* so that when she spoke one had to listen even if one disagreed with her. Plausibility refers to the personal, communal, and social embodiment of the life of the kingdom so that when Christians do speak they are listened to.

Plausibility is closely related to worldview. Several years after I was converted, a landmark in my coming to grips with apartheid South Africa as a

---

[20]Bosch, *Believing in the Future*, 48.

[21]Andrew Walker, *Telling the Story: Gospel, Mission, Culture* (London: SPCK, 1996), 190.

Christian was the dawning insight that Christianity is a worldview; it relates to all of life as God has made it. The last chapter of David Bosch's *Believing in the Future* is called "The Impossibility of Not Believing." What he means by this is that everyone by virtue of being human has a worldview, whether conscious of it or not. A worldview is like a pair of glasses—we all wear them (worldviews, that is!), but because we look *through* glasses *at the world* we are generally not conscious of the glasses we wear. Indeed, Michael Polanyi makes the point that it is often only a change in worldview that makes us aware of just how strong our previous worldview has been. He uses two examples, one of a former Marxist and one of a former Freudian.[22]

The challenge—and it is particularly urgent nowadays—for Christians is to develop an integrally biblical Christian worldview and to live creatively and thus plausibly from this perspective in our particular contexts. We need to become conscious of our glasses and to actively ensure that as far as possible we look with integrally Christian eyes at our world.

The challenges of our day are significant, to put it mildly. As Wendell Berry so aptly expresses it, we are called to "difficult hope"[23] amid the vortex of forces that often seem completely out of control. But "in Christ" we are not without hope, and, as in Revelation 1:12-20, Christ continues to walk amid his people, called to be lampstands, shining the Christ light into a world that is often desperately dark and cold. But it is his world for which he died, and we can therefore be confident that there is everything to be gained in doing what we can to initiate approximations in our contexts of God's coming kingdom.

But where will we find resources for this journey? As we will see, the answer is preeminently by living deeply into Christ. A spirituality with deep roots will be indispensable, but so too will be thinking deeply and acting wisely. For all these elements we do not need to reinvent the wheel, since we are heirs to a great tradition of Christian practice and thought that we can and must distill into the present. When it comes to *worldview* in Christian thought, there were two nineteenth-century Reformed thinkers who reached for the word in order

---

[22]See Michael Polanyi, *Personal Knowledge: Towards a Post-Critical Philosophy* (Chicago: University of Chicago Press, 1958), 288.

[23]See, e.g., Wendell Berry, "A Poem of Difficult Hope," in *What Are People For?* (New York: North Point, 1990), 58-63.

to articulate what it was Christians needed to be about if they were to face the challenges of modernity. Almost simultaneously Scottish theologian James Orr (1844–1913) and Dutch pastor, theologian, journalist, politician, prime minister, and cultural critic Abraham Kuyper (1837–1920) appropriated *worldview* to give expression to the comprehensive range of orthodox Christian faith. I agree with Orr in preferring to call this a *Christian* worldview as opposed to Kuyper's calling it a *Calvinistic* worldview. However, in terms of developing and embodying this idea, Kuyper is far more significant. Orr remained in theology, whereas Kuyper ranged across life, seeking to give expression to what it means to follow Christ in every sphere of life. In his *Lectures on Calvinism*, Kuyper stirringly writes,

> If everything that is, exists for the sake of God, then it follows that the whole creation must give glory to God. The sun, moon, and stars in the firmament, the birds of the air, the whole of nature around us, but, above all, man himself, who priest-like,[24] must consecrate to God the whole of creation, and all life thriving in it. . . . The sacred anointing of the priest of creation must reach down to his beard and to the hem of his garment. . . . Wherever man may stand, whatever he may do, to whatever he may apply his hand, in agriculture, in commerce, and in industry, or his mind, in the world of art and science, he is, in whatsoever it may be, constantly standing before the face of God, he is employed in the service of God, he has strictly to obey his God, and above all, he has to aim at the glory of his God.[25]

This quote gives us a taste of the feast of thought and practice that Kuyper has bequeathed to us. Kuyper was far from perfect, and in our discussion of his views on race and the Boers in South Africa we will, for example, find him wanting on the issue of racial purity. However, I argue in this book that in Kuyper's thought and the tradition flowing from him there are rich resources that can help Christians in their calling to be the salt of the earth and the light of the world today, including in South Africa.[26]

---

[24]Note here how Kuyper invokes the priesthood of humankind in ways similar to that of Orthodox theologian Alexander Schmemann, *For the Life of the World: Sacraments and Orthodoxy*, 2nd ed. (Crestwood, New York: St. Vladimir's Seminary Press, 1973).

[25]Abraham Kuyper, *Lectures on Calvinism* (Peabody, MA: Hendrickson, 2008), 41-42.

[26]John Bolt, *A Free Church, a Holy Nation: Abraham Kuyper's American Public Theology* (Grand Rapids: Eerdmans, 2001), xx-xxi, tells of attending a luncheon in Grand Rapids in 1997 with African theologian Kwame Bediako of Ghana. After hearing him describe the chaotic political condition of West Africa and after having watched two evenings full of a PBS documentary on Thomas Jefferson, Bolt asked Bediako

Others have written in detail about the life of Kuyper; the aim of this book is to analyze the systematic contours of Kuyper's thought, with appropriate reference to that of his coworkers and followers, with a view to asking how we can learn from it today.[27]

---

whether West Africa was not urgently in need of its own Thomas Jefferson. Bediako smiled and replied, "What Africa needs even more today is its own Abraham Kuyper."

[27]In English, most recently *AK* on the life of Kuyper.

ABRAHAM KUYPER'S
CONVERSION

*The entire story of the failure of upper-middle-class nerve
in modernity is one of the loss of a place to stand.*

JOHN CARROLL, *EGO AND SOUL*

ABRAHAM KUYPER'S ACHIEVEMENTS WERE EXTRAORDINARY.
He was a pastor, a fine theologian, a political activist, a leader of the Anti-Revolutionary Party in Holland, prime minister, cofounder of the Free University of Amsterdam, a prolific journalist, an author of numerous books, a church reformer, and so on. But where did the motivation come from in all that he did and achieved? Doubtless human motivation is complex and multifaceted, and certainly Abraham Kuyper was a complex individual. In modernity, however, there is a tendency in scholarship and often in culture to draw a firm line between people's private lives and their public achievements and scholarship. Ultimately this stems from the myth of religious neutrality, the belief that our public lives are independent of our life stories and beliefs. Kuyper rightly resists any absolutizing of this boundary. As he correctly states, "Our way of thinking is inevitably rooted in our own life-course, in what we each have experienced in our heart and life."[1]

One simply cannot understand Kuyper or his achievements without knowing his story and in particular the story of his conversion. Fortunately, Kuyper wrote about this in some detail in his "Confidentially."[2]

---

[1]*AK:CR*, 46.
[2]*AK:CR*, 45-61. Cf. George Puchinger, *Abraham Kuyper: De Jonge Kuyper (1837–1867)* (Franeker, Nether-

Kuyper's Conversion

Kuyper was the son of a Reformed pastor of the national Dutch Reformed Church (NHK).[3] Under King William II (1772–1839) a new constitution was introduced, under which the national church was reorganized in a hierarchical way and responsible to a cabinet minister. Many Dutch Protestants deplored this. Within the national church two parties worked for internal reform. One was those of the Groningen school, which found resources in the Renaissance humanist Erasmus and in medieval mysticism for a Dutch ecumenical Protestantism that would be relaxed about traditional doctrine.[4] By the mid-nineteenth century Groningen theology dominated preparation of Dutch clergy. The second group was made up of adherents of the Dutch wing of the Réveil, whose most notable representatives were Isaac da Costa (1798–1860) and Guillaume Groen van Prinsterer (1801–1876), the latter of whom was to have a major influence on Kuyper's life.[5] In 1834 minister Hendrik de Cock of the town of Ulrum seceded from the NHK in response to growing theological liberalism, and this separation led to 120 churches leaving the NHK. A new political constitution in 1848 severed ties between state and church, but the hierarchal structure was not changed.

Kuyper's father was called to a church in Leiden, where he had done his theological studies, and he remained there as a pastor for twenty-six years. As a churchman Jan Frederik Kuyper disliked extremes and worked for unity in the congregation, and he absorbed from Isaac da Costa an earnest evangelical spirit. Looking back, Kuyper was highly critical of the sort of Christianity he grew up in, noting that in his youth he found himself repulsed by the church. "The church there [in Leiden] was not really a church. The spirit was absent, and my heart could feel no sympathy either for a church that so blatantly dishonored itself or for a religion that was represented by such a church."[6]

---

lands: T. Wever, 1987). George Puchinger, *Abraham Kuyper: His Early Journey of Faith*, ed. George Harinck (Amsterdam: VU University Press, 1988), 9, notes, "When his [Kuyper's] religious spark was kindled, Kuyper's emotional self turned out to be a cultural powder keg that, once it was brought to explosion, would leave its mark in the Netherlands to this day."

[3]The Nederlandse Hervormde Kerk, which emerged out of the Reformation.

[4]Cf. Herman Bavinck, "Recent Dogmatic Thought in the Netherlands," *Presbyterian and Reformed Review* 10 (April 1892): 209-28.

[5]*Réveil* means "renewal" or "restoration." This movement for Christian renewal drew from sources in Switzerland and England and worked particularly among the upper class. The father figure of this movement in the Netherlands was the great poet William Bilderdijk (1756–1831).

[6]*AK:CR*, 46-47.

Kuyper had an excellent education at the Leiden gymnasium and then went to Leiden University, where he earned his baccalaureate in 1858 and his doctorate in 1862. He was a theology student, but his real interests were more in history and literature than theology.[7] When he looked back at his spiritual state during that time, he saw that he had been defenseless against criticism of the faith and recognized that the problem lay deep within him: "My faith was not deeply rooted in my unconverted, self-centered soul and was bound to wither once exposed to the scorching heat of the spirit of doubt."[8]

In the summer of 1858 Kuyper met his future wife, Johanna Schaay. While Johanna was preparing for profession of faith and being catechized, Kuyper kept pushing her on why she believed what she was learning to profess, betraying his growing distance from traditional Christian faith. Bratt notes, "From their correspondence Kuyper's theology during his doctoral studies can best be described as Unitarian with pronounced Calvinist and moralist accents."[9] Kuyper denied the eternal deity of Christ and insisted that Jesus was purely a man. "The rational and religious feeling in us is God, who reveals Himself overall and thus also in man."[10] His unorthodoxy manifested itself across the doctrinal spectrum: on immortality, he felt the need for such a belief but could not grasp it clearly; on the atonement, he found forgiveness through Christ's blood unintelligible; on revelation, he questioned how we could know what Jesus actually said, and anyway he was only a man; he gave the forms of church practice short shrift; he argued that what really matters is God's holiness and virtue.

If this sounds all too familiar, there is a good reason for it. Kuyper was studying theology at the time when historical criticism was gaining traction in Europe, and Kuyper's mentor was Joannes Henricus Scholten (1811–1885), the pioneer of modernist theology in Holland. Scholten embraced a rigorous naturalism that viewed nature not in romantic categories but as a long struggle of spirit over flesh, of morality over willfulness. Religion was part of this process and would yield as reason progressed. Scholten and his colleagues embraced

---

[7]Kuyper's love of literature affected him throughout his life and especially as an author and rhetorician. John Bolt, *A Free Church, A Holy Nation: Abraham Kuyper's Public Theology* (Grand Rapids: Eerdmans, 2001), touches on this when he evocatively describes Kuyper as a "poet."

[8]*AK:CR*, 47.

[9]*AK*, 26.

[10]Quoted in *AK*, 26.

German higher criticism, with its denigration of the historicity of the Bible. The Bible and theology were viewed as an allegory of human development toward autonomy. Abraham Kuenen (1828–1891) was Scholten's foremost contemporary, a major figure in the development of historical criticism.[11]

Students from all faculties flocked to hear Scholten. What attracted them, as one of Scholten's successors perceptively notes, was witnessing "one great, fully fledged world and life view [being] built up before their eyes." It was "an all-inclusive monism . . . wherein all questions had an answer, wherein no divisions remained for human thought, but wherein everything flowed out from God 'as the power of all powers, the life of all life.'"[12] Scholten had been a village pastor, and there he had been impressed by the robustness of classic Reformed theology. As would Kuyper, he sought to develop it for his day, though, as we will see, Kuyper took it in a very different direction from that of Scholten.

In his "Confidentially" Kuyper relates three events that moved him toward God. The first was a theology competition in which as an undergraduate he was providentially able to get hold of primary sources of Polish theologian Jan Laski (1499–1560) and won a competition with his 320-page essay comparing John Calvin's and Jan Laski's views of the church.[13] Kuyper saw, at least in retrospect, God's intervention in enabling him to get hold of the primary sources.

The real turning point for Kuyper came from a book Johanna sent him, namely, *The Heir of Redclyffe* by Charlotte Yonge (1823–1901), a bestselling British novel of 1853.[14] As Kuyper says, "This masterpiece was the instrument that broke my smug, rebellious heart."[15] In England a revival of Anglo-Catholicism was underway, spearheaded by John Keble, Edward Pusey, and John Henry Newman. Keble (1792–1866) became vicar of Hersley and rector of

---

[11]See chapter three.

[12]Quoted in *AK*, 29.

[13]See *AK*, 35-37. On Laski see Michael S. Springer, *Restoring Christ's Church: John a Lasco and the Forma ac ratio* (Aldershot, UK: Ashgate, 2007); Henning P. Jürgens, *Johannes a Lasco in Ostfriesland: der Werdegang eines europäischen Reformators* (Tübingen: Mohr Siebeck, 2002). For Kuyper's essay see Jasper Vree, *Abraham Kuyper's "Commentatio" (1860): The Young Kuyper About Calvin, a Lasco, and the Church*, 2 vols. (Leiden: Brill, 2005). Springer, *Restoring Christ's Church*, 6, notes, "The nineteenth-century Dutch theologian, Abraham Kuyper, was among the first modern scholars to attempt a study of Lasco." Jasper Vree refers to Kuyper's edited collection of Laski's works as "the foundation stone of modern Lasco research" (Springer, *Restoring Christ's Church*, 6).

[14]Charlotte M. Yonge, *The Heir of Redclyffe*, Wordsworth Classics (Ware, UK: Wordsworth, 1998). Yonge was the author of more than one hundred books. For information about Charlotte Yonge and access to her letters, see the Charlotte Mary Yonge Fellowship Website, www.cmyf.org.uk.

[15]*AK:CR*, 51.

Otterbourne, the latter being the parish in which Yonge's family lived.[16] Yonge was a firm advocate of Anglo-Catholicism and was mentored by Keble as an author.[17]

The main characters in the novel are two cousins, Philip de Morville and the orphaned Guy de Morville, and the novel revolves around their tense relationship. Philip is proud and ambitious, rigid and inflexible. Guy is tender and sensitive, and strong in his faith. He is accommodating and self-sacrificial. The novel presents two diametrically opposing characters who clash repeatedly.

The unconverted Kuyper, however, was fascinated by Philip's character and identified with him as his hero. In the novel, Philip falls sick with malaria fever in Italy and, ironically, is saved by his cousin Guy, whom he has been manipulating and undermining for most of the novel. Through his sacrificial care of Phillip, Guy contracts and dies from the same fever from which Philip recovered. Kuyper notes that in the novel, "almost imperceptibly, automatically, the roles are reversed so that the once so extraordinary Philip is disclosed in all his vanity and inner emptiness while Guy excels in a true greatness and inner strength."[18] Guy is typically Romantic, full of deep feeling and honor, and impulsive, but he channels Romantic passion into pure love. "Guy brought the *Sturm und Drang* to quiet harbor."[19]

Philip is plunged into remorse, and Kuyper with him. Yonge describes Guy's burial service in words that must have moved Kuyper greatly: "The blessing of peace came in the precious English burial service, as they laid him to rest in the earth, beneath the spreading chestnut tree, rendered a home by those words of his Mother Church—the mother who had guided his steps in his orphaned life."[20] During his convalescence Philip looks back over his life with deep regret and lives restlessly through "the stings of a profound repentance."[21] He returns to England to stay with his sister during his recovery

---

[16]See Charlotte Mary Yonge, *John Keble's Parishes: A History of Hursley and Otterbourne* (London: Macmillan, 1898).

[17]On Keble's influence on Yonge as an author see Ellen Jordan, Charlotte Mitchell, and Helen Schinske, "'A Handmaid to the Church': How John Keble Shaped the Career of Charlotte Yonge, the 'Novelist of the Oxford Movement,'" in Kirstie Blair, ed., *John Keble in Context* (London: Anthem, 2004), 175-91. On Yonge as an author and her fiction see Tamara S. Wagner, ed., *Charlotte Yonge: Reading Domestic Religious Fiction* (Abingdon, UK: Routledge, 2012). For Yonge's view of writing see her "Authorship," *The Monthly Packet*, September 1892, available online at http://community.dur.ac.uk/c.e.schultze/index.html.

[18]*AK:CR*, 53.

[19]*AK*, 40. *Sturm und Drang* is the German for "Storm and Stress," the movement out of which Romanticism emerged.

[20]Yonge, *Heir of Redclyffe*, 421.

[21]Ibid., 452.

and one day rides out to his childhood home in Stylehurst. He enters the village church and "He knelt down, with bowed head and hands clasped."[22] This marks his turning from despair to hope, his finding his way home to God, and Kuyper notes, "I read that Philip knelt, and before I knew it, I was kneeling in front of my chair with folded hands. Oh, what my soul experienced at that moment I fully understood only later. Yet, from that moment on I despised what I used to admire and sought what I had dared to despise."[23] As Kuyper himself later wrote, "to obtain real peace, an unshakeable faith, and full development of powers, our soul must, in the depth of depths and forsaken of all men, depend on God Almighty alone."[24]

Thus Kuyper entered the kingdom of God, a doctoral student in theology at last finding his way home. In "Confidentially" he makes a passing comment that reveals how far he had been from the faith as a theology student: "I had become acquainted with Calvin and à Lasco [Jan Laski], but in reading them it never occurred to me that this might be the truth."[25] We noted above Kuyper's love of literature, and there is something wonderfully human in the Spirit using a novel to bring him home to God.

Kuyper learned other lessons from the novel. The learned Philip abused and controlled his fiancée, and Kuyper similarly had pressured and manipulated Johanna; he repented of his sin against her. He was also struck by the role of the Anglican Church as the mother of believers in the novel, as noted above, and according to him it was from this point on that he similarly longed for a sanctified church.[26]

In 1863 Kuyper received his first call to the Dutch Reformed church in the village of Beesd. His experiences there marked a third formative phase in his life. If his work on Jan Laski alerted Kuyper to God's sovereignty and the reality of his interventions in history, his encounter with *The Heir of Redclyffe*

---

[22]Ibid., 461.

[23]Quoted in *AK*, 39.

[24]Abraham Kuyper, "The Biblical Criticism of the Present Day," trans. J. Hendrik de Vries, *Bibliothecra Sacra* LXI (1904): 678.

[25]*AK:CR*, 56.

[26]For a comparison of Kuyper and Newman see George Puchinger, "Newman en Kuyper," in *Ontmoetingen met theologen* (Zutphen, Netherlands: Terra, 1980), 94-105. Puchinger notes that we have no idea whether Kuyper was aware of the work of Newman and Pusey. However, Puchinger, "Newman en Kuyper," 105, concludes that Kuyper's contact with Anglicanism through Yonge's novel must not be forgotten. Bearing in mind the profound effect of Yonge's novel on Kuyper, it would be surprising if he was not aware of Newman, Keeble, and Pusey.

brought him firmly into what C. S. Lewis calls the hall of Christianity, "the grand Christian vision of reality, which transcends denominational differences."[27] Leading off this hall are multiple rooms representing the various denominations. C. S. Lewis says that his *Mere Christianity* is about this hall, a hall that has many rooms connected to it. Lewis's aim is not to tell readers which room to enter, that is, which denomination or tradition, but to invite them into *mere* Christianity.[28] Kuyper was now in the hall, just as C. S. Lewis, after a long period of reflection and dialogue, got onto a bus not a Christian and got off converted! In Beesd (1863–1867) Kuyper found out which room to enter.

Kuyper arrived at Beesd with the new sense of spiritual intimacy with God from his conversion. In his first sermon there he stressed that fellowship with God was "the highest aspiration of the human heart" and concluded with a vital point that he never lost sight of again: "Religion is always a matter of the heart, and in that heart God the Holy Spirit speaks according to his divine good pleasure."[29] At the same time his preaching reflected that of the emerging ethical school in Dutch theology, which sought to find a via media between Scholten's modernism and the strict confessionalism of those who had seceded.[30] Kuyper's awareness of the social dimension of the gospel manifested itself early on as he worked with the National Society for the General Welfare to set up a bank for small savers.

Kuyper describes his congregation in Beesd as "characterized by a rigid conservatism, orthodox in appearance but without the genuine glow of spiritual vitality."[31] He was made aware of a small group of malcontents in the congregation and warned off them. He found it impossible, however, to ignore them. As he got to know them he was deeply impressed by their conviction, their deep interest in spiritual matters, their knowledge of the Bible, their possession of a well-ordered worldview, and their emphasis on "full sovereign grace." This group brought Kuyper firmly into the Reformed room of Christianity as he embraced their emphasis on sovereign grace. However, he found

---

[27]Alister McGrath, *C. S. Lewis—A Life: Eccentric Genius, Reluctant Prophet* (Carol Stream, IL: Tyndale House, 2013), 221.

[28]Lewis got this expression from the Puritan Richard Baxter. See McGrath, *C. S. Lewis—A Life*, 218-29.

[29]Quoted in *AK*, 43.

[30]Kuyper, "Biblical Criticism of the Present Day," 436, sees Schleiermacher as the father of the ethical school.

[31]*AK:CR*, 55.

that they were too locked into the world and time of the Reformation and that he needed more. He reached for works by Johannes H. Gunning (1829–1905) and Daniel Chantepie de la Saussaye (1818–1874), leading proponents of the ethical school.[32] He found them fascinating but inadequate. Finally,

> It was Calvin himself... who first disclosed to me those solid, unwavering lines that only need to be traced to inspire full confidence. I saw at once that we had to advance exegetically, psychologically, and historically beyond him, but nonetheless here I found the foundations which, banning all doubt, permitted the edifice of faith to be constructed in a completely logical style—and with the surprising result that the most consistent ethic ruled in its inner chambers.[33]

And having (re)discovered Calvin, Kuyper saw that it was this tradition that the malcontents in Beesd had mediated to him: "And Calvin had so taught that, centuries after his death, in a foreign land, in an obscure village, in a room with a stone floor, people with a common laborer's brain could still *understand* him."[34]

Kuyper further connected his discovery of Calvin with the church and with *The Heir of Redclyffe*. This mediation of Calvinism to Kuyper via the poor laborers in his church meant that Calvin had founded a church and through the form given it had spread blessings far and wide in Europe and beyond, even among the poor and uneducated. Kuyper lauds Calvin's description of God as our Father and the church as our Mother,[35] and this, of course, reminded him of the description of the funeral liturgy in *Redclyffe*.

> And now, I saw in actual persons, in very fact, what miraculous, unutterable, almost unbelievable power a spiritually organized church may yet reveal, silently and unobtrusively, even amid the disintegration we had suffered, so long as she knows what she wants and allows her word to be the form of her essential thought.... The restoration of a "church that could be our Mother" had to become the goal of my life.[36]

---

[32]See http://poortman.kb.nl, the website of the Koninglijke Bibliotheek, Nationale bibliotheek van Nederland, for a list of Gunning's publications. Cf. A. de Lange and J. H. Gunning Jr., *Brochures en brieven uit zijn Leidse tijd (1889–1899)* (Kampen: Kok, 1984); Daniël Chantepie de la Saussaye, *Verzameld werk. Een keuze uit het werk van Daniël Chantepie de la Saussaye*, selected and annotated by F. G. M. Broeyer, H. W. de Knijff, and H. Veldhuis, 3 vols. (Zoetermeer, Netherlands: Boekencentrum, 1997–2003).

[33]*AK:CR*, 58-59. For a fascinating lecture by Herman Bavinck on Calvin see Herman Bavinck, "John Calvin: A Lecture on the Occasion of His 400th Birthday, July 10, 1509–1909," trans. John Bolt, *The Bavinck Review* 1 (2010): 57-85.

[34]*AK:CR*, 59.

[35]John Calvin, *Institutes of the Christian Religion* (Philadelphia: Westminster, 1960), IV.1.1.

[36]*AK:CR*, 61.

KUYPER AND MODERNISM

Now staunchly Reformed, Kuyper's reaction to modernism in theology was further provoked by the publication in 1864 of a study of the Gospel of John by his old mentor Scholten,[37] who completely reversed his earlier view of its Johannine authorship. Kuyper notes that Scholten himself acknowledged that this radical change was rooted in his shift from a Platonic to more of an Aristotelian worldview, "thereby himself acknowledging the apriori as the guiding star of his critique."[38] Kuyper stresses that he is by no means opposed to progress, to new insights, "But we must dispel the sacred haze in which a critique dares to hide while it remains alien to the essence of things and, demanding the subordination of all, toys with the *corpus vile* according to the whim of its apriori."[39]

Then, in 1865, Allard Pierson, a leading member of the Dutch Reformed Church, left the ministry because of modernist principles. Pierson argued that if Christianity were to be superseded by culture, why not move ahead and devote oneself to science and education. In a series of three sermons in 1865 Kuyper tackled these issues head-on. Pierson was correct in his logic; the church *was* confronted with a stark choice between humanism and Christianity, and there was no middle ground. Of course, Kuyper wanted Christianity rather than humanism. For Kuyper not only was the church at stake in the challenge of modernism, but the very existence of the soul, indeed of any reality transcending the material. "The specter of blank materialism would represent, from now on, the deepest horror of Kuyper's imagination, the ultimate in a remorseless, meaningless world."[40]

In 1867 Kuyper took up a church in Utrecht. There he fell foul of the conservatives.[41] However, if an ultraconservatism was the challenge on one side, on the other was modernism, and in 1871, the year after he left Utrecht for Amsterdam, Kuyper addressed this head-on in his "Modernism: A Fata Morgana in the Christian Domain."

---

[37]J. H. Scholten, *Het Evangelie naar Johannes: kritisch, historisch onderzoek* (Leiden: P. Engels, 1864).
[38]*AK:CR*, 115n34.
[39]*AK:CR*, 115.
[40]*AK*, 47.
[41]See Abraham Kuyper, "Conservatism and Orthodoxy: False and True Preservation," in *AK:CR*, 65-85.

Kuyper was perhaps the first to use *modernism* in its implied sense of modernity.[42] It is important to note that there was much in modernism that Kuyper admired, namely its intellectual scope, courage, and consistency. Modernism set a standard he wanted orthodoxy to meet. Kuyper recognized, however, as did James Orr, the comprehensiveness of the challenge of modernism: "The most firmly laid foundations are being battered, our deepest and dearest principles uprooted. It almost seems as if the shrieks of the French revolution in 1793 were but the prelude to the mighty battle march now being played in our hearing."[43] For Kuyper, as for Edmund Burke (1729–1797), modernism was the theory in which the polemic against Christianity has created its most coherent system.[44] This meant that resistance was a duty. "You cannot walk away from your own time but must take it as it is, and the times demand that we either accept the unsettling of our faith or enter the fray. Given this choice, the committed person does not hesitate." With typical rhetorical flourish he asserted, "The honeymoon of spiritual impassivity is over."[45]

How we resist, though, was important to Kuyper. We do not battle modernism by belittling or vilifying it. Intriguingly, Kuyper argues that modernism *had to appear.* In almost the same decade, it summoned its apostles everywhere: in Germany, Strauss; in Switzerland, Baur; in the United States, Parker; in the Cape in South Africa, Colenso.[46] Modernism is a Christian heresy in that it refracts the beams of Christianity in the spiritual atmosphere of its age, as do all heresies. It is not new, but "it has never *ruled* as now, never achieved the central importance it has today."[47]

What, Kuyper asks, is it in the spiritual atmosphere of the age that gave rise to modernism? He discerns four causes: first, the bankruptcy of contemporary

---

[42]Malcolm Bull, "Who Was the First to Make a Pact with the Devil?," *London Review of Books* (May 14, 1992): 22-23. Bull asserts, "If, for the sake of clarity, we take the modern era to include at least the period from the mid-19th century to the mid-20th century, we can define modernity in terms of the social conditions of life in the West during that period, and modernism as the positive cultural response to the experience of modernity. It is perhaps easiest to start with modernism, which must, of necessity, already contain an implicit definition of modernity." He notes that in this period modernism is particularly associated with the arts and theology. It is indisputably in theology that the first reference is found, and in this respect Bull refers to Kuyper's denunciation of modernism in theology in his "Fata Morgana."

[43]Abraham Kuyper, "Modernism: A Fata Morgana in the Christian Domain," in *AK:CR*, 89.

[44]See Edmund Burke, *Reflections on the Revolution in France* (New York: Bobbs Merrill, 1955).

[45]*AK:CR*, 89-90.

[46]David Friedrich Strauss (1808–1874), Ferdinand Christian Baur (1792–1860), Theodore Parker (1810–1860), and Bishop John William Colenso (1814–1883) were all leading figures in the emergence of historical criticism, which raised questions about the truth of the Bible.

[47]*AK:CR*, 98.

philosophy; second, the impotence of revolution; third, the enormous expansion of the study of nature; and fourth, the somnolence of the church. Modernism, according to Kuyper, is a form of realism, but one well on the way to the abyss of materialism. Ironically, (theological) modernism arose to defend Christian faith against materialism. It attempted to mediate—or we might today say *correlate*—Christian faith with modern culture. Kuyper says, "How grandly that effort might have been rewarded if people had only let themselves be led to the realism of Scripture, taking as their motto Baader's own statement that 'corporeality is the end of the road of God.'"[48]

Theological modernism, Kuyper notes, claims the name of Protestantism and seeks to represent itself and Protestantism as branches of the same tree! However, as regards faith modernism takes human authority and autonomy as its starting point, the precise thing Protestantism railed against. Consequently modernism only concerns itself with the visible realm and not the things of heaven. It effectively erased the boundary line separating the sacred from the profane.

Against the religious standpoint of modernists Kuyper raises the following charges:

1. Their God of eternally beautiful love is an abstraction and miles away from the living Word, the God who speaks.

2. They view prayer not as petitioning but merely as an outpouring of the soul.

3. If consistent, they deny the reality of divine government.

4. Their view of morality is problematic. They reject the special creation of humankind and end up with no real concept of sin. In their view of morality, we rise toward an ideal, whereas in biblical Christianity the ideal comes down to us in Christ.

5. Their theology is flawed. They attend to history, but through a flawed lens that tries to squeeze everything into its idea; into "that idea, not derived from reality but born from an illicit union of the sacred and the profane."[49] The result is that what Scripture says of Jesus cannot be true.

Kuyper sums up the modernist creed as follows:

---

[48]*AK:CR*, 102. Franz van Baader (1765–1841) was a mystical Roman Catholic theologian whose thought Kuyper regarded as global, cosmic in nature.
[49]*AK:CR*, 114.

I, a modernist, believe in a God who is Father of all humankind, and in Jesus, not the Christ, but the rabbi from Nazareth. I believe in a humanity which is by nature good but needs to strive after improvement. I believe that sin is only relative and hence that forgiveness is merely something of human invention. I believe in the hope of a better life and, without judgment, the salvation of every soul.[50]

On the modernist view of the church, Kuyper comments, "No real God, no real prayer, no real divine government, the reality of human life under threat, no real sin, no real ideal, no genuine history, no true criticism, no dogma that could withstand scrutiny, nor a real church."[51]

Startlingly, Kuyper argues that modernism has saved orthodoxy in the church, as in the healing of a sick person by an injection of poison, or a terrible defeat that rouses the life of a nation. He compares the challenge of modernism to the early heresy of Arianism and exhorts his listeners to have no fear; the church has overcome before and can do so again.

Modernity is a complex phenomenon, and Kuyper does differentiate in his writings between *pantheism* and *evolution*. He accuses pantheism of blurring the boundaries: first, that most fundamental boundary between the world and God, and then, consequently, all other boundaries.[52] Intriguingly, Kuyper picks up on the motif of "dividing" in Genesis 1 as central to its theology of creation and thus of God-given boundaries, an insight that several recent scholars have highlighted.[53] Kuyper is adamant that pantheism's blurring of the boundary between God and the world has fatal consequences: "if the boundary between God and the world is removed and in the holy Trinity you can no longer adore the fullness of the richest personal life, the mainspring of your own personal life is bound to break."[54]

Kuyper's treatment of evolution is remarkable in its even-handedness. He repeatedly foregrounds the insights of evolution. Positively, he sees it as a welcome response to the empiricism and an emphasis on the unknowable that for too long had dominated philosophy. Second, it has stimulated a careful

---

[50]*AK:CR*, 116.

[51]*AK:CR*, 118.

[52]Abraham Kuyper, "The Blurring of the Boundaries," in *AK:CR*, 363-402, 374.

[53]Cf., for example, Paul Beauchamp, *Création et Séparation: étude exégétique du chapitre premier de la Genèse* (Paris: Aubier Montaigne-Éditions du Cerf, 1969); Leon R. Kass, *The Beginnings of Wisdom: Reading Genesis* (Chicago: University of Chicago Press, 2003), 31-36.

[54]*AK:CR*, 387.

study of nature. Third, it has discovered a unity of design in organic life, and fourth, it has illumined variations in species. Its error, however, stems from extending its legitimate scientific explorations to all of life as a worldview and thinking it has thereby solved the riddle of the universe. As a *worldview* it attempts to explain the entire cosmos and thus becomes opposed to Christianity. Kuyper evokes the antithesis between evolution as a worldview and Christianity with a series of "over against" statements:[55]

1. Over against Nietzsche, whom Kuyper sees as an embodiment of evolution as a worldview, Kuyper sets Christ, who seeks the lost and has mercy on the weak: "Certainly if there is anyone who is a radical protest against the very idea of evolution, it is he who came down from the Father of lights to manifest himself as God in the flesh. Christ is the miracle."[56]

2. Over against the undirected mechanism of evolution, he sets that eternal being who works all things after the counsel of his will.

3. Over against species selection, he sets election.

4. Over against the annihilation of the person in the grave, he sets coming judgment and eternal glory.

Kuyper explores the implications of evolution as a worldview for aesthetics and ethics. Its implications as a worldview for ethics are devastating: the moral ideal, world order, and law, their concomitant sense of duty, and their source in God all fall away, and thus we lose the interconnected ideas of sin, atonement, redemption, and repentance.[57] Kuyper connects Nietzsche with evolution and notes that as a worldview evolution confronts us, as does Nietzsche, with whether the stronger must have mercy on or crush the weaker. The logical outcome of evolution is absolute nihilism.

A Place to Stand

The effect of Kuyper's conversion is remarkable. It gave him a place to stand and from which to engage the fast-changing world of his day, the emerging modern world to which we are heirs. In his "Blurring the Boundaries" he poses the question of how to respond to the challenge of the day. He identifies

---

[55]*AK:CR*, 429-30, 439.
[56]*AK:CR*, 389.
[57]*AK:CR*, 434.

three approaches being tried. First is that of apologetics. He notes, "no argument will avail where Reason is both a party to the dispute and its judge."[58] Second is the approach—typical of what Kuyper calls (theological) modernism—that seeks to mediate between faith and the emerging worldview/s. Proponents of such mediation exhaust their energies in making a monstrous marriage! Third are the amphibians who seek to separate head and heart. Such dualism is of no avail, because logic and ethics only have one mind at their disposal.

Instead Kuyper proposes we follow the example of God calling Abraham apart and of Christ forming the church by calling the Twelve apart to accompany him in his public ministry. He argues that those who retain faith and understand the danger of blurring the boundaries should begin by drawing a boundary around their own circle, by developing their own lives within that circle, so that they can mature to the point where they will be ready for the struggle that is at hand.[59]

Scripture is fundamental to Kuyper's call for separation: "You are clear, then, on the purport of our system I am arguing for. A *life-sphere* of our own on the foundation of *palingenesia*, and a *life-view* of our own thanks to the light that the Holy Spirit kindles on the candelabra of Scripture."[60] Kuyper refers to a life-sphere based on *palingenesia*, a New Testament Greek word that merits explanation. The word means rebirth, and in a footnote Kuyper explains why he retains this word: "I deliberately use the Greek word because it covers both personal rebirth (Tit. 3:5) and the re-creation of heaven and earth (Matt. 19:28)."[61]

On the authority of Scripture Kuyper is unequivocal. He refers with approval to Kant's statement that if we should ever allow Scripture to lose its authority, no comparable authority could ever emerge again.[62] Kuyper notes of this statement,

> Long ago when I read that statement I felt the deep truth of it. In Scripture we confront a cedar tree of spiritual authority that for eighteen centuries has pushed its roots into the soil of our human consciousness; in its shadow the

---

[58]*AK:CR,* 396.
[59]*AK:CR,* 396.
[60]*AK:CR,* 400.
[61]*AK:CR,* 398.
[62]*AK:CR,* 399.

religious and moral life of humanity has immeasurably increased in dignity and worth. Now chop that cedar down. For a little while some green shoots will still bud out from its trunk, but who will give us another tree, who will provide future generations with a shade like this? This is why—not as a consequence of erudition but with the naiveté of the little child—I have bowed my head in simple faith before that Scripture, have devoted my energies to its cause, and now rejoice inwardly and thank God when I see faith in that Scripture again increasing. You know that I am not conservative, but this indeed is my conservatism: I will attempt to save the abundant cover of that cedar for our people, so that in future they will not sit down in a scorching desert without shade.[63]

Notice that Kuyper's call for separation is not in order never to reengage; rather, we separate so that we as Christians acquire the maturity needed for the struggle we must engage. This is withdrawal *for mission*, not withdrawal for the sake of withdrawal. Kuyper is adamant that faith affects all of life, including the life of the mind. "Those who believe receive not only another impression of *life* but are also reoriented in the world of *thought*."[64] He movingly quotes Augustine's *Confessions* 10.6, in which Augustine interrogates the different parts of creation, who all reply "I am not he." Finally, with a loud voice they cry out "*It is he who made us.*" As Kuyper notes, Augustine was now another person, and so he heard and thought differently.

PALINGENESIS AS THE KEY TO THE KUYPERIAN TRADITION

Kuyper's conversion contains in seed form all the great themes that will dominate his life and which we will explore in the following chapters. For now, we focus on those elements that are utterly foundational to the Kuyperian—and other—traditions and yet are easily overlooked. As the Kuyperian tradition was transplanted to North America, South Africa, and elsewhere, a danger has emerged, of ethnicism, with Dutch enclaves developing with the concomitant danger of being characterized primarily by Dutch descent rather than first by Christian faith.[65] The effect of such ethnicism is invariably a loss of the missional vision central to the Kuyperian tradition and then of trust in Scripture as God's Word. At the same time, some converts to the Kuyperian tradition become so enamored with its public vision that they despair of and

---

[63]*AK:CR*, 399-400.
[64]*AK:CR*, 398.
[65]See my dialogue with Michael Goheen at the end of chapter eight.

neglect the church. To reverse this process, the following elements need to be attended to as truly foundational to this tradition.

Conversion. The great danger for Kuyper was that he grew up as a pastor's son in the established church. I say *danger* because, apart from its many gifts, it presented the grave danger that he would assume he was a Christian because of his background, his involvement in the church, and his being a student of theology. Certainly prior to his conversion he relates to Johanna as though he were an authority on all things Christian. This is *the* danger that is central to the thought of Danish philosopher Søren Kierkegaard (1813–1855).[66] Kierkegaard lived in Copenhagen, and he tirelessly sought to awaken his fellow citizens from the slumber of *Christendom*—namely, assuming because they were part of a Christian nation and the national church that all was well in their relationship with God.

Apart from his conversion, Kuyper would never have achieved what he did. His conversion enabled him to see that utterly central to the Christian life is a living relationship with God through Christ and that this comes about through the work of the Spirit in one's heart. Kuyper reached for the New Testament Greek word *palingenesis* to express this and more. Kuyper himself refers to Titus 3:5 and Matthew 19:28. It is worth quoting Titus 3:5 in its context:

> At one time we too were foolish, disobedient, deceived and enslaved by all kinds of passions and pleasures. We lived in malice and envy, being hated and hating one another. But when the kindness and love of God our Savior appeared, he saved us, not because of righteous things we had done, but because of his mercy. He saved us through the washing of rebirth and renewal by the Holy Spirit, whom he poured out on us generously through Jesus Christ our Savior, so that, having been justified by his grace, we might become heirs having the hope of eternal life. This is a trustworthy saying. And I want you to stress these things, so that those who have trusted in God may be careful to devote themselves to doing what is good. These things are excellent and profitable for everyone. (Tit 3:3-8)

Several points are worth noting. First, Titus 3:3 shows what we were like before our conversion. Kuyper would have identified with this. He thought he was righteous and wise, but he came to see, like Philip de Morville, that he was arrogant and foolish. Second, we need to be saved, rescued from this condition,

---

[66]See, e.g., John W. Elrod, *Kierkegaard and Christendom* (Princeton, NJ: Princeton University Press, 1981).

and this is entirely by the mercy of God through "Jesus Christ our Savior."
Third, salvation is the work of the Holy Spirit through the washing of palingenesis (rebirth) and renewal. Salvation is a supernatural event of rebirth and
decidedly not something that humans can achieve. By God's grace we are declared righteous in Christ before him and thus become heirs, having the hope
of eternal life.

Although John 3 does not use the word *palingenesis*, it deals with the same
territory as Titus 3. Nicodemus, a deeply religious man, comes to Jesus by
night, affirming that he is a teacher from God. Jesus replies in well-known
words, "Very truly I tell you, no one can see the kingdom of God unless they
are born again" (Jn 3:3). Again in John 3:5 Jesus says, "Very truly I tell you, no
one can enter the kingdom of God unless they are born of water and the Spirit."
In John 3:8 he speaks of being "born of the Spirit." It is this high view of conversion that Kuyper saw as essential to being a Christian.

We are witnessing a renewal of interest in the Kuyperian tradition way
beyond its traditional homelands in Reformed churches in the Netherlands
and in those Reformed churches set up by Dutch immigrants in North
America. Many evangelicals who have discovered the Kuyperian tradition in
recent years will need no reminder that we all need to be converted.[67] What
will excite such readers is the connection between being born again and the
kingdom of God, as we will see below.

However, in the Reformed churches in North America, church, school, and
university easily remain predominantly Dutch.[68] This is precisely not what
Kuyper meant when he spoke of "a *life-sphere* of our own on the foundation of
palingenesia, and a *life-view* of our own thanks to the light that the Holy Spirit
kindles on the candelabra of Scripture." The basis for "a life-sphere of our own"
is palingenesis and not ethnicity! When a life-sphere of our own gets caught
up in ethnicity and a failure to recognize the need for conversion, the life-
sphere takes on a life of its own, and mission and the kingdom soon get rele-
gated to a secondary place. As many Reformed churches and institutions seem
to have lost interest in Kuyperianism, one suspects that it is only through a

---

[67]In Western fashion I am assuming conversion is individual. But see Diogenes Allen, *Spiritual Theology:
The Theology of Yesterday for Spiritual Help Today* (Cambridge, MA: Cowley, 1997), 37-63.

[68]This was certainly not always intentionally so. Cf. H. Evan Runner, "Lecture I: Scientific and Pre-Scientific,"
in *Christian Perspectives 1961* (Hamilton, ON: Guardian Publishing, 1961), 13-15.

fresh breeze of the Spirit that this interest and reengagement with *their* tradition will take place. The kingdom is exciting because of the King, and without a living relationship with the King religion will be about many things but will lack that missional vision of the kingdom, passionately concerned with spreading the fragrance of the King throughout the creation that is rightly his.

Scripture.

> And then, I say it frankly and unhesitatingly, to us Christians of the Reformed faith, the Bible is the Word and the Scripture of our God. When in private or at the family-altar I read the Holy Scripture, neither Moses nor John addresses me, but the Lord my God.[69]

One of the things the Spirit does when a person is converted is to assure them that Scripture is the Word of God and that God speaks to us through his Word by his Spirit. Kuyper's journey is telling in this respect. Prior to his conversion he embraced the emerging liberal view of Scripture, according to which it is assessed for its value through the lens of the modern worldview. Conversion led Kuyper to a hermeneutic of suspicion in regard to himself and a hermeneutic of trust in regard to Scripture, whereas previously it had been the other way around. This does not for a moment mean that conversion solved all the problems Kuyper found in Scripture. On the contrary, he acknowledges that there are many problems he has no idea how to resolve. But such problems are now placed in the context of a childlike faith in Scripture as that great oak tree beneath which one can find shade and rest.

We noted above Kuyper's call for a "*life-sphere* of our own on the foundation of *palingenesia*, and a *life-view* of our own thanks to the light that the Holy Spirit kindles on the candelabra of Scripture." Kuyper here uses imagery for Scripture that reminds one of Calvin's image of Scripture as a pair of spectacles that enables us to see the world aright. Those of us who need glasses will understand this all too well. I need glasses to see at a distance, and it is amazing the change my glasses make to my vision. Apart from Scripture the world is out of focus, and we cannot see it as it is, as the theater of God's glory.

The Kuyperian tradition has made a major contribution to Christian faith and thought in alerting us, with James Orr and others, to the fact that

---

[69]Abraham Kuyper, "The Biblical Criticism of the Present Day," 422.

Christianity involves a *worldview*. It is utterly comprehensive in its outlook, just like the kingdom of God. When George Marsden speaks of the triumph of Kuyperianism in North American evangelicalism, it is undoubtedly this that he is referring to, as evangelicals have rightly come to see the lordship of Christ as claiming and embracing the whole of creation.[70] We must not forget that a worldview is Christian *only* insofar as it views the world in "the light that the Holy Spirit kindles on the candelabra of *Scripture*." Scripture, and not our worldview, is the Word of God, and our worldview must be normed and authorized by Scripture. Utterly central to the Kuyperian tradition is this trust in Scripture as the infallible Word of God, and we should not budge from this position.

Palingenesis. Kuyper is reminiscent of the great Christian philosopher J. G. Hamann (1730–1788)[71] in his immediate recognition that Scripture interprets ourselves to ourselves and casts its light on the whole of creation *as creation*. Many of us become Christians and then discover the comprehensiveness of the gospel years later in a kind of second conversion. For Hamann and Kuyper it came with conversion.

This is the genius of Kuyper's reaching for palingenesis, for, as Kuyper notes, the word not only is used in the New Testament of our personal rebirth, but also in Matthew 19:28 for the rebirth of the entire cosmos. And, as Kuyper so perceptively saw, the two are integrally connected.

The ESV translates *palingenesis* as "in the new world" in Matthew 19:28. This is the time when the Son of Man will sit on his glorious throne, and his followers will also reign. In this passage Jesus is speaking of his second coming, of the consummation of history, and he uses his favorite self-designation, the Son of Man. This title has its primary background in Daniel 7, where one like a son of man comes to the Ancient of Days: "He was given authority, glory and sovereign power; all nations and peoples of every language worshiped him. His dominion is an everlasting dominion that will not pass away, and his kingdom is one that will never be destroyed" (Dan 7:14).

---

[70]George Marsden, "The State of Evangelical Christian Scholarship," *Reformed Journal* 37 (1987): 14, speaks of "The triumph—or nearly so—of what may be loosely called Kuyperian presuppositionalism in the evangelical (academic) community."

[71]See Craig G. Bartholomew and Michael W. Goheen, *Christian Philosophy: A Systematic and Narrative Introduction* (Grand Rapids: Baker Academic, 2013); John R. Betz, *After Enlightenment: The Post-Secular Vision of J. G. Hamann* (Chichester, UK: Wiley-Blackwell, 2012).

Clearly, from Daniel 7, Son of Man is a royal title par excellence. Christ's dominion is over everything. The rebirth is the means by which one enters the kingdom (cf. Jn 3:5), but the kingdom of God, the main theme of Jesus' teaching, is about far more than conversion and the church, although the church is of great importance as a sign of the kingdom. The kingdom is all about the reign of Israel's God, about his climactic breaking into history in and through Jesus in order to recover his purposes for his whole creation. The rebirth of conversion thus involves becoming an active participant in the *missio Dei*: "Christianity aims at a new creation, but the new from the old, a new-fashioned from the fallen world that already exists."[72]

This makes being "born again" a far more significant thing than has often been the case in contemporary evangelicalism, which rightly stresses that we must be born again but too often fails to connect this experience with the kingdom of God. Jesus, by comparison, asserts that we cannot *see or enter* the kingdom of God unless we are born again of the Spirit. The comprehensiveness of the kingdom is a major theme in the biblical and Kuyperian tradition, but it is vital that we not neglect the element of conversion in relation to it. There is no value in being about "kingdom business" if one has not been born again! The kingdom is first about coming into a right and living relation to the King, and cultural engagement follows from and always builds on this experience. It is the great delight of the Spirit to open sinners to the reality of what God has done in Christ and through the response of repentance and faith to enable them to enter the kingdom, a synonym for becoming a Christian.

Two dangers confront contemporary Christianity. One is to rightly emphasize conversion but wrongly to fail to connect conversion to the kingdom of God and God's purposes to lead his creation forward to its climax in a new heaven and a new earth. Conversion thus becomes individualistic, related almost exclusively to the institutional church and focused on going to heaven with no concern for the world. Kuyper is scathing in his critique of such a view: "Life forms in all its rich ramifications one high and holy temple in which the fragrance of the eternal must rise, and whoever wishes to serve at the altar of his soul but not at the altar of life's temple has perhaps been consecrated a priest by himself or by others but certainly not by Christ."[73] The

---

[72]AK:CR, 69.
[73]AK:CR, 83.

sacred/secular dichotomies that have plagued evangelicalism are an embodiment of this problem, as is the debate over whether evangelism has priority over sociopolitical involvement in the mission of the church. We will discuss this in detail in chapter nine.

The second danger is to so emphasize cultural engagement that one forgets that it is citizens of the kingdom who need to be culturally engaged, and that no one is born a citizen but must *enter the kingdom* through being born again. If the first danger is preeminently that of evangelicalism, the second is preeminently that of liberal, ecumenical Christianity. We will have much to say in this book about Kuyper's genius for cultural engagement, but in our excitement about the breadth of his vision we must never forget that participation in that vision begins on our knees before God and returns there again and again.

The church. As we have seen, integral to Kuyper's conversion was a concern for the church, for a church that can truly be the believer's mother in the faith, as Calvin so eloquently put it. Kuyper wrestled with this issue from the time of his prize-winning essay on Calvin's and Laski's views of the church, and his conversion made the issue more and not less important. He would go on to participate, controversially, in founding a new denomination, the Doleantie, and in chapter six we will explore his lifelong passion for the church in more detail.

Suffice it here to note the vital importance of the institutional church for Kuyper. In his social theory Kuyper is best known for his doctrine of sphere sovereignty, according to which society is by God's design divided into separate spheres such as government, family, education, institutional church, and so on. We will examine this theory in chapter five. For now, we note that Kuyper never lost sight of the unique importance of the sphere of the institutional church. In his 1870 farewell sermon to his congregation in Utrecht, Kuyper was clear: "the problem of the church is none other than the problem of Christianity itself."[74]

We have seen how Kuyper took a stand against the emerging theological liberalism; he could be equally critical of a dead conservatism. Kuyper saw that the church was rightly and inherently conservative in its duty to hold on to the gospel once delivered to the church by the apostles. "'Preservation,' therefore, must remain its rallying cry, since without that drive to preserve it

---

[74]*AK:CR*, 69.

would also lose the precious pearl." Unlike revolution, Christianity aims to restore and not to destroy. But "Precisely because it seeks to save, Christianity detests a false conservatism that adorns itself with the name of Christianity but is devoid of its power."[75]

Kuyper wanted an orthodox church, but a living orthodoxy and one that would develop its resources in relation to the needs of the day. In today's language we would say he abhorred any attempt to undermine the gospel but longed for its contextualization. "One can aim at preserving either that which has so far emerged from that principle or the principle itself."[76] For Kuyper there was no dilemma; one must opt for the principle itself, and that is Christ:

> *All* power in the church of Christ must forever be traced back to Christ. He and He alone is our King. To Him alone is given all power in heaven and on earth. And just as the sun has been set in the sky above as the greater light to rule the day, so the Sun of righteousness shines out from above to exercise lordship over the church militant on earth. He is the Immanuel, beside Him there is no other. He is the ruler in Israel, but only after letting Himself be trampled to give his life as a ransom for many.[77]

CONCLUSION

At the beginning of the chapter we quoted John Carroll to the effect that "The entire story of the failure of upper-middle-class nerve in modernity is one of the loss of a place to stand." There, at the very outset of modernity, Kuyper never made this mistake. By grace he took his stand firmly "in Christ," and from that place was able to bring a Christian perspective to bear across the sweep of European culture. In this he has much to teach us today.

---

[75]*AK:CR*, 71, 79.
[76]*AK:CR*, 81.
[77]*AK:CR*, 131.

CREATION AND REDEMPTION

*For the past few decades, one problem has dominated the exegesis and theology
of the Old Testament: what degree of independence is to be accorded the
doctrine of creation in relation to the fundamental soteriological affirmation
that is assumed to run through both testaments of the Bible. . . . Within
Christian communities, then, the stakes of this discussion are high.*

PAUL RICOEUR, "THINKING CREATION"

*However rich the dispensation of grace may be, it ever remains a bandage
applied to the injured part of the body, and is never that vital part itself.*

ABRAHAM KUYPER, *PRINCIPLES OF SACRED THEOLOGY*

*The cross of Christ divides history into two parts . . . but in both parts,
from the creation to the cross and from the cross to the advent, it is
one whole, one uninterrupted work of God. Christianity . . . embraces
the whole man, all humanity, and the totality of the world. . . . And
it has its heart and centre in the person and work of Christ.*

HERMAN BAVINCK, *PHILOSOPHY OF REVELATION*

God has loved not individuals nor nations, but the world.

ABRAHAM KUYPER, *PRINCIPLES OF SACRED THEOLOGY*

AT THE HEART OF THE KUYPERIAN TRADITION is the sovereign
God, who has come to us in Christ. The Kuyperian tradition is thus trinitarian
and christocentric. It shares these characteristics, of course, with all other

orthodox Christian traditions. However, when we seek to explain the work achieved by God in Christ, the distinctives of the Kuyperian tradition move to the foreground. The distinctives of the Kuyperian tradition can be explored in this respect via a variety of questions:

- What is achieved through the saving work of Christ?[1]
- What is the relationship between redemption and creation?
- What is the relationship between the fall and salvation in Christ?
- What is the relationship between nature and grace?
- What is the relationship between general and special revelation?
- What are the major themes of the biblical story, and how do they evoke the *missio Dei*, the work of God with his creation?
- What happens to the creation at Christ's second coming?

Kuyper was well aware that the way we answer the above questions has profound implications for how we think about the Christian life and obedience in this time between the coming of the kingdom and its final consummation. Thus it is not surprising that he attends to such questions closely and mainly, although not exclusively, in terms of the relationship between nature and grace, our fourth question above. We will begin with Kuyper and then move on to Bavinck, who is a master at articulating answers to the above. Then we will follow Al Wolters in developing a typology of different views of the nature-grace relationship. Finally, we will take note of the developing convergence around the Kuyperian view that grace restores nature.

ABRAHAM KUYPER

Like Karl Barth, Kuyper sees God as abundantly gracious in his relationship to the creation from its outset and not only after the fall. Kuyper notes that it is "impossible to imagine man even for a moment in paradise without grace hovering around him and permeating him."[2] The *particular grace* that is involved in the salvation of the elect presupposes what Kuyper calls *common grace*, God's preserving of his creation after the fall.[3]

---

[1]Cf. Craig G. Bartholomew, "Wisdom and Atonement," forthcoming.
[2]*CG*, 1:263.
[3]Kuyper was preceded in his discussion of common grace by Herman Bavinck, who gave a rectorial

For Kuyper, we should not make the mistake of thinking that God preserves his creation only in order to make possible the salvation of the elect. The mistake in this view is to make the elect the focus rather than Christ. Kuyper points out that in the Reformed confessions it is clear that everything in this world has Christ as its aim and that the body of Christ is at the center of God's work in history so that we can and must say that "the church of Christ constitutes the center of world history."[4] The church is this center because of Christ and who he is:

> No, Christ takes first position here. He through whom all things are, and we through him. He, the reflection of God's glory and the express image of his substance, of whom we confess that all things have been created through him, whether visible or invisible, in heaven and on earth, in whom even now all things hold together [see Col 1:16-17]. Everything revolves around this Christ because in him the fullness of God dwells bodily [see Col 2:9], and before him every knee must bow and he must be confessed by every tongue as Christ the Lord, to the glory of God the Father [see Phil 2:10-11].[5]

Kuyper points out that in order to grasp this and the interrelationships between particular grace and common grace we must focus on a vital issue, namely *the relationship between nature and grace.*

Kuyper does this by asking our first question above, namely, what precisely is achieved through the work of Christ? Is it "only" the expiation of guilt? Kuyper's answer is clear: "The notion that the Christ had no other significance than that he died for our sin as the Lamb of God cannot be sustained when we consult Scripture."[6] Christ is not only given for our justification and sanctification but also for wisdom and "perfect redemption." Kuyper poses a series of rhetorical questions:

---

address in 1894 at the Theological School in Kampen titled "Common Grace." See "Herman Bavinck's 'Common Grace,'" trans. Raymond van Leeuwen, *CTJ* 24, no. 1 (1989): 35-65. For a critique of Kuyper's view of common grace see Simon J. Ridderbos, "De theologische cultuurbeschouwing van Abraham Kuyper," PhD diss., Free University of Amsterdam, 1947; S. U. Zuidema, "Common Grace and Christian Action in Abraham Kuyper," in *Communication and Confrontation* (Toronto: Wedge, 1972), 52-105. Zuidema argues that there is a tension in Kuyper's work between common and particular grace. However, he sees Kuyper breaking through this tension especially in his *Pro Rege.* Cf. Craig G. Bartholomew, "Not So Common," introductory essay for Abraham Kuyper, *Common Grace* II (Bellingham, WA: Lexham Press, forthcoming).

[4]*CG* 1:266.
[5]*CG* 1:266.
[6]*CG* 1:267.

Shall we say that Christ is given only for our justification and sanctification, or shall we continue to confess with the apostle in 1 Corinthians 1:30 that Christ is given to us from God also for *wisdom* and *perfect redemption*? Shall we say that we have in him only atonement for our sin, or shall we continue to acknowledge that it is he who will one day transform our lowly bodies to be like his glorified body "by the power that enables him even to subject all things to himself" [Phil 3:21]? Shall we consider the work of the Christ on Golgotha as finished, or shall we with Scripture and with the whole church of the first centuries continue to expect our Lord from heaven in order to bring the present situation to an end and lead it to a new heaven and a new earth? To put it succinctly, shall we imagine that the Redeemer of our soul is enough for us, or shall we continue to confess a Christ of God as the Savior of both soul and body and as re-creator, not only of the things that are invisible but also of the things that are visible and apparent to our eyes? Does Christ have significance only for the spiritual, or also for the natural and visible? Does the fact that he overcame the world mean that one day he will cast the world back into nothingness in order to be left with only the souls of the elect, or does it mean that the world will also be his prize, the trophy of his glory?[7]

Kuyper makes clear through this chain of questions that the work of Christ extends beyond the salvation of individuals to include the renewal of the entire creation. God's grace in Christ thus certainly saves individuals but is also aimed at restoring the creation and leading history toward that destination for which it was always intended.

The practical implications of this are significant, and Kuyper is in no doubt about them. He asks his reader to reflect on the danger of receiving Christ only for one's soul and thus seeing one's life in the world as something positioned alongside one's faith and thus not being governed by it. The result is that Christianity is only relevant to "spiritual" matters such as church and mission, and all the other areas of life are seen as outside Christ. This leads to a false dualism with radical ethical implications: "In the world you do as others do. The world is a less holy, almost unholy area that should take care of itself as best it can."[8]

Academic work, the arts, business, politics: all become unholy. A type of unhelpful dualism emerges in the Christian life:

---

[7]CG 1:267-68.
[8]CG 1:269.

You end up living in two spheres of thought. On the one hand the very narrow, reduced line of thought involving your soul's salvation, and on the other hand the broad, spacious, life-encompassing sphere of thought involving the world. Your Christ then belongs comfortably in that first, reduced sphere of thinking, but not in the broad one. And then from that antithesis and false proportionality proceed all narrow-mindedness, inner untruthfulness, not to mention pious insincerity and impotence.[9]

Kuyper places his finger here on what in more recent thought has become known as a sacred/secular dualism. Church activities such as worship, prayer, preaching, and evangelism are regarded as spiritual or sacred, whereas other areas of created life such as education, politics, agriculture, leisure, sports, and so on, are regarded as "secular" and thus second-rate in comparison to the primary spiritual activities. Much of twentieth-century evangelicalism was pervaded by such dualism, and its influence lingers.[10] Theologically such a view is problematic because it leaves salvation unconnected to creation:

> Particular grace is treated too much in isolation while neglecting its foundation in common grace and its ultimate goal: the salvation of the world that was created, maintained, and never abandoned by God. The sad consequence of this error is that particular grace floats in the air; the salvation of our soul is dissociated from our position and our life in the world; the floodgates open for the influx of Jewish particularism; and our Christian people are hindered from arriving at a thoroughly sound, truly Christian world- and lifeview that impassions their faith and steels their resilience.[11]

An example of how the sacred/secular approach manifests itself in so much church life is its influence on how we think about vocation. It yields what John Stott referred to as a *vocational pyramid*, which can be represented as shown in figure 1.

As one ascends the vocational pyramid, one's spirituality increases, and only the top two tiers are in the "full-time" service of God. Business is useful only insofar as it provides the funding for spiritual activities. Health care has its place, but *the soul* is what really matters. And so on and so forth. Large swaths of life

---

[9]CG 1:269.
[10]See the important book by David W. Smith, *Transforming the World? The Social Impact of British Evangelicalism* (Carlisle, UK: Paternoster, 1998).
[11]CG 1:377.

are left to go their own way, and Christianity in effect has no relevance to what most Christians spend most of their time doing.[12] One ends up in the disastrous situation described by David Smith in his *Transforming the World? The Social Impact of British Evangelicalism*. While Scottish theologians such as James Orr were engaging critically with modernity and appropriating the concept of "worldview" in order to do so, the Cambridge University Christian Union was hosting an American evangelist whose preaching amounted to an emotional sentimentality. A soloist sang a song with the words "Tell Mother I'll Be There," and Charles Alexander asked undergraduates to stand if they wanted to meet their mothers in heaven. As Smith observes, "The Christian Union had clearly abandoned any attempt to speak the word of God meaningfully in a university permeated by secular thought and a mission which resorted to such frankly subjectivistic techniques was bound to confirm the intelligentsia in their belief that religious faith was irrational and impossible."[13]

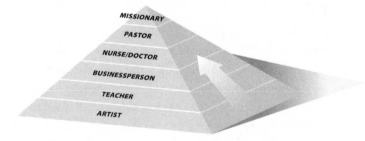

Figure 1. Vocational pyramid

Kuyper will have none of this, yet neither does he make the mistake of reactively letting the pendulum swing to the other extreme. He is quite clear that the question "What must I do to be saved?" (Acts 16:30) has to be kept front and center in our thinking and practice. He is also clear that the comprehensive extent of God's salvation does not equate to universalism in terms of salvation for all. At the same time,

> we must confess with equal clarity and explicitness how this same Christ who has
> been given to us for justification and sanctification is also given to us for wisdom

---

[12]Cf. the salient comments in this respect by Wendell Berry, *What Are People For?* (New York: North Point, 1990), 96-97.

[13]Smith, *Transforming the World?*, 74.

and complete redemption, that is to say, for the re-creation of our whole being, soul and body, and all of this together with the inclusion of the whole world we live in, the world that belongs to and is inseparably linked to our existence.[14]

Grace, according to Kuyper, must not be seen as external to nature. It is not like oil poured on water and remaining separate from it, like a lifeboat into which the drowning person can find refuge from the world. "We cannot grasp *grace* in all its richness if we do not notice that the fibers of its roots penetrate into the joints and cracks of the life of nature."[15]

This view of grace *penetrating nature* stems from our view of Christ's work:

If, on the other hand, it is definitely true that Christ our Savior is dealing not only with our soul but also with our body; that all things in the world are Christ's and are claimed by him; that he will one day triumph over all enemies in that world; and that the culmination will be not that Christ will gather around himself some individual souls, as is presently the case, but that he will reign as King upon a new earth under a new heaven—then of course all this becomes entirely different and it becomes immediately apparent that grace is inseparably linked to nature, that grace and nature belong together.[16]

This holistic view, of course, stems not only from Christ's work but also from his *identity*. The firstborn from the dead is also the firstborn of creation, as in Colossians 1, and the incarnate Word remains the same eternal Word that was with God and was God, of whom John writes that apart from him nothing was made that has been made.

If, as Matthew 5 tells us, disciples of Jesus are the salt of the earth and the light of the world, then a great deal is at stake in developing a right view of the relationship between nature and grace. The well-being of the world depends on it. A dualistic worldview prevents salt being rubbed into the decaying meat of the world or light radiating out into its darkness. Kuyper is well aware of this, but he rightly keeps the focus elsewhere. It is not just the well-being of the world that is at stake but the glory of God. Like the biblical prophets, he is seized by a holy indignation: "Once we have grasped this, we sense something of holy indignation vibrate within us when we hear this grand distinction between *new* creation and *re*-creation being presented as something of

---

[14]*CG* 1:270.
[15]*CG* 1:270.
[16]*CG* 1:270.

secondary importance." Again, "But nevertheless it hurts to see how people in such circles are so minimally concerned with the honor of God."[17] Kuyper finds support for his biblical sense that the honor of God is foremost in that after the fall God addresses the *protevangelium* not to Adam and Eve but to the serpent in order to preserve his reputation and honor over that of the serpent.

Our view of the relationship between nature and grace also reveals itself in what we think will happen when Christ returns. What will then become of the creation? Did God's work of creation fail? Kuyper rightly argues, "God's honor depended on the fact that his glorious work of creation would ultimately be shown not to have failed but to have served the glorification of his name."[18] Thus Kuyper argues for re-creation, or what Wolters calls "creation regained," as the goal that Christ will facilitate when he returns:

> But if we move away for a single moment from the governing notion of *re*-creation and slip into the false notion of a kind of creating *anew*, then any reasonable motive for all of this falls away; everything acquires an absurd character, and we get the impression of mere arbitrariness, so that any impulse to worship is transformed into a dull and meaningless dumbfoundedness.[19]

In his book on Revelation Kuyper is clear that, when it comes to our world,

> It is, and always shall be, the world which God Almighty has created, which He, in spite of all the sins of angels and of men, has in its broad dimensions upheld and maintained, and which at the time of the end He will so bring out to a perfect form of life, that it will perfectly correspond to His purpose of creation, and which, in spite of the sins of angels and of men shall make His original plan—now no more susceptible of corruption—shine forth resplendently in fullness and richness of form.[20]

Kuyper thus strongly affirms *re-creation*, but his articulation of it is more complex than that. He takes 2 Peter 3:10 to be saying literally that the creation will perish: "First everything that exists will perish, and only then the new order will emerge out of that apparent chaos." In an effort to distinguish between what will perish and what will be re-created, Kuyper makes a somewhat unhelpful

---

[17]*CG* 1:290.
[18]*CG* 1:209.
[19]*CG* 1:291.
[20]Abraham Kuyper, *The Revelation of St. John*, trans. John H. de Vries (Grand Rapids: Eerdmans, 1963), 344.

distinction between form and essence: "There is no doubt that what exists now will one day perish and disappear, except that what will perish will be not the essence but only the form, and the essence itself will emerge in new and more glorious forms."[21] Kuyper invokes 1 Corinthians 15 as decisive in this respect: everything belonging to our human nature or essence by virtue of creation will reemerge the second time, but now with more abundance and greater glory.

> Entirely in the same way we have to imagine that all the forms in which the fruit of common grace blossoms now will one day perish, but the powerful germ that lies at the foundation of all of these things will not perish but abides, and one day will be carried into the new kingdom of glory, and God will supply this all with a new form that is in sacred harmony with the glory of his kingdom.[22]

Kuyper ends up with a tension between perishing and re-creation in his thought. He insists that the new earth will be a visible, material reality and that it will develop out of the existing world and correspond to it "in kind."[23] But it is hard to see how this relates to this creation "perishing." Nevertheless, overall Kuyper's view is rich and insightful. He summarizes it as follows:

> Originally God created his universe as one connected organic whole. This artwork of the supreme Artist was ripped apart and wrecked by sin. As a result, it appeared as though the creation had been a mistake and God's purpose with that creation was thwarted, and this is what people thought for many centuries. But there was a mystery, a secret with God. Formerly people did not understand that secret, but it is revealed in Christ. And this secret consists in this, that the original plan of God was *not* neutralized, but continues full of majesty, and that God will thereby realize his world plan, that one day in Christ he will once again connect those parts and pieces of his creation, taken here as heaven and earth, *under one head*, that is, once again into one entirely organic, integrated, and connected entity.[24]

EVALUATION

Kuyper's thought on the relationship between nature and grace is rich indeed. First, we should note how important it is that he *recognizes* this issue as of fundamental importance. Alas, it remains one too little explored.

---

[21]*CG* 1:544, 572.
[22]*CG* 1:549.
[23]*CG* 1:572.
[24]*CG* 1:577.

Second, Kuyper rightly keeps drawing us back to Christ and the glory of God. At the end of the day, life is about God and his glory and not about us, but as we decenter ourselves and "let" God be God we—ironically—find ourselves. As Bavinck perceptively notes, "Conversion is a turning back to God, but at the same time a coming to one's self."[25]

Third, Kuyper never lets go of the importance of individual salvation, even as he insists that the grace that saves us is also aimed at saving the entire creation. Fourth, Christology is wonderfully central to Kuyper's comprehensive vision. Kuyper opens up for us a huge, biblical vision of the Christ, who is both creator and redeemer.

Fifth, Kuyper is attentive to the practical consequences for the view we hold of the relationship between nature and grace. This is no secondary issue but gets to the core of Christian practice and witness in the world. Sixth, Kuyper sees clearly that grace is not external to creation but penetrates to its core.

Seventh, Kuyper's view of the telos of creation as re-creation is biblical, but his view of the creation perishing needs to be refined. Recent studies have argued that 2 Peter 3:7 is not talking about the destruction of the creation but about its purification from the damaging toxins of sin and evil.[26] Although one cannot speak with precision about the exact points of continuity and discontinuity between this creation and the new heavens and the new earth, we can speak with assurance about the renewal of this creation and that as such it will not perish.

Eighth, *eschatology* could be a stronger element in Kuyper's view of nature and grace.[27] Kuyper notes in regard to nature and grace that we "have only to seek to answer the question concerning what conceivable connection exists between the nature of this temporal life and the character of eternal life," but he fails to explore "eternal life" as the life of the age to come, which has already broken into the creation with the coming of Christ.[28]

Ninth, there are tensions in Kuyper's articulation of the relationship between particular grace and common grace. Kuyper argues, "The Reformed

---

[25]*PR*, 258.

[26]See Craig G. Bartholomew, *Where Mortals Dwell: A Christian View of Place for Today* (Grand Rapids: Baker Academic, 2011), 152-56.

[27]But cf. *PST*, 371; Abraham Kuyper, *The Revelation of St. John* (Eugene, OR: Wipf and Stock, 1999); Abraham Kuyper, *Van de voleinding*, 4 vols. (Kampen: Kok, 1929–1931).

[28]*CG* 1:570.

person looks through grace to the nature behind and underneath it and therefore takes into account both common grace and particular grace," but tensions remain in his view of the interrelationship between particular and common grace.[29] S. U. Zuidema, as noted above, argues that Kuyper broke through this tension in his later work and especially in his *Pro Rege*, leaving behind a view of common grace as somehow independent of particular grace. As Zuidema writes, "Rather, common grace would then be confessed as a work of God whereby He upholds His creation, maintains his creation ordinances, and thus opens the way for the militant as well as suffering church to fight her warfare *pro Rege*, throughout this age, with the weapons God in His common grace has provided her."[30]

If we return to the questions with which we began, we can see that to one extent or another all of them have been answered by Kuyper.

HERMAN BAVINCK ON NATURE AND GRACE

Herman Bavinck was a younger contemporary of Kuyper.[31] After several times refusing the invitation to come to the Free University of Amsterdam, finally in 1902 he accepted and succeeded Kuyper as professor of theology. Thus Bavinck moved to Amsterdam, with his first edition of his multivolume *Reformed Dogmatics* already published. He remained at the Free University for the remainder of his teaching career.

Intriguingly, in an essay published in 1888 on the theology of Albrecht Ritschl (1822–1889), Herman Bavinck confesses that he does not know how to combine the view of salvation as separating us from the world with Ritschl's view of salvation as equipping us to fulfill our earthly vocations.[32] This was the same year in which Bavinck published his rectorial address on the catholicity of the church, inter alia a beautiful articulation of the relationship

[29]CG 1:380.

[30]Zuidema, "Common Grace and Christian Action in Abraham Kuyper," 100-101.

[31]See the major work by Dirk van Keulen, *Bijbel en dogmatiek: Schriftbeschouwing en schriftgebruik in het dogmatisch werk van A. Kuyper, H. Bavinck, en G.C. Berkouwer* (Kampen: Kok, 2003).

[32]Herman Bavinck, "The Theology of Albrecht Ritschl," trans. John Bolt, *The Bavinck Review* 3 (2012): 123-63. Bavinck states: "Personally, I do not yet see any way of combining the two points of view, but I do know that there is much that is excellent in both, and that both contain undeniable truth" (157). See Jan Veenhof, *Nature and Grace in Herman Bavinck*, trans. Al Wolters (Sioux Center, IA: Dordt College Press, 2006), 8-9. Albrecht Ritschl (1822–1889) was a German theologian who made significant use of worldview. Cf. Clifford B. Anderson, "Jesus and the 'Christian Worldview': A Comparative Analysis of Abraham Kuyper and Karl Barth," *Cultural Encounters* 6, no. 1 (2006): 61-80.

between nature and grace.[33] It would appear that Ritschl's work provoked
Bavinck to attend closely to this issue, and that, once solved, it became abso-
lutely central to his theology and is to be found everywhere in his writings.
Indeed, he reduces the differences in Christian traditions to this issue:

> Every Christian must take into account two factors: creation and re-creation,
> nature and grace, earthly and heavenly vocation, etc.; and in accordance with
> the different relationship in which he puts these to each other, his religious life
> assumes a different character. . . . Whoever breaks the divinely appointed con-
> nection between nature and grace is led to sacrifice one to the other.[34]

Bavinck sees the relationship between nature and grace as central to the Reformation and to the thought of Calvin in particular. The Reformation, through
its recalibration of theology, brought the cosmos firmly back into view as the
theater of God's glory. "The natural is not something of lesser value. . . . It is
just as divine as the church, though it owes its origin not to recreation but
creation, though it is not from the Son but from the Father."[35]

Bavinck recognizes the important priority in pietism of one's relationship
with God. However, he is alert to the danger of a disengaged Christianity that
leaves the world to itself. Bavinck is wonderfully clear that the problem with
the world is *sin* and that grace has come to deal with this problem. Jesus, says
Bavinck, was not a statesman, a new legislator, a philosopher, but only Jesus,
that is, *Savior*! "But *that* he was completely and entirely . . . in the full, deep,
broad Reformed sense. . . . The love of God, the grace of the Son and the fellowship of the Holy Spirit extend as far as sin." He regularly quotes 1 Timothy
4:4-5 and 1 John 3:8, which he summarizes as: "the Son of God was manifested, not that he might destroy the works of the Father, but that he might
destroy the works of the devil, in order thus to restore the works of the Father."
In Bavinck's memorable words, "grace does not abolish nature, but affirms and
restores it."[36]

Bavinck is deeply attuned to the practical implications of a right understanding of the relationship between nature and grace. He never blurs the importance of conversion and relationship with Christ, and he is rightly alert to

---

[33]Herman Bavinck, "The Catholicity of Christianity and the Church," *CTJ* 27 (1992): 220-51.
[34]Herman Bavinck, *De Bazuin* XLVIII, no. 12 (March 23, 1900). Quoted in Veenhof, *Nature and Grace*, 8.
[35]Quoted in Veenhof, *Nature and Grace*, 12.
[36]Quoted in ibid., 20, 17.

the danger of a sort of messianism whereby we think we will introduce the kingdom: "Nowadays we are out to convert the whole world, to conquer all areas of life for Christ. But we often neglect to ask whether we ourselves are truly converted and whether we belong to Christ in life and in death." However, from a position of faith in Christ, the believer "can now freely look around and enjoy all the good gifts and the perfect gift that descends from the Father of lights. Everything is his because he is Christ's and Christ is God's. The whole world becomes material for his duty."[37] Veenhof summarizes Bavinck's view as follows:

> The soteriological concentration of Christ's work and word, and the universal range and scope that is based upon it, must be reflected in the lives of believers in such a way that the faith-relation with Christ constitutes not only the decisive pre-condition but also the driving force for the unfolding of created reality in meaningful cultural work. The faith-relation with Christ through the gospel is primary. Man must first become son of God again, before he can become "a cultural creature" in the true sense of the word. But once he *is* son of God, he can also dedicate himself to culture again.[38]

Bavinck opens his chapter "Revelation and Culture" in his *Philosophy of Revelation* with an instructive quote from the preacher J. Chr. Blumhardt: "man must be twice converted, first from the natural to the spiritual life, and then from the spiritual to the natural."[39]

Bavinck's theology is *trinitarian* through and through, and he expresses a trinitarian view of nature and grace more concisely and integrally than does Kuyper:

> The essence of the Christian religion consists in the reality that the creation of the Father, ruined by sin, is restored in the death of the Son of God and re-created by the grace of the Holy Spirit into a kingdom of God. Dogmatics shows us how God, who is all-sufficient in himself, nevertheless glorifies himself in his creation, which, even when it is torn apart by sin, is gathered up again in Christ (Eph. 1:10). It describes for us God, always God, from beginning to end—God in his being, God in his creation, God against sin, God in Christ, God breaking down all resistance through the Holy Spirit and

---

[37]Herman Bavinck, *The Certainty of Faith*, trans. Harry der Nederlanden (St. Catherines, ON: Paideia, 1980), 94, 95.
[38]Veenhof, *Nature and Grace*, 28-29.
[39]PR, 242.

guiding the whole of creation back to the objective he decreed for it: the glory of his name.[40]

Bavinck's theology of nature and grace is also christological. In words strongly reminiscent of Oliver O'Donovan's statement that resurrection is the reaffirmation of creation, he asserts, "The resurrection is the fundamental restoration of all culture."[41] "The bodily resurrection of Christ from the dead is conclusive proof that Christianity does not adopt a hostile attitude toward anything human or natural, but intends only to deliver creation from all that is sinful, and to sanctify it completely."[42] One is reminded here also of Tom Wright's work. Wright says, for example,

> The deepest meanings of the resurrection have to do with new creation. . . . As Paul saw so clearly in Romans 8, it was the sign that the whole creation would have its exodus, would shake off its corruption and decay, its enslavement to entropy. . . . Because of this hope, the resurrection of Jesus means that the present time is shot through with great significance. What is done to the glory of God in the present is genuinely building for God's future.[43]

Both Kuyper and Bavinck make much of the incarnation in their theologies, an emphasis that needs to be recovered.[44] Bavinck notes that a docetic Christology always follows from a dualistic view of nature and grace. First John, which Bavinck regularly quotes, is a firm corrective to Docetism. He asserts that the affirmation of Christ's humanity implies a correct understanding of the nature-grace relationship; one cannot affirm the incarnation and denigrate nature. Scripture, Bavinck argues, "maintains, also in the incarnation, the goodness of creation and the divine origin of matter." In principle the incarnation implies "the overcoming of all dualism, and the condemnation of asceticism."[45]

Using neo-Thomist categories, Bavinck argues that sin and grace are not *substantial*; they are not of the essence of things but adhere to the essence.[46]

---

[40]RD 1:112.

[41]Oliver O'Donovan, *Resurrection and Moral Order: An Outline for Evangelical Ethics* (Grand Rapids: Eerdmans, 1986, 1994), 15; *PR*, 267.

[42]Quoted in Veenhof, *Nature and Grace*, 21.

[43]N. T. Wright in Wright and Marcus J. Borg, *The Meaning of Jesus* (London: SPCK, 1999), 126.

[44]Cf. Athanasius, *On the Incarnation*. See, for example, Richard J. Mouw and Douglas A. Sweeney, *The Suffering and Victorious Christ: Toward a More Compassionate Christology* (Grand Rapids: Baker Academic, 2013).

[45]Quoted in Veenhof, *Nature and Grace*, 21-22.

[46]See Wolters's insightful comments in ibid., 3, on how Vollenhoven and Dooyeweerd developed a

Consequently, sin can be eradicated without destroying the good creation, and grace can restore the creation without creating anew: "Sin does not lie in matter, nor in nature, nor in the substance of things, but it belongs to the will of the creature; it is of ethical nature, and thus capable of being expiated, effaced, extinguished. It can be separated from the creature, so that it disappears and the creature remains intact, yea, much more, is restored and glorified."[47] Bavinck also connects his view of nature and grace with Kuyper in affirming *reformation* of a society, but not revolution. Revolution destroys the good with the bad, whereas reformation goes after sin alone. We will revisit this issue in chapter seven.

Bavinck sees the telos of creation as *restoration* and not repristination. The move in Scripture is from garden to city and not a move from garden to garden. God leads his creation toward the destiny he intended for it from the very beginning.

As is well-known, Bavinck wrote far more theology than Kuyper. In his *Reformed Dogmatics* he has a rich discussion of general and special revelation, and readers are referred to that discussion.[48] Here it should be noted that Bavinck's articulation of general and special revelation is more systematic and nuanced than Kuyper's and, in my view, more helpful than Kuyper's use of common grace. Bavinck also has a stronger stress on eschatology:

> In no way should the Christian faith be represented as otherworldly or anti-creation. Rather, grace and nature are united in the Christian faith, and general revelation links the kingdom of heaven and the kingdom of earth—it joins creation and redemption together in one great eschatological cantata of praise. Grace restores nature, a religious life is woven into the very fabric of ordinary human experience. Finally, God is one and the same living God in creation and redemption; grace restores nature.[49]

If we were to revisit our questions at the outset of this chapter we would see that, like Kuyper, Bavinck answers nearly all of them, and in remarkably

---

vocabulary of their own that does better justice to Kuyper's and Bavinck's insights on nature and grace. Particularly relevant are their concepts of law, subject, and direction. For an excellent discussion of structure and direction see Albert M. Wolters, *Creation Regained: Biblical Basics for a Reformational Worldview*, 2nd ed. (Grand Rapids: Eerdmans, 2005).

[47]PR, 307. Cf. PST, 346; Brian G. Mattson, *Restored to Our Destiny: Eschatology and the Image of God in Herman Bavinck's Reformed Dogmatics*, Studies in Reformed Theology (Leiden: Brill, 2012).

[48]RD 1:301-85.

[49]RD 1:302, emphasis original.

similar, though more systematic, ways. As regards the second coming Bavinck notes, "*The day of our Lord's return brings about the resurrection of believers, the judgment of unbelievers, and the renewal of creation.*"[50]

OPPOSING VIEWS OF NATURE AND GRACE

All orthodox Christian traditions believe in creation, fall, and redemption. The issue the Kuyperian tradition raises is how different traditions construe the relationships between these three or, as Kuyper and Bavinck would express it, between nature and grace. In Kuyper's writings one regularly finds him distinguishing between Calvinist, Lutheran, and Catholic perspectives. Such distinctions are more systematic in Bavinck's writings, and his approach has been developed and honed by Al Wolters, who distinguishes five different categories for ways in which the Christian tradition has understood the relationship between nature and grace:[51]

1. grace against nature (*gratia contra naturam*) (Anabaptism)

2. grace over nature (*gratia supra naturam*) (Roman Catholicism)

3. grace alongside nature (*gratia iuxta naturam*) (Lutheranism)

4. grace within nature (*gratia intra naturam*) (Calvinism)

5. grace equals nature (*gratia instar naturae*) (liberalism)

Wolters understands *nature* to refer to creation, including human life and culture,[52] and *grace* to refer to new life in Jesus Christ, to redemption and salvation.[53] From a Kuyperian perspective the way one construes the nature-grace

---

[50]*RD* 4:691, emphasis original. See this volume for Bavinck's theology of the last things.

[51]See, e.g., Herman Bavinck, "The Catholicity of Christianity and the Church." Wolters writes against the background of H. R. Niebuhr's seminal work, *Christ and Culture* (New York: Harper & Row, 1951). See Al Wolters, "On the Idea of Worldview and Its Relation to Philosophy," in Paul Marshall, Sander Griffioen, and Richard J. Mouw, eds., *Stained Glass: Worldviews and Social Science* (Lanham, MD: University Press of America, 1983), 14-25. Cf. Albert Wolters, "Nature and Grace in the Interpretation of Proverbs 31:10-31," *CTJ* 19 (1984): 153-66.

[52]Cf. Henri de Lubac, *A Brief Catechism on Nature and Grace*, trans. Br. Richard Arnandez (San Francisco: Igantius, 1984), 13, who notes the elusiveness of the meanings of the word *nature* but argues that its theological use does not pose difficulties. De Lubac quotes G. Martelet with approval: "Anything that does not derive from divine adoption in man, even if it does derive from the spirit and liberty in him, can be called natural." However, de Lubac's discussion (9-22) indicates that his view of nature differs from Wolter's equation of nature with creation. For de Lubac humankind cannot be reduced to nature; it goes beyond nature. One could not say this if by *nature* one meant "creation."

[53]Al Wolters, "The Nature of Fundamentalism," *Pro Rege*, September 1986, 7.

relationship is foundational and inevitably manifests itself in a whole range of other issues, such as one's view of the relationship between gospel and law, between gospel and culture, of God's order for creation or natural law and how we know it, of rationality and epistemology, education, politics, and so on.[54]

Such a typology is just that; it is an attempt to discern the major models while being aware that in reality views will diverge and overlap. A typology of this sort identifies tendencies and not always strictly defined categories. We also live in a day in which diverse views of the nature-grace relationship are found *within* confessional traditions so that, for example, one should certainly not assume from the above typology that we are saying that all Lutherans today hold to a view of grace alongside nature. Historically, grace alongside nature in Lutheran thought manifested itself in the doctrine of two kingdoms. Such language remains common among Lutherans, but ironically, one of the most ardent advocates for such a view today is Reformed theologian David VanDrunen![55] At the same time, Lutheran theologians have revisited just what Luther's view of nature was, and, for example, well-known Lutheran theologian Oswald Bayer argues that far more attention needs to be given to Luther's doctrine of the three estates—church, the household, and politics; indeed, "The story of Luther's discovery of the positive meaning of world and nature is still to be written."[56]

The Thomist tradition, with which we associate the grace-above-nature type, is similar. There is ample evidence for this type among many Catholic scholars, as we will see below, but it is by no means confined to them. At the same time Thomas Aquinas's view on this matter is disputed, with some

---

[54]On gospel and law, cf. Herman Dooyeweerd, *A New Critique of Theoretical Thought* (Jordan Station, ON: Paideia, 1984), 1:511-13. On philosophy and rationality, see Al Wolters, "Dutch Neo-Calvinism: Worldview, Philosophy and Rationality," in H. Hart, J. van der Hoeven, and Nicholas Wolterstorff, eds., *Rationality in the Calvinian Tradition* (Toronto: University Press of America, 1983), 113-31.

[55]David VanDrunen, *Living in God's Two Kingdoms* (Wheaton, IL: Crossway, 2010); *Natural Law and the Two Kingdoms: A Study in the Development of Reformed Social Thought*, Emory University Studies in Law and Tradition (Grand Rapids: Eerdmans, 2010).

[56]Oswald Bayer, *Freedom in Response: Lutheran Ethics: Sources and Controversies*, trans. Jeffrey F. Cayzer (Oxford: Oxford University Press, 2007), 99. Bayer, 95, asserts that "It is very noticeable that in contrast to the strict distinction of the spiritual and worldly governments which marks the two kingdoms doctrine, the doctrine of the three estates sets the spiritual alongside the other two in sequence, and so treats it together with that 'worldly' realm to which at other times it is so sharply opposed." Cf. also Dietrich Bonhoeffer, *Ethics* (London: SCM Press, 1955), 62-72, who as a Lutheran theologian strongly distances himself from a doctrine of two spheres; Uwe Simon-Netto, *The Fabricated Luther: Refuting Nazi Connections and Other Modern Myths*, 2nd ed. (St. Louis: Concordia, 1995, 2007).

arguing that a firm nature-grace distinction is characteristic of his followers, who misrepresented Thomas's view.

While we will argue for the grace-restoring-nature view, there is much to be learned from each of the traditions representing the different views.

Gratia contra naturam. Anabaptists are most commonly associated with this view. Anabaptism emerged in the Reformation and post-Reformation period and was subject to terrible persecution.[57] Anabaptist theology has a strong emphasis on the church as the new people of God and tends to equate the church with the kingdom of God. Gross, for example, observes, "The Anabaptists . . . held to an ultimate responsibility for the kingdom of God, which they held to be separate from the world."[58] Historically, it is not hard to find statements in the Anabaptist tradition that denigrate the world and see the effects of sin as making involvement in the world impossible. Around 1577 Bishop Peter Walpot (1521–1578), for example, writes in the *Great Article Book* of the Hutterites,

> Between the Christian and the world there exists a vast difference like that between heaven and earth. The world is the world, always remains the world, behaves like the world and all the world is nothing but world. The Christian, on the other hand, has been called away from the world. He has been called never to conform to the world, never to be a consort, never to run along with the crowd of the world and never to pull its yoke.[59]

Robert Webber comments, "The striking point of the Anabaptist theology of the kingdom is the absolute antithesis it sees between the kingdom of Christ and the kingdom of this world."[60] The new creation and the kingdom are identified with the church. Thomas Finger alerts us to the centrality of the "new creation" theme in Anabaptist theology, but when he unpacks this in terms of the three dimensions of personal, communal, and missional, communal is discussed entirely in relation to the institutional church. In his discussion of the missional dimension of the church, Finger notes that "Duane Friesen challenges

---

[57]For a comprehensive introduction to Anabaptism including its history see Thomas N. Finger, *A Contemporary Anabaptist Theology: Biblical, Historical, Constructive* (Downers Grove, IL: IVP Academic, 2004).

[58]Leonard Gross, "Sixteenth Century Hutterian Mission," in Wilbert R. Shenk, ed., *Anabaptism and Mission* (Scottdale, PA: Herald, 1984), 97-118, on 98.

[59]Quoted in Robert E. Webber, *The Church in the World: Opposition, Tension, or Transformation?* (Grand Rapids: Zondervan, 1986), 87.

[60]Ibid., 88.

Anabaptist church-world dualism by considering *creation, a theme Anabaptists seldom have touched.*"[61] Notably, Finger *himself* includes no substantial discussion of creation in his comprehensive volume. And this presents a problem: if one has no clear idea of creation and the effect of the fall on God's good creation, then redemption is left hanging and reduced to the church, so that one potentially ends up with a grace-against-nature position. In the Anabaptist tradition there is also a strong tendency to see the telos of creation as spiritual rather than leading to a new heavens and a new earth.[62]

It must, however, be noted that *contemporary Anabaptist thought* is far more nuanced than the position described above. To be sure, one still finds statements like "A church-world dualism is basic to Anabaptist thought, brought about internally by the vision of building a church 'without spot or wrinkle,' and externally by the threat of persecution."[63] However, the author immediately moves on to explore ways in which Anabaptists take seriously their mission for the world.

In line with Walter Wink and others, Finger refers to the forces at work in the creation as "powers." He poses the question, "Are the powers being redeemed?" and argues that only Colossians 1:20 comes close to affirming this possibility. He notes that elsewhere in Scripture the evil powers are implacably opposed to God and acknowledges that historically Anabaptists understood *world* in this sense. To his credit Finger examines the different meanings of *world* in Scripture and concludes,

> Since God endowed humans with creative capacities, the world is also a process, or age, and also resembles a plot line, which humans can develop in many directions. In its basic intended direction this process is "very good." Consequently the original creation's structures, processes and goals cannot be vastly different from the new creation's. New as the new creation is, it does not abolish life's basic structures. It fulfills their potentialities, even if its consummation will somehow transcend them.[64]

---

[61]Finger, *Anabaptist*, 157-254, emphasis added; 305. The reference to Friesen is to his *Christian Peacemaking and International Conflict* (Scottdale, PA: Herald, 1986), 58. For a summary of Friesen's view see Finger, *Anabaptist*, 305-6.

[62]See Finger, *Anabaptist*, 512-61.

[63]Cornelius J. Dyck, "The Anabaptist Understanding of Good News," in Shenk, *Anabaptism and Mission*, 24-39, on 31.

[64]Finger, *Anabaptist*, 316.

We see here a move toward a more integral understanding of creation, fall, and redemption. In his view of the world as a process, in which he positions the structures of creation, Finger is closer to Groen van Prinsterer than Kuyper, who grounds the structures in creation. The language of "powers" is, however, unhelpful in my view, since in Colossians 1:8, 15 they have negative connotations, so that such language easily collapses creation into fall and obscures the important distinction between structure and direction.[65]

In *Things Hold Together*, Branson Parler argues that John Howard Yoder, a theologian associated with the Anabaptist tradition, is unfairly accused of dualistically separating Christ and creation. Parler's defense of Yoder is fascinating and provides an important dialogue partner for the Kuyperian tradition. He argues that in Yoder's trinitarian theology redemption is the redemption of creation.

Yoder also uses the language of "the powers," and Parler defines them as "the nexus of earthly and heavenly powers, both the visible and invisible spiritual forces that, for good or for ill, enable ordered human life." The dynamic rather than static quality of the language of "powers" attracts Yoder. However, the powers are not arbitrary but ordered, and Yoder compares them to the Reformed doctrine of creation order. "With the Reformed doctrine of the orders of creation, [Hendrikus] Berkhof's Paul affirms that all human being is structured, that that structured quality is, itself, not an accident nor the fall, but a part of the divinely given creatureliness so that the whole is always more than its parts." The fall involves the fall of power so that the fall is also the fall of culture. This fallenness goes deep, according to Yoder: "[It] is structural: they are warped. It is functional: they do not do their duty. It is noetic: we are not able to perceive by looking at things as they are what they really should be."[66]

Parler argues that for Yoder Jesus' power reestablishes the power and thus the politics of creation. Humans were created to exercise peaceful, Christlike power, and the powers were created to be flourishing, dynamic servants of peace. The transformation of culture depends on the work of the Spirit in relation to the in-breaking of God's kingdom. When the powers of creation are

---

[65]See Wolters, *Creation Regained*, 87-114. Structure comes with creation, but the fall opens up the possibility of the good structures of creation being misdirected.

[66]Yoder, quoted in Branson L. Parler, *Things Hold Together: John Howard Yoder's Trinitarian Theology of Culture* (Scottdale, PA: Herald, 2012), 134, 138, 146-47. Yoder engaged in a fascinating correspondence with John Stott about the powers.

unleashed by the Spirit, the public practices of the church exert a transformative effect in all of human culture. Thus, redemption does not annihilate the powers; redemption rehabilitates true human power and the powers. "Living in line with the Lamb's victory is not alien or in contradiction to creation, but coheres with creation at the most basic level. Because God created the world and continues to be involved in history, creation is from the beginning oriented toward an 'open future.'"[67] The new relationship between Christ and the powers opens the way for authentic cultural transformation. The kingdom involves a reinstatement of God's original purpose.

The in-breaking of God's kingdom is centered in the life of the church and also flows from there into the surrounding world as well. "So when we talk about how Christ redeems culture, we must remember that this has first to do with the very life of the church itself." "So the church marches under the banner of the champion and pioneer of the true humanity, who exercises the power of creation as the true *imago Dei*."[68]

Clearly Parler's reading of Yoder is a far closer view to that of the Kuyperian tradition, and it is a fertile dialogue partner. Creation and redemption are held closely together, and a far more nuanced view of the powers is presented. Questions remain about how the public practices of the church influence culture, as well as the precise nature of the structures of creation. As is typical of the Anabaptist tradition, the institutional church remains central, and a pacifist position is defended.

Where the Kuyperian tradition needs to listen carefully to the Anabaptist tradition is in its stress on the extent to which the fall penetrates public life. Especially in separatist groups such as the Amish, we often witness a radical alternative to the global consumer culture of which most Christians in the West form a relatively uncritical part. The Anabaptist tradition prophetically provides a conscience for Kuyperians in terms of the extent to which we have *uncritically* become complicit in the *misdirected* structures of creation. Kuyperians readily affirm cultural development, but amid global consumerism and the industrial military complex, groups such as the Amish and the Anabaptists in general raise in an acute fashion the question of the creational norms for development.

---

[67]Ibid., 156.
[68]Ibid., 200, 154.

Gratia instar naturae. The example of this type is theological liberalism, which too readily accommodates itself to the spirit of the age, overconfident that God is at work in it, so that grace easily ends up equated with what is going on in the world. Our first model, grace against nature, is at the opposite end of the spectrum to theological liberalism and could hardly be more different. *Instar* here means equals, indicating that in this view grace and nature are held very closely together, with little sense of the effects of the fall on creation.

This is a view that Kuyper and Bavinck encountered firsthand and rejected, as we saw in chapter one.[69] But, as we have seen, Kuyper insisted that there was much to be learned from the emergent modernism, and not least that orthodox Christians needed to produce works of the same caliber as liberals. Kuyper himself learned much from Friedrich Schleiermacher, the father of modern liberal theology, in his doctrine of the church.

Gratia iuxta naturam. The view that grace flanks or runs alongside nature is associated with the Lutheran tradition and Luther's doctrine of the two kingdoms, the kingdom of the world and the kingdom of God. However, lest we succumb to nineteenth- and twentieth-century caricatures of Luther's view, it must be noted that Luther broke with the medieval dualism of matter and spirit, insisting that the fundamental dichotomy is between faith and works and not between matter and spirit.[70] Luther's break with the medieval dichotomy of spirit and matter opens up a far more positive view of the creation. For Luther, all created things are really masks of God (*larvae Dei*); on Galatians 2:6, for example, Luther comments, "Now the whole creation is a face or mask of God . . . there must be masks or social positions, for God has given them and they are his creatures." This implies the contingency of all things but also that these masks, which include created objects *as well as* stations in life such as magistrate, schoolteacher, parent, and so on, should be honored as a means through which God may be revered. The God revealed in Jesus is for Luther also the creator who is constantly active in and among all his creatures.[71] As is well-known, Luther articulated a rich theology of vocation or callings.

---

[69]Scholten's theology would be an example from Kuyper's day of this view.

[70]William A. Dyrness, *Reformed Theology and Visual Culture: The Protestant Imagination from Calvin to Edwards* (Cambridge: Cambridge University Press, 2004), 51. Cf. William J. Wright, *Martin Luther's Understanding of God's Two Kingdoms: A Response to the Challenge of Skepticism*, Texts and Studies in Reformation and Post-Reformation Thought (Grand Rapids: Baker Academic, 2010), 17-43.

[71]Quoted in Dyrness, *Reformed Theology*, 52.

Indeed, it is for good reason that it was the Lutheran Reformers who broke the back of Jerome's *contemptus mundi* reading of Ecclesiastes, a reading that had dominated interpretation of Ecclesiastes for a thousand years. Their theology of creation and positive view of life in the world opened the way for a far more positive and biblically centered reading of Ecclesiastes to emerge.[72]

Nevertheless, a dualism remains in the Lutheran view. William Wright notes, "Luther's understanding of God's two kingdoms represented his basic premise about the nature of reality. In short, it was his Christian worldview."[73] Luther distinguishes between the kingdom of Satan or the world and the kingdom of God. But this is not for a moment to say there are two kings; the trinitarian God rules over both, directly over the spiritual kingdom and indirectly over the worldly kingdom, by means of his three orders or stations, namely daily life, including marriage, household, or domestic affairs and livelihood; worldly government or state; and the church.

Where, in my view, the dualism comes to the fore is in the Lutheran view of *natural law*.[74] According to David Steinmetz, "God, who rules the Church through the gospel, rules this disordered world through the instruments available to the state—namely, human reason, wisdom, natural law, and the application of violent coercion."[75] Certainly, from a Lutheran perspective, Christians are called to be good citizens and thereby salt and light in the kingdom of the world. As Berndt Wannenwetsch notes, Luther viewed faith as the station above all stations, and "the primacy of this one station *in all stations* ensured that the gospel permeated every aspect of human social life."[76] But the question emerges of the extent to which the gospel shapes our view of the state, of rationality, of education, and so on. According to Steinmetz, for Luther, "Reason and natural law provide adequate norms for a well-run state.

---

[72]See Craig G. Bartholomew, *Ecclesiastes* (Grand Rapids: Baker Academic, 2009), 31-33.

[73]William J. Wright, *Martin Luther's Understanding*, 114. Berndt Wannenwetsch, "Luther's Moral Theology," in Donald K. McKim, ed., *The Cambridge Companion to Martin Luther* (Cambridge: Cambridge University Press, 2003), 120-35, on 132, however, argues that Luther's doctrine of two kingdoms "served a merely emancipatory purpose in Luther's theology, directed against the conflation of secular and ecclesial authority and illegitimate borrowings of one side from the other."

[74]For a carefully nuanced, Lutheran perspective see Carl E. Braaten, "Natural Law in Theology and Ethics," in Carl E. Braaten and Robert W. Jenson, eds., *The Two Cities of God: The Church's Responsibility for the Earthly City* (Grand Rapids: Eerdmans, 1997), 42-58. For Braaten, "Social ethics will necessarily correlate eschatology and natural law, or it will forfeit its right to be considered a biblically Christian viewpoint" (56).

[75]David Steinmetz, *Luther in Context*, 2nd ed. (Grand Rapids: Baker Academic, 1995, 2002), 114.

[76]Wannenwetsch, "Luther's Moral Theology," 132.

There is no need for a divine political polity revealed in the Bible, a polity which can only be interpreted correctly by true believers."[77]

In a fascinating book titled *Christ and Culture in Dialogue: Constructive Themes and Practical Applications*, a group of authors, mainly Lutherans, revisit Niebuhr's type of Lutheran theology as Christ and culture in paradox—the paradoxical vision—and vigorously defend this Lutheran perspective as most relevant to Christian engagement with culture today. Carl Braaten writes the foreword, in which he identifies belief in two kingdoms and a proper distinction between gospel and law as central to the paradoxical vision. Braaten warns against the mistake of separating the two kingdoms and argues that the paradoxical vision is particularly well suited to enable the church to avoid both the model of Christendom and that of a secularized church. Braaten asserts,

> The two kingdoms are both anchored in God's will, so that what goes on in the world is as much God's concern as what goes on in the church. There is no such thing as a secular world spinning on its own axis, no such thing as autonomous social, political, and economic structures following their own laws, no such things as secular authorities who can become a law unto themselves. They are all God's agents in the drama of the world-historical process.[78]

Well and good. But what exactly does a two-kingdom approach look like in practice? Gene Veith's chapter in this book provides us with a glimpse into contemporary, practical application of Luther's vision.[79] Veith stresses the importance of cultural involvement for Christians but notes,

> Christians exercising their vocations in the secular culture must assess their activity in secular terms, which are also under God's sovereignty. Christian artists may well express their faith in their work, but the quality of the art lies primarily not in its theological message but in its aesthetic excellence, since the laws of aesthetics have been ordained by God in His creation. There is no need for a distinctly Christian approach to music, plumbing, computer science, physics, or wood-carving, because all of these things, no matter how secular or non-religious they appear, already fall under God's sovereignty.[80]

---

[77]Steinmetz, *Luther*, 124-25.

[78]Carl Braaten, "Foreword," in Angus J. L. Menuge, ed., *Christ and Culture in Dialogue: Constructive Themes and Practical Applications* (St. Louis: Concordia Academic Press, 1999).

[79]Gene Veith, "Two Kingdoms Under One King: Towards a Lutheran Approach to Culture," in Mengue, *Christ and Culture in Dialogue*, 129-44.

[80]Ibid., 140.

For Veith, Christians in politics should play by political rules, "whether hardball power plays or the arts of compromise and consensus building." At the same time Christians in politics must exercise power in accord with God's law. Veith is quite clear that "the secular kingdom, again, must be kept separate from the spiritual kingdom."[81]

In the final chapter of *Christ and Culture in Dialogue*, Robert Benne addresses the issue of a Lutheran approach to education. He maintains that the Lutheran tradition espouses an epistemological autonomy at the worldly level so that

> reason and experience are generally trustworthy tools of knowing, although they too can become idolatrous and claim too much for themselves. This epistemological autonomy, however, is not an ontological autonomy. Reason and experience, and the world they explore, are creations of God. They do not stand independently of the divine reality. Second, reason and experience are given autonomy solely in the worldly or horizontal sphere.

Thus, for Benne, a Luther college or university is a place where there is "an ongoing and unresolved conversation between the two poles of the dialectic, the Christian and the cultural."[82]

Benne and others in this volume take brief account of the Kuyperian vision but label this transformative approach as somewhat useful but in danger of being utopian, underestimating the power of sin, being totalist and thus potentially oppressive, and so on. For Benne, "The Lutheran tradition, operating from more paradoxical theological roots, is most promising in holding Christian revelation and cultural knowledge in creative tension."[83]

From a Kuyperian perspective a significant, lingering dualism is evident in Benne's explication of a Lutheran theology of education, which embraces the epistemic autonomy of the disciplines, thus removing them from the inner reformation of the sciences advocated by Kuyperians. Reason and experience are treated as neutral, and the need of the light of the gospel to rightly

---

[81]Ibid., 140-41.

[82]Robert Benne, "A Lutheran Vision of Christian Humanism," in Menuge, *Christ and Culture in Dialogue*, 314-32. Cf. also Robert Benne, *Quality with Soul: How Six Premier Colleges and Universities Keep Faith with Their Religious Traditions* (Grand Rapids: Eerdmans, 2010); *A Paradoxical Vision: A Public Theology for the Twenty-First Century* (Minneapolis: Augsburg Fortress, 1995).

[83]Ibid., 325. See also Robert Benne, *Good and Bad Ways to Think About Politics* (Grand Rapids: Eerdmans, 2010), esp. 51-60.

understand politics, the nature of society, science, the arts, and so on, is denied. Benne's dialectic is deeply problematic, trusting that from a dialectic starting from very different epistemologies truth and wisdom will emerge. This is precisely the danger of which Michael J. Buckley warns in his *At the Origins of Modern Atheism*, arguing that a major mistake Christians made at the outset of modernity was to concede the epistemic foundations to Enlightenment thinkers and then try to work toward conclusions that agree with a Christian perspective.[84]

Readers should note that the Lutheran view of nature and grace is an ongoing discussion among Lutheran theologians.[85] Wannenwetsch, in contrast to comments above, for example, asserts that "Luther does not entertain the idea of the autonomy of professional reason."[86] And Paul R. Hinlicky, in his massive *Beloved Community: Critical Dogmatics After Christendom*, creatively revisits this issue in the light of Oswald Bayer's and others' ongoing research, and our situation in the West today.[87] There are great strengths in Luther's view, but the tension between the two kingdoms as manifest in the Lutheran espousal of natural law is real and does not, in my view, open wide the door for grace to penetrate all of culture.[88]

In terms of the Lutheran tradition, one of the most fertile theologies for a reassessment of the relationship between nature and grace is that of Dietrich Bonhoeffer. Bonhoeffer's thought certainly has its complexities and must be understood in his context of Nazi Germany. In April 1932 at the Berlin Youth Conference, Bonhoeffer denounced any appeal to the "orders of creation" in discussions of peace and war. He was wary of the extent to which we could know the good creation orders and spoke rather of "orders of preservation." Hinlicky and others take a similar view, arguing for a dynamic view of such orders or mandates, and remain wary of a doctrine of creation order as too

---

[84]Michael J. Buckley, *At the Origins of Modern Atheism* (New Haven, CT: Yale University Press, 1990).

[85]See, e.g., Ulrich Duchnow, ed., *Lutheran Churches—Salt or Mirror of Society* (Geneva: Lutheran World Federation, 1977); Karl H. Hertz, ed., *Two Kingdoms and the World* (Minneapolis: Augsburg, 1976); Oswald Bayer, *Freedom in Response. Lutheran Ethics: Sources and Controversies* (Oxford: Oxford University Press, 2007).

[86]Wannenwetsch, "Luther's Moral Theology," 133.

[87]Paul R. Hinlicky, *Beloved Community: Critical Dogmatics After Christendom* (Grand Rapids: Eerdmans, 2015), 791-814.

[88]After World War II Luther's doctrine of two kingdoms came in for close scrutiny. See Heinz Zahrnt, *The Question of God: Protestant Theology in the Twentieth Century*, trans. R. A. Wilson (London: Collins, 1969), 171-201.

static. As regards the Kuyperian tradition, such a view is closer to that of Groen van Prinsterer, who saw God's normative order as given in history, unlike Kuyper, who firmly grounded it in creation.

Where Bonhoeffer is helpful, and here he is closer to Wannenwetsch, is in his rejection of any concept of a two-spheres approach to the world.[89] Bonhoeffer is quite clear that "there are not two realities, but only one reality, and that reality is the reality of God, which has become manifest in Christ in the reality of the world.... The reality of Christ comprises the reality of the world within itself."[90] Bonhoeffer's theology is profoundly ecclesial: "the history of the church is the hidden center of world history."[91] In Christ God has claimed space in the world, and even though it be only an inn, "then in this narrow space He comprises together the whole reality of the world at once and reveals the ultimate basis of reality." As the community of Christ the church always reaches beyond itself; it is the place where witness is borne to the foundation of all reality in Christ. "If one wishes to speak, then, of the space or sphere of the Church, one must bear in mind that the confines of this space are at every moment being overrun and broken down by the testimony of the Church to Jesus Christ." The place of the church is not intended to deprive the world of territory "but precisely in order to prove to the world that it is still the world, the world which is loved by God and reconciled with Him.... The only way in which the Church can defend her own territory is by fighting not for it but for the salvation of the world."[92]

Withdrawal from the world is not an option for Bonhoeffer. Darkness and evil—and Bonhoeffer is under no illusion about the extent of these—must not be abandoned; every area of life must be claimed for Christ because "Christ gives up nothing of what He has won. He holds it fast in His hands." The incarnation is for Bonhoeffer the ultimate affirmation of finite reality: "Christ died for the world, and it is only in the midst of the world that Christ is Christ."[93] In terms of the form that human life takes in the world, Bonhoeffer identifies four divine mandates: labor, marriage, government, and

[89]Cf. footnote 73 above.
[90]Bonhoeffer, *Ethics*, 62-72.
[91]Dietrich Bonhoeffer, *Sanctorum Communio: A Theological Study of the Sociology of the Church*, Dietrich Bonhoeffer's Works 1 (Minneapolis: Augsburg Fortress, 1998), 142-43.
[92]Bonhoeffer, *Ethics*, 68, 69.
[93]Ibid., 70, 71.

church. God's will is that the reality of Christ with us and in our world becomes real. Bonhoeffer's theology is strongly eschatological, and he describes
the time between the coming of Christ and the consummation of the kingdom
as the "penultimate." This does not downplay the importance of life today;
indeed, the penultimate receives its profound meaning from the ultimate.

Bonhoeffer recognizes that the penultimate is characterized by an antithesis, but Christians should not abandon the "secular"; opposition to the
secular must only be in the quest for a "better secularity." "It is only in this
sense, as a polemical unity, that Luther's doctrine of the two kingdoms is to
be accepted, and it was no doubt in this sense that it was originally intended."
The penultimate it characterized by a preparing of the way for the return of
Christ, and this preparation is not only inward but "a formative activity on the
very greatest visible scale." Bonhoeffer deplores the loss of "the natural" in
Protestant theology and seeks to recover it.[94] The natural is what is, after the
fall, directed toward the coming of Christ, whereas the unnatural is what
closes its doors to Christ.

For Bonhoeffer the world is *the place* of *concrete* responsibility, which is
given to us in Christ. He articulates a keen sense of the particularity of im-
placement: our task is not to transform the world but "to do what is necessary
at the given place and with a due consideration of reality." Grace comes to the
human in his or her place, and it is in this place that we are called to hear and
respond to Christ's call. "The calling is the call of Jesus Christ to belong wholly
to Him; it is the laying claim to me by Christ at the place at which this call has
found me; it embraces work with things and relations with persons; it demands a 'limited field of accomplishments,' yet never as a value in itself, but in
responsibility towards Jesus Christ."[95]

Bonhoeffer's theology seems to me far closer to a transformational
worldview than to the paradoxical vision. Similar trends are visible in contemporary Lutheran thinkers. Contemporary Lutheran theologian Paul Santmire,
for example, has written a series of groundbreaking books on the theology of
nature, helping many of us develop a robust theology of the environment for
engagement in "the kingdom of the world." In his work I discern no restricting
of such an issue to reason and experience but rather a full engagement of the

---

[94]Ibid., 65, 66, 93, 101-41.
[95]Ibid., 203, 225.

biblical story. In Old Testament studies Terence Fretheim's work is similarly noteworthy. He observes,

> Generally speaking, God's goal for the creation is not redemption; God's redemption is a means to a new creation, and salvation will be the key characteristic of that new reality. . . . The creation is not something that is left behind as God works on more important matters, such as redemption. . . . The objective of God's redemptive activity is to transform the creation as it moves towards its eschatological goal. God's goal is a new creation, not a new redemption. There must be redemption if creation is to be and become what God intends it to be, but the redemption is not an end in itself; it has finally to do with creation, a new creation.[96]

Fretheim's emphasis on transformation is significant, and he here expresses a view of nature and grace akin to that we find in Kuyper and Bavinck.

As I read Bonhoeffer and contemporary Lutheran theologians such as Oswald Bayer and Paul Hinlicky, it seems to me that the time is ripe for a fresh dialogue about the relationship between nature and grace between Lutherans and Kuyperians. In my view tensions remain in the Lutheran view, but contemporary Lutheran theologians have provided important nuance to a Lutheran perspective, and there are signs of reassessment of the tradition, particularly in our late modern context.

Gratia supra naturam. The view of grace above—or perfecting nature—is associated with Roman Catholicism and goes back to the great medieval theologian Thomas Aquinas. In question 1 of his *Summa Theologiae*, for example, he comments: "As grace does not abolish nature but brings it to perfection, natural reason should assist faith as the natural inclination of the will yields to charity."[97] Aquinas's quest was to incorporate the philosophy of Aristotle with its focus on the earthly realm into the prevailing Augustinian theological tradition with its focus on the heavenly realm. "The task presented by the age itself, then, was this: to effect a legitimate union between the two realms that threatened to break apart by their own mutual repulsion."[98]

---

[96]Terence E. Fretheim, *God and World in the Old Testament: A Relational Theology of Creation* (Nashville: Abingdon, 2005), 12.

[97]Thomas Aquinas, *Summa Theologiae: Questions on God*, ed. Brian Davies and Brian Leftow, Cambridge Texts in the History of Philosophy (Cambridge: Cambridge University Press, 2006), 15.

[98]Josef Pieper, *Guide to Thomas Aquinas* (San Francisco: Ignatius, 1991), 120. Among scholars there has been much discussion about the precise relationship between Aquinas and Aristotle. In his introduction

Thomas is quite clear that the whole of the world is God's good creation, and it is ordered throughout by his law. G. K. Chesterton perceptively notes that St. Francis and Thomas were after the same thing: a recovery of the incarnation and thus the natural world as inherently good.[99] Aquinas affirms that there are three different uses of the word *world*, and two are positive: the world as created good and the world as renewed by Christ. The third use is the "creation" as it is twisted by sin.[100] Thus, the created world is good: sexuality is good, the body is good, sensuality and passion, even anger is good.[101] God created the world with its order, each creature with its own nature, and humanity in God's image with the rational capability of understanding this world. Thomas affirms the natural world not only on the basis of the good creation but also on the basis of the incarnation and sacraments—both are material in nature.

In all of this the Kuyperian tradition and the Thomistic one are in agreement. Where the difference moves to the fore is in the area of epistemology, or in what Thomas means by "natural reason" in the quote above. Thomas's thought is complex, and scholars continue to debate its shape and contours.[102] For our purposes Ralph McInerny's extracts from Aquinas's *On Boethius' "On the Trinity,"* published in 1257, will suffice.[103]

This work is particularly interesting because in it Thomas discusses the extent to which illumination from God is required for knowledge of the truth. As is typical of the scholastic method, Thomas first explores the view contrary to his own, a view that is a lot like the Kuyperian view and that argues that divine illumination is required for knowledge of the world. Under question 1, article 1, one finds repeatedly statements like: "No more then can the human intellect know truth unless it is illumined by the light of the invisible sun which is God."[104]

to *Thomas Aquinas: Selected Writings*, ed. and trans. Ralph McInerny (New York: Penguin, 1998), Ralph McInerny reviews this discussion and states, "The assumption of the following selections is that the philosophy of Thomas Aquinas is fundamentally Aristotelian."

[99]G. K. Chesterton, *Saint Thomas Aquinas* (Garden City, NY: Doubleday, 1933, 1956), 1-28. On 17 Chesterton asserts, "They were strengthening that staggering doctrine of incarnation."

[100]Thomas Aquinas, *Commentary on The Gospel of St. John*, part 1: chapters 1-7, trans. James A. Weisheipl (New York: Magi, 1998), 1, Lecture 5, 128. Commentary on John 1:10.

[101]See Pieper, *Aquinas*, 122, 174, for references in Aquinas.

[102]See the works by Etienne Gilson, Brian Davies, Brian Leftow, Ralph McInerny, Eleonore Stump, Stephen A. Long, etc.

[103]McInerny, *Thomas Aquinas: Selected Writings*, 109-41.

[104]Ibid., 110.

But this is the view that Thomas proceeds to argue against: "That is, the human mind by its natural light, without any other superadded, can know the truth." For Thomas, unlike Augustine in my view, the human mind is illumined by a natural light by virtue of its creation by God. And it is here that the nature-grace dualism between theology and philosophy enters: "Sacred doctrine is based on the light of faith just as philosophy is based on the light of natural reason. Hence it is impossible that what pertains to philosophy should be contrary to what is of faith, though they fall short of it."[105]

Thus, at the very least a case can be made that Thomas relates the natural realm of Aristotle to the spiritual realm of the Augustinian theological tradition in a hierarchical way. There are two realms, but the upper spiritual realm of grace is needed to make up the deficiencies of the lower realm of nature. There is the natural and the supernatural. Thomas's "starting point is to be two spheres, two levels of knowledge, metaphorically *two storeys*, which are clearly distinguished but not simply separated: one of higher certainty, the other fundamental and rationally clearly superior, both of which are in the last resort not contradictory but in fundamental accord."[106] Reason functions in the lower realm to gain knowledge, and faith in the upper realm; natural law gives knowledge in the lower realm, revelation in the upper realm; philosophical knowledge founded on the natural light of reason is proper to the lower realm, and theology is the product of faith in revelation in the upper realm. In this synthesis *grace perfects and completes nature* but does not destroy it.

> Revelation does not basically oppose human philosophy (though it will oppose *false*, incorrect philosophy), but rather supplements it and brings it to completion and perfection. Thomas's system is like a two-storey house: Aristotelian philosophy provides the foundation and the first storey; Catholic theology perfects and completes it by adding the second storey and the roof (with the assistance of philosophy).[107]

Grace completes, supplements, perfects, fulfills nature. All these words indicate that the lower storey is not twisted and corrupted but simply incomplete. Reason will take you so far (reliably) but is insufficient, and so faith and

---

[105]Ibid., 112, 136.

[106]Hans Küng, *Great Christian Thinkers: Paul, Origen, Augustine, Aquinas, Luther, Schleiermacher, Barth* (London: Bloomsbury, 1994), 111, emphasis original.

[107]Tony Lane, *The Lion Concise Book of Christian Thought* (Herts, UK: Lion, 1984), 94-95.

revelation must add more and complete it. Philosophy can take you so far up the ladder of truth, but theology takes you the rest of the way.

Debate continues as to the right understanding of Thomas and the Thomistic tradition on the relationship between nature and grace, a debate that I cannot solve here![108] Suffice it here to take note of a modern example of where this view of "Thomas" can lead. Historian James Turner, in a dialogue with Mark Noll, notes that while scholasticism is dead and neo-Thomism diminished,

> Yet Catholic intellectuals by and large still share the conviction that in matters of human reason we all stand on the same ground, regardless of religious faith. . . . Outside the order of salvation, Christians and non-Christians stand on exactly the same footing: knowledge of reality is accessible to all on the same terms. . . . Faith gives no *epistemological edge*.[109]

Turner is no expert on Thomas, but it is not hard to see how such a view could develop from Thomas's commentary on Boethius. Clearly Turner expresses a nature/grace dualism that limits the potential for transformative Christian witness and is far from the view of Kuyper and Bavinck.

In our late modern age it has become very difficult to see how in any discipline one could simply appeal to the objective rules of the discipline and do history—or any other subject—as any other historian does it.[110] There is no longer any such agreed hermeneutic, and the question must be posed as to whether one's faith illumines the way forward in history, in other disciplines, and in the crises of culture facing the West. In this respect the work of Catholic theologian John Betz on Christian philosopher J. G. Hamann is well worth noting. Hamann manifests many similarities to the Kuyperian tradition, and at the end of *After Enlightenment* Betz has a fascinating chapter titled "After Postmodernity: Hamann Before the Postmodern Triumvirate."[111]

---

[108]Cf. B. Wentsel, *Natuur en Genade: Een introductie in en confrontatie met de jongste onwikkelingen in de Rooms-Katholieke theologie inzake dit thema* (Kampen: Kok, 1970); the several important works by Henri de Lubac on this topic; John Milbank, *The Suspended Middle: Henri de Lubac and the Debate Concerning the Supernatural* (Grand Rapids: Eerdmans, 2005).

[109]Mark Noll and James Turner, *The Future of Christian Learning: An Evangelical and Catholic Dialogue*, ed. Thomas A. Howard (Grand Rapids: Brazos, 2008), 105-6. In my view a far more productive view is articulated by John R. Betz at the conclusion of his *After Enlightenment: The Post-Secular Vision of J. G. Hamann* (Chichester, UK: Wiley-Blackwell, 2008).

[110]Hinlicky, *Beloved Community*, 800, similarly struggles with natural law in today's context. Of course, it could be argued that today's wild pluralism requires precisely a renewed emphasis on natural law or common grace. Cf. Richard Mouw, *He Shines in All That's Fair: Culture and Common Grace* (Grand Rapids: Eerdmans, 2001).

[111]Betz, *After Enlightenment*, 312-40.

Betz recognizes in Hamann resources for moving beyond postmodernism and argues that after the enlightenment there are only two options: some form of secular postmodernity or a postsecular theology. In Betz's words:

> But if Hamann's metacritique forecloses the possibility of a return to the Enlightenment, it does so also—and here is the catch for theology—for any return to a *neo*-scholasticism (which is to be distinguished in important respects from much of the scholasticism of the Middle Ages) that would attempt to isolate reason and faith, nature and grace, into airtight compartments, believing . . . that reason apart from faith can infallibly establish not only certain metaphysical principles, but also the theological origin and end of all things. In other words, Hamann's metacritique cuts both ways: while it deflates the Enlightenment's overblown doctrine of reason . . . it also demands a more modest estimation of the possibilities of a purely rational metaphysics or a purely natural (or philosophical) theology.[112]

As a Catholic theologian Betz, through his engagement with Hamann, arrives at a place much closer to that of Kuyper and Bavinck than does Turner.

Gratia intra naturam. The Kuyperian tradition represents the view of grace working *inside* nature, healing it of the disease of sin. The early sections of this chapter elaborate that view, and we will not repeat them here.

CONVERGING VIEWS FROM DIFFERENT TRADITIONS

Our typology above illumines important and lingering *differences* but also shows a developing *convergence* among views previously regarded as opposing. This is an exciting and important time, exciting because it indicates that there is room for widespread agreement among Christians of diverse traditions on the nature-grace relationship. Clearly in this context the Kuyperian tradition has much to offer and much to learn! This time is also important, because cultural engagement cannot afford a church that is endlessly split in factions and unable to cooperate in being salt and light in Western and global culture. At the outset of this chapter we quoted Paul Ricoeur on the vital importance for the church of the relationship between creation and salvation. Resolution of this question has immense practical implications, and we have seen how a variety of traditions show signs of approximating the central Kuyperian insight

---

[112]Ibid., 317.

that grace restores nature. Of course, adherents of such traditions might state this move somewhat differently! The tasks required of the church today are simply too great for one tradition, so ecumenical cooperation is imperative. However, it needs to be an ecumenical cooperation with theological and practical teeth, and convergence around the relationship between nature and grace could provide just that.

Amid orthodox theology today there are so many signs of adherence to the basic insight that grace restores nature that we cannot discuss most of them here. Suffice it to note in conclusion a few of these. Claus Westermann has done what is probably the most rigorous work on the book of Genesis in our day. He adheres to classic historical criticism and would probably fall, broadly speaking, in the liberal theological tradition. However, he is quite clear that "God who sent the Savior remains the creator; the New Testament can only speak of a new creation because God remains the creator."[113]

Anglican theologian Oliver O'Donovan is one of the leading ethicists of our day. His *Resurrection and Moral Order* is a tour de force. He is worth quoting at length on the relationship between creation and redemption:

> Creation and redemption each has its ontological and its epistemological aspect. There is the created order and there is natural knowledge; there is the new creation and there is revelation in Christ. This has encouraged a confusion of the ontological and epistemological in much modern theology, so that we are constantly presented with the unacceptably polarized choice between an ethic that is revealed and has no ontological grounding and an ethic that is based on creation and so is naturally known. . . . If . . . it is the gospel of the resurrection that assures us of the stability and permanence of the world which God has made, then neither of the polarized options is right. In the sphere of revelation, we will conclude, and only there, can we see the natural order as it really is and overcome the epistemological barriers to an ethic that conforms to nature. This nature involves all men, and indeed, as we shall see later, does not exclude a certain "natural knowledge" which is also part of man's created endowment. And yet only in Christ do we apprehend that order in which we stand and that knowledge of it with which we have been endowed.[114]

---

[113]Claus Westermann, *Genesis 1–11: A Commentary*, trans. John J. Scullion (Minneapolis: Augsburg, 1984), 177.

[114]Oliver O'Donovan, *Resurrection and Moral Order: An Outline for Evangelical Ethics* (Grand Rapids: Eerdmans, 1986), 19-20.

CONCLUSION

Bavinck asserts, "Finally, the purpose and goal of special revelation is God's own trinitarian glory, his delight in himself. The aim of revelation is to re-create humanity after the image of God, to establish the kingdom of God on earth, to redeem the world from the power of sin, and thus to glorify the name of the Lord in all his creatures."[115] The whole world belongs to God. At the same time, all of reality is under the curse of sin—and all of reality lies within range of redemption in and through Jesus Christ. In Kuyper's justly celebrated words: "There is not a square inch of the entire world of which Christ does not rightly say, 'That is mine.'" There is a good creational structure for everything, but after the fall the serious possibility of misdirection is opened up in all areas of life. Kuyperianism rightly does not recognize any conflict between gospel and creation. Kuyperians understand the gospel to be the healing power that restores creation, in line with God's original design and toward its originally intended consummation. This is a penetrating insight and one with important ecumenical resources for today.[116]

EXCURSUS: NATURE AND GRACE IN THE BIBLE

Evangelical readers might well be persuaded by the logic of Kuyper's and Bavinck's view of grace restoring nature, but they also might well ask, is it biblical? Both Kuyper and Bavinck take Scripture seriously in their examination of nature and grace, and I encourage readers to read them in this regard. Their works are peppered with biblical insights! Nevertheless, as we note in chapter three, both were aware of the need for far more rigorous, orthodox biblical exegesis than was available in their day. The Free University of Amsterdam and Kampen Seminary served as the home for a range of significant biblical scholars whose work also needs to be retrieved today.[117] Here I will draw attention to some of the most significant recent biblical scholarship that grounds their view of nature and grace exegetically.

Kuyper's and Bavinck's work alerts us to the importance of understanding Scripture in its totality and not just piecemeal. In this respect the major biblical

---

[115]*RD* 1.

[116]For a fascinating and certainly not uncritical collection of essays closely related to South Africa see Ernst M. Conradie, ed., *Creation and Salvation: Dialogue on Abraham Kuyper's Legacy for Contemporary Ecotheology* (Leiden: Brill, 2011).

[117]For example, G. Ch. Aalders (1880–1961), W. H. Gispen (1900–1986), F. W. Grosheide (1881–1972), H. N. Ridderbos (1909–2007), etc.

themes are *covenant* and *the kingdom of God*. Years ago Karl Barth already argued that creation is the external basis of covenant, and covenant the internal side of creation.[118] This is correct, in my view, and it adds considerable biblical ballast to the Kuyperian view of nature and grace when we see that the foundational covenantal text is Genesis 1:1–2:3. Both Kuyper and Bavinck work with the Reformed categories of a covenant of works and, after the fall, a covenant of grace. Bavinck, in my view, is more insightful than Kuyper in this respect,[119] with his recognition that even though the word *covenant* does not occur in Genesis 1–2 humankind's religious life before the fall has the character of a covenant.[120] Recent work in biblical theology has been particularly helpful in showing with exegetical precision that Genesis 1:1–2:3 is the foundational covenantal text in the Old Testament.

Covenant. The most rigorous exegetical support for this view has come from Australian biblical scholar William Dumbrell.[121] The word for "covenant" (*berit*) first occurs in Genesis 6:18: "But I will establish my covenant with you." Dumbrell notes that an examination of the three secular instances of the use of covenant in Genesis (Gen 21:22-32; 26:26-33; 31:43-54) is instructive, because the covenants referred to do not initiate the already existing relationship but provide them with a quasi-legal backing and provide assurance of their continuation.[122] This is important for our interpretation of Genesis 6:18 because it means that we must look for the origin of the relationship referred to by "covenant" in prior circumstances. When a covenant is initiated, the usual word used is *karat* (to cut), and since this is not used in Genesis 6:17-18 or the related passage in Genesis 9:9-13, again we are pushed to look behind the covenant with Noah to a preexisting relationship. The terms of the covenant with Noah are notably creation-wide, and the verb used instead of *karat*, namely "established" (Hebrew "caused to stand"), further supports the view

---

[118]CD III/1.

[119]Cf. Abraham Kuyper, *Dictaten Dogmatiek III*, "Locus de Foedere"; Uit het Woord, Tweede Serie, and Tweede Bundel, *De Leer der Verbonden* (Amsterdam: J. H. Kruyt, 1885).

[120]RD 2:569. See also the older work of Anthony A. Hoekema, *Herman Bavinck's Doctrine of the Covenant* (Clover, SC: Full Bible Publications, 2007).

[121]For a defense of Dumbrell's view see Craig G. Bartholomew, "Covenant and Creation: Covenantal Overload or Covenantal Deconstruction," *CTJ* 30, no. 1 (April 1995): 11-33.

[122]Dumbrell, "Covenant," unpublished article. For Dumbrell's full defense of his view see his *Covenant and Creation: An Old Testament Covenantal Theology* (Exeter, UK: Paternoster, 1984). A second edition has recently been published by Paternoster.

that a preexisting relationship is in view. The terms of the covenant with Noah and the language used thus push us back to Genesis 1–2 as the context in which the relationship was initiated, that is, by creation.

A crucial step in the Old Testament is God's covenant with Abraham. The fivefold occurrence of the Hebrew root for "bless" in Genesis 12:1-3 is deliberately set against the fivefold occurrence of the root for "curse" in Genesis 1–11, signifying clearly that through Abraham and his descendants God will recover his purpose of blessing for his whole creation.[123] "In covenantal terms we have seen Genesis 12:1-3 as the divine response to Genesis 3–11. The kingdom of God established in global terms is the goal of the Abrahamic covenant." The Sinai covenant is presented against the Abrahamic background so that Israel is portrayed as in some sense the "holder of the creation charge given to Adam, finally and fully to be expressed by the redeemed."[124] In terms of Israel, Dumbrell notes,

> The biblical plan of redemption does not finally focus upon a saved people so much as it does upon a governed world.... Though Israel is certainly the nation which the Abrahamic promises have immediately in view, Israel as a nation, as a symbol of divine rule manifested within a political framework, was intended to be an image of the shape of final world government, a symbol pointing beyond itself to the reality yet to be.[125]

Dumbrell traces the theme of covenant through the Bible in considerable exegetical detail, and we cannot pursue his entire argument here. Suffice it to note that he identifies as central to the new covenant in Jeremiah Yahweh's statement "I will forgive their iniquity and remember their sin no more." "When Yahweh remembers sin no more, no further action would be needed to forgive sin, no more atonement required, no more confession verbalized! Sin would no longer be a problem in the life and experience of believers! At once we see that this goes beyond the present experience of the Christian believer."[126]

Covenant, Dumbrell rightly argues, continues as a major theme in the New Testament. In Revelation 4 the rainbow around the throne (cf. Gen 9:13)

---

[123]On "blessing" see Claus Westermann, *Blessing in the Bible and the Life of the Church* (Minneapolis: Fortress, 1978).

[124]Dumbrell, *Covenant and Creation*, 78; Dumbrell, "Covenant."

[125]Dumbrell, *Covenant and Creation*, 66-67.

[126]Dumbrell, "Covenant."

reveals that God's covenant purposes for creation have prevailed. All agree that God's covenants are integral to his work of redemption. What Dumbrell's work demonstrates is that redemption through covenant involves a recovery of God's original purposes for his creation. Or, as Bernard Zylstra says, "The covenant is as wide as creation."[127] Isaac Watts, in his well-known hymn, has us joyfully sing that Christ's redemption extends "far as the curse is found." Redemption is "creation regained."

Kingdom. Dumbrell is right that in the New Testament covenant continues as a major theme,[128] and it is closely related to the major theme of Jesus' teaching—namely, "the kingdom of God."[129] Indeed, Gordon Spykman argues that covenant and kingdom are flip sides of the same coin, as it were.[130] J. H. Bavinck did important work in excavating the theme of the kingdom of God and its implications for mission. As a New Testament scholar, Herman Ridderbos's work on kingdom remains essential reading.[131] However, probably the most significant recent work on the kingdom of God in the New Testament is that by Tom Wright, and in particular his *Jesus and the Victory of God*. Indeed, a significant achievement of New Testament scholarship and missiology over the last century has been the recovery of kingdom as the major theme of Jesus' teaching.[132] It is clear, at least according to the Synoptics, that the kingdom of God/heaven was *the* major theme of Jesus' teaching.[133] The evidence for this is overwhelming; suffice it here to note Mark's summary of

---

[127]Bernard Zylstra, "Preface to Runner," in H. Evan Runner, *The Relation of the Bible to Learning* (Jordan Station, ON: Paideia, 1982), 30. This is the view of Klaas Schilder.

[128]This is disputed, but see N. T. Wright, *The Climax of the Covenant: Christ and the Law in Pauline Theology* (Edinburgh: T&T Clark, 1991).

[129]Cf. Herman Bavinck, "The Kingdom of God, the Highest Good," trans. Nelson D. Kloosterman, *The Bavinck Review* 2 (2011): 133-70.

[130]Gordon J. Spykman, *Reformational Theology: A New Paradigm for Doing Dogmatics* (Grand Rapids: Eerdmans, 1992), 11.

[131]Herman Ridderbos, *The Coming of the Kingdom* (Phillipsburg, NJ: Presbyterian and Reformed, 1962).

[132]A very useful overview of the kingdom of God in twentieth-century missiology and its relevance today is Lesslie Newbigin, *Sign of the Kingdom* (Grand Rapids: Eerdmans, 1981). An immense amount has been and continues to be published on the kingdom of God/heaven. See Bartholomew, *Where Mortals Dwell*.

[133]In John's Gospel "the kingdom of God" occurs only twice, in Jn 3:3, 15. John's equivalent phrase to the kingdom of God in the Synoptics is "eternal life." A. N. Wilder, "Preface," in *The Kingdom of God in 20th Century Interpretation* (Peabody, MA: Hendrickson, 1987), notes of John, "with his categories of eternal life, light, and truth, this evangelist does not forfeit in any way the celebration of the New Age and the travail of its advent" (ix). R. Brown, "Translating the Whole Concept of the Kingdom," *Notes on Translation* 14, no. 2 (2000): 43, rightly notes that the different components of the "complex multistage concept" of the kingdom of God find expression in the New Testament in a *variety* of terms but still relate to the concept of the kingdom.

Jesus teaching in Mark 1:14, "After John was put in prison, Jesus went into Galilee, proclaiming the good news of God. 'The time has come,' he said. 'The *kingdom of God* has come near. Repent and believe the good news!'"

As Wright notes, "We may therefore safely conclude that Jesus habitually went about from village to village, speaking of the kingdom of the god of Israel, and celebrating this kingdom in various ways, not least in sharing meals with all and sundry."[134] But what did Jesus mean by the kingdom of God? He never defines it but appears to assume an understanding on the part of his audience, so we are compelled to explore the Old Testament background, the background in the Judaism of Jesus' day, and most importantly the variety of ways in which Jesus explains the kingdom.[135]

Historically, we cannot be sure when the idea of God as king emerged clearly in the life of Israel. Canonically, however, it is there from the very beginning. Genesis 1 portrays God as a great king, with humans as his royal stewards. Genesis 3 represents rebellion against this rule, and Genesis 12 onward indicates God's plans to recover his purposes for his world through the line of Abraham. Thus written deeply into the narrative of the Old Testament is kingdom theology; as creator, God is king over all. After the fall he rules in particular over his people, Israel, who are called to be a *royal* priesthood (cf. Ex 19:6), living actively under his reign and demonstrating to the world what normative creaturely life looks like. As Israel slides down toward exile, the prophets look toward the time when God will act decisively to fulfill his purposes with Israel and his creation. Martin Buber rightly notes, "This is what it comes to: the realization of the all-embracing rulership of God is the Proton and Eschaton of Israel." "The messianic faith of Israel is . . . according to its central content the being-oriented-toward the fulfillment of the relation between God and world in a consummated kingly rule of God."[136]

In the intertestamental Jewish literature we do find the expression the kingdom of God, and kingdom of heaven occurs twice in the Mishnah.[137]

---

[134]N. T. Wright, *Jesus and the Victory of God* (London: SPCK, 1996), 150.

[135]Ridderbos, *Coming of the Kingdom*, 3, notes that Jesus "did not give any further explanation or description of the coming event, at least according to the tradition that has come down to us. This is an indication that the expression . . . was not unknown to those to whom this message was addressed, but was rather calculated to find an immediate response with them."

[136]Martin Buber, *Kingship of God*, 3rd ed. (Atlantic Highlands, NJ: Humanities Press International, 1990), 58, 14-15.

[137]See N. T. Wright, *The New Testament and the People of God*, Christian Origins and the Question of God

Thus, as Wright notes,

> But at least we can be sure of this: anyone who was heard talking about the reign
> of Israel's god would be assumed to be referring to the fulfillment of Israel's
> long-held hope. The covenant god would act to reconstitute his people, to end
> their exile, to forgive their sins. When that happened, Israel would no longer be
> dominated by the pagans. She would be free. The means of liberation were no
> doubt open to debate. The goal was not.[138]

A crucial insight of Wright's is that while Jesus assumes the basic Jewish
framework in his proclamation of the kingdom, he nevertheless consistently
redefined the contours of the fulfillment of the reign of God. Jesus' proclamation of the kingdom was *eschatological* and *apocalyptic*:

> The expression "The time is fulfilled" will thus have to be understood as the
> indication that the threshold of the great future has been reached, that the door
> has been opened, and that the prerequisites of the realization of the divine
> work of consummation are present; so that now the concluding divine drama
> can start. . . .
>
> The future, as it were, penetrates into the present. The world of God's re-
> demption, the great whole of his concluding and consummative works pushes
> its way into the present time of the world.[139]

Jesus saw his arrival as the climax of Israel's history, involving events that
only the metaphors of end of the world language are adequate to express, but
resulting in a new phase *within* history. "Kingdom is a social word first of all.
'Kingdom' indicates that God is about to do a big world event and not just a
big *individual* event—a cosmic thing and not just a heart thing. What happens
when *God* comes is not going to be grapeshot; it is going to be nuclear, a kind
of explosion, a reshaping of the earth."[140]

Jesus proclaimed the arrival of the kingdom and its future consummation.
This tension between the presence and the future of the kingdom involves the
reworking of Jewish apocalyptic, but decidedly not in terms of substituting

---

1 (Minneapolis: Fortress, 1992), 302-7; Jonathan T. Pennington, *Heaven and Earth in the Gospel of Mat-*
   thew (Grand Rapids: Baker Academic, 2009), 258-68.

[138]Wright, *Jesus and the Victory of God*, 151.

[139]Ridderbos, *Coming of the Kingdom*, 48, 55.

[140]Frederick D. Bruner, *The Christbook: A Historical/Theological Commentary. Matthew 1–12* (Grand Rapids: Eerdmans, 1987), 87.

the vertical eschatology of private devotion for the horizontal eschatology of Jewish thought. "The point of the present kingdom is that it is the firstfruits of the future kingdom; and the future kingdom involves the abolition, not of space, time, or the cosmos itself, but rather of that which threatens space, time, and creation, namely, sin and death." In Jesus' reworking of the eschatology of the Jewish story Wright notes that the typical Jewish symbols are missing. "The answers to the worldview *questions* can be given in terms of a redeemed humanity and cosmos, rather than in terms simply of Israel and her national hope." In Acts 1:8 Luke reveals that "the newly inaugurated kingdom claims as its sacred turf, not a single piece of territory, but the entire globe."[141]

G. B. Caird observes, "Obviously the understanding of the Kingdom of God in Jesus' teaching depends on the presuppositions with which one begins."[142] This is particularly true of the biblical-theological framework within which one interprets the kingdom of God. If one takes the canonical shape of Scripture seriously leading from creation through fall and redemption to new creation, as well as the embeddedness of Jesus in first-century Judaism, then the realm of the king's reign in kingdom is blindingly obvious; it is the entire creation.

In this way the great themes of covenant and kingdom provide exegetical support for the Kuyperian view that grace restores nature.

---

[141]Wright, *Jesus and the Victory of God*, 218.

[142]George B. Caird, *New Testament Theology*, completed and ed. L. D. Hurst (Oxford: Clarendon, 1994), 368.

SCRIPTURE

*The ignorance of the Bible that is abroad today is so great that to
preach the gospel one must begin at the very beginning.*

J. H. BAVINCK, AN INTRODUCTION TO THE SCIENCE OF MISSIONS

*The historical critique of Scripture that emerges fully in the
eighteenth century has its dogmatic base, as our brief look at
Spinoza has shown, in the Enlightenment's faith in reason.*

HANS-GEORG GADAMER, TRUTH AND METHOD

*As the curtain begins to descend on the twentieth century, we who find ourselves
still on the stage, are, truth to tell, more than a little befuddled about how to act
and what to think. To be sure, we seem to speak our lines and play our parts
no less than did our ancestors. But we barely remember the name of the drama,
much less its meaning or its purpose. The playwright is apparently dead and
cannot be consulted as to his original intention. Cultural memory still holds
gingerly a tattered script, but many of its pages are missing and the guidance it
provides us is barely audible and, even then, delivered in what appears to us to
be a foreign tongue. Armed with new-fangled, electronically delivered images
and phrases, we are never at a loss for words. But we are at a loss for meaning.*

LEON R. KASS, THE HUNGRY SOUL

THE LETTER TO THE HEBREWS (Heb 1:1-2) begins with the assertion
that "In the past God spoke to our ancestors through the prophets at many
times and in various ways, but in these last days he has spoken to us by his Son,
whom he appointed heir of all things, and through whom also he made the

universe." This conviction, that God has spoken authoritatively and finally in Jesus and that we find his fully trustworthy Word in the Bible, which is normative for all of life, is at the heart of the Kuyperian tradition. It is, however, a conviction that modernity challenged again and again. Like a tsunami, modernity swept all of culture along with it, and, inevitably, the modern worldview was soon brought to bear on Scripture, resulting in the historical-critical approach to the Bible. Historical criticism developed in Germany in the second half of the nineteenth century and was dominant in Europe and America early in the twentieth century.[1]

We live a century after the emergence of historical criticism, a century during which historical criticism has been carefully evaluated, relativized, and critiqued by literary and theological interpretation, so that it is far easier for us today to receive its insights while rejecting many of its presuppositions.[2] For Kuyper and Bavinck, the situation was far different. The Netherlands lagged behind the rest of Europe in the development of historical criticism, but this changed decisively in the decade 1850–1860, with the change spearheaded from Leiden University by Jan Hendrik Scholten (1811–1885) and Abraham Kuenen (1821–1891).

Both Kuyper and Bavinck were taught at Leiden by Scholten and Kuenen. They had, as it were, front-row seats as historical criticism took hold in the Netherlands. As a young man, I still recall the challenge of going to study at Oxford University and being inducted into the major methods of historical criticism and then being taught to apply them to the Bible. However, it is hard to imagine how Kuyper and Bavinck must have felt as this new, critical approach to the Bible opened up in front of them through professors they admired and respected.

LEIDEN UNIVERSITY: DUTCH MODERNIST THEOLOGY

Scholten studied at Utrecht University, was appointed professor of theology at Franeker in 1840, and from there went to Leiden University, where he

---

[1]This is not to say that there was only one type of historical criticism, but it is to say that the different types shared the application of the modern worldview to the Bible. See the quote from Gadamer in the epigraph to this chapter.

[2]See Craig G. Bartholomew, *Introducing Biblical Hermeneutics: A Comprehensive Framework for Hearing God in Scripture* (Grand Rapids: Baker Academic, 2015); Craig G. Bartholomew and Heath A. Thomas, eds., *A Manifesto for Theological Interpretation* (Grand Rapids: Baker Academic, 2016).

remained until his retirement. As a theologian Scholten published his *Principles of the Theology of the Reformed Church*.[3] However, he also worked on the New Testament, and in 1864 he published his *Critical Study of the Gospel of John*, the book that, as we saw in chapter one, helped convince Kuyper of the deep problems with modernist theology.[4]

Students flocked to Scholten's lectures, and through him Abraham Kuenen, one of his students, was attracted to theology. Kuenen was awarded his doctorate for his work on an edition of thirty-four chapters of Genesis from the Arabic version of the Samaritan Pentateuch. In 1853 he was appointed professor *extraordinarius* of theology at Leiden, and full professor in 1855. He married a daughter of Willem Muurling, a founder of the Groningen school, whose break with Calvinistic theology in the Reformed Church of the Netherlands we noted in chapter one. Kuenen became a major proponent of modernist theology, of which Cornelis Willem Opzoomer (1821–1892) and Scholten were the chief founders in the Netherlands, and of which Leiden was the headquarters. These scholars created a movement resembling that of the Tübingen school in Germany.[5] From their theology began to rise "a different type of spirit, the spirit of absolute antisupernaturalism of the German idealistic kind."[6]

Kuenen's first major work, *Historical-Critical Investigation of the Origin and Collection of the Books of the Old Testament*, followed the lines of the German school of Heinrich Ewald (1803–1875).[7] Ewald was one of the teachers of Julius Wellhausen, the father of Pentateuchal criticism, and has been described as "one of the greatest Old Testament scholars of all time."[8] Ewald was

---

[3]Jan Hendrik Scholten, *Principles of the Theology of the Reformed Church*, 2 vols. (1848–1850); 4th ed., 1861–1862.

[4]Cf. *RD* 1:366. The reference is to J. H. Scholten, *Het Evangelie naar Johannes* (Leiden: P. Engels, 1864). An account of Scholten's theological development is provided in his *Afscheidsrede bij het Neerleggen van het Hoogleeraarsambt* (1881), and in the biography written by Abraham Kuenen, *Levensbericht van J. Henricus Scholten* (1885).

[5]See George Harinck, "Twin Sisters with a Changing Character: How Neo-Calvinists Dealt with the Modern Discrepancy Between the Bible and Modern Science," in Jitse M. van der Meer and Scott Mandelbrote, eds., *Nature and Scripture in the Abrahamic Religions* (Leiden: Brill, 2008), 1:317-70.

[6]Gerrit J. Tenzythoff, *Sources of Secession: The Netherlands Hervormde Kerk on the Eve of the Dutch Immigration to the Midwest*, Historical Series of the Reformed Church in America 17 (Grand Rapids: Eerdmans, 1987), 102.

[7]Abraham Kuenen, *Historisch-Kritisch Onderzoek naar het ontstaan en de verzameling van de Boeken des Ouden Verbonds*, 3 vols. (1861–1865); 2nd ed., 1885–1893.

[8]John Rogerson, *Old Testament Criticism in the Nineteenth Century: England and Germany* (London: SPCK, 1984), 91.

professor of Oriental languages at Göttingen University. In 1838 he moved to
Tübingen University as part of the philosophical faculty there. In 1841 he
moved into the theological faculty. In terms of Pentateuchal criticism, Ewald
advocated a supplementary hypothesis. The Elohist source, a basic source
(*Grundschrift*) starting at Genesis 1, runs through the Pentateuch and into
Joshua. An editor expanded this basic source with insertions from an originally separate J (Yahweh) source. Ewald thus played a major role in what has
become known as the JEDP source-critical approach to the Pentateuch.
Kuenen played a significant role in the emerging discussions about the sources
underlying the Pentateuch.[9]

In 1869–1870 Kuenen published a book on the religion of Israel, which was
followed in 1875 by a study of Hebrew prophecy, largely polemical in its scope,
and especially directed against those who based theological doctrines on the
fulfillment of prophecy.[10] In 1882 Kuenen traveled to England to deliver the
Hibbert lectures on the subject "National Religions and Universal Religion."[11]
Through his travels, the translations of his writings, and his correspondence,
Kuenen became far better known internationally than Scholten. His correspondence demonstrates that he was in dialogue with the major critical
scholars of the day, including Bishop Colenso in the Cape (South Africa),
William Robertson Smith in Scotland, and Julius Wellhausen.[12] The translation
of his books into German and English indicates the breadth of his influence.[13]

---

[9]See Ernest Nicholson, *The Pentateuch in the Twentieth Century: The Legacy of Julius Wellhausen* (Oxford:
Clarendon, 1998), 6-15; Rudolph Smend, "The Work of Abraham Kuenen and Julius Wellhausen," in M.
Sabø, ed., *HB/OT* 3, 1:424-53; Simon J. De Vries, "Hexateuchal Criticism of Abraham Kuenen," *Journal
of Biblical Literature* 82, no. 1 (1963): 31-57.

[10]Abraham Kuenen, *De Godsdienst tot den ondergang van den Joodschen staat* (Eng. trans. 1874–1875); *De
profeten en de profetie onder Israël* (Eng. trans. 1877).

[11]Several of Kuenen's books are available online in English: *An Historico-Critical Inquiry into the Origin and
Composition of the Hexateuch* (Pentateuch and book of Joshua); *National Religions and Universal Religions:
Lectures Delivered at Oxford and in London, in April and May, 1882; The Religion of Israel to the Fall of the
Jewish State* (3 vols.).

[12]John W. Rogerson, "J. W. Colenso's Correspondence with Abraham Kuenen, 1863–1878," in W. P. Stephens, ed., *The Bible, the Reformation and the Church: Essays in Honour of James Atkinson*, Journal for the
Study of the New Testament Supplement 105 (Sheffield: Sheffield Academic Press, 1995), 190-223; Cor-
nelius Houtman, "Abraham Kuenen and William Robertson Smith: Their Correspondence," *Nederlands
Archief voor Kerkgeschiedenis* 80 (2000): 221-40; R. Smend, "Kuenen and Wellhausen," in Peter W. Dirksen
and Aad W. van der Kooij, eds., *Abraham Kuenen (1828–1891): His Major Contributions to the Study of the
Old Testament: A Collection of Old Testament Studies Published on the Occasion of the Centenary of Abraham
Kuenen's Death (10 December 1991)*, Oudtestamentische Studiën 29 (Leiden: Brill, 1993), 113-27.

[13]See the essays in Dirksen and van der Kooij, *Abraham Kuenen*.

Kuenen's work takes us deeply into the emergence of modern biblical criticism, and doubtless readers who are unfamiliar with this territory are wondering about its relevance. We cannot here elaborate further on Kuenen's and Scholten's work; the point of our foray into it is to demonstrate that what Kuyper and Bavinck were exposed to was not trivial explorations into modern biblical criticism but critical biblical scholarship at the forefront of modern developments. Neither Kuyper nor Bavinck were biblical scholars, but they knew what they were talking about when they spoke of modernist theology and biblical criticism.

It is important to note that the new criticism immediately affected the church.[14] Kuenen is a coauthor of *The Bible for Learners*, a book in which students and laity are introduced to biblical criticism and the effort made to bridge it by reading the Bible as Scripture. Much of the Bible is classified as myth and legend, but, as with Wilhelm de Wette (1780–1849), the father of modern biblical criticism, it is argued that this in no way detracts from the religious value of the Bible. Of the transfiguration, for example, the authors note that "if we looked to the Transfiguration on the mount for light on the history of Jesus, we should be bitterly disappointed."[15]

REFORMED RESPONSES

Kuyper was by no means the first to respond to the challenges of modernism at Leiden. In 1857 Isaac da Costa published his "De profeet Hosea te recht staande voor den hoogleraar Kuenen" ["The prophet Hosea standing trial before professor Kuenen"].[16] Houtman notes in relation to da Costa's critique,

> To what extent the Orthodox and the Moderns lived in two separate worlds and to what extent the two were characterized by differing points of departure and presuppositions has been strikingly described by Pierson in *Oudere tijdgenooten*, in which he informs the reader of the view of Scripture and the use of Scripture that prevailed in Réveil circles, and gives his own opinion on the matter.[17]

---

[14]Cf. Abraham Kuyper, "The Biblical Criticism of the Present Day," trans. J. Hendrik de Vries, *Bibliothecra Sacra* LXI (1904): 410-42, 666-88, on 676-77, for his fear that among the ethical school the modernizers are better known than the orthodox.

[15]Henricus Oort, Isaäc Hooykaas, and Abraham Kuenen, *The Old Testament for Learners* (Boston: Little, Brown, 1900), 10.

[16]Isaac da Costa, *De Heraut* (1857), 6.

[17]C. Houtman, "Die Wirkung der Arbeit Kuenens in den Niederlanden," in Dirksen and van der Kooij, *Abraham Kuenen*, 34. German: "Wie sehr Orthodoxe und Moderne in zwei voneinander getrennten

Allard Pierson (1831–1896) came from an influential Réveil family, and da Costa was a regular visitor at his parental home. Pierson was a leading light in the national church, but then, in 1865, having lost patience with the church and much enamored by modernism, he left the church to become a professor of aesthetics. For Pierson, if Christianity were to be replaced by Culture and were merely an expression of human evolution, then why wait; why not leap ahead and devote oneself to education and science?

Like Pierson, Kuyper recognized the clash of worldviews at work in modernism and the church. In a series of three sermons in November and December 1865, Kuyper declared that Pierson's logic was right! The church was confronted with a choice between humanism and Christianity, and there could be no compromise between the two. "Not only was the church as a body at issue, but the very existence of the soul itself, or of any reality beyond the material realm. The specter of blank materialism would represent, from now on, the deepest horror of Kuyper's imagination, the ultimate in a remorseless, meaningless world."[18]

Kuenen did not respond to da Costa's critique; instead he chose the work of a German Old Testament scholar on messianic interpretation of the Psalms, E. Böhl (1836–1903) at Wien, as his target.[19] Kuenen's attack on Böhl enabled him to demonstrate to the Dutch public his view of orthodox exegesis without attacking a Dutchman directly.

KUYPER: "THE BIBLICAL CRITICISM OF THE PRESENT DAY"

In the fall of 1881 Kuyper chose the occasion of handing over the rectorship of the Free University of Amsterdam to address the issue of biblical criticism in his "The Biblical Criticism of the Present Day." At the outset he makes his position crystal clear: biblical criticism is damaging to the church because it undermines its theology, robs it of the Scriptures, and destroys its freedom in

---

Welten lebten und wie sehr beide durch unterschiedliche Ausgangspunkte und Voraussetzungen gekennzeichnet waren, ist von Pierson treffend in *Oudere tijdgenooten* beschrieben worden, wo er den Leser mit den Schriftauffassung und dem Schriftgebrauch in den Kreisen des Réveil vertraut macht und seine Meinung dazu äussert."

[18]*AK*, 47.

[19]E. Böhl's (1836–1903) *Zwölf messianische Psalmen: Nebst einer grundlegenden christologischen Einleitung* (Basel, 1862). See Ulrich Gäbler, "Eduard Böhls Auseinandersetzung mit dem Holländer Abraham Kuenen über die rechte Auslegung des Alten Testaments, 1864," *Jahrbuch für die Geschichte des Protestantismus in Österreich* 96, parts 1-3 (Vienna: Verlag des Evangelischen Presseverbandes in Österreich, 1980), 101-16.

Christ. Kuyper knew that modern biblical criticism now dominated European universities, and this was one of the reasons for establishing a university like the Free University of Amsterdam. As he notes, "And therefore, in behalf of that misappreciated and theology-robbed church, we have planted in this new University a slip of the old plant, with the prayer that God may give it increase."[20] Kuyper develops three major critiques of biblical criticism:

1. It tears apart theology and substitutes for it something that is not theology (his encyclopedic argument).

2. It robs Christians of their Bible (his dogmatic argument).

3. It leads to an unhelpful clericalism in the church (his argument about Christian liberty).

We will review each of these in detail.

The encyclopedic argument. Kuyper devoted considerable energy to the encyclopedia of theology, a topic on which he would publish a three-volume work.[21] Biblical studies, for Kuyper, is part of the encyclopedia of theology, and he sees the biblical criticism of his day as destructive of the vital ecology of theology.

For Kuyper theology differs from other sciences in that its object is God, and God can only be known through his revelation of himself: "in all other sciences man observes and thoughtfully investigates the object, and subjects it to himself, but in theology the object itself is active; it does not stand open, but gives itself to be seen; does not allow itself to be investigated, but reveals itself; and employs man as instrument only to cause the knowledge of his Being to radiate."[22]

Theology is a unity and is born from the impulse of the Holy Spirit. It has a vital role to play among God's people: God "wills that the knowledge of his Being shall be received by us; and that, having been cast into the furrows of our minds and hearts, it shall germinate; and having germinated, that it shall bear fruit to the honor of his name."[23]

For Kuyper *dogmatics* is the heart of theology, with critical-literary studies lying furthest away from the center, and with exegesis, pastoral theology, and

---

[20]Kuyper, "Biblical Criticism of the Present Day," 410, 421.
[21]Partially translated into English by J. Hendrik de Vries as *Principles of Sacred Theology* (Grand Rapids: Baker, 1980). See chapter ten.
[22]Kuyper, "Biblical Criticism of the Present Day," 411.
[23]Ibid.

church history lying in a constellation around the center. The center ought to receive the greatest energy, a priority that biblical criticism turns upside down: it "makes that which is subordinate principal; devotes the finest energies to that which lies nearer the circumference; withdraws its best heads and best hours from the central study of theology, and thus occasions the birth of a monstrous hydrocephal." Kuyper is ever a master rhetorician, and he likens the effect of biblical criticism to a royal banquet in which the threads of the table linens have been numbered, every spot on the golden goblets recorded, but there is no wine! For Kuyper something is seriously wrong when much is said *about* "introduction to Scripture" but little said *on* the authority of Scripture. The result is that "by far the greater part of the theological domain is still untilled ground; the real theological sense is dulled; and most of those who call themselves theologians declare their study already ended when the portal which leads from the outer sanctuarium of the sancta theologia still waits their steps."[24]

Biblical criticism has thus subverted the governing principle of theology of revelation, and once we let go of the governing principle "that course of studies governs us, and subjects us unconsciously to the power of that other principle, from which the impulse to this divergence in the course of studies was born."[25] For Kuyper biblical criticism is a manifestation of the spirits of the day, and its emergence and dominance is no accident:

> It was rather a general disposition of the spirits, which, in all countries of Europe, almost simultaneously raised very similar presumptions against the Scripture. The Schleiermachers and Robertson Smiths, the Kuenens and Colensos, are but the most accurate interpreters, on Scripture grounds, of the spirit which, as a reformer of the once current conceptions, has transposed the entire human consciousness in every department of life; even the revolution in theology, such as we have already witnessed in politics and in social and domestic relations.[26]

For Kuyper this new spirit often comes clothed in the forms of orthodox Protestantism. He is thus critical of the ethical approach stemming from Groningen, which continues to use the language of Zion but has given us an

---

[24]Ibid., 412, 414.
[25]Ibid., 415.
[26]Ibid.

entirely different theology.[27] He argues that the "'science of religion' has been allowed to ascend the throne of the *sancta theologia,* and that as willing priests you offer it the services of your splendid talents, and as willing choir-boys bring to it the incense of your homage." Kuyper is insightful here because a major shift in modern biblical studies has indeed been the replacement of theological interpretation of the Bible with a *history of religions* approach. As Kuyper notes of Old Testament studies, "The simple change of name by which henceforth all idolatry, however defiant its character might be to the only true God, is called 'religion,' is a criticism on the Old Covenant that condemns its entire world-view."[28]

Kuyper is ever aware of the implications of biblical criticism for the church. In his view it is very damaging to the church because the church needs a healthy theology; indeed, theology is a gift from God. "In brief, she needs a theology which, while it differs not specifically, but only gradually, from the knowledge of sacred things on the part of the laity, does not stand outside of it, but in the service of the Holy Spirit, blooms and flourishes with it upon one root." And this, says Kuyper, the biblical critics, "the vivisectors," withhold from it.[29]

The dogmatic argument. Second, Kuyper argues that biblical criticism robs the church of its Bible. He poses the critical question, when does the church have a Bible and when not? Kuyper seeks to answer this crucial question "plainly as a day-laborer, because the Holy Scripture is a divine jewel common to the day-laborer and professor."[30]

Kuyper confesses that when he reads the Bible in private or family devotions he reads it not as Moses or John addressing him, but the Lord God. He is worth quoting at length at this point:

> He it is who then narrates to me the origin of all things and the calamitous fall of man. God tells me with silent majesty how he has appointed salvation to our fallen race. I hear him himself relate the wonders which he wrought for our deliverance and that of the people of his choice, and how, when that people rebelled against him, he afflicted them in his wrath, and when chastened restored them again to his favor, the whilst they sought the day of the coming of

---

[27]Cf. also ibid., 433-42.
[28]Ibid., 420, 674.
[29]Ibid., 420.
[30]Ibid., 422.

the Son of his love. In the midst of that sacred history I hear the Holy Spirit singing to my spiritual ear in the Psalms, which discloses the depths of my own soul; in the prophets I hear him repeat what he whispered in the soul of Israel's seers; and in which my own soul is refreshed by a perspective which is most inspiring and beautiful. Till at length, in the pages of the New Testament, God himself brings out to me the Expected One, the Desire of the fathers; shows me the place where the manger stood; points out to me the tracks of his footsteps; and on Golgotha lets me see, how the Son of his unique love, for me poor doomed one, died the death of the cross. And, finally, it is the same God, the Holy Spirit, who, as it were, reads off to me what he caused to be preached by Jesus' disciples concerning the riches of that cross, and closes the record of this drama in the Apocalypse with the enchanting Hosanna from the heaven of heavens. Call this, if you will, an almost childish faith, outgrown by your larger wisdom, but I cannot better it. Such is my Bible to me, and such it was in the bygone ages, and such it is still, the Scripture of the church of the living God. The human authors must fall away; in the Bible God himself must tell the narrative, sing, prophesy, correct, comfort, and jubilate in the ear of the soul. The majesty of the Lord God is the point in question, and that only.[31]

Kuyper clearly has a very high view of the Bible. However, he avoids bibliolatry. Scripture becomes the Word of God only when the Spirit facilitates God's address to one in and through Scripture. Kuyper affirms *inspiration* as the mode by which God caused Scripture to originate. He carefully differentiates revelation from inspiration. He affirms with "those backward ones" that God wrote the law upon the tablets of stone, spoke audibly at Sinai, predicted the future through his prophets, and so on. Scripture should, however, not be equated with revelation, since it provides us with only so much from God's revelation of himself to be kept in the inscripturated Word for the church of all ages.[32] Kuyper rejects a magical, dictation view of inspiration: "I take the writers as entirely instrumental in the service of the Holy Spirit, including everything they knew, together with the entire result of their previous training, even to their surroundings and credentials, and maintain that the Holy Spirit has used this whole person, with everything belonging to him."[33] Kuyper

---

[31]Ibid., 422-23.
[32]Cf. *RD* 1:381.
[33]Kuyper, "Biblical Criticism of the Present Day," 430. Cf. *RD* 1:431, critique of a mechanical approach to inspiration.

rejects the distinction some make between Scripture and the Word of God.[34] As a whole and in its parts Scripture is God's Word. Scripture is infallible, and one cannot separate the thoughts from the words, as some German theologians in Kuyper's day were wont to do. Kuyper thus affirms what nowadays we call the plenary verbal inspiration of the Bible: "it was also a verbal inspiration,—not mechanically by whispering into the fleshly ear, but organically by calling forth the words from man's own consciousness." Kuyper allows for some incoherence in one's theory of inspiration, provided the fact of Scripture's inspiration is left intact. "The divine fixedness over against the uncertainty of all human ponderings, is chiefly that which makes the Holy Scripture 'holy,' i.e., a bible for the church of God."[35]

Kuyper is by no means a fundamentalist, opposed to every aspect of biblical criticism.[36] He affirms the critics' close attention to the Bible and their exploration of the history of its production. Under God's grace even the most extreme vivisection of Scripture will lead to good. He is quite open about the difficulties he finds in the Bible and urges that these must be faced squarely with four provisos:

1. We do not have the autographs available to us.

2. The genres of Scripture must be taken seriously.

3. Rigorous apologetic work remains important.

4. Where difficulties remain, we choose to profess ignorance over a proud scientism that rejects the infallibility of Scripture.[37]

In response to those who would still remind Kuyper that he acknowledges errors in Scripture, he reaches for an intriguing illustration. If one held a cup of pure gold whose edge was slightly damaged, who would not choose this over a cup of gold that is not real?[38]

As in other areas of culture, Kuyper certainly does not plead for conservatism, but what he objects to is the abandonment of the basic principle of theology. Kuyper insists on reading the world through the Word and notes

---

[34]Cf. *RD* 1:443: "Scripture is the word of God; it not only contains but *is* the word of God."
[35]Kuyper, "Biblical Criticism of the Present Day," 432, 433.
[36]Cf. Harinck, "Twin Sisters"; Al Wolters, "The Nature of Fundamentalism," *Pro Rege*, September 1986, 2-9.
[37]Kuyper, "Biblical Criticism of the Present Day," 675-76.
[38]Ibid., 677.

that the Word alerts us to the antithesis in the world. Scripture condemns "the world" and its spirit, and

> hence nothing can be more natural than that this spirit of the world, which has made itself so strongly felt in this age, should bend its energies toward the breaking-down of the authority of Scripture. Either it must bend before the Scripture or Scripture must bend to it, and it cannot be otherwise than that the spirit which inspires the world, must wage inexorable war against the spirit that inspired the Scripture. The antithesis formed by the two is diametrical.[39]

Only the Spirit can teach us wisdom, and thus every creaturely spirit must subject itself to the Holy Spirit. "This places us before an absolute dilemma; a choice with no way of escape." The self-witness of the Spirit must be trusted over fallible human judgments of the work of the Spirit in inspiring Scripture. Kuyper notes that scholars who attach no particular significance to Scripture now devote their lives to its study. Theology thus needs to be on its guard, "And therefore I make no appeal at the bar of conservatism, but ask the encyclopedia of our science, what the proper principle of theology here both allows and disallows." In theology it is the spirit of the object and not the subject that is the "active investigator." Kuyper observes that the witness of the Spirit produces a particular view of the world so that "every critical study of the Holy Scripture must be rejected as being foreign to theology, which is governed by a philosophical principle which evidently reacts against the principle of the Holy Spirit."[40] The spiritual impulse of the day to transpose the "Deus homo" into the "Homo-deus" is bound to lead to a casting off of Scripture, or when piety exercises some restraint, to rend the map of Scripture and put it together again in a different composition until "Scripture" affirms the wisdom of the world. The end result: the church is robbed of the Bible.

The clerical argument. Third, Kuyper argues that biblical criticism deprives the church of its liberty and makes it captive to an intellectual clericalism. The troubled soul needs to be shepherded toward God and set on the *"Rock of the Word."*[41] Only in dependence on God alone does the troubled soul find peace, and the Spirit ministers to God's people through God's Word. "That same Holy Spirit has ever afterward himself interpreted that Word through the

---

[39]Ibid., 668. Cf. *RD* 1:439-40.
[40]Ibid., 671, 669, 672.
[41]Ibid., 678, emphasis original. Cf. *RD* 1:461.

official preaching, and has mingled it with faith in those that are called unto life." Kuyper stresses that the same Spirit who oversaw the production of the canon of Scripture tends to its ongoing life. "And, finally, as to the exegesis of the Scripture, here also the Holy Spirit is the real exegete and, in difference of opinion, the *Supremus Judex*." The witness of the Spirit provides certainty that Scripture is God's Word, thereby providing true liberty to the believer. This is the fulfillment of the prophecy according to which a person has no need to say to his or her neighbor "Know the Lord," for all shall know him. "Or, if you please, call it the holy, divine, and only real equality which brings the pro-foundest scholar to his knees by the side of the humblest house-mother, with an assurance in the heart which is absolutely similar and unmoveable."[42]

The problem with biblical criticism is that it undermines this beautiful order of things: "It turns loose what was fast; it lifts each piece of the Scripture out of its grooves; and, unwilling and helpless, the laity are delivered into the hands of the men of Semitic and classical studies."[43] Christians are left as sheep without a shepherd and are made captive to the "learned" opinions of clerics.

Conclusion. Kuyper, in conclusion, defends the rights of non-Christian scholars to work as they choose in biblical studies and theology:

> But I deplore that in the domain of the church of Christ, and in the very temple of the sacred theology, the Holy Scripture has been so roughly handled by those who profess themselves to be Christian theologians, that at their hand the Holy Bible has been recklessly and unsparingly carved and torn loose in its several parts, and has had its organism remodeled after philosophical hypotheses.[44]

Kuyper is acutely aware of the philosophical underpinnings of the biblical criticism of his day, and he appeals to the ethical theologians: "Smelt away the philosophical alloy from the pure gold which still hides in the kernel of your faith. Be done with limping on two mutually excluding principles."[45] To the younger scholars who might hear Kuyper's call as one to do violence to their scientific conscience, he denies this; he urges them to do violence to an in-flated sense of human reason but to be rich in the Spirit.

---

[42]Kuyper, "Biblical Criticism of the Present Day," 679, 682, 684.
[43]Ibid.
[44]Ibid., 686.
[45]Ibid., 687-88.

HERMAN BAVINCK (1854–1921) AND THE BIBLE

We saw above how Kuyper compared his reading of Scripture to that of a child. Bavinck uses a similar analogy:

> There is nothing humiliating nor anything that in any way detracts from a person's freedom, in listening to the word of God like a child and obeying it. Believing God at his word, i.e., on his authority, is in no way inconsistent with human dignity, anymore than it dishonors a child to rely with unlimited trust on the word of his or her father. So far from gradually outgrowing this authority, Christian believers rather progressively learn to believe God at his word and to renounce all their own wisdom. On earth believers never move beyond the viewpoint of faith and authority. To the degree that they increase in faith, they cling all the more firmly to the authority of God in his word.[46]

As with Kuyper this does not lead to a fundamentalist view of Scripture but to a robust doctrine of inspiration and a serious engagement with the challenges of biblical criticism.

Bavinck stresses that in the revelation of Scripture word and fact go together. Christian revelation is and has to be *history*, as is particularly evident in the incarnation. "To be able fully to enter the life of humankind and for it fully to become its possession, revelation assumes the form (μορφη) and fashion (σχημα) of Scripture. Scripture is the servant form of revelation. Indeed, the central fact of revelation, i.e., the incarnation, leads to Scripture." Scripture is thus the continuation of the incarnation of Christ, "the way by which Christ makes his home in the church, the preparation to the full indwelling of God."[47] Christ is God's final word, but it is through Scripture that Christ now enters into the whole of life and history.

As with Kuyper, but in a more expanded fashion, Bavinck argues for an organic view of inspiration.[48] He notes that awareness of the historical and psychological mediation of Scripture is a fruit of modernity so that a mechanical view of inspiration has rightly made way for an organic one. Far from an organic view detracting from the Bible as Scripture, it enables Scripture to

---

[46]*RD* 1:464.

[47]*RD* 1:380-81.

[48]Dirk van Keulen, "The Internal Tension in Kuyper's Doctrine of Organic Inspiration of Scripture," in Cornelis van der Kooi and Jan de Bruijn, eds., *Kuyper Reconsidered: Aspects of His Life and Work* (Amsterdam: VU Uitgeverij, 1999), 123-30, discerns a tension in Kuyper's view of inspiration stemming from Kuyper's quest for certainty. I am not persuaded by the argument.

come more fully into its own. Organic inspiration has been used to undermine inspiration and God as the primary author of Scripture, "But just as Christ's human nature, however weak and lowly, remained free from sin, so also Scripture is 'conceived without defect or stain': totally human in all its parts but also divine in all its parts."[49]

Many objections to this approach are raised, objections that largely derive from historical criticism. Bavinck notes that if Scripture is God's Word it is bound to arouse opposition:

> Of course not all opposition to Scripture can be explained in terms of this [spiritual hostility]. Still, the attacks to which Scripture is exposed in this century must not be viewed on their own. They are undoubtedly an integral part of the intellectual trend of this age. . . . It is unlikely that today it is only the head that speaks and that the heart remains completely outside of it. . . . The connection between sin and error often lies deep below the surface of the conscious life. . . . The battle against the Bible is, in the first place, a revelation of the hostility of the human heart.[50]

Just as Kuyper argues against a dead conservatism and an unbelieving criticism, so too Bavinck sees not just historical criticism but dead orthodoxy as a problem.

Bavinck pleads for a hermeneutic of trust and humility. He refers to a beautiful incident in the life of Augustine. A rhetorician, when asked what the chief rule is in eloquence, replied, first "delivery," second "delivery," and third "delivery!" Augustine responds that if asked what the main precepts are of the Christian religion he would reply, first humility, second humility, and third humility! Bavinck also quotes Pascal: "Humble yourself, powerless reason! Be silent, stupid nature! . . . Listen to God!" This is not to deny the difficulties we face in Scripture: "There are intellectual problems (*cruces*) in Scripture that cannot be ignored and that will probably never be resolved."[51] However, what we do in the face of such challenges is crucial. Bavinck notes that theology is not alone in its encounter with mystery; other sciences face a similar challenge.

It is vital that we are clear on the purpose of Scripture, which is religious-ethical. Bavinck notes, "Historical criticism has utterly forgotten this purpose

---

[49]*RD* 1:431, 435.
[50]*RD* 1:440.
[51]*RD* 1:441, 442.

of Scripture."[52] Scripture is not a manual for the special sciences, and we can neither construct a life of Jesus nor a history of Israel from the Bible. Scripture, furthermore, does not satisfy the demand for exact knowledge as we do in mathematics, astronomy, and so on. Biblical historiography has a character of its own, but it does not follow that it is untrue and unreliable.

Although Scripture is not a manual for the sciences, "Precisely as the book of the knowledge of God, Scripture has much to say also to the other sciences. It is a light on our path and a lamp for our feet, also with respect to science and art." Indeed, "the authority of Scripture extends to the whole person and over all humankind. . . . Its authority, being divine, is absolute." Bavinck develops a wonderfully nuanced view of biblical apologetics, noting inter alia that "the Christian worldview alone is the one that fits the reality of the world and of life."[53]

Kuyper's Successors and the Bible

Neither Kuyper nor Bavinck were biblical scholars, though the work of both is saturated with Scripture, and Kuyper wrote volumes of devotionals. Bavinck in particular recognized the need for substantial biblical work. In his preface to the Dutch translation of Matthew Henry's *Commentary on the Bible* he writes: "It would be too much to expect this commentary of Henry to satisfy the present needs in all respects. But in this area we are still extremely poor. . . . However much we may lament it, we must still live from what the past offers us."[54]

The *Korte Verklaring* ["Short exposition"] commentary series made a major contribution in filling the gap identified by Bavinck and includes work by such luminaries as G. Ch. Aalders (1880–1961), W. H. Gispen (1900–1986), Herman Ridderbos (1909–2007), and so on.[55] The *Korte Verklaring* commentaries are by no means so "kort" (short) as the title suggests. Aalders's commentary on Genesis, for example, consists of three volumes and engages seriously with the biblical criticism of his day. Biblical scholars at the Free University of Amsterdam and at the Reformed seminaries in the Netherlands

---

[52]*RD* 1:444.
[53]*RD* 1:445, 465, 515.
[54]Matthew Henry, *Letterlijke en Practicale Verklaring van het N.T.*, with introduction by Herman Bavinck (Kampen: Kok, 1909), vii. Quoted in Sidney Greidanus, *Sola Scriptura: Problems and Principles in Preaching Historical Texts* (Toronto: Wedge, 1970; repr., Wipf and Stock, 2001), 25.
[55]Presently under translation into English.

produced not only commentaries but substantial works on biblical themes, introductions, and so on. An example, which remains a useful work, is Aalders's *Introduction to the Pentateuch*. These works remain a treasury of insight and need to be retrieved, recovered, and developed in our day.

Kuyper died in 1920, and after his death, between World War I and World War II, a significant new development in Reformed biblical hermeneutics took place, namely, the emergence of the *redemptive-historical* school. This movement has its roots in Kuyper and Bavinck and other Dutch scholars but was new in important aspects. The movement was initiated by Klaas Schilder with a series of articles and books in the 1930s, including *Christ in His Suffering*.[56] The movement was constructive in its quest for a way of reading Scripture with God and Christ at its heart, but also developed in reaction to the perceived ahistoricism of the early Barth and the dominance of "exemplary preaching" in the Reformed churches.[57]

The following elements characterize the redemptive-historical approach:

1. Redemptive history *is* history, and this approach opposes the distinction between secular and redemptive history. Schilder insists in his *What Is Heaven?* that "God's redemptive work does not produce a different history, separate from the 'profane,' but it enters into history and executes itself with and through it. It compels history to become what it already is."[58] In Christ God recovers his purposes for his world.

2. Redemptive history is a *unity*. Among proponents of the redemptive-historical approach, God's eternal counsel is presupposed so that he has planned all things according to his will, and thus history as it unfolds is a unity, a unity of which Christ is the center. Thus in 1946 Schilder defined redemptive history as "God's successive realization of his thoughts of peace for us in time according to a fixed plan, and the fulfillment of what Father, Son and Spirit, with mutual counsel between one another, decided upon as their program, decided 'before' time, and executed in time."[59]

---

[56]Klaas Schilder, *Christus in zijn lijden*. ET *Christ in His Suffering*, 3 vols., trans. Henry Zylstra (Grand Rapids: Eerdmans, 1954).

[57]See Greidanus, *Sola Scriptura*, 8-18, on exemplary preaching. On the exemplary/redemptive historical controversy in Holland, see ibid., 22-120.

[58]Klaas Schilder, *Wat is de Hemel?* (Kampen: Kok, 1935), 68.

[59]Quoted in Greidanus, *Sola Scriptua*, 123-24n14, my translation.

3. "God's successive realization" expresses the *progressive* element of the redemptive-historical approach. "History always means unity and progress
   simultaneously."[60] According to Schilder, "In every subsequent epoch
   there is a decisive entrance of something new, an inevitable increase in
   atmospheric pressure, a rise in temperature, a drawing near of Bethlehem."[61]
   All the mysteries of God are known to God eternally, but their content is
   revealed successively to humankind in history.[62] There was controversy
   about the extent to which one can plot the progressive nature of God's
   revelation, but even Schilder could write, "To follow redemptive history
   in all its phases always means to confront a mystery."[63] The emphasis is
   thus more on eschatology as central to Scripture than on tracking the
   precise details of the progress of God's revelation.

4. It will be obvious that the redemptive-historical hermeneutic is *theological*
   through and through. What is noteworthy is that it arises out of a concern
   with how to *preach* Scripture so that God's address is heard in the church
   in all its creation-wide and redemptive power. Doubtless the proponents
   of the redemptive-historical approach would have affirmed ecclesial reception of the Word as the primary context for its reception. Biblical studies's role is to deepen this reception.

A leader in this movement, B. Holwerda,[64] summarized this redemptive-
historical approach in 1940 as follows:

> The Bible does not contain many histories but *one* history—the one history of
> God's constantly advancing revelation, the one history of God's ever pro-
> gressing redemptive work. And the various persons named in the Bible have all
> received their own peculiar place in this one history and have their peculiar
> meaning for this history. We must, therefore, try to understand all the accounts
> in their relation with each other, in their coherence with the centre of re-
> demptive history, Jesus Christ.[65]

---

[60]B. Holwerda, "... *Begonnen Hebbende van Mozes* ..." (Terneuzen: D. H. Littooij, 1953), 89.

[61]Quoted in Greidanus, *Sola Scriptura*, 124.

[62]Schilder, *Wat is de Hemel*, 253.

[63]Quoted in Greidanus, *Sola Scriptura*, 129.

[64]See George Harinck, ed., *Holwerda herdacht: Bijdragen over leven en werk van Benne Holwerda (1909–1952)* (Barneveld: De Vuurbaak, 2005).

[65]Translated and quoted in Sidney Greidanus, *Sola Scriptura*, 41.

There are many excellent resources to be excavated in this tradition, but one of the outstanding exponents of this approach was Herman Ridderbos (1909–2007),[66] whose books *The Coming of the Kingdom* and *Paul* remain classics. He did his doctorate on the Sermon on the Mount at the Free University of Amsterdam and went on to produce an astonishing corpus of work, much of which remains untranslated.

The new approach to Paul, with its controversial recontextualization of justification, is receiving much attention among New Testament scholars and Christians today.[67] In this context it is fascinating to read Ridderbos on Paul. For example, he poses this question of the edifice of Paul's corpus: "It is clear that there are all sorts of doors leading into it. But which of these is the main entrance?" The Reformers found the main entrance in *justification*, later exegetes in *"being-in-Christ,"* so that Pauline Spirit-mysticism became the main entrance. The effect of the latter was to disrupt the unity of Paul's teaching with that of Jesus. Ridderbos resists setting the mystical against the forensic and asserts, "The term 'redemptive-historical' . . . expresses a new and broader outlook on the general character of Paul's preaching."[68] Ridderbos contrasts Luther's conversion with that of Paul: for Luther it involved the reversal of his understanding of the *ordo salutis*, whereas for Paul it involved the *historia salutis*.

> God revealed to him, on the road to Damascus, that Jesus of Nazareth, crucified and persecuted by Paul, is the Messiah sent by God. This is the new, overpowering certainty, that in the crucified and risen Savior the great turning-point in God's times has come. . . . The nature of his mission and ministry, therefore, is defined by the history of redemption. . . . He is the one who, together with the other apostles, is to accompany and explain the penetration of the new aeon into the present time with his testimony.[69]

---

[66]The Ridderbos family is reminiscent of the Wenham family in the UK. John Wenham, the father, wrote several important books, including *Elements of New Testament Greek*, and produced three sons—a pastor, a New Testament scholar (David), and an Old Testament scholar (Gordon). Herman Ridderbos's father, Jan, was professor in Old Testament in the Theological Seminary at Kampen, where Herman worked, and his brother N. H. Ridderbos was professor of Old Testament at the Free University of Amsterdam.

[67]For an introduction see Kent L. Yinger, *The New Perspective on Paul: An Introduction* (Eugene, OR: Cascade Books, 2011).

[68]Herman N. Ridderbos, *When the Time Had Fully Come: Studies in New Testament Theology* (Grand Rapids: Eerdmans, 1957), 44, 47.

[69]Ibid., 48.

Justification, for Ridderbos, must be understood in this larger, redemptive-historical context.

ASSESSMENT

The Kuyperian tradition holds rich resources for a recovery of Scripture today. In the context of the emergence into sharp focus of the modern world, Kuyper and Bavinck saw with crystal clarity the importance of holding fast to Scripture as God's infallible word. Contrary to so much biblical study today, they affirm a hermeneutic of trust *in Scripture* and a hermeneutic of suspicion *in relation to ourselves* and cultural trends, not least in relation to modernism. Both rightly affirm an *organic view of inspiration,* and Bavinck develops this in detail.

Neither Kuyper nor Bavinck were conservatives in the sense of getting stuck in a particular time in church history. Both saw the need to update the Reformed tradition for their day. Kuyper's "Conservatism and Orthodoxy: False and True Preservation" is essential reading in this respect.[70] Kuyper notes that in a certain respect conservatism lies in the very DNA of the church: "Christianity aims at a new creation, but the new from the old, a new-fashioned from the old fallen world that already exists." Christianity is decidedly not revolutionary: "Unlike the revolution which it opposes, it lives not by hollow ideas but by real power; it does not conjure up castles in the air but builds a solid home on the *given* foundation from the materials at hand." And Scripture and the Christ of Scripture are utterly central to this foundation. Christianity is an historical phenomenon, "a revelation of the eternal *in time*" recorded in Scripture, so that preservation is essential, lest the church lose the pearl of great price. "I've pointed out how a tenacious hold on tradition is synonymous with religion and how 'salvation by resurrection' is the theme song of the Christian."[71]

However, a false conservatism holds on to the tradition but lets go of the living Christ and thereby becomes powerless. "Still it is our calling to hold fast what we have in Christ *in our own time,* not in theirs, and so it is from our own time that we must take the material with which to prepare that form today."[72] For Kuyper this means that on the firm basis of an infallible Scripture, Christians need to work out what it means to live for God *today.*

---

[70]*AK:CR*, 65-85.
[71]*AK:CR*, 69, 70, 78.
[72]*AK:CR*, 82.

Consequently, Kuyper, Bavinck, and their followers took seriously the development and triumph of biblical criticism across Europe. And they did not simply write it off. Despite his disagreements with Scholten, Kuyper remained in a dialogue with him, and Bavinck was drawn to Kuenen as one of his professors. Both recognize that there is much to be learned from biblical criticism, but neither is prepared to concede the *epistemological ground* to biblical criticism, expressive as it was of the larger shifts in culture, much of which were deeply anti-Christian. It is the genius of Kuyper and Bavinck to penetrate behind biblical criticism to the worldviews and philosophies informing it, the soil out of which it grew, and to insist on testing the spirits of that soil.[73] Wellhausen argued that philosophy never preceded but only followed on from biblical criticism, but Kuyper and Bavinck rightly saw that this was simply not the case. Recent developments in biblical studies, especially with the emergence of so-called postmodernism, have shown Kuyper and Bavinck to be right, though it is astonishing how entrenched the view remains that biblical criticism is somehow neutral and autonomous.

Although they were not biblical scholars, both Kuyper and Bavinck saw the need for orthodox scholars to catch up to historical critics in terms of rigorous work on the Bible, albeit from the basis of a very different epistemology. During the twentieth century Dutch Kuyperian scholars made significant progress in this respect, and we identified the development of the redemptive-historical hermeneutic as noteworthy. A danger of the redemptive-historical approach might be that it fails to account adequately for the radically new element in God's revelation in Christ, but it is really helpful in discerning the grand story of Scripture and in seeing that Jesus is the son of Abraham, the one through whom God will recover his purpose of blessing for his entire creation (cf. Gen 12:1-3; Mt 1:1).[74]

Toward the end of the twentieth century mainstream biblical criticism largely triumphed in the Netherlands, and to this day much of the work of Kuyper and his followers in biblical studies is ignored or unknown. This, in

---

[73]Cf. Harinck, "Twin Sisters."

[74]Parallels between the redemptive-historical hermeneutic, the biblical theology movement, the work of Geerhardus Vos at Princeton, and the works of scholars such as John Bright, *The Kingdom of God*, need to be noted. Cf. George Harinck, "Gerhardus Vos as Introducer of Kuyper in America," in Hans Krabbendam and Larry J. Wagenaar, eds., *The Dutch-American Experience: Essays in Honor of Robert P. Swieringa* (Amsterdam: VU, 2000), 242-62.

my view, is a mistake. Certainly the Kuyperian tradition in biblical studies needs to be updated and to be reformed in relation to further developments; Kuyper himself would have strongly affirmed this. But the basic building blocks put in place need to be retained, retrieved, and renewed.

Bavinck's attention to the focus of Scripture as religious-ethical, for example, is a poignant insight, as is his point that this focus is forgotten by too many biblical critics whose work does everything except help us hear Scripture as God's address. Jewish biblical scholar Jon Levenson, in an important work, perceptively notes,

> Most Christians involved in the historical criticism of the Hebrew Bible today, however, seem to have ceased to want their work to be considered distinctively Christian. They do the essential philological, historical, and archaeological work without concern for the larger constructive issues or for the theological implications of their labors. They are Christians everywhere except in the classroom and at the writing table, where they are simply honest historians striving for an unbiased view of the past. Even in the world of Old Testament theology, however, there has grown over the last twenty years or so considerable awareness that the historical-critical enterprise is in tension with the demands of Christian proclamation.[75]

The implications of this could not be more serious. As Bavinck notes, "With the fall of Holy Scripture, therefore, all of revelation falls as well, as does the person of Christ."[76]

Bavinck rightly resists both *dualism*—in which Scripture only addresses issues of "faith"—and *biblicism*, according to which Scripture is seen as a manual for the sciences. He rightly notes that Scriptures' orientation toward the world is authoritative for all of life. Or, as Lesslie Newbigin notes, Christ is the clue to all that is.[77] The clue needs to be pursued in all areas of life, but one cannot find one's way if one does not start with *the* clue.

In terms of development of this tradition, Sidney Greidanus has done important work in relation to the Bible and preaching, with his multiple publications. From the 1970s onward in biblical studies, we witnessed the literary turn

---

[75]Jon D. Levenson, *The Hebrew Bible, the Old Testament, and Historical Criticism: Jews and Christians in Biblical Studies* (Louisville: Westminster John Knox, 1993), 29.

[76]*RD*, 1:382.

[77]Lesslie Newbigin, *The Gospel in a Pluralist Society* (Grand Rapids: Eerdmans, 1989), 103-15.

with its (re)discovery of the Bible as literature. The best insights of the literary and narrative approach provide important insights that the redemptive-historical hermeneutic needs to take into account, and in *The Drama of Scripture: Finding Our Place in the Biblical Story*, Mike Goheen and I attempted to update the tradition in this respect.[78] Intriguingly, as noted above, when Kuyper recounts how he reads Scripture, he resorts to a narrative, dramatic approach, with God, through Scripture, telling him the true story of the whole world. We thus find strong correlations between the Kuyperian tradition and the work of scholars such as Richard Bauckham, Chris Wright, and Tom Wright, especially with the latter's model of the Bible as a drama in multiple acts.

Scripture is that field in which is hid the pearl of great price. We have seen in this chapter that without Scripture as its foundation, the Kuyperian tradition ceases to be genuinely Kuyperian. As the Kuyperian tradition developed in the Netherlands and in North America, there has been a worrisome tendency to loosen its hold on Scripture as God's infallible Word. This is a mistake and will lead to an intellectual tradition that is vacuous at its heart and vulnerable to the spirits of the age. In British evangelicalism too, after Lausanne in 1974, many evangelicals rediscovered cultural engagement, a thoroughly Kuyperian enterprise, but once again there have been signs of a laxity in relation to Scripture and a consequent succumbing to unhealthy cultural trends. Kuyper calls us back to Scripture and then out into the world, to being thoroughly biblical *and* thoroughly culturally engaged.

---

[78]Craig Bartholomew and Michael Goheen, *The Drama of Scripture: Finding Our Place in the Biblical Story*, 2nd ed. (Grand Rapids: Baker Academic, 2014).

WORLDVIEW

Scripture . . . is itself the interpretation of reality, the shaper of a distinct worldview.

HERMAN BAVINCK, *REFORMED DOGMATICS*

The Christian faith is the only worldview that fits the reality of life.

HERMAN BAVINCK, *REFORMED DOGMATICS*

GROWING UP IN THE ERA OF APARTHEID in South Africa, I was converted around the age of fourteen. I sensed when I was converted that my faith provided a key to understanding the world as a whole, but the Christianity I was converted into, while vital and alive, was *dualist* in its almost exclusive concern with the institutional church and evangelism.[1] As Kuyper might say, to a newborn Christian the church as my mother in the faith interpreted God and the world to me in a particular way. When one becomes a Christian, it is almost impossible to distinguish the voice of the mother (church) from the voice of the Father (God). A crucial point in my development came several years later, when as a youth pastor I revisited the works of Francis Schaeffer (1912–1984) and Hans Rookmaaker (1922–1977), discovering in the process that Christianity is a *worldview*.[2] I still recall the illumination and excitement

---

[1]Note that in philosophy *dualism* is used in a variety of ways. In this chapter I use it, as does Kuyper in *LC*, to refer to dividing the world up into sacred and secular areas, with church on the sacred side and activities such as politics and economics on the secular side.

[2]See Edith Schaeffer, *The Tapestry: The Life and Times of Edith and Francis Schaeffer* (Waco, TX: Word, 1985), for the delightful story of L'Abri. Rookmaaker was the founder of the art history department at the Free University of Amsterdam.

that came from being able to name my faith as a worldview. Eugene Peterson talks about the insight that comes from being able to name something you only know intuitively.[3] This is how I experienced *worldview*. Naming it was huge; it enabled me to see that the gospel is comprehensive and relates to all of life as God has made it, including politics, which was the rubicon one dared not cross as an ordinary South African evangelical. I had been locked into a type of Christianity that provided a *church* view, but now the whole of creation opened up before me as *the theater of God's glory*. My faith remained as real, but the vista before me opened up immeasurably.[4]

As we will see in chapter eight, perhaps Kuyper's least helpful reflections relate to race in South Africa. It never occurred to me, however, that the Kuyperian tradition and a Christian worldview could be used to support apartheid. In fact, quite the reverse; it enabled me to see that the gospel could and should be brought to bear critically on all aspects of life, including the racism of apartheid in South Africa.

Worldview is widely used in Christian thought today, though, as we will see below, it is not without its critics. I discovered worldview through Schaeffer and Rookmaaker. Rookmaaker received it through his Dutch context and thus from Kuyper and Bavinck.

James Orr, Abraham Kuyper, and Worldview

When Orr, Kuyper, and Bavinck reached for the term *worldview* to express the comprehensive vision of the Christian faith, they chose a term already well-known and widely used in academia.[5] We will begin, therefore, with some background to this term.

The origins and use of the term **worldview**.[6] *Worldview* is a translation of the German word *Weltanschauung*. It was coined by the German philosopher Immanuel Kant in his 1790 publication *Critique of Judgement*. In Kant's *idealism*

---

[3]Eugene Peterson, *Working the Angles: The Shape of Pastoral Integrity* (Grand Rapids: Eerdmans, 1987), 55n3. See also Eugene Peterson, *Answering God: The Psalms as Tools for Prayer* (New York: HarperCollins, 1989), 10.

[4]See in this regard my booklet *Church and Society* (Pinetown, South Africa: CESA, 1998).

[5]Cf. Herman Bavinck, *Christilijke Wereldbeschouwing* [Christian Worldview] (Kampen: Kok, 1913). Bavinck's wrestling with the theology of Albert Ritschl might have played an important role in his embrace of worldview. See note 32 in chapter two.

[6]The history of the term *worldview* has been mapped in detail in several German articles. In English the definitive treatment is by David Naugle, *Worldview: The History of a Concept* (Grand Rapids: Eerdmans, 2002). Cf. Michael W. Goheen and Craig G. Bartholomew, *Living at the Crossroads: An Introduction to Christian Worldview* (Grand Rapids: Baker Academic, 2008), chap. 2.

there is a single set of determining categories in rational minds by which humans interpret and view the world. Thus, though Kant believed that we cannot know the world as it is in itself—what he called the "noumenon"—the makeup of the human mind makes a single view of the world as "phenomenon" possible and the goal of scientific endeavor. *Weltanschauung* is not developed as a concept in Kant's philosophy, and it was Friedrich Wilhelm Joseph von Schelling (1775–1854) who gave it its more familiar meaning of the way in which humans understand and interpret the world around them.[7]

The Enlightenment shifted the starting point in philosophy from *ontology*— the nature of the world around us—to *epistemology*—how *we* go about knowing something so that we can trust the results of the knowing process. From a Christian perspective this was a significant shift. We *should* start with ontology—this is our Father's world, and we are creatures made in his image— and then move on to epistemology—as his creatures, how do we go about knowing this world truly? But the Enlightenment, and Kant in particular, turned this order on its head, with humanity and not God now firmly in the center. *Worldview* thus has an inauspicious beginning, nestled as it is in the turn to human autonomy clearly evident in Kant's and other Enlightenment philosophies. As David Naugle notes, "Kant's Copernican revolution in philosophy, with its emphasis on the knowing and willing self as the cognitive and moral center of the universe, created the conceptual space in which the notion of worldview could flourish."[8]

And flourish worldview certainly did. In the early nineteenth century *worldview* entered the vocabulary of German theologians, philosophers, and poets, and from them it spread to other disciplines. During the nineteenth century worldview established itself as a major theoretical concept. From Germany it spread through Europe and then to the UK and to the United States, reaching the height of its reputation at the start of the twentieth century, when a large number of books and articles used it in their titles.[9]

Once history was added to the notion of worldview, as it was in G. W. F. Hegel, it started to become apparent, contra Kant, that there are a variety of

---

[7]Martin Heidegger, *The Basic Problems of Phenomenology* (Bloomington: Indiana University Press, 1982), 4, describes Schelling's understanding of worldview as "a self-realized, productive as well as conscious way of apprehending and interpreting the universe of beings."

[8]Naugle, *Worldview*, 59.

[9]Ibid., 62.

worldviews. Richard Rorty is thus correct when he states that "the notion of alternative conceptual frameworks has been a commonplace of our culture since Hegel."[10] Sooner or later this would raise the question of *how* we know or even *whether* we can know which is the right worldview. The conjunction of history and worldview would thus also raise the problem of *relativism*—do we all just have different worldviews, or is there one right way to view the world?

Important background to Orr and Kuyper's use of worldview is the use made of it by liberal theologians, and in particular Friedrich Schleiermacher (1768–1834) and Albrecht Ritschl (1822–1889).[11] According to Eilert Herms,

> In the history of the problem of worldview within Protestant theology, the positions of Schleiermacher and Ritschl actually constitute the base point and a turning point. Schleiermacher was the very first theologian who used the concept of worldview in a theoretically concise setting. And Ritschl then elevated the concept to a central instrument of theological theory construction.[12]

James Orr. In the context of Christian thought the appropriation of "worldview" to express the orthodox Christian vision of the world was the particular achievement of James Orr (1844–1913), a Scottish theologian, and Abraham Kuyper.[13] It is thus through Reformed Protestantism that worldview has come to be widely used to articulate the comprehensive shape of the Christian faith today.

Both Orr and Kuyper reached for the concept of worldview in response to the post-Enlightenment culture that was coming to dominate the West. Orr's Kerr lectures were published in 1893 as *The Christian View of God and the World.* Orr was familiar with the use of worldview in German thought and its pervasive attempt to articulate a comprehensive view of the whole of reality.[14]

---

[10]Ibid., 73.

[11]This is an important insight of Clifford Blake Anderson, "Jesus and the 'Christian Worldview': A Comparative Analysis of Abraham Kuyper and Karl Barth," *Cultural Encounters* 6, no. 1 (2006): 61-80, who points out that *worldview* was first used by liberal theologians and Albrecht Ritschl in particular.

[12]Eilert Herms, ">>Weltanschauung<< bei F. Schleiermacher and A. Ritschl," in *Theorie für die Praxis* (München: Chr. Kaiser Verlag, 1982), 123. Quoted in and translated by Anderson, "Jesus and the 'Christian Worldview,'" 67.

[13]*AK*, 207, notes that they appear to have come to this use of *worldview* independently of each other. Anderson, "Jesus and the 'Christian Worldview,'" explores the possibility of Ritschl's influence on Orr and Kuyper in this respect. The evidence for Ritschl's influence in relation to worldview is stronger for Herman Bavinck than it is for Kuyper. See note 32 in chapter two.

[14]James Orr, *The Christian View of God and the World*, 2nd ed. (Edinburgh: Andrew Elliot, 1893), 42-48, in appendix 2, "Idea of the 'Weltanschauung,'" discusses its use by Ritschl and other German authors.

He realized that piecemeal responses to the worldviews of modernity were inadequate; what the time needed was a demonstration that Christianity was in itself a comprehensive vision of the whole of life: "It is the Christian view of things in general which is attacked, and it is by an exposition and vindication of the Christian view of things as a whole that the attack can most successfully be met."[15]

According to Orr a Christian worldview is christocentric, embracing as Christ did the Old Testament view of creation, with salvation history finding its fulfilment in Christ himself.[16] Commitment to Christ thus carries with it a view of God, of humankind, of sin, of redemption, of the purpose of God in creation and history, and of human destiny. This forms a worldview.[17]

For Orr humans need to form worldviews at a theoretical level because they seek unity in their understanding of life as a whole, and practically in order to answer the big, existential questions of life. Orr was alert to the difference between the philosophical, theoretical worldviews of his day and Christianity, which, by contrast, was rooted in divine revelation and aimed at salvation. However, he argued that religions too express worldviews and insisted that in the Christian faith we find a particular view of the world that has a coherence and unity of its own, which is rationally defensible and stands or falls in its integrality.[18] For Orr such a view of Christian faith enables the differences between it and alternative modern theories to emerge into bold relief so that their antisupernaturalist presuppositions are exposed for what they are.

Abraham Kuyper. Kuyper believed passionately that Calvinism, the tradition of Protestant thought originating from sixteenth-century reformer John Calvin, related to the whole of life and that Calvinists should work tirelessly to relate God's sovereign law to all of life. Kuyper used his Stone lectures at Princeton in 1898 to give expression to this as a worldview, subsequently published and repeatedly reprinted as *Lectures on Calvinism*.[19] Kuyper's first

---

[15]Orr, *Christian View of God and the World*, 4.

[16]Ibid., 378, says of Christ, "What did Christ come for, if not to impart a new life to humanity, which, working from within outwards, is destined to transform all human relations, all family and social life, all industry and commerce, all art and literature, all government and relations among people—till the kingdoms of this world are become the kingdoms of our Lord and of His Christ."

[17]Ibid., 4, 5.

[18]Ibid., 17, 18.

[19]For a detailed study of these lectures see Peter S. Heslam, *Creating a Christian Worldview: Abraham Kuyper's Lectures on Calvinism* (Grand Rapids: Eerdmans, 1998).

Stone lecture, "Calvinism as Life-System," is the most important source for Kuyper's concept of worldview.

Kuyper had used the concept of worldview before, but in a loose way, and it was only in his Stone lectures at Princeton that he drew on it to give expression to his body of thought. For the published version of his *Lectures on Calvinism* in English, Kuyper changed the title of chapter one from "Calvinism in History" to "Calvinism as a Life-System." In a footnote in this chapter Kuyper interacts with Orr's use of "view of the world" but decides against it because in English it is associated mainly with physical nature. Kuyper elects to use "life-system" and "life- and worldview" interchangeably, noting that the German *Weltanschauung* has no precise equivalent in English.[20]

As we will see in chapter ten, on theology, Kuyper was a brilliant scholar and certainly capable of rigorous and precise systematic thought. However, as a public intellectual he was far less precise with his concepts. We will see, for example, in chapter five that he never developed a logically tight theory of sphere sovereignty, even though it was central to his social philosophy. The same is true of his use of worldview. He makes substantial use of it in his *Lectures on Calvinism*, but, apart from his footnote engaging with Orr, he never attempts to define it carefully. This task, as we will see below, fell to later scholars.

What Kuyper does say is that underlying a worldview is a unifying spiritual principle that has been allowed to come to free and full expression. He thinks this is not true of Lutheranism and thus does not regard it as one of the major worldviews of his day.[21] Calvinism, on the other hand, is a worldview because it developed a distinctive theology and church order, and then a form for political and social life, through which one could interpret the world order, and finally a distinctive approach to art and science. Along with Calvinism, Kuyper identifies paganism, Islam, and Roman Catholicism as the four major worldviews of his day: "four entirely different worlds in the one collective world of human life."[22]

As with Orr, Kuyper argued that modernity had given rise to a worldview deeply opposed to the Christian tradition that underlay North American and European culture. In his *Lectures on Calvinism* he uses *modernism* to refer to

---

[20]*LC*, 3n1.
[21]*LC*, 9.
[22]*LC*, 8.

what we nowadays call modernity, a more encompassing usage compared to his description of the emergent liberal theology as modernism. For Kuyper, however, the roots of the two were the same.

At the outset of his *Lectures on Calvinism* he asserts, "the storm of Modernism has now arisen with violent intensity."[23] Following Groen van Prinsterer, Kuyper argues that in the French Revolution—thus 1789—the turning point was reached. He never denies that in such events there were elements of progress and that God used them in this respect, but in *principle* the Revolution was profoundly anti-Christian and since 1789 has spread like cancer, so that

> Two life systems are wrestling with one another, in mortal combat. Modernism is bound to build a world of its own from the data of the natural man, and to construct man himself from the data of nature; while, on the other hand, all those who reverently bend the knee to Christ and worship Him as the Son of the living God, and God Himself, are bent upon saving the "Christian Heritage." This is the struggle in Europe, this is the struggle in America.[24]

Again like Orr, Kuyper dismissed piecemeal apologetics; the very foundations of life and thought were at stake, and it was at this level of worldview that the battle needed to be fought:

> Modernism now confronts Christianity; and against this deadly danger, ye, Christians, cannot successfully defend your sanctuary, but by placing in opposition to all this, *a life–and world-view of your own, founded as firmly on the base of your own principle, wrought out with the same clearness and glittering in an equal logical consistency.*[25]

For Kuyper the only adequate Christian approach to this challenge was to be found in Calvinism. However, it is important to note that he discerns four meanings of Calvinism but is using the term in a far broader way than the narrow confessional interpretation.[26] For Kuyper Calvinism in this respect is a *worldview*.[27]

---

[23]*LC*, 2.

[24]*LC*, 3.

[25]*LC*, 182, emphasis original.

[26]The four are: in a sectarian sense, in a confessional sense, as a denominational title, and as a scientific name. Kuyper uses it in the fourth sense. See *LC*, 4-5.

[27]See *LC*, 13-14, for Kuyper's comparison between Calvin and Luther. Kuyper addresses here the question

Modernity rose up as a unity, and the reason for "our" weakness before it was our lack of an equally unified life-conception.[28] What conditions need to be met for an approach to life to qualify as a unified life-conception or a worldview? For Kuyper there are three: from a special principle, insight must be gained into the basic relations of humankind, namely, (1) our relationship to God, (2) our relationship to humankind, and (3) our relationship to the world. For Kuyper the special principle is the sovereignty of the trinitarian God as revealed in Scripture.

Relationship to God. A worldview springs forth from the root of our lives, from our *hearts,* and thus reflects and is informed by the *antithesis.* The antithesis is an important theme in Kuyperian thought. Here Kuyper uses it to refer to the gap between our finitude and God's infinity. Kuyper uses our *heart* to refer to the deepest part of our being, where "the rays of our life converge as in one focus"[29] and there regain the harmony we so easily lose amid daily life.

This use of *antithesis* by Kuyper is closely related to a second way in which he uses the term, namely to refer to the spiritual warfare between the kingdom of God and that of Satan. Each lays claim to the whole of creation. Albert Wolters defines the antithesis as follows:

> ANTITHESIS—Used by Dooyeweerd (following Abraham Kuyper) in a specifically religious sense to refer to the fundamental spiritual opposition between the Kingdom of God and the kingdom of darkness. Cf. Galatians 5:17. Since this is an opposition between regimes, not realms, it runs through every department of human life and culture, including philosophy and the academic enterprise as a whole, and through the heart of every believer as he struggles to live a life of undivided allegiance to God.[30]

For Kuyper and in the Kuyperian tradition, such is the nature of humankind as *homo religiosis* that our hearts are always directed toward the living God or

---

of whether what he claims for Calvinism is not true of Protestantism as a whole. Kuyper acknowledges the extraordinary contribution of Luther and that Calvin was not possible without Luther. However, their starting points were different: for Luther it was justification, whereas for Calvin it was the comprehensive principle of the sovereignty of God. According to *LC,* 14, "Lutheranism restricted itself to an exclusively ecclesiastical and theological character, while Calvinism put its impress in and outside the church upon every department of life. Hence Lutheranism is nowhere spoken of as the creator of a peculiar life-form."

[28]*LC,* 10. On how modernity answers the first requirement of a worldview see *LC,* 14-15.

[29]*LC,* 11.

[30]Albert M. Wolters, "Glossary," in L. Kalsbeek, *Contours of a Christian Philosophy: An Introduction to Herman Dooyeweerd's Thought* (Amsterdam: Buijten and Schipperheijn, 1975), 347.

an idol. Our worldview issues forth out of our heart so that a Christian worldview requires a regenerate heart that is continually disclosing itself to the eternal One. A deep spirituality is thus an essential component of a Christian worldview. Kuyper stresses that "in prayer lies not only our unity with God, but also the unity of our personal life."[31] Kuyper argues that only movements that spring from such a unified heart endure in history.

According to Kuyper, Calvinism does not locate God in part of the creation; it does not isolate God from the creature, as does Islam, nor does it mediate communion with God, as does Catholicism. In Calvinism God enters into immediate fellowship with humans by his Spirit. "This is even the heart and kernel of the Calvinistic confession of predestination. There is communion with God, but only in entire accord with his counsel of peace from all eternity."[32] Calvinism thus fulfills the first requirement of a worldview.

In his second lecture Kuyper expands on this first requirement in his discussion of Calvinism and religion. First, he argues that creation exists *for the sake of God*. Of course, it produces a blessing for humankind, but God does not exist for the creation; the creation exists for God. Indeed, God has placed a religious impression on the whole of creation, though religion finds its clearest expression in humankind. Following Calvin, Kuyper speaks of the *semen religionis* placed in humankind by God.[33] In an evocative metaphor, Kuyper notes that God causes this to strike the chords on the harp of the human person's soul. Sin, however, has profoundly affected the functioning of the *semen religionis*. When it comes to religion, "God alone is here the goal, the point of departure and the point of arrival, the fountain, from which the waters flow, and at the same time the ocean into which they finally return."[34] Kuyper rightly evokes passages such as the Lord's Prayer, in Matthew 6:9-13: "Hallowed be your name. . . . Yours is the kingdom and the power and the glory forever." In Calvinism the confession of the absolute sovereignty of God comes first so that prayer is the deepest expression of religious life. The relationship between God and the believer operates directly, and the only mediator is Christ, whose mediatorial work is confirmed by the Spirit. This is essential for real freedom.

---

[31]*LC*, 11.
[32]*LC*, 12.
[33]John Calvin, *Institutes of the Christian Religion* (Philadelphia: Westminster, 1960), I.1.3.
[34]*LC*, 36.

Religion for Kuyper embraces the whole of our personal being. He rejects the view that religion must retire from the precinct of the intellect, reducing it to the feelings and the will. He traces such an emphasis back to Kant, who, "by his *du Sollst* . . . limited the sphere of religion to the ethical life." This limitation of religion to the nonlogical or nonrational is paralleled by the sacred/secular dualism, which ends up viewing nine-tenths of practical life as outside religion. Rather than this dualism, which Kuyper associates especially with the Roman Catholic Church, humankind must in a priest-like way consecrate to God the whole of creation. "The sacred anointing of the priest of creation must reach down to his beard and to the hem of his garment."[35] This could *never* exclude one's reason:

> To possess his God for the underground world of his feelings, and in the out-works of the exertion of his will, but not in his inner self, in the very center of his consciousness, and his thoughts; to have fixed starting points for the study of nature and axiomatic strongholds for practical life, but to have no fixed support in his thoughts about the Creator himself—all of this was, for the Calvinist, the very denying of the eternal Logos.[36]

For Kuyper, God has established laws and ordinances for all of life so that humankind is called to obedience in all of life (see below). "With the Psalmist, he [Calvin] calls upon heaven and earth, he calls upon all peoples and nations to give glory to God." Only in this way, "every *labora* [work] shall be permeated with its *ora* in fervent and ceaseless prayer." "All partial religion drives the wedges of dualism into life, but the true Calvinist never forsakes the standard of religious monism."[37]

True religion reveals the current state of the world and of humankind as abnormal. Humankind in its present condition is not normal; humans have fallen into sin, and Calvinism is rooted in a consciousness of the holiness of God and of sin, and thus of the necessity of regeneration and revelation. It is sin that makes Scripture necessary: "an artificial light must be kindled for us—and such a light God has kindled for us in his holy Word." Through the testimony of the Spirit we know that Scripture is God's Word; through regeneration God rekindles in our heart the lamp sin has blown out, and now in

---

[35]*LC*, 40, 41; cf. 58.
[36]*LC*, 41-42.
[37]*LC*, 42, 43.

Scripture God reveals "to the regenerate, a world of thought, a world of energies, a world of full and beautiful life, which stands in direct opposition to his ordinary world, but which proves to agree in a wonderful way with the new life that has sprung up in his heart."[38]

Within this second lecture Kuyper then moves on to a discussion of the church, the subject of chapter seven of this book. As we will see there, Kuyper saw a vibrant institutional church as absolutely integral to the Calvinist worldview. Suffice it here to note his stress on the indispensability of the institutional church:

> Only when hundreds of candles are burning from one candelabrum, can the full brightness of the soft candlelight strike us and in the same way it is the communion of saints which has to unite the many small lights of the single believers so that they may mutually increase their brightness, and Christ, walking in the midst of the seven candlesticks, may sacramentally purify the glow of their brightness to a still more brilliant fervor. Thus the purpose of the church does not lie in us, but in God, and in the glory of his name.[39]

The relationship to one another: A social tradition of liberty. We noted above that for Kuyper one reason that Calvinism is a worldview is that it has developed a form for political and social life. It is this Kuyper is referring to by our relationship to humankind. Kuyper recognizes the immense diversity among human beings. However, in relation to the basic principle of Calvinism of the sovereignty of God, Kuyper discerns a unique emphasis in Calvinism on the equality of human beings, which has given rise to a unique view of society and politics.

Kuyper notes that Calvinism, by placing our entire life *coram deo*, ensures that all humans, rich and poor, brilliant and average, weak and strong, are equal in the sight of God and have no right to lord it over each other. Thus "we cannot recognize any distinction among men, save such as has been imposed by God himself, in that he gave one authority over the other, or enriched one with more talents than the other, in order that the man of more talents should serve the man with less, and in him serve his God."[40] Consequently, Calvinism condemns all open slavery and systems of caste, but also covert slavery of women and oppression of the poor.

---

[38]*LC,* 46.
[39]*LC,* 54-55.
[40]*LC,* 18.

For Kuyper Calvinism was therefore "bound to find its utterance in the democratic interpretation of life; to proclaim the liberty of nations; and not to rest until both politically and socially every man, simply because he is man, should be recognized, respected, and dealt with as a creature after the divine likeness."[41] This theme is taken up in detail in Kuyper's third lecture, on "Calvinism and Politics," in which he discusses how Calvinism's principle of the sovereignty of God comes to fruition in its view of the sovereignty of the state, sovereignty in society, and sovereignty in the church. In the process Kuyper outlines his theory of sphere sovereignty, which we will come to in the next chapter, and to the church and public life, which we will address in chapters six and seven.

Encompassing the world. For Kuyper, in relation to the third requirement, paganism elevates the world too highly, whereas Islam deprecates it, reaching after a sensual paradise as its goal. In the Middle Ages, under Rome, the church was set *against* the world, with a view to setting the church *over* the world. The result was that the church was corrupted by the world, and free development of life was constrained. Calvinism radically restructured this model, withdrawing the control of the church so that all of life under God could emerge. The cultural mandate of Genesis 1 was rediscovered and with it a doctrine of vocation so that God is to be served in all areas of life. "To praise God in the church and serve him in the world became the inspiring impulse, and, in the church, strength was to be gathered by which to resist temptation and sin in the world." It remained the distinctive characteristic of Calvinism that it positioned the believer *coram deo*, and not only in church but also in one's personal, family, work, social, and political life.[42]

Kuyper summarizes the Calvinist worldview as follows:

> For our relation to God: an immediate fellowship of man with the Eternal, independently of priest or church. For the relation of man to man: the recognition in each person of human worth, which is his by virtue of his creation after the divine likeness, and therefore of the equality of all men before God and his magistrate. And for our relation to the world: the recognition that in the whole world the curse is restrained by grace, that the life of the world is to be honoured in its independence, and that we must, in every domain, discover the treasures and develop the potencies hidden by God in nature and human life.[43]

---

[41]*LC*, 18.
[42]*LC*, 21, 57.
[43]*LC*, 22.

Worldview and reason. For Kuyper the conflict or antithesis between modernism and Christianity manifests itself in *all* cultural and social dimensions of life; however, he argues that this conflict is especially poignant in what the Germans called *Wissenschaft*, often translated as "science" but with a broader reference to theorizing or academic work in the disciplines that make up the modern university. In other writings Kuyper argues that there are two types of science, arising out of those who theorize on the basis of conversion to Christ and those who do not. He asserts "that there are two kinds of *people* occasions of necessity the fact of two kinds of human *life* and *consciousness* of life, and of two kinds of science."[44]

We will explore this in more detail in chapter eleven. It may be that Kuyper here is oversimplistic in his discernment of two types of science, but a crucial contribution of Kuyper to worldviewish thinking is the clear rejection of the *autonomy of reason.* Here he differs from Orr, as well as other key twentieth-century proponents of a Christian worldview, namely Carl Henry and Francis Schaeffer.[45] Henry and Schaeffer did a tremendous amount to promote a Christian worldview, and their substantial contribution needs to be acknowledged. However, in terms of the Reformed tradition, they side with the view that neutral reason operating properly will support a Christian perspective of the world. In other words, they concede a common epistemological ground with non-Christians. Kuyper will have none of this and argues that one's epistemology is itself a development of one's worldview. In this respect Kuyper adopts an approach more in line with the contemporary Catholic philosopher

---

[44]*PST*, 154.

[45]See Carl F. H. Henry, *God, Revelation and Authority*, vol. 5, *God Who Stands and Stays*, part 1 (Waco, TX: Word, 1982), chap. 20, "Man's Mind and God's Mind." Henry asserts, "The relevance of the mind's rational structure . . . lies, rather, in the fact that the mind enables us within limits to know reality as God preserves and knows it" (387).

There is some debate about whether Schaeffer was a rationalist. See Bryan A. Follis, *Truth with Love: The Apologetics of Francis Schaeffer* (Wheaton, IL: Crossway, 2006), chap. 3, "Rationality and Spirituality." Schaeffer used the concept of worldview in apologetics, his main concern, but never wrote systematically about it. While I am sympathetic with Schaeffer's apologetic, I would argue that the best apologetic is a well-articulated and incarnated Christian worldview. Also of interest here is the relationship between Kuyper and Benjamin B. Warfield. George Marsden, "The Collapse of American Evangelical Academia," in Alvin Plantinga and Nicholas Wolterstorff, eds., *Faith and Rationality* (Notre Dame: University of Notre Dame Press, 1983), 219-64, on 247, observes that "the evidentialist [Warfield] and the Kuyperian traditions are two of the strongest influences on American thought and reason." On the Kuyper-Warfield relationship see Heslam, *Creating a Christian Worldview*, 12-14, 126-32, 186-90, 251-56; Owen Anderson, *Reason and Worldviews: Warfield, Kuyper, Van Til and Plantinga on the Clarity of General Revelation and the Function of Apologetics* (Lanham, MD: University Press of America, 2008).

Alasdair MacIntyre, who argues that rationality is inevitably *traditioned*, that is, it always functions in the context of a particular tradition or story, or what we call worldview.[46] Alvin Plantinga and Nicholas Wolterstorff have developed this Kuyperian tradition by arguing for the legitimacy of a Christian starting point in theorizing.[47] We will discuss Plantinga's and Wolterstorff's work in chapter ten.

CONTEMPORARY CHRISTIAN APPROPRIATION OF WORLDVIEW

In recent decades the idea of Christian faith as a worldview has become widely popular, especially in evangelical circles. Francis and Edith Schaeffer, with their base at L'Abri in Switzerland, played a major role in introducing generations of students to such an approach, and more recently John Stott, Al Wolters and Michael Goheen, Chuck Colson and Nancy Pearcey, Brian Walsh and Richard Middleton, and many others have contributed to the spread of worldviewish thinking.[48]

We cannot survey these many works on worldview here, but suffice it to take note of the works of James Sire, who has been a tireless advocate of a Christian worldview over the years. One of Sire's earlier works is his delightful *How to Read Slowly: Reading for Comprehension.*[49] He explores how to read a variety of genres of literature and includes creative reflections on how to know what to read and how to stay abreast of contemporary thought. Reading slowly involves reading for the worldview that is embodied in literature.

---

[46]See Alasdair MacIntyre, *Whose Justice? Which Rationality?* (Notre Dame, IN: University of Notre Dame Press, 1988). Note also Buckley's view that a major error Christian thinkers made at the outset of modernity was to concede the epistemic ground to non-Christians: "In an effort to secure its basis, religion unknowingly fathered its own estrangement." M. J. Buckley, *At the Origins of Modern Atheism* (New Haven, CT: Yale University Press, 1987), 359.

[47]See, e.g., James F. Sennet, ed., *The Analytic Theist: An Alvin Plantinga Reader* (Grand Rapids: Eerdmans, 1998); Nicholas Wolterstorff, *Reason Within the Bounds of Religion* (Grand Rapids: Eerdmans, 1976). For an introduction to so-called Reformed epistemology, of which Wolterstorff and Plantinga are leading figures, see Dewey J. Hoitenga, *Faith and Reason from Plato to Plantinga: An Introduction to Reformed Epistemology* (New York: SUNY Press, 1991).

[48]Charles Colson and Nancy Pearcey, *How Now Shall We Live* (Wheaton, IL: Tyndale, 1999); Nancy Pearcey, *Total Truth: Liberating Christianity from Its Cultural Captivity* (Wheaton, IL: Crossway, 2004). Brian J. Walsh and J. Richard Middleton's *The Transforming Vision: Shaping a Christian Worldview* (Downers Grove, IL: InterVarsity Press, 1984, 2009) has been very influential.

[49]James Sire, *How to Read Slowly: Reading for Comprehension* (Downers Grove, IL: InterVarsity Press, 1978).

Sire's best-known work on worldview is *The Universe Next Door*, which is now in its fifth edition and has been translated into twenty languages.[50] The title of Sire's book is reminiscent of Kuyper's description of "four entirely different worlds in the one collective world of human life." It evokes the diversity of worldviews that surround us in our pluralistic cultures—our neighbor may see the world in a very different way and thus live "in a different universe"!

For Sire a worldview is "a set of presuppositions which we hold—consciously or unconsciously—about the world in which we live."[51] An important insight is that a worldview might not be *conscious*. It is like a pair of glasses; we look through them at the world, and only rarely do we look at the glasses themselves. Thus it is easy to think that we see the world in an unmediated, objective, neutral fashion, until one becomes conscious that one's perspective on the world is mediated through one's worldview.

In the most recent edition of *The Universe Next Door* Sire identifies seven main worldviews: Christian theism; deism, which is what remains of theism once a personal God is abandoned; naturalism, which abandons belief in God but retains its trust in human autonomy; nihilism, which flows from naturalism once the trust in human reason is eroded; existentialism, which attempts to move beyond nihilism through the power of the individual to will into existence its own conception of the good, the true, and the beautiful; Eastern pantheistic monism, in which New Age thought is combined with the existentialists' sense of the self; and finally postmodernism, which denies that we can know reality as it is but belives that we can manage without such knowledge, especially through our use of language. "Pragmatic knowledge is all one can have and all one needs."[52]

For Sire a service Christians can provide is to help people become conscious of their worldview. Sire has developed a series of diagnostic questions that can bring the unconscious to consciousness. These are:[53]

- What is prime reality?

- What is the nature of the world around us?

---

[50]James Sire, *The Universe Next Door*, 4th ed. (Downers Grove, IL: InterVarsity Press, 2004).

[51]James Sire, *The Universe Next Door*, 3rd ed. (Downers Grove, IL: InterVarsity Press, 1997), 16.

[52]James Sire, *Naming the Elephant: Worldview as a Concept* (Downers Grove, IL: InterVarsity Press, 2004), 12.

[53]Sire, *Universe Next Door*, 4th ed., 20.

- What does it mean to be human?

- What happens at death?

- Why is it possible to know anything at all?

- How do we tell what is right and wrong?

- What is history about?

In his *Naming the Elephant* Sire reviews more recent thinking among Christians on worldview. He expresses dissatisfaction with his previous definition of a worldview and, in the light of more recent work and reflection, redefines it as follows:

> A worldview is a commitment, a fundamental orientation of the heart, that can
> be expressed as a story or in a set of presuppositions (assumptions which may be
> true, partially true or entirely false) which we hold (consciously or subcon-
> sciously, consistently or inconsistently) about the basic constitution of reality,
> and that provides the foundation on which we live and move and have our being.[54]

There are several notable developments in Sire's revised definition:

First, his emphasis on commitment and the heart resonates with Kuyper's view that a worldview is not firstly intellectual and propositional; it is foundationally a matter of the heart, of spiritual orientation, of religion. Like Kuyper, Sire embraces the view that at the core of our being every human is oriented religiously, either toward the true God or an idol. "In my estimation, simply by being alive in the world, everyone makes and lives out of a religious commitment."[55]

Second, Sire has recognized that we often encounter a worldview as a grand story or master narrative. His definition leaves it open as to whether or not this is always the case with worldviews, but his recovery of story is significant, especially as regards a Christian worldview. As we saw in chapter three, such an approach to the Bible is implicit in Kuyper's description of how he reads Scripture, but neither he nor Bavinck attends to the storied nature of worldviews.

Third, Sire has introduced an emphasis on the embodied nature of a worldview. A worldview might be unconscious, but it will manifest itself in how we live.

---

[54]Sire, *Naming*, 122, and *Universe Next Door*, 4th ed., 16-19.
[55]Sire, *Naming*, 124.

It is mainly through Reformed Protestants and evangelicals such as James Sire that worldview has been appropriated to express the comprehensive vision of the gospel, but such thinking is by no means absent from other Christian traditions. In Roman Catholic circles the use of worldview is particularly associated with Italian-born German priest and theologian Romano Guardini,[56] and with Alexander Schmemann in Orthodoxy.[57] Schmemann grounds his exposition of the Orthodox view of the world in liturgy and sacrament. He develops his worldview around the metaphor of eating—Adam and Eve sinned by eating the forbidden fruit, and, of course, central to the Eucharist is our eating and drinking of Christ. Schmemann conceives of the world sacramentally:

> The world, be it in its totality as cosmos, or in its life and becoming as time and history, is an epiphany of God, a means of His revelation, presence and power, In other words, it not only posits the idea of God as a rationally acceptable cause of its existence, but truly speaks of Him and is in itself an essential means both of the knowledge of God and communion with Him, and to be so is its true nature and ultimate destiny.[58]

Like Kuyper, Schmemann calls us to think of humans as *priests* who bless God in thanksgiving and worship and by filling the world with the Eucharist to transform life into communion with God. The fall involves the loss of this sacramental, priestly perspective on life, but redemption involves its renewal. In Christ, "the true life that was lost by man was restored, for redemption as new creation means 'that in Christ, life,—life in all its totality—was returned to man, given again as sacrament and communion, made Eucharist.' . . . In redemption, the world is restored as God's creation and human beings resume their priestly vocation."[59] From this basis Schmemann exhorts Christians to witness to the reality of the world as God's good creation and to be busy with transforming every aspect of life.

---

[56]Cf. Romano Guardini, *Christliche Weltanschauung und mensliche Existenz* (Regensburg: Pustet, 1999). Guardini held a chair in philosophy of religion and Christian *Weltanschauungen* at the University of Berlin, after World War II at the University of Tübingen, and finally at the University of Munich. See Heinz R. Kuehn, "Introduction," in Romano Guardini, *The Essential Guardini: An Anthology of the Writings of Romano Guardini* (Chicago: Liturgy Training Publications, 1997), 1-12.

[57]Alexander Schmemann, *For the Life of the World*, 2nd ed. (Crestwood, NY: St. Vladimir's Seminary Press, 1973).

[58]Ibid., 120.

[59]Naugle, *Worldview*, 52.

CRITICISMS OF WORLDVIEW

Despite the widespread use of worldview, it is not without its critics. Some of the major criticisms that are leveled against appropriating worldview in this way are as follows.

1. It intellectualizes the gospel. An idol of modernity has been autonomous human reason. Scientific reason and not experience has been seen as the royal route to truth about the world. In order to confront the challenge of modernity, it was essential for Christians to give an adequate—and in this context *rational*—account of their hope in Christ. In his celebrated book *The Christian Mind*, Harry Blamires saw, in line with Orr, Kuyper, Henry, and Schaeffer, that Christians desperately needed a Christian mind. Demonstrating that the gospel was intellectually credible was crucial, and the development of a Christian worldview has been an important way of showing this to be the case. However, a constant danger is of mirroring modernity by reducing the gospel to an intellectual framework and playing down the roots of a Christian worldview in the biblical story and in a living relationship with Christ. No one that I have come across warns more clearly of this danger than twentieth-century Catholic monk Thomas Merton. For Merton,

> It is not enough for meditation to investigate the cosmic order and situate me in this order. Meditation is something more than gaining command of a *Welt-anschauung* (a philosophical view of the cosmos and of life). . . . Such a medi-tation may be out of contact with the deepest truths of Christianity. It consists in learning a few rational formulas, explanations. . . . We should let ourselves be brought naked and defenceless into the center of that dread where we stand alone before God in our nothingness, without explanation, without theories, completely dependent upon his providential care, in dire need of the gift of his grace, his mercy and the light of faith.[60]

Within the Orthodox tradition, Schmemann similarly insists that a worldview be rooted in liturgy and worship. And we have seen above how Kuyper connects a worldview with the heart and prayer. Christians nurtured in a dualistic worldview have rightly experienced the discovery of faith as a worldview as akin to a second conversion. However, it sometimes leads to a concentration on the gospel as an intellectually credible *system* divorced from a deep spirituality, which

---

[60]Thomas Merton, *Contemplative Prayer* (London: DLT, 1969), 85.

is the wellspring of a truly Christian worldview.[61] The result is that one dualism—sacred/secular—is replaced by another—heart/mind.

Thinking Christianly—"faith seeking understanding"—is a vital part of a Christian worldview, but it is only a part and never the whole. If it becomes disconnected from the whole, then it leads to a distorted, intellectualized Christianity that lacks grace and humility. In my opinion too much evangelical work on worldview has tended to be strong on the intellectual side but weak on the side of spirituality.[62] Thus the danger of a worldview becoming scholastic, dry, and arid is real, but clearly a distortion of a worldview emerging from the drama of Scripture.

Under the present heading of the danger of intellectualizing the gospel, we will also take account of Karl Barth's implacable hostility toward Christians appropriating worldview to articulate the gospel.[63] Barth is *the* great Reformed theologian of the twentieth century, and it is alarming to find him so opposed to the development of a Christian worldview.

In his discussion of the doctrine of creation, Barth lists six reasons why the Christian theology of creation can never become a worldview.[64] The crucial point to note is that they all rest on Barth's definition of a worldview. He rightly asserts that the Christian doctrine of creation is based on divine revelation but proceeds to argue that, whereas theology is

> concerned only with divine revelation . . . the latter [world-view], as nontheological thinking, reckons only with such apprehension of the cosmos as is possible to unaided reason. . . . Theology has to recognize and confess creation as benefit because it is the work of God in Jesus Christ, whereas philosophy is intrinsically incapable of doing this.[65]

Barth is surely right that if a worldview can only reckon with insights on the creation gained via reason alone, then the gospel and a worldview are indeed irreconcilable. However, the whole point of a Christian worldview is precisely *not* to rely on reason alone but to take fully into account and to make its starting point God's revelation of himself to us in Christ.

---

[61]Søren Kierkegaard is a helpful antidote here, with his insistence on personal appropriation of the truth and his—in my view somewhat excessive—wariness of systems.

[62]However, see Mark Noll, *The Scandal of the Evangelical Mind* (Grand Rapids: Eerdmans, 1994).

[63]See *CD* III/1, 343-44; III/3, 55-56; IV/3.1.

[64]See *CD* III/1, 343-44.

[65]*CD* III/1, 343.

In *The Doctrine of Reconciliation* Barth sees worldviews as an attempt to escape from Jesus. When it comes to the living Lord, the King, the Prophet, "this Jesus Christ is of no value for the purposes of a world-view." Barth lists in this context five characteristics of a worldview:[66]

1. Humans grasp via worldviews at seeing the totality of the world from a distance.

2. It is the world that is viewed via a worldview, closed in on itself.

3. Worldviews deal with general states, relationships, and consequences.

4. Worldviews are doctrines that humans compose from what they see.

5. Worldviews are an attempt by humans to come to grips with themselves.

Barth's negative reaction to the use of worldview developed out of his re-action to liberal theology.[67] By means of his reaction he seeks to preserve the event-aspect of encounter with Jesus and the lived aspect of the Christian life. Both are vital elements of Christian faith, elements that are stressed in this book. However, all these points relate to Barth's definition of a worldview above, and once one rejects his definition, it is hard to see the problem with developing a worldview. Barth's critique might bear on Kuyper's insistence that a worldview be grounded in a *principle*, but, as we have seen above, more recent advocates of a Christian worldview ground it in living faith and the narrative shape of Scripture.

2. It universalizes the gospel.[68] This criticism of the use of worldview to express the gospel is already present in Barth, who associates worldview with philosophy, which involves the analysis of "pure becoming" and thus subverts the particularity of the gospel by falsely universalizing it. However, it is in Rudolph Bultmann's (1884–1976) dialectical theology that we find this crit-icism far more fully articulated.[69]

In order to grasp Bultmann's staunch opposition to worldview, we need to understand his views of faith and of God. For Bultmann, "Faith is not a worldview [*Weltanschauung*], in which the concept of God serves as a principle

---

[66]CD IV/3.1, 255-57.

[67]Cf. Anderson's very useful article "Jesus and the 'Christian Worldview.'"

[68]I am indebted to David Congdon for alerting me to this challenge to worldview.

[69]Bultmann's thought is complex, and I am dependent here on David W. Congdon's lucid exposition in his *The Mission of Demythologizing: Rudolf Bultmann's Dialectical Theology* (Minneapolis: Fortress, 2015), esp. 374-407.

for the explanation of the world [*Welterklärung*], and in which the meaning of human existence develops from a general understanding of the world [*Weltverständnis*]."[70] Instead, faith is the existential position of the human being before God. God, according to Bultmann, is eschatological, transcendent, and wholly other, always on the way to new situations. His nature is such that he cannot be objectified and is never available for theoretical analysis and knowledge.[71] For Bultmann it is just such theoretical analysis of God that is central to a worldview. It abandons the historicity and particularity of talk about God and thereby abandons a relationship to the eschatological God. Universalization is utterly central to a worldview: "It is a comprehensive view of the world that at the same time proposes a comprehensive philosophy of life. In that sense a *Weltanschauung* is a theory or science of existence that purports to have universal validity."[72]

Much in Bultmann's argument hinges on how he conceives of theology.[73] Bultmann agrees with orthodox theologians that the object of theology is God, but he argues that orthodoxy confuses kerygma and theory in its search for universalizing faith embodied in a worldview, thereby turning the transcendent, other God into a principle for our own security: "Worldviews deny the concrete historicity of the human person and attempt to describe what is the case always and everywhere." By contrast, true faith unsettles us and sets us free to participate in the contingencies of history.[74] Bultmann ends up with a view of theology as a paradox; on the one hand, we must speak of faith in an objectifying way; on the other hand, simultaneously such speaking has meaning only in the sublation (*Aufhebung*) of the objectification.

Congdon notes the centrality of a view of the nature-grace relationship in Bultmann's critique of worldview.[75] It seems to me that Bultmann's theology is an example of the Lutheran worldview of Christ and culture in paradox, with the paradoxical emphasis considerably sharpened. Within the Kuyperian tradition it is, inter alia, theologian Gerrit C. Berkouwer who engages directly

[70]Bultmann, quoted in ibid., 393.

[71]On objectification see David W. Congdon, *Rudolph Bultmann: A Companion to His Theology*, Cascade Companions (Eugene, OR: Cascade Books, 2015), chap. 3.

[72]Congdon, *Mission*, 389.

[73]See Rudolf Bultmann, *What Is Theology?*, trans. Roy A. Harrisville, Fortress Texts in Modern Theology (Minneapolis: Fortress, 1997).

[74]Congdon, *Mission*, 391, 392.

[75]Ibid., 379.

with Bultmann. In his *General Revelation*, Berkouwer argues that the whole point of revelation is that what was hidden now becomes known. Thus, "It is impossible to construct a *contrast* between God's Word and God's deed, between 'knowing' and 'taking place.' With respect to a viewpoint [such] as Bultmann's we wonder whether the result of the 'biblical theology' is a reverting to a *separation* between Word-revelation and deed-revelation."[76] In Alvin Plantinga's terms, there is a noetic and an affective dimension to faith, and these need to be held together.

Bultmann is quite correct about a worldview seeking to universalize faith, or, more accurately, to tease out the universal implications given in faith. However, both Barth and Bultmann equate such a universalization with philosophy, whereas, certainly for contemporary Kuyperians, a worldview is of a *pretheoretical* nature, though most would hold that it can be developed into a philosophy or mined for philosophical insights. Bultmann and Barth are valuable in alerting us to potential dangers in such an enterprise, but so long as faith, the heart, and existential openness to God are maintained as central to a Christian worldview, I do not find their objections compelling.

3. It relativizes the gospel. Much of postmodernism has abandoned the quest for what Francis Schaeffer calls *true Truth* as simply not attainable. Postmodernism thus tends to be strongly antirealistic. Rather than despairing, these brands of postmodernism tend to celebrate our limitations along the lines of a cheerful nihilism. The genuine insight of such views is that they recognize that we are all situated historically, that we all view the world through particular lenses, which are inescapable, and that these lenses always influence the way we view and interpret the world. The danger is the inevitable slide into relativism.

Relativism *is* a real temptation in a pluralistic context, but one we can and must resist. Christ is *the* revelation of God and, as Newbigin puts it, *the* clue to all that is. This is not to deny that other worldviews have genuine and profound insights, so that we ought to be in critical dialogue with other perspectives, but it is to assert that Christ is the way, the truth, and the life. The biblical story is not just one story alongside others but the true story of the world. As Tom Wright says, "in principle the whole point of Christianity is that is offers

---

[76]Gerrit C. Berkouwer, *General Revelation* (Grand Rapids: Eerdmans, 1955), 100.

a story which is the story of the whole world. It is public truth."[77] James Sire expresses this sentiment clearly when he writes:

> Traditional Christians are not about to give up the idea of objective truth. I do not think I speak only for myself when I say that every fiber of my being cries out for a worldview that is not just my own story, my own set of propositions, my own interpretation of life, but one that is universally, objectively true, one in which the really real is the God Who is There, and in which human beings are truly made in his image and capable of knowing at least some of "the way things actually are."[78]

Thus, while relativism is a danger, it need not be one. Of course, *our* articulation of a Christian worldview must not be equated with the Bible, which alone is God's infallible Word, but we should affirm that the biblical story is the true story of the world, and insofar as our worldview approximates to that story, it too will embody the true story of the world.

4. It becomes disconnected from Scripture and thus becomes vulnerable to the spirits of the age. The kind of framework that a worldview yields is powerful and can become a free-floating entity loosened from its roots in Scripture. It then becomes vulnerable to being absorbed into stories other than the biblical one. However, this is certainly not inevitable. A worldview emerging from the biblical drama should lead us back again and again, ever more deeply into the biblical story, rather than away from it. Scripture is God's Word, and a Christian worldview must emerge from, be seen to emerge from, and return to Scripture.[79]

5. Rather than leading to the transformation of society, a worldview entrenches middle-class Christianity and leads to unhealthy messianic activism. A real danger with a Christian worldview is that we start to think that *we* will usher in the kingdom, and we become hectically busy trying to transform the world.[80] In this regard Bultmann's critique of a worldview as a search for false security rings true. We mistakenly appropriate the vision of progress central to modernity and think that if *we* just work hard enough we will usher in the

---

[77]N. T. Wright, *The New Testament and the People of God* (Minneapolis: Fortress, 1992), 41-42.
[78]Sire, *Naming*, 118, 119.
[79]Hence the importance of the excursus at the end of chapter two.
[80]See, for example, R. A. Swenson, *Margin* (Colorado Springs: NavPress, 1992), for an acute analysis of the problem of activism in our culture.

kingdom in our generation. Because of the intellectual dimension of a worldview, such activism is too often directed at the mainstream, middle-class elements of our culture. Worldviewish Christians insist on working from within to transform our cultures, but the danger of contamination remains real, with the salt losing its saltiness.

Provided the heart and spirituality are kept central to a Christian worldview, these problems are not inherent to a Christian worldview, but they do provide a call to being self-critical as an essential component of a healthy worldview.

Thus, in my view, as long as we are conscious of the shadow side of the concept of worldview, it remains a rich and useful word for articulating the comprehensive, unified vision embodied in the kingdom of God.

A WORLDVIEW: WHAT IT IS AND WHY IT MATTERS

Defining a Christian worldview. In the literature on Christian worldview, definitions abound. In *Living at the Crossroads* Michael Goheen and I, working in the Kuyperian tradition, define a worldview as follows: "Worldview is an articulation of the basic beliefs embedded in a shared grand story which are rooted in a faith commitment and which give shape and direction to the whole of our individual and corporate lives."[81]

Several points must be noted in relation to this definition. First, because humans are creatures—and not the Creator—we will always orient ourselves toward the world in some way, the only question being which way. It is this sense of a basic orientation toward the world that is fundamental to being human and creaturely that I find the word *worldview* useful to name.[82]

Second, because we are human creatures, at its deepest level a worldview emerges from our hearts and a faith commitment. The religious center of our being, our heart, is either directed toward the living God or toward an idol, and the grand story or metanarrative we indwell flows from this direction of our heart. Worldviews are grounded at their deepest level in faith, whether in the living God, in human ability, in an aspect of God's creation, or in any one of the multitude of idols humans manufacture.

Third, because the creation is timed and thus historical, and humans are embedded in history, a worldview will always come to expression in one or

---

[81]Goheen and Bartholomew, *Living at the Crossroads*, 23.

[82]In this respect, strange as it may sound, our view of worldview will depend itself *on our worldview.*

another grand story or metanarrative about the world. God intended us finite creatures to find meaning in our lives through being part of a larger story that gives purpose and direction to our lives and explains our world. It is important to note, therefore, that one who rejects the Christian story will not simply live without a grand story but will find an alternative grand story and live by it. Even the postmodern view—that there is no grand story—is itself a whopper of a grand story!

Fourth, because our world is fallen and broken, once we take worldviews seriously we are inevitably confronted with their plurality and rivalry. Again and again in modernity, worldviews try to assert their neutral objectivity and deny their status as worldviews, but, as has become clear, every worldview has its own "prejudices" or, in Gadamer's sense, prejudgments; and, as Dilthey notes, their foundations rest on faith rather than rationally proved assertions.[83] Worldviews are not easily or at all reconcilable. Because of general revelation they will overlap in myriad ways because they all seek to make sense of the world common to all, but inevitably they aim to tell the story of the world from their perspective and as such are incommensurable.

What we must resist in this context is relativism, as if a worldview is merely a matter of personal preference. A Christian worldview must retain a deep commitment to the fact that Scripture alone tells the true story of the whole world.

Fifth, because we are communal creatures, these grand stories are inevitably shared among us. This is one reason individuals often hold them unconsciously. Roy Clouser notes, "The enormous influence of religious beliefs remains, however, largely hidden from casual view; its relation to the rest of life is like that of the great geological plates of earth's surface to the continents and oceans."[84] As Christians, we are aware that we are part of "one holy, catholic and apostolic church," part of the people of God down through the ages and on into the future. With all Christians, we share the basic story of the Bible. We live as part of a community committed to the truth of that story. Hence, Kuyper is absolutely right to include a discussion of the church in his second Stone lecture, "Calvinism and Religion."

---

[83]Hans-Georg Gadamer, *Truth and Method* (London: Bloomsbury, 2013); Wilhelm Dilthey, *Selected Writings*, ed. and trans. H. P. Rickman (Cambridge: Cambridge University Press, 1976), 141.

[84]Roy Clouser, *The Myth of Religious Neutrality: An Essay on the Hidden Role of Religious Beliefs in Theories* (Notre Dame, IN: University of Notre Dame Press, 1991), 1.

Sixth, embedded in all such grand stories are fundamental beliefs about the world, answers to questions of ultimate significance: What is life all about? Who are we? What kind of world do we live in? What's wrong with the world? How can it be fixed?[85] The answers to such questions are not first of all philosophical concepts: they are beliefs, often not even consciously articulated, embedded in the particular "grand story" we share, and they achieve coherence through being part of a unified vision of the world arising from that story. We can become increasingly conscious of those foundational beliefs and their impact by: (1) articulating the grand story that we take to be the true story of the world; (2) lifting out and articulating the fundamental beliefs of that story; and (3) articulating and explicating those beliefs. A worldview is an analysis of such beliefs and their interrelatedness.

A worldview is distinct from philosophy, because a worldview is *pretheoretical*. By pretheoretical we mean that it is not a logical, systematic theory, as is found in traditional philosophy. Beliefs are distinct from opinions or feelings because they make a cognitive claim. They are also committed in the sense that they are not just opinions or hypotheses. The beliefs constituting a worldview are also basic because they deal with matters of ultimate significance, such as what life is all about, what happens at death, the problem of evil, and so on and so forth. However, these basic beliefs are *not* philosophical concepts but are concepts embedded firmly in the drama of Scripture and form a framework in the sense that they hang together in a coherent way.

In this respect a worldview is similar to the Apostles' Creed, a short, pithy statement of the key elements in Christian faith, but more expansive in seeking to articulate the way in which the key elements of the faith hang together. This, for me, is what a Christian worldview is all about: at a pretheoretical level—it

---

[85]Richard Middleton and Brian Walsh have helpfully phrased four worldview questions: Where am I? Who am I? What's wrong? What's the remedy? (*Transforming Vision*, 35). N. T. Wright has suggested that we change the singular "I" to the plural "we" to indicate the communal sharing of worldview beliefs. He has also suggested the adding of a fifth question, "What time is it?" to indicate that worldview is a narrative in which we find our place (*Jesus and the Victory of God* [London: SPCK, 1996], 443n1; see also 467-72). J. H. Bavinck notes that the human being "by virtue of his place in the world, must always and everywhere give answers to the same questions. He has to struggle with the basic problems which his existence itself entails" (*The Church Between Temple and Mosque* [Grand Rapids: Eerdmans, 1961], 31). He formulates those questions in terms of five magnetic points that are found in all world religions. He speaks of "I and the cosmos," "I and the religious norm," "I and the riddle of my existence," "I and salvation," and "I and the Supreme Power."

lacks the tight theoretical rigor of philosophy—it sets out the main elements or beliefs that constitute the biblical story and shows how they fit together in a coherent framework. These beliefs can, of course, be analyzed at a theoretical level in theological and philosophical categories. The point of a Christian worldview, however, is that the biblical story embodies and implies a framework of beliefs that can be set out and be appropriated by ordinary Christians. The framework of basic beliefs inherent to the biblical story is not for scholars alone, though it certainly includes them, but for all the people of God.

Seventh, a worldview is thus an abstraction from Scripture and can *never* replace Scripture. It will be Christian insofar as it emerges clearly from the biblical drama, and will be of value insofar as it not only emerges from Scripture but, like a good systematic theology, leads us back deeply into Scripture again and again.[86] Indeed, we always read Scripture itself through the lens of our worldview, and the more our worldview is shaped by Scripture the more refreshing we will find our immersion in Scripture.

Eighth, we need to understand and appropriate our worldview at a personal and existential level, a major emphasis of Søren Kierkegaard. For humans in the *imago Dei*, indwelling a worldview is inescapable. But Kierkegaard's emphasis is helpful in that the whole point of exploring the contours of a Christian worldview is to help Christians to actively appropriate a distinctively Christian worldview centered in a personal relationship with Christ. And as Kierkegaard would remind us, this is no quick or simple task but a lifelong struggle with costly consequences.

Why worldview matters. If being human means that we all have worldviews, then it follows that as Christians we *should* have a Christian worldview. How could anyone pray the Lord's Prayer, for example, and think otherwise? This is a duty, but a wonderful one. The gospel opens our eyes to God's good but fallen and being-redeemed world, for which Christ died. How can we follow the Christ without learning to see the world as he sees it? His glory is at stake in how we see and live in the world, and so too is the well-being of humankind. We owe it to God, to our neighbor, to ourselves, and to his world to allow Scripture to polish the lenses of our glasses until they too are aflame with the grandeur of God and his revelation in his creation.

---

[86]As with Calvin, *Institutes*, I.3-5, which was the purpose of his *Institutes*.

We have already seen how Orr and Kuyper were driven to articulate the gospel as a worldview in response to the powerful challenges of their cultural contexts. In other words, their impulse in this direction was a *missional one*— in order to engage their culture with the gospel and to bear a credible witness to Christ, they needed to demonstrate that the gospel embodied a worldview that provided a viable alternative to the powerful worldviews of their day. Living at the crossroads of the biblical story and their cultural story necessitated such a move. Bratt rightly notes of Kuyper,

> By the 1890s, however, an acute sense of crisis in European high culture drove more thinkers than ever to entertain the concept [of worldview] as a solution to two components in that crisis: the question of cultural authority and the question of cultural coherence. As those issues were perpetually atop Kuyper's intellectual agenda, "worldview" offered him a way to put Calvinism at the cutting edge of cultural discourse while simultaneously showing his followers that they had as legitimate a voice in that conversation as their self-proclaimed superiors.[87]

And it has always been so throughout the history of the church. Not that the early church fathers made use of worldview, but it soon became apparent to them that if they were to witness to Christ in their Greco-Roman context, then they would need to articulate the basic Christian beliefs and show how they hang together as a credible system. Indeed, this is one of the great achievements of the church fathers: "Early Christian thought is biblical, and one of the lasting accomplishments of the patristic period was to forge a way of thinking, scriptural in language and inspiration, that gave to the church and to Western civilization a unified and coherent interpretation of the Bible as a whole."[88]

The point is that throughout history Christians have found it a missional imperative to explain to nonbelievers the coherence of the biblical message and to relate it in a logical and coherent way to the cultures of their day. Proof texting is simply inadequate in this respect—what is needed is a sense of how the major beliefs of the drama of Scripture hang together and how one can build on them to develop a Christian understanding and critique of the culture of the day.

---

[87]*AK*, 205.
[88]Robert L. Wilken, *The Spirit of Early Christian Thought* (New Haven, CT: Yale University Press, 2003), xvii-xviii.

Apologetics—engaging the worldviews of the day intelligently and thus bearing witness to Christ with credibility—and cultural engagement *require* an explanation of the logic of the gospel that moves beyond the great story of Scripture. At an academic *as well as* at a practical level, serious Christian engagement with life and culture—that is, mission—requires the development of a Christian worldview. We live and think *out of* our worldviews, so it is not a question of whether one has a worldview or not, but the question of which worldview one thinks from, lives from, and works from. Failure to consciously develop and indwell a Christian worldview will merely leave us captive to the ideological worldviews of our day. If we are serious about bearing witness to the Lord Christ with the integrity and depth such witness requires in our late-modern day, the development and appropriation of a Christian worldview rooted in the drama of Scripture will be a priority. Simply put: mission demands it.

Acknowledged as one of the greatest missiologists of the twentieth century, David Bosch attends to our postmodern Western culture in his posthumous *Believing in the Future: Toward a Missiology of Western Culture*. In the final chapter, before his conclusion, Bosch asks the question, "What is it that we have to communicate to the Western 'post-Christian' public?" His answer: "It seems to me that we must demonstrate the role that plausibility structures, or rather, *worldviews*, play in people's lives."[89]

Conclusion

Kuyper reached for the concept of worldview at a crucial point in the history of the West and put it to work with extraordinary versatility. Typical of Kuyper, immersed as he was in so many projects, he never paused to examine it in much detail. Since Kuyper a rich resource of reflection on worldview has developed and is now available to Christians. This is a node in the Kuyperian tradition that we need to appropriate and develop further. In a day of wild pluralism, it offers "a mandate for critical Christian comprehensiveness" and coherence.[90]

For example, as I have argued elsewhere, a developed view of worldview and of Christian worldview in particular provides a useful resource for engaging Islam in our day, probably the most urgent issue of our time.[91] Islam

---

[89]David Bosch, *Believing in the Future: Toward a Missiology of Western Culture* (Valley Forge, PA: Trinity Press International, 1995), 48, emphasis added.

[90]*AK*, 208.

[91]See chapter eleven and Craig Bartholomew, "The Challenge of Islam in Africa," *Journal of Interdisciplinary*

is the one religion that has most resisted the privatization of religion that characterizes modernity. In this, moderate Muslims could work with Christians as cobelligerents exposing the naked public square of Western life now adrift in capitalist consumerism. At the same time worldview tunes us in to the pluralism of contemporary culture and the need for democracies to create genuine space for different worldviews to come to fruition. Here worldview provides a challenge to majority Muslim countries to respect alternative religions and traditions, even as they should expect their religion to be respected in non-majority-Muslim countries. As far as we can see into the future, we urgently need Christians fully equipped with a biblical, Christian worldview, fully aware of how this critiques our Western culture, and able to open up dialogue with alternative worldviews.[92] Nothing less than the well-being of the world and the glory of God are at stake.

Studies 6 (1994): 129-46. Kuyper did reflect deeply on Islam, and one of the volumes in Lexham's Abraham Kuyper Collected Works in Public Theology will be devoted to Kuyper on Islam. See also John Bolt, "Herman Bavinck and Islam," The Bavinck Review 2 (2011): 171-73.

[92]Cf. Philip Jenkins, The Next Christendom: The Coming of Global Christianity, 3rd ed. (Oxford: Oxford University Press, 2011).

SPHERE SOVEREIGNTY

Kuyper's Philosophy of Society

CULTURAL ENGAGEMENT *requires* a philosophy of society. Of course it is quite possible for a believer to intuitively engage one's culture in profoundly transformative ways. I doubt, for example, that Mother Teresa—one of my heroes!—had a developed philosophy of society, and yet her impact has been immeasurable. Nevertheless, one of the reasons that Christians fail to influence their contexts is that they lack a framework for understanding their context and thus, even if they have consistent ethical views, they are unable to work out with nuance how the gospel might and should impact their culture as a whole. In our pluralistic cultures the need for such a philosophy of society has increased. Kuyper was nothing if not culturally and socially engaged. Central to Kuyper's dreams was the establishment of the Free University of Amsterdam, and appropriately on the occasion of its inauguration (October 20, 1880) he spoke on sphere sovereignty, his philosophy of society.

EARLY ANTICIPATIONS OF SPHERE SOVEREIGNTY

Kuyper did not develop his theory of sphere sovereignty de novo. He built on the work of Calvin, and of his predecessors, and especially that of his close friend and mentor, Guillaume Groen van Prinsterer (1801–1876). In his study of the development of sphere sovereignty, Jan Dengerink traces its development through the thought of German legal scholar Friedrich Julius Stahl (1802–1861), Groen van Prinsterer, Kuyper, and then on into the philosophy of Herman Dooyeweerd.[1] To this list should be added Johannes Althusius (c. 1563–1638), German jurist and Calvinist political philosopher.[2]

The overwhelming background of Kuyper's concept of sphere sovereignty is the reconstruction of nations and societies that developed out of the Enlightenment.[3] For Groen van Prinsterer and Kuyper, this spirit of *revolution*, rebuilding whole societies from the ground up by the light of "reason," was embodied most clearly in the French Revolution and what followed in France.[4] They saw this same spirit at work across Europe, and they identified it as deeply anti-Christian and profoundly dangerous. Their challenge was to develop an alternative, modern, Christian philosophy of society, and this culminated in the doctrine of sphere sovereignty.

John Calvin. Already we find in Calvin an *organic* view of state, church, and the individual.[5] Central to Calvin's thought, as to that of Groen van Prinsterer and Kuyper, is the sovereignty of God. Calvin's approach was to ask how humanity as a whole could fulfill its purpose under God's sovereignty. God has provided spiritual and temporal authorities as part of his plan for his world.[6] Church and government should coexist in close harmony, not as united under the dominion of the church but as equal organs of authority under God. Dominance of either by the other is tyrannical. Skillen notes,

> What we see here is a further enlargement of Calvin's conviction that different spheres of human life have their own internal order of authority and freedom under God. The private citizen may be the responsible head of his home, the owner of his own shop, or even an elder in the Church, but if he holds no political office his responsibility with regard to civil law and magistrate is simply to obey. Another man may have no authority in the Church or in

---

[1]Jan D. Dengerink, *Critisch-Historisch Onderzoek Naar de Sociologische Ontwikkeling van het Beginsel der "Sovereiniteit in Eigen Kring" in de 19e en 20e Eeuw* (Kampen: Kok, 1948).

[2]See James W. Skillen, "The Development of Calvinistic Political Theory in the Netherlands, with Special Reference to the Thought of Herman Dooyeweerd" (PhD diss., Duke University, 1993), 191-217.

[3]For an expansive review of the background see ibid., 22-179.

[4]See Harry Van Dyke, *Groen van Prinsterer's Lectures on Unbelief and Revolution* (Jordan Station, ON: Wedge, 1989). This masterly work includes a translation of Groen van Prinsterer's *Lectures*. For a detailed analysis of developments in political theory and practice in the Netherlands, including Groen van Prinsterer and Kuyper, see John W. Sap, *Paving the Way for the Revolution: Calvinism and the Struggle for a Democratic Constitutional State*, VU Studies on Protestant History 6 (Amsterdam: Vrije Universiteit, 2001). See also James Eglinton and George Harinck, eds., *Neo-Calvinism and the French Revolution* (London: Bloomsbury, 2014).

[5]On Calvin see Skillen, "Development," 180-91.

[6]John Calvin, *Institutes of the Christian Religion* (Philadelphia: Westminster, 1960), IV.6.1102-18.

business, but if he holds a political office he has responsibility before God to serve both the king and his citizens by maintaining justice. Such a man, because of his office, must not only prosecute law-breakers, but also be prepared, together with other civil authorities, to resist injustice even if that injustice originates with the king.[7]

Skillen identifies eight features of Calvin's political thought that Groen van Prinsterer and Kuyper drew on:[8]

1. the sovereignty of God;

2. God's authority over human and state life;

3. the relative freedom of each sphere of life under God;

4. the divine origin of the state to preserve humankind in the face of sin;

5. the mutual obligation of rulers and subjects in constituting civil society;

6. the antirevolutionary spirit of obedience on behalf of the citizens;

7. the necessity of positive civil law; and

8. the possibility of just government flowing from the common grace of God.

All of these elements were deeply influential in the development of sphere sovereignty.

Johannes Althusius.[9] Althusius's *Politica* represents the climax of sixteenth-century efforts to demarcate the limits of monarchy. Drawing on Scripture and Christian and classical sources, Althusius developed "a comprehensive covenantal theory of the state and society."[10] "Politica," for Althusius, "is the art of associating (*consociandi*) men for the purpose of establishing, cultivating, and conserving social life among them. Whence it is called 'symbiotics.'"[11] Althusius explores the concept of symbiosis as the way in which humans live

---

[7]Skillen, "Development," 189.

[8]Ibid., 190-91. Skillen's points are understandably oriented toward Kuyper and Dooyeweerd. His point three is less clear to me from Calvin. On Calvin and politics see Dolf Britz, "Politics and Social Life," in *The Calvin Handbook*, ed. Herman J. Selderhuis (Grand Rapids: Eerdmans, 2009), 437-48.

[9]See Thomas O. Hueglin, *Early Modern Concepts for a Late Modern World: Althusius on Communalism and Federalism* (Waterloo, ON: Wilfred Laurier University Press, 1999), for the context, content, and contemporary relevance of Althusius's political theory.

[10]John Witte Jr., *God's Joust, God's Justice* (Grand Rapids: Eerdmans, 2006), 350. See Heinrich Jannssen, *Die Bibel als Grundlage der Politischen Theorie des Johannes Althusius* (Frankfurt: Peter Lang, 1992).

[11]Johannes Althusius, *Politica*, abridged, ed. and trans. with introduction by Frederick S. Carney (Indianapolis: Liberty Fund, 1995), 17, http://oll.libertyfund.org/titles/althusius-politica. Althusius is here citing Aristotle in the first part of this quote.

together comprehensively, and then goes on to discuss family, private organizations, church, and governmental organizations. We are not just fellow citizens but coworkers in this symbiosis, since the human is by nature a social creature, created so by God to love and serve. The different associations each have a holy vocation; they are life communities to be perfected by their participants.

It is especially Althusius's concept of *symbiotic communities* that anticipates sphere sovereignty. In chapters two and three he discusses the family. It is a *natural* association, whereas the state is a *civil* association. In chapter four he moves on to the "collegium," which includes bakers, tailors, builders, merchants, philosophers, and so on, each association having separate laws. He refers to laws "according to the nature and necessities of each association."[12] Dooyeweerd asserts, "This utterance may be considered the first modern formulation of the principle of internal sphere-sovereignty in the societal relationships."[13] In chapters five through eight he moves on to public associations such as towns, cities, provinces. He argues that public citizenship enhances and does not erase the previous spheres. At the highest level of church and state, neither reigns over the other, and both claim the whole person. The only monism in Althusius's thought is the glory of God and the welfare of neighbor. All sovereignty goes back to God.[14]

Friedrich Julius Stahl. Raised strictly in the Jewish religion, Stahl was allowed to attend the gymnasium and was baptized into the Lutheran Church at the age of seventeen, to which faith he remained deeply committed until his death. In 1840 he was appointed professor of ecclesiastical law and polity at Berlin. Stahl came under the influence of Friedrich Wilhelm Joseph von Schelling (1755–1854),[15] and at the latter's encouragement began in 1827 his great work: *Die Philosophie des Rechts nach geschichtlicher Ansicht* (*The Philosophy of Law in Historical Perspective*). Along with it *The Doctrine of Law and State on the Basis of the Christian World-View* constitute Stahl's magnum opus, *The Philosophy of Law*.[16]

---

[12]Ibid., 22.

[13]Herman Dooyeweerd, *A New Critique of Theoretical Thought*, 4 vols. (Jordan Station, ON: Paideia, 1984), 3:623.

[14]We do not know for sure why Kuyper does not appeal to Althusius. Cf. *AK*, 134.

[15]Friedrich Schelling's most important work in this respect is his *System of Transcendental Idealism* (1800), trans. Peter Heath (Charlottesville: University of Virginia Press, 1978).

[16]Friedrich Julius Stahl, *The Philosophy of Law*, trans. Ruben Alvarado (Aalten, Netherlands: Wordbridge, 2007).

Stahl based law and political science on Christian revelation, rejected rationalism, and maintained that a state church should be strictly confessional. Groen van Prinsterer was only dimly aware of Stahl when he gave his lectures *Unbelief and Revolution,* but his discovery of Stahl's work shortly thereafter alerted him to a kindred spirit, especially in evaluating the antirevolutionary theories of Karl Ludwig von Haller (1768–1854).[17] Von Haller was a Swiss Jurist who initially embraced the revolutionary theories of his day but later changed his mind, became antirevolutionary, and joined the Catholic Church. Otto Pflanze describes von Haller's philosophy of society as follows:

> Haller maintained that the natural and therefore God-ordained condition of man was one of inequality and dependence, the stronger over the weaker. The microcosm of society was the family. As the father rules over wife and children, the master governs his servants, the landowner his peasants, the teacher his pupils, the leader his followers, the prince his subjects. The entire social fabric was woven from such dependent relationships based upon mutual duty and service more than upon force. The prince alone was independent, subject only to God. The state he ruled was simply the highest in a pyramid of contractual relationships, which were matters of private, not public law.[18]

There are several emphases in Stahl's work that resonate with Groen van Prinsterer and Kuyper, such as[19]

1. the binding of humans to creation order;

2. history as an outworking of God's plan culminating in the second coming;

3. his resistance to revolution; and[20]

4. in particular, in contrast to von Haller, Stahl's resistance to *state absolutism.* Creation answers to God, and he recognizes the positive role of the state but insists that the state cannot interfere in the domains of the other communities, the church, family, possibly business, indeed in the enterprises of culture, other than in relation to injustice.

---

[17]Von Haller was a Swiss nobleman and a member of the supreme council of Berne. His major work was *Restauration der Staatswissenschaft,* which appeared in six volumes between 1816 and 1834. On von Haller's theory of the state see Skillen, "Development," 219-20. Groen van Prinsterer was initially sympathetic to von Haller's monarchist views but later became more sympathetic to those of Stahl. Cf. Sap, *Paving the Way,* 295-305.

[18]Otto Pflanze, *Bismarck and the Development of Germany: The Period of Unification 1815–1871* (Princeton, NJ: Princeton University Press, 1968), 30.

[19]Cf. Dengerink, "Critisch-Historisch," 13-68.

[20]See Groen van Prinsterer's engagement with Stahl toward the end of lecture VI of his *Lectures.*

Groen van Prinsterer. Guillaume Groen van Prinsterer was of aristocratic birth and position. He came to faith gradually between 1827 and 1833, largely through the influence of members of the Dutch Réveil (1820–1850), including the ministry of the court chaplain Merle d'Aubigné.[21] The Réveil stressed a personal faith in Christ but also developed a concern for social and political issues, well over a hundred years before the Lausanne Congress and Covenant of 1974; the latter made major progress among evangelicals by insisting on the importance of both evangelism and sociopolitical involvement. Some members of the Réveil formed an Abolition Society to help end slavery. Groen van Prinsterer himself would make personal visits to the homes of the poor, and such contact strengthened his and his friends' resolve to work to improve their conditions and to improve the schools. Church reform and school reform were major issues on Groen van Prinsterer's agenda. As Christianity became more diluted and marginalized in public schools, Groen van Prinsterer labored to create the space for Protestant schools, an issue Kuyper took up with extraordinary energy.

The French Revolution was still in the forefront of the European mind at this time. In his *Unbelief and Revolution* Groen van Prinsterer argued that the deepest conflict of the time was between truth as found in Scripture, and revolution, which confessed no authority higher than man. "In the lectures, Groen developed a unique and profound interpretation. The case he argued was that the root cause of the malaise of his age was *unbelief*—unbelief as it was first elaborated into a system and then applied in a wholesale social experiment."[22] Humans create out of their own philosophy a new world order, disregarding the past. Through his diagnosis Groen van Prinsterer redefined the battleground for much of Dutch Calvinism, leading to the emergence under Kuyper of the Anti-Revolutionary Party, whose effect on the Netherlands continues to resonate to this day. Groen van Prinsterer drew the battle line at the level of antithetical principles without articulating a new philosophy of society, but precisely as a catalyst his importance should not be underestimated. Indeed, in our days, in which, in the West, it is still hard to have faith or religion taken seriously, it is just the kind of catalyst that we need. Faith, Groen van Prinsterer would remind us, really matters, and for all of life.

---

[21]See van Dyke, *Groen*, 39-52.
[22]Ibid., 3.

As a good Calvinist, for Groen van Prinsterer God is sovereign, and all authority comes from him and should be subject to him. He remained a monarchist and advocated against separating church and state.[23] He did not emphasize distinct spheres over against the state. He defended some autonomy in the lower spheres but viewed society as a hierarchy around the central organ of the state. In his battle for education reform, he stressed the rights of parents and sought to decentralize control of schools, arguing for the control of provinces and local communities as opposed to central government; he did not, however, recognize the nonpolitical character of family life and education.

Groen van Prinsterer did have a strong sense of the moral world order[24] but imbibed historicism from Stahl, and Skillen notes, "Groen insisted that all earthly authority is obliged to comply with God's revealed will, but he never conceived of the different private and public spheres of society as owing their defined order to the creational will of God. The actual structure of society, according to Groen, is the result of historical unfolding."[25] Groen van Prinsterer does, however, suggest that church and state are two spheres both under God.

SPHERE SOVEREIGNTY IN THE KUYPERIAN TRADITION

As we will see in chapter eleven, the reform of schooling and education in the Netherlands was one of Kuyper's earliest areas of activism and an ongoing one. He fought for government-funded "nonpublic" schools, a battle the Anti-Revolutionary party eventually won. A cherished project of his was the establishment of a Reformed Christian university, and it was at the inauguration of the Free University of Amsterdam that Kuyper gave his celebrated address on sphere sovereignty.

Kuyper begins by arguing that the new university is being founded out of duty for Christ's sake and the importance of it for people and country. He says to his audience, "You expect me, then, to tell you how the school we are introducing fits into the Dutch garden, why it brandishes the liberty cap on the tip of its lance, and why it peers so intently into the book of Reformed religion."[26]

This he proceeds to do. Like Groen van Prinsterer, Kuyper argues that the crisis of the day is ultimately a crisis of faith and centers on Jesus as the bearer of

---

[23]On Groen van Prinsterer's development in this respect see Sap, *Paving the Way*, 295-305.
[24]Van Dyke, *Groen*, 232.
[25]Skillen, "Development," 221-22.
[26]*AK:CR*, 464.

all sovereignty. "That King of the Jews is either the saving truth to which all peoples say Amen or the principial lie which all people should oppose."[27]

Kuyper poses the question, what is sovereignty? and answers that it is the authority that has the right to break and avenge all resistance to its will, so that original, absolute authority must reside in God's majesty. The triune God is the only sovereign. For Kuyper, belief in God's sovereignty does not lead to determinism but is the basis for genuine human freedom, as Augustine similarly argued.[28] However, God created in such a way that he delegates his authority to human beings, and thus we always witness God's authority exercised in human office—but how? Does God delegate his authority to one person or to a limited sphere?

As with Groen van Prinsterer, Kuyper argues that everything depends on one's view of revelation. On the one side the power of the state is seen as absolute and unlimited. Kuyper refers in this respect to Caesar and to Hegel's system of the state as the "immanent God."[29] On the other side, from a Christian perspective, the Messiah alone has absolute sovereignty, and this changes everything.

Human life is an infinitely complex organism made up of many spheres:

> Call the parts of this one great machine "cogwheels," spring-driven on their own axles, or "spheres," each animated with its own spirit. The name or image is unimportant, so long as we recognize that there are in life as many spheres as there are constellations in the sky and that the circumference of each has been drawn on a fixed radius from the center of a unique principle, namely the apostolic injunction *hekastos en toi idioi tagmati* ["each in its own order": 1 Cor 15:23]. Just as we speak of a "moral world," a "scientific world," a "business world," the "world of art," so we can more properly speak of a "sphere" of morality, of the family, of social life, each with its own domain. And because each comprises its own domain, each has its own Sovereign within its bounds.[30]

God, on this view, challenges absolute authority among humans by dividing life into separate spheres, each with its own sovereignty. In the domain of

---

[27]*AK:CR*, 464.
[28]See *LC*.
[29]*AK:CR*, 466.
[30]*AK:CR*, 467.

nature, fixed laws apply that cannot be disobeyed. But there are creational laws also for the different spheres of human life, laws that can be disobeyed, but only with dire consequences. The spheres engage with one another; the cogwheels turn, interact with each other, and thus the rich, multifaceted multiformity of human life emerges, akin to Althusius's symbiosis.

In this social ecology there is always a danger that one sphere might encroach unfairly on its neighbor; hence the need for the state. The special authority of the state is *public justice*, by which the state defines the mutual relations between spheres so that the state is a kind of sphere of the spheres. There is no earthly power above the state, and thus the vitality of the life spheres is crucial if the state is to be constrained to play its role without undue interference in the spheres. Kuyper is clear that God instituted the state to mediate his justice on earth. But it cannot and should not interfere in the tasks of the other spheres. However, when one sphere violates the boundaries of another, it is the state's duty to intervene and protect the boundaries of the different spheres.[31]

Kuyper argues that beliefs about sovereignty are just that, *beliefs*. One's views of sovereignty emerge from life convictions and not just from theories. A gulf lies—what Kuyper calls the antithesis—between confession of Jesus as Messiah and the view of such a confession as a harmful delusion. These are diametrically opposed confessions leading to opposed views of power and sovereignty:

> Sphere sovereignty defending itself against State sovereignty: that is the course of world history even back before the Messiah's sovereignty was proclaimed. For though the Royal Child of Bethlehem protects sphere sovereignty with His shield, He did not create it. It existed of old. It lay in the order of creation, in the structure of human life; it was there before State sovereignty arose.[32]

If interference from the state is one challenge to the life of the spheres, another is disease within the spheres: "*Sin* threatens freedom within each sphere just as strongly as *State-power* does at the boundary."[33] There is for Kuyper thus a structural dimension to the spheres—their potential is built into the creation—and a directional element, their healthy functioning. The chief culprit for their dysfunction, according to Kuyper, is the citizen.

---

[31]Abraham Kuyper, *Christianity and the Class Struggle*, trans. Dirk Jellema (Grand Rapids: Piet Hein, 1950), 57-64. Skillen, "Development," 225-73.

[32]*AK:CR*, 469.

[33]*AK:CR*, 473.

History is plagued with the suppression of the spheres. But

> Then Jesus the Nazarene, through the supernatural power of faith, once again
> created a free sphere with a free sovereignty within the iron ring of uniformity.
> With God in his heart, one with God, himself God, He withstood Caesar, broke
> down the iron gates, and posited the sovereignty of faith as the deepest piling
> upon which all sphere sovereignty rests. Neither Pharisee nor disciple under-
> stood that His cry "It is finished" entailed, beyond the salvation of the elect, also
> a *soteria tou kosmou* [salvation of the cosmos], a liberation of the world, a world
> of freedoms. But Jesus discerned it. Hence the sign *Basileus* [King] upon His
> cross. He appeared as Sovereign. . . . Then began that glorious life, crowned with
> nobility, exhibiting in the ever richer organism of guilds and free communities
> all the energy and glory that sphere sovereignty implies.[34]

The tide of royalism was followed by revolution, revolution born from an understandable thirst for freedom but also hatred for the Messiah. However, in the Netherlands the Messiah saved the day, according to Kuyper, through the Réveil of 1815–1870. Out of the Réveil the Anti-Revolutionary party emerged, with Kuyper at the helm, and the struggle for sphere sovereignty was fully engaged. In particular, there was the struggle for the sphere of education, the school: "For there the sovereignty of conscience, and of the family, and of pedagogy, and of the spiritual circle were all equally threatened."[35]

Now the day had come for the founding of the Free University of Amsterdam, "the launching of this vessel, small and unseaworthy to be sure, but chartered under the sovereignty of King Jesus and expecting to show in every port of knowledge the flag of 'sphere sovereignty'!"[36]

Faith/unbelief and society. A profound insight of Groen van Prinsterer and Kuyper is that at the deepest level of the different views of how to shape culture and society is belief or unbelief. Either God is viewed as sovereign or something else is, usually the state or the people, and this has a formative affect on our philosophy of society. Of course to see this in any detail we need to dig deeply into the views of society shaping our world today.[37] But at a basic level it is obvious that if we view God as the final authority, it will profoundly change the

---

[34]*AK:CR*, 469-70.

[35]*AK:CR*, 472.

[36]*AK:CR*, 472.

[37]See Bob Goudzwaard and Craig G. Bartholomew, *Beyond the Modern Age: An Archaeology of Contemporary Culture* (Downers Grove, IL: IVP Academic, 2017).

way we develop a society. Groen van Prinsterer and Kuyper saw so clearly and correctly that it will mean, for example, that we can never absolutize the state.

Jewish sociologist Philip Rieff perceptively notes that culture-making always involves the translation of *sacred order into social order*.[38] He rightly argues that the health of a society depends on its having a "vertical in authority," which he playfully abbreviates as a *via*. Rieff argues that there cannot be a healthy culture without it having some sense of *transgression*, that to which the society says a firm "no."

Worryingly, Rieff argues that we are in a "third age," an age that for the first time in history is trying to form societies without a *via*. Not surprisingly, therefore, he titles the first volume of his trilogy Sacred Order/Social Order *My Life Among the Deathworks*. The point is that when a culture loses a sense of vertical authority, then it is in severe danger, with a host of "demons" moving to fill the gap left by the *via*.

This is not for a moment to argue that we should reinvent Christendom. But it is to argue that we need to think hard about *how faith informs culture making* and that we also need to think hard about *how diverse faiths can coexist* in a culture that is just and fair and that can flourish as such.

Contingency. At the heart of sphere sovereignty is the recognition that the creation is just that, creation, and is never *self*-sufficient but utterly dependent on its creator for its existence, meaning, and flourishing. In theological language it is *contingent*. This, in my view, is a major insight of the book of Ecclesiastes. Ultimately meaning cannot be found within the creation but only in God: "Remember your creator . . ."

It is the genius of Groen van Prinsterer and Kuyper to have seen this with such clarity. Human authority is all *delegated* authority, all under and responsible to God. In the ancient Near East, it was common for the king or pharaoh to be regarded as having final authority, often equated with divine authority. In parts of the ancient Near East the king alone was seen as the image of the god/s. Genesis 1 will have none of this and democratizes the concept of the image so that *all humans are image bearers*, in that all humans have (delegated) authority together to steward and develop the creation so that it develops to God's glory.

It is this kind of insight that supports sphere sovereignty. Authority for public justice is delegated to government, for family life to parents, for church

---

[38]See ibid. for a discussion of Rieff and references to his work.

to church leadership, and so on. Different Christians develop this in different ways, but the basic principle is surely correct.

Delineation of the roles of other spheres. Sphere sovereignty enables us to distinguish the different areas of a culture and to ask questions such as, What is education? What is sport? What is business? What should church life consist of? and so on. These are crucial questions, and if we fail to ask them we will simply emulate the models of our culture. Take business for example. Many business practitioners, in practice if not in theory, see business as a way to make as much money as possible. The goal of business thus becomes wealth, and you sell whatever will sell and make as much money as possible. We will say more about this below, but for now we should note that this is an unbiblical and an extremely destructive view of business that misdirects the sphere of business. Business is there to provide a service so that commodities in a society can be shared and the needs of a community met. Of course, in the process, a business needs to make a profit so that it can continue to serve, but it is a distortion of a lovely field of service when profit dominates the whole enterprise and starts to colonize the other spheres.

Education is a wonderful thing, a great gift, as Kuyper stresses in his inaugural speech for the Free University of Amsterdam. But what exactly is education? In my view it involves primarily *the formation of the mind* so that children and students are equipped mentally to play a full role as citizens in their culture. While humans are far more than minds, the mind is a powerful instrument; ideas have legs and have a habit of running into and shaping history. *That* the mind is formed is vital; so too is *how* it is formed. Take homeschooling, for example. Especially as many Christians have become wary of public education, many have resorted to homeschooling. At its best this is a very good thing, but it must be home*schooling*. Memorizing Bible verses and doing Bible study, both admirable activities, are insufficient. Schooling has to involve . . . well, *schooling*: math, literacy, science, history, and so on. Formation of the mind is never neutral, and we will say more about this below in relation to *how* the mind is formed.

Interaction—symbiosis and enkapsis. It is important to note that the spheres are constantly in interaction with one another so that *symbiosis* is a good word for describing their relationship.[39] In the Kuyperian tradition the

---

[39]Cf. R. D. Henderson, *Illuminating Law: The Construction of Herman Dooyeweerd's Philosophy 1918–1928* (Amsterdam: Buijten and Schipperheij, 1994), 164-81, for a discussion of coherence among the spheres.

word that has come to be used for this is *enkapsis*, referring to "structural interlacements which can exist between things, plants, animals, and societal structures."[40] In response to the question of how social structures relate to each other, Jonathan Chaplin responds: "they relate to each other in terms of *sphere sovereignty*, 'an inner sovereignty of each structure within its own orbit,' balanced, however, by the enkaptic interlacement of each with others."[41] Thus when a father works as a school principal he does not cease to be a father, but his "office" as principal dominates in his life in the school in which he works. Things can be more complex than this. In the home a husband might occupy the role of head of the household, but at his work as a police officer he might work under his wife as his superintendent.[42]

Furthermore, the boundaries between spheres are far from absolute. Kuyper, for example, goes to great lengths to emphasize the independence from the church of the sphere of education, and there is validity in this, but it is by no means as straightforward as Kuyper suggests in his inaugural. When the Christian Reformed Church joined the Doleantie they now had two training places for ministers: the seminary at Kampen, under the control of the church, and the theology faculty at the Free University of Amsterdam, under no church control. Kuyper and Bavinck were both keen to unite the two, but under whose control? For me it is hard to see how a denomination should not be allowed to control its seminary, but clearly a seminary is for education and pastoral formation. It operates thus across the ecclesial and the educational spheres! Bavinck worked hard to resolve this issue, and his inability in this respect was one reason he left Kampen for the Free University.

While it does seem right that church authorities should not control a Christian university like the Free University of Amsterdam, a moot question remains regarding the role of church confessions in a Christian university. As confessions, creeds such as the Apostles' Creed and the Nicene Creed are universal in their scope, and one cannot have a situation where a Christian confesses these on Sunday but feels entirely free to do his or her academic

---

[40]Albert M. Wolters, "Glossary," in L. Kalsbeek, *Contours of a Christian Philosophy: An Introduction to Herman Dooyeweerd's Thought* (Amsterdam: Buijten and Schipperheijn, 1975), 347-48.

[41]Jonathan Chaplin, *Herman Dooyeweerd: Christian Philosopher of State and Civil Society* (Notre Dame, IN: University of Notre Dame Press, 2011), 316, and see chaps. 5-7.

[42]I realize that the notion of headship in the family is controversial, but in some way it seems to me that this is clearly taught in the epistles. In my view it should be emphasized that as with Christ this is a *servant* headship.

work on Monday to Friday without any sense of the authority of such confessions.[43] The danger here of sphere sovereignty, if pushed in this direction, is that of *dualism*, where one perspective on reality reigns in one's church life and another in the academy. Clearly very close cooperation between the spheres is imperative if this sort of dualism is not to gain traction. Indeed, it is an irony that, more than one hundred years after the foundation of the Free University, it is now confessedly a postmodern university, largely secular with pockets of the remnants of its founding intention.

Herman Dooyeweerd saw the need for the Kuyperian tradition to develop an integrally Christian philosophy.[44] Dooyeweerd's philosophy of society leaned heavily on Kuyper's doctrine of sphere sovereignty, but in the process sphere sovereignty becomes a far more complex idea. A major development of Kuyper's philosophy of sphere sovereignty by Dooyeweerd was Dooyeweerd's theory of societal *differentiation*, whereby it is normative for a primitive, undifferentiated culture to differentiate into diverse spheres.[45]

Separate Christian organizations. Kuyper not only wanted us to recognize the different spheres in society but to be intensely aware that different worldviews will shape life in these spheres *differently*. Take sport, for example. Sport is a wonderful, entertaining gift from God, but we are now in a situation where young sportsmen and -women earn unbelievable salaries in certain sports, way beyond what one would judge as appropriate. They have become the rock stars of our day. With this goes an ethos of competitiveness that led one famous sportsman to say, "Winning is not the main thing, it is the only thing!" The result is the sort of tragedy we witnessed in gifted cyclist Lance Armstrong, repeated again and again as sports become rife with illegal drugs in the quest to win *at all costs*. An idolatry has entered in here, and it represents a *misdirection* of the good sphere of sports and entertainment.

When it comes to the spheres, therefore, we need to be sensitive to their structure rooted in creation and their potential misdirection. Sex is good, a gift from God, but it can be and is being radically misdirected. The Christian responsibility is to engage in these spheres in such a way that they become healthier and directed rightly so that they flourish in the best sense of the word.

---

[43]Cf. Marcel E. Verburg, *Herman Dooyeweerd: The Life and Work of a Christian Philosopher*, trans. Harry Van Dyke (Grand Rapids: Paideia, 2009), 348-54.

[44]See chapter nine.

[45]Cf. Chaplin, *Herman Dooyeweerd*, 71-85.

Kuyper saw this with crystal clarity, and he and his colleagues fought for the possibility of alternative Christian organizations in all spheres of life: education, politics, broadcasting, youth organizations, and so on.[46] To a great extent I think he was right. For the Christian mind to flourish, for example, it has to be given the space to develop to maturity, and this requires separate Christian educational institutions. However, a note of caution is in place here. Withdrawal from the mainstream is often necessary, but *only and always* to reengage more powerfully and more constructively. The church in its institutional and organic senses is *missional* through and through, and mission is rendered ineffective when Christians withdraw without constantly remaining engaged with their culture.

The Implications of Sphere Sovereignty

Sphere sovereignty and higher education. In his *Our Program* Kuyper fleshes out the implications of sphere sovereignty for government and other areas of life.[47] In his inaugural for the Free University of Amsterdam, he focuses on higher education, as we will here.

For Kuyper, academic work is characterized by "sanctified intellectual power," and scholarship is at the forefront of defending freedom. Of academic work he comments, "In its authentic form God sent it to us as an angel of light." Human wisdom is thus a gift from God, and human ideas have a powerful effect on history and its development. The Christian ought, therefore, to take intellectual life with the utmost seriousness.[48]

Kuyper is insistent that scholarship should remain sovereign in its own sphere and not be allowed to degenerate under the guardianship of the state or the church. In his view, as scholarship develops, it forms its own life sphere, in which truth is sovereign. Any violation of this would be sin. In this respect Kuyper affirms Baruch Spinoza, who left the synagogue rather than sacrifice academic freedom, and denigrates Desiderius Erasmus for being unwilling to follow his conclusions through and join the Reformation. "We must therefore

---

[46]It is here that Barth and Kuyper part ways. See Clifford Blake Anderson, "Jesus and the 'Christian Worldview': A Comparative Analysis of Abraham Kuyper and Karl Barth," *Cultural Encounters* 6, no. 1 (2006): 61-80, esp. 74-80.

[47]Abraham Kuyper, *Our Program: A Christian Political Manifesto*, trans. Harry Van Dyke, Collected Works in Public Theology (Bellingham, WA: Lexham, 2015).

[48]*AK:CR*, 475, 476.

resist tooth and nail any imposition upon learning by the church of Christ."[49]
The state is the master planner but should not interfere in academic freedom.
Kuyper invokes the prophets of Israel and the school of wisdom in Jerusalem
as biblical examples of such freedom.

Some Christians have proposed setting up Christian chairs at secular universities, but Kuyper replies, "No, what we need is . . . a plant of scholarship
growing from a Christian root. To satisfy ourselves with the role of sauntering
around another garden, clipper in hand, is to throw away the dignity of the
Christian religion." We need knowledge that generates wisdom, culminating
in adoration of the only wise God.[50]

In the third section of his inaugural Kuyper argues that sphere sovereignty
is distinctively Reformed, with its emphasis on the sovereignty of God. Scripturally, he invokes Hebron's tribal law for David's coronation, Elijah's resistance to Ahab's tyranny, the disciples' refusal to yield to Jerusalem's police
regulations, and Jesus' memorable saying "Render to Caesar what is Caesar's
and to God what is God's." He finds the principle of sphere sovereignty in
Presbyterian church order and in the government of Reformed nations that
have inclined toward a confederative form of government.

For Kuyper it is Reformed to insist that we should not make a covenant of
neutrality with learning proceeding from a principle other than our own.[51]
He recognizes that his opponents will see this as self-deception, but so be it.

> Not that he is our inferior in knowledge; he is probably our superior. But because
> he takes to be no fact that which for us stands fast as a fact in Christ. . . . Faith in
> God's Word, objectively infallible in Scripture and subjectively offered to us by
> the Holy Spirit—there is the line of demarcation. Not as if knowledge of others
> rests on intellectual certainty and ours only on faith. For all knowledge proceeds
> from faith of whatever kind. . . . The person who does not believe does not exist.[52]

In scholarship the starting point and direction need to be clear. For Kuyper it
is ridiculous to imagine that one must think through all confessions and
systems and only then decide which is the best one.[53]

---

[49]AK:CR, 477.
[50]AK:CR, 479, 476.
[51]AK:CR, 481.
[52]AK:CR, 485-86.
[53]AK:CR, 486.

In conclusion, Kuyper explores the difference a Reformed perspective makes to a medical faculty, to a law school, and to study of the natural sciences. He asks, "Does not the study of Semitic languages change depending upon whether I regard Israel as the people of absolute revelation or merely as a people with a genius for piety?" One of his best-known sayings occurs in this inaugural address, but the start of it is not nearly as commonly noted: "Oh, no single piece of our mental world is to be hermetically sealed off from the rest, and there is not a square inch in the whole domain of our human existence over which Christ, who is Sovereign over *all*, does not cry: 'Mine!'"[54] The honor of Christ and well-being of his people are thus at stake in the founding of institutions like the Free University of Amsterdam.

Politics: The state between absolutization and libertarianism. In the twentieth century we saw what happens when God is rejected and the state assumes absolute authority, particularly in the horrors of National Socialism and Communism. The result was what many regard as the most brutal century in history.

Sphere sovereignty is insightful in its recognition of the importance of government as a gift from God to restrain evil and establish public justice. Inherently, the Kuyperian tradition is thus positive toward government and has much vested in encouraging Christians to respect the state and to be model citizens. But it unequivocally rejects any absolutization of the state, since this would be to bow the knee to Caesar. The state has a unique but limited role. It is the sphere of spheres in the sense that it is there to ensure the freedom of the different spheres and to ensure that they do not unfairly encroach on each other.

In this respect sphere sovereignty lines up with Paul's view of government in Romans 13. Government is there to punish evil and to reward good, and as such is appointed by God. But Paul is clear that government is God's "servant" and thus can never assume the authority of God himself. Its authority is always a delegated authority, which can be, and often is, removed by God.

Inherent in this approach is the possibility of civil disobedience. Groen van Prinsterer and Kuyper were understandably wary of revolution, which seeks violently to overthrow and to rebuild from scratch. But they were equally

---

[54]*AK:CR*, 488.

aware of the need for civil resistance and to use all legal means to oppose governments when they acted unjustly. What both wanted was an active, vibrant civil culture in which citizens and Christians in particular took a vested interest in their society and held government accountable. Kuyper wanted the spheres functioning at full capacity and playing an active role in society.

The church. Sphere sovereignty is particularly helpful in delineating a sphere that all Christians have a vested interest in, namely the institutional church. It is vital to distinguish between the gathered church for worship (the institutional church) and the life of the people of God as a whole. The institutional church is qualified philosophically as a structure by *faith* and is all about worship in the narrow sense of the word, about the Word, faith, prayer, sacraments. The institutional church is there as our mother in the faith to continually nurture our trust in and dependence on the living God, who has come to us in Jesus Christ. A church can engage in many activities, but worship and the formation of disciples through Word and sacrament must always be central to its life.

I worked at one stage of my life as a youth pastor. In youth ministry one is always facing the issue of how to plan and develop a vibrant youth program for a church. The temptation is to turn youth *ministry* into entertainment in order to attract as many young people as possible. In the process one tries to ape youth culture and often sets up a wall between the young person and the church that is funding the youth ministry! It is not that youth ministry should be boring, and it is not that it should be irrelevant to the needs of young people, but it must remain part of the institutional church's ministry. Thus worship and discipleship must be at its heart. I learned early on that numbers in attendance would fluctuate greatly, and so I selected a group of twelve in whose lives I thought I discerned the Spirit working. I then discipled this group intensively, and to this day I am aware of where most of those twelve are and what they are doing. As one author puts it, in youth ministry we need to beware of spending so much time entertaining the goats that we fail to feed the sheep!

Activity. Kuyper and his fellows Calvinists were very industrious. They got involved! We cannot usher in God's kingdom, but we can get alongside God in what he is doing in his world. According to sphere sovereignty, no one sphere is better than another; all are unique in their own way. The institutional church is thus not better than the family, but it is indispensable in terms of its unique role. You can have families without the church, but for both to flourish they need each other. And both soon discover that if government is not functioning well, both suffer and are adversely affected. And so on and so forth.

Central to this vision is that we are all as Christians God's full-time servants. As Eugene Peterson puts it, "Every Christian takes holy orders."[55] All of us are called to serve God full time in every aspect of our life: some as teachers, some as politicians, some as parents, some as students, some as pastors, some as nurses, and so on. Of course, each of these roles are different and each important. What we must avoid is either discounting the importance of the pastor and missionary or thinking that they *alone* are in full-time service. The pastor is appointed by the sheep to spend his or her time entirely devoted to keeping the flock's attention focused on the great Shepherd. One of the roles of the pastor is to keep reminding the sheep that they are in God's service every day and every hour of their lives.

Indeed, when you think about it, we are all *already* involved in many of the spheres of our societies. Sphere sovereignty should help us to be involved consciously and not *individualistically*, but to *seek the welfare of our city*, to seek to promote the flourishing of our main spheres of involvement so that these spheres flourish to the benefit of all citizens. This will mean developing leadership gifts where we have them and exercising them not just in the institutional church but in all spheres of life.

The economics of globalization. Sphere sovereignty is also insightful in alerting us to beware of one sphere dominating others. Groen van Prinsterer and Kuyper were particularly aware of the danger of *the state* absolutizing its control over all other areas. In our day this remains a danger in many countries, but in the West, indeed globally, a great danger is of the *economic sphere* controlling all others. Indeed, with the development of globalization it is becoming harder to conceive of the individual nation-state that has been so central to modernity. Under global consumer capitalism the economy has taken on a life of its own, and corporations are fast becoming fluid, international entities with no obligation to any particular country. In the process we are witnessing an extraordinary dominance of all spheres by the economic one.

---

[55]Eugene Peterson, *Leap over a Wall: Earthly Spirituality for Everyday Christians* (New York: HarperCollins, 1997), 32.

There is hardly an area of life that has not become a product by which someone seeks to make a profit. Courtesy of the Internet, sex and pornography have become such a major international industry that there seems little political will to control them. The food chain has become a product, with inadequate concern for the well-being of animals or the health of humans. Eugene Peterson, in his masterful *Working the Angles*, points out how pastors are abandoning their calling in droves, not by leaving the church but by turning the church into a business. While there are undoubted benefits to globalization, global consumerism is creating a north-south economic apartheid that leaves far too many in poverty while chanting the mantra of "free trade." Joseph Stiglitz perceptively points out that it is not that free trade has not worked; it has just never really been tried![56] The house has become an asset and a commodity rather than a home, and as Wendell Berry provocatively points out, a house that is for sale is not a home.[57]

René Girard has pointed out the central role of desire in human life and culture.[58] Girard notes the uniqueness of the Bible in its exposure of the mechanics of desire and in its constraint of them in the Tenth Commandment and especially its overcoming of false desire in the Gospels. Consumer culture, however, seeks no constraint of desire but fans its flames in order to encourage greater and greater consumption.[59] We know that this is unsustainable in all sorts of ways, and yet, when the bottom nearly fell out of the US economy in 2008, Americans were encouraged to get out and shop, to consume. They were not encouraged to be frugal, to tighten their belts, but to reignite the consumer economy. Girard in an interview speaks nowadays of a whirlwind of desire at work in our world.[60] The dangers should be obvious. Unbridled consumerism is a recipe for rivalry, violence, and conflict. What we urgently need is to rethink the economy and how it fits in relation to all the spheres of life. As Bob Goudzwaard and Harry De Lange have argued, we need to move *Beyond Poverty and Affluence* toward an "economy of care," which distributes resources fairly and justly.[61]

---

[56]Joseph E. Stiglitz, *Making Globalization Work* (New York: Norton, 2006), 62.

[57]Wendell Berry, *The Mad Farmer Poems* (Berkeley, CA: Counterpoint, 2008), 19.

[58]For a discussion of Girard see Goudzwaard and Bartholomew, *Beyond the Modern Age*.

[59]See Craig G. Bartholomew and Thorsten Moritz, eds., *Christ and Consumerism: A Critical Analysis of the Spirit of the Age* (Carlisle, UK: Paternoster, 2000).

[60]See "Insights with Rene Girard," YouTube video, December 9, 2009, www.youtube.com /watch?v=BNkSBy5wWDk.

[61]See Bob Goudzwaard and Harry De Lange, *Beyond Poverty and Affluence: Toward an Economy of Care*. There are several editions of this work.

Islam. Several years ago now in an article titled "The Challenge of Islam in Africa," I suggested that the Kuyperian tradition could be of great help in the relationship between Islam and Christianity and the role of Islam in the West.[62] Since writing that article 9/11 intervened, and the issue becomes a more urgent one by the day. I suggested then, and continue to argue today, that moderate Islam in particular could be an ally, a cobelligerent with Christianity in opposing the privatization of religion in the West. Islam has shown more grit in resisting Western-style modernity in this regard than any other religion. Of course we would need to wake up to the fact that Western nations are *not* Christian nations and make that perfectly clear in dialogue with Muslims. Increasingly Western nations are governed by a secular elite that is too often anti-Christian.

At the same time sphere sovereignty can be used to challenge Muslim-dominated nations to work for the same freedoms of minority groups in their nations that Muslims enjoy in Western nations. It is ridiculous to have militant Muslims using the freedoms of Western nations to plan attacks on the West while Christians are being denied basic rights in far too many Muslim nations. Government is there to ensure public justice for all its citizens, and pressure needs to be put on Muslim nations to come into line in this respect or to face the consequences via political pressure, trade embargoes, and so on.

There is abundant and carefully researched evidence now that Christians are the most persecuted religion in the world today.[63] In *The Global War on Christians* distinguished Catholic journalist John Allen lists the twenty-five most hazardous nations in which to be a Christian today, and then notes that eighteen of the twenty-five are majority-Muslim nations.[64] Similarly, Brian Grim and Roger Finke note, "Religious persecution is not only more prevalent among Muslim-majority countries, but it also occurs at more severe levels."[65]

---

[62]Craig Bartholomew, "The Challenge of Islam in Africa," *Journal of Interdisciplinary Studies* 6, no. 1/2 (1994): 129-46.

[63]See, for example, Brian J. Grim and Roger Finke, *The Price of Freedom Denied: Religious Persecution and Conflict in the Twenty-First Century* (Cambridge: Cambridge University Press, 2011); Paul Marshall and Nina Shea, *Silence: How Apostasy and Blasphemy Codes Are Choking Freedom Worldwide* (Oxford: Oxford University Press, 2011).

[64]John L. Allen, *The Global War on Christians: Dispatches from the Front Lines of Anti-Christian Persecution* (New York: Image, 2013), 41.

[65]Ibid., 169.

This is completely unacceptable, and it is a scandal that Western leaders are not leading the campaign against such persecution. The tragedy of 9/11 has forced the West to realize that religion is a public force, but our secular leaders still find it desperately hard to take religion, let alone Christianity, seriously. This needs to change, and change will probably have to come from the ground up in the West as Christians and cobelligerents in a variety of societal spheres exert pressure in diverse ways to change this situation. Blasphemy laws are being used to enforce an attitude of noncriticism of Islam in the West while Christians are oppressed and persecuted in too many majority-Muslim countries.[66]

Sphere sovereignty can certainly help here. If a religion or a country wants its citizens to have the freedom to meet and exercise their faith in other countries, then justice demands that it exercises the same courtesies to minority groups and religions on its home turf. With its doctrine of societal structures and societal pluralism, the Kuyperian tradition proposes a model that allows religions to come to full fruition in all areas of life while granting the same freedom to other groups, including secular humanists. What it resists is the coercive dominance of one religious group over another. If this is what proponents of shari'a law are after, then they need to be clear about it but should not then expect to trade off the freedoms of other cultures in which much greater degrees of religious freedom are granted.

Sphere Sovereignty and Apartheid

As I noted in the introduction to this book, the Kuyperian tradition is controversial in South Africa because of its use to support apartheid. Kuyper himself is partially responsible for this. Martin Bossenbroek has written the first book to tell the story of the Anglo-Boer Wars from the Dutch perspective.[67] Prior to the initial defeat of the British by the Boers of the Transvaal at Majuba Hill in 1881, the latter were not well thought of in the Netherlands. According to Bossenbroek, the Boers

> deliberately frustrated the efforts of missionaries who tried to convert the black population to Christianity. So it was mainly the missionary societies that were critical of the Boers and turned public opinion against them, first in Britain and later in the rest of Europe as well. The most incriminating evidence was revealed

[66]See Marshall and Shea, *Silence*.
[67]Martin Bossenbroek, *The Boer War*, trans. Yvette Rosenberg (Auckland Park, South Africa: Jacana, 2015).

in the Netherlands by the clergyman Pierre Huet in 1869. Huet had been a missionary for 12 years and had written at length about the plundering, murder and other atrocities committed by the Boers.[68]

The initial defeat of the British changed everything, and Kuyper was among those who championed the rights of the Boers against English imperialism. His critique of British arrogance and imperialism is valid, but disastrously, in his defense of the Boers, he affirms as a virtue their refusal to socialize with "inferior" black Africans:[69]

> The Boers are not sentimental but men of practical genius. They understood that the Hottentots and the Bantus were an inferior race, and that to put them on a footing of equality with the whites, in their families, in society, and in politics, would be simple folly. They have understood, further, the danger of mixed *liaisons,* and to save their sons from this scourge they have inculcated the idea that to have carnal intercourse with the Kaffir woman is to commit incest. But on the other hand they have treated their slaves as good children; they have habituated them to work; have softened their manners; and in South Africa you will find no man more skillful in dealing with the Natives than a Boer patriarch.[70]

Kuyper, furthermore, clearly articulates the *swart gevaar* (black danger), the cry that carried the Afrikaner Nationalists to victory after World War II: "The Blacks are increasing in South Africa to an extent which may well give cause for uneasiness."[71] This forms a contrast with Kuyper's celebration of mixed blood in America in his *Lectures on Calvinism,* and, though his views reflect the times, they mark one low—if not *the* lowest—point in Kuyper's thought.[72] Such comments were wrong and profoundly unhelpful in terms of the future of South Africa, a future, of course, of which Kuyper could not be aware.

---

[68]Ibid., 2.

[69]See George Harinck, "Abraham Kuyper, South Africa, and Apartheid," in Steve Bishop and John H. Kok, eds., *On Kuyper: A Collection of Readings on the Life, Work, and Legacy of Abraham Kuyper* (Sioux Center, IA: Dordt College Press, 2013), 419-22, for Kuyper's more enlightened approach to Dutch imperialism.

[70]Abraham Kuyper, *The South-African Crisis,* 4th ed., trans. A. E. Fletcher (London: Stop the War Committee, 1900), 24-25.

[71]Ibid., 26.

[72]The contrast is not as strong as this may suggest, because Kuyper refers to the mixing of the blood of the lines of Noah's sons Shem and Japeth, but not of Ham, from whom black races were thought to descend. However, earlier in his first lecture Kuyper is clear that Calvinism opposes all hierarchy as well as slavery of women and the poor.

However, they were also profoundly unhelpful in terms of the South Africa—and United States—of Kuyper's time.[73] In the United States in 1903, W. E. B. Du Bois penned his most famous aphorism in one of his essays: "the problem of the Twentieth Century is the problem of the color-line."[74] At the very time when Kuyper was writing his racist remarks, emerging black Christian South African leaders such as John L. Dube (1871–1946), the founding president of the African National Congress, were visiting America and struggling to find their and their people's place amid Western-style civilization.[75] Dube was a product of missionary education, and the work and witness of many of the missionaries in South Africa must be taken seriously, as must the very different viewpoints held about race in South Africa by some of Kuyper's contemporaries. In so many ways it is hard to imagine two more different personalities than Kuyper and Bishop John Colenso of Natal (1814–1883).[76] Colenso, however, manifested a far more Christian attitude to the blacks of South Africa. For example, Wyn Rees, in his edited volume *Colenso: Letters from Natal*, notes,

> The Bishop was over-optimistic, but he always regarded the Zulus of Natal as subjects of the Queen, potentially equal in rights to Her Majesty's white subjects. It was for this, and humanitarian reasons, that he intervened in the Langalibalele affair. A popular Lieutenant-Governor was recalled, the Shepstone system of native administration was shaken to its foundations and reformed, the colonial Charter was revised, and the demands of the settlers for responsible government were checked. As for the Bishop, he became the most hated man in Natal.[77]

In the nineteenth and twentieth centuries it was especially among the liberal tradition in South Africa, much of which was Christian, that voices could be

---

[73]Herman Bavinck was far more helpful in his approach, writing in RD 2:525, "While the existence of races and peoples is a fact, the determination of their boundaries is nevertheless so difficult that it generates immense disputes."

[74]W. E. B. Du Bois, *The Souls of Black Folk*, ed. David W. Blight and Robert Gooding-Williams, Bedford Series in History and Culture (Boston and New York: Bedford Books, 1997), 34.

[75]Heather Hughes, *First President: A Life of John L. Dubbe, Founding President of the ANC* (Auckland Park, South Africa: Jacana, 2011); Martin Plaut, *Promise and Despair: The First Struggle for a Non-Racial South Africa* (Auckland Park, South Africa: Jacana, 2016); André Odendaal, *The Founders: The Origins of the ANC and the Struggle for Democracy in South Africa* (Auckland Park, South Africa: Jacana, 2012).

[76]Kuyper, *South-African Crisis*, 22, refers to Colenso.

[77]Wyn Rees, ed., *Colenso: Letters from Natal* (Pietermaritzburg, South Africa: Shuter and Shooter, 1958), 259. For the details of Langalibalele and the rebellion see 258-89.

heard calling for justice for all in South Africa.[78] Alan Paton (1903–1988) was one such voice. In his *Hope for South Africa* he perceptively comments,

> For the Christian liberal the choice should be simple, being between obedience to God and obedience to man, but will not thereby be made easier. And we must face the position soberly that many white Christians in South Africa find it easier as time goes on, and as the Government becomes more powerful, to believe that apartheid and the great commandments can be happily reconciled, and that Christ would approve apartheid had he been here. They therefore cease to fight or to protest against injustice, because they dare not admit that it exists. Furthermore it becomes easier for them to dismiss supporters of human rights as subversive and communistic, or if they do not wish to go that far, as unrealistic and impractical.[79]

Paton wrote the biography of an earlier Christian liberal, J. H. Hofmeyr (1894–1948). Hofmeyr's formative Christian experience was in a Baptist church under a protégé of Spurgeon's, sent out by him to minister in the Cape. Paton comments, "Perhaps if he had experienced what is known as Christian National Education, he might not have felt that exclusiveness and Christianity were irreconcilable. However, he had learned his religion in a church that was not much concerned with race."[80]

There are now many good books available on the history of apartheid.[81] Even within Afrikanerdom there were always prophetic voices raised against it, one of them being B. B. Keet, who did his doctorate under the supervision of Herman Bavinck.[82] Having come to power in 1948 the Afrikaner Nationalists systematically enacted a form of Christianity subservient to their nationalist, exclusivist ideology. Paton narrates a telling incident in 1936 debates in South Africa about the Native Bill. J. B. M. Herzog (1866–1942) was expounding the view that white South Africa's two great fears were black

---

[78]In the Dutch tradition the work of J. H. Bavinck's successor, Johannes Verkuyl, *Break Down the Walls: A Christian Cry for Racial Justice*, trans. Lewis B. Smedes (Grand Rapids: Eerdmans, 1973), stands out as an acute critique of apartheid from a theological perspective.

[79]Alan Paton, *Hope for South Africa* (London: Pall Mall Press, 1958), 64-65.

[80]Alan Paton, *Hofmeyr* (Oxford: Oxford University Press, 1964), 87.

[81]See, e.g., David Welsh, *The Rise and Fall of Apartheid* (Johannesburg and Cape Town: Jonathan Ball, 2009).

[82]See, e.g., B. B. Keet, *Whither South Africa?*, trans. N. J. Marquard (Stellenbosch and Grahamstown, South Africa: University Publishers and Booksellers, 1956), a trenchant theological critique of apartheid originally written in Afrikaans. I am indebted for this information about Keet's relationship with Bavinck to George Harinck.

domination and the intermingling of blood—both of which fears were voiced earlier by Kuyper—and Herzog argued that his view was firmly based on Christian principles, and in particular the principle of self-preservation for a nation. Paton comments,

> Herzog then went on to utter one of the most plausible of Christian heresies; he said there was a principle of self-preservation for a nation.... "It is a sacred principle, a Christian principle just the same as any other principle, and it stands equally high—I place that principle still higher, it is the only principle, that of self-preservation, that of self-defence, by which humanity itself and Christianity itself will ever be able to protect itself."
>
> So Herzog placed the defence of the good higher than the good itself, and made Christianity one of the warring factions, the survival of which was in the last resort dependent on the use of power.[83]

The evil and tragedy of apartheid is indisputable. For our purposes, the central question is whether Kuyper's thought can legitimately be used to support it. W. A. de Klerk, in his *The Puritans in Africa: A Story of Afrikanerdom*, thinks the answer is straightforward: "It is a relatively simple matter to see how Kuyper's 'sovereignty in the individual social spheres,' as fully extended to a 'life system' by Dooyeweerd and others came to be used as the most powerful of the neo-Calvinist supports for the secular faith of the Revolutionary Afrikaners."[84] In my view this is by no means as clear as de Klerk suggests.[85] Reformational philosophers such as Hendrik G. Stoker (1899–1993) in South Africa did use Reformational philosophy to defend apartheid, but there is no direct line between sphere sovereignty and apartheid. Kuyper did believe that nations were created by God and celebrated such diversity, but the directional pluralism he seeks in the spheres of society is religious and decidedly not ethnic.[86] Indeed, we saw in our discussion of Kuyper on worldview that he sees equality of persons as a fruit politically of Calvinism. The view of the state as being there to provide public justice for all citizens runs entirely counter to the sort of oppression of the majority experienced under apartheid. It is a

---

[83]Paton, *Hofmeyr*, 224.

[84]W. A. de Klerk, *The Puritans in Africa: A Story of Afrikanerdom* (Middlesex, UK: Penguin, 1975), 258.

[85]Cf. Harinck, "Abraham Kuyper, South Africa, and Apartheid," for a nuanced view.

[86]See Gerrit Schutte, *A Family Feud: Afrikaner Nationalism and Dutch Neo-Calvinism* (Amsterdam: Rozen-berg, 2010), 88-100.

tragedy and a scar on Kuyper's thought that he was so inconsistent when it came to black Africans.

EVALUATION

It is obvious from the above that I consider sphere sovereignty a useful heuristic for exploring the shape of society. But it needs further development and thought. In particular, the issue of sphere sovereignty and enkapsis needs to be thought through as thoroughly as has been sphere *sovereignty*. Once again the image of symbiosis comes to mind. Suffice it here to problematize some aspects of sphere sovereignty in order to demonstrate the need for further work.

Kuyper, as we saw in his inaugural, is adamant about the sovereignty of the educational sphere. However, he sees education as primarily the responsibility of parents and wanted parents to have the choice as to the type of education their children receive. Here we witness the symbiosis between the family and the school. Parents delegate the education of their children to schools, but they remain responsible for it. There is thus a far more intricate relationship between family and school than sphere sovereignty might at first blush suggest, and we would expect parents to play a formative role in boards that govern schools.

As regards higher education, we discussed above the question of the relationship between church and academy. Kuyperians tends to be averse to "church schools" because of sphere sovereignty, but once again we see that the relationship is far more nuanced than simply keeping the institutional church's influence out of the school or university. The church *should* have a vested interest in a Reformed or Christian university remaining genuinely Reformed or Christian. This is not to argue that minsters should govern a school or university, but that representation on the board and regular dialogue and reporting is crucial if the confessional stance of a school or university is to be maintained. The relationship needs to be symbiotic rather than one of strict boundaries.

Another issue that needs clarification is the precise nature of a sphere and the number of spheres. How many spheres are there? As with worldview, Kuyper's language is loose in this respect, sometimes referring to an endless number, whereas at other times he focuses on spheres such as church, family, schools, universities, politics, and economics. Dooyeweerd's notion of differentiation is helpful here, but we need to develop criteria for healthy, normative development, as opposed to modern progress that espouses "development" too often uncritically.[87]

Conclusion: The Questions to Ask

We began this chapter by noting the importance of a philosophy of society. As a university professor my goal is always to encourage my students to ask their questions and in the process to learn to ask the questions that will open up a topic or problem. Indeed, I have on my shelves a book about the university titled *Love the Question*! If one thinks about it, one will find that one always works with some view of society, but alas, among too many Christians, this view is underdeveloped and largely functions unconsciously. For example, it is far too easy to work with a basic framework of "church and society" so that one is left, at best, asking questions like, How does the church relate to society? This is an important question, but it does not get one very far. One needs to dig deeper to ask questions like, What is the church? What is society, and what parts make it up? We will attend to the church in chapter six, but for now it is vital, for example, to work out whether we are talking about the institutional church or the life of the people of God as a whole when we pose such questions.

Sphere sovereignty allows one to approach society and cultural engagement with nuance and so avoid the sort of blunders in this area that dog Christian engagement with culture. For example, a hot issue nowadays is that of gay marriage. What is a Christian approach to gay relationships and marriage? Let us assume, as I do, that Scripture is clear on this issue, that same-sex relationships are ruled out by Scripture, and that heterosexual marriage is the norm.[88] If this is the case, then certainly in the church this should be clear and upheld. However, this only *begins* to deal with the issue. While Christians should not, from my perspective, recommend or promote gay behavior, what about the civil rights of gays? This is another issue altogether. The church now lives scattered among the nations so that their societies are no longer theocracies, as with Israel. We live in pluralist cultures in which a variety of worldviews jostle

---

[87]See C. T. McIntire's nuanced critique in his "Dooyeweerd's Philosophy of History," in C. T. McIntire, ed., *The Legacy of Herman Dooyeweerd: Reflections on Critical Philosophy in the Christian Tradition* (Lanham, MD: University Press of America, 1985), 81-117.

[88]See George Hobson, *The Episcopal Church, Homosexuality, and the Context of Technology* (Eugene, OR: Pickwick, 2013).

together. What does justice look like in such a context, and how should the state legislate in order to protect the freedoms of all groups? This is doubtless complex, but one can see how sphere sovereignty can help. Without affirming gay relationships one can, as I would, affirm and seek to protect the *civil* rights of gay citizens. So too with Islam. I would not recommend to anyone to become a Muslim, but I would advocate for the freedom of Muslims to practice their faith within our cultures.

Another example is the education of one's children. Whose responsibility is this? Is it the parents' or the state's? We far too quickly assume that it is the state's responsibility and then wonder why our children so easily lose their faith at public schools and universities. Kuyper would argue that it is the responsibility of the parents and that they (should) choose a school to carry out large parts, albeit not all, of this duty *on their behalf.* Thus parents have a responsibility to know what and how their children are being taught and to ensure that God's Word is taken seriously in their education.

THE CHURCH

A life and death struggle for the confessional center is going on in
all Protestant denominations. The confessional center is not the
concoction of conservatives but simply the evangelical catholic faith
in continuity with the Scriptures and the apostolic tradition.

CARL BRAATEN, *MOTHER CHURCH: ECCLESIOLOGY AND ECUMENISM*

A BIG, BIBLICAL VIEW OF CHRIST will result in a big view of the
church. Too often, far too often, despite what we confess, our church practices
reveal a small, truncated view of Christ. This is why I love the titles of two of
Michael Griffiths's books: *Cinderella with Amnesia: A Practical Discussion of the
Relevance of the Church* and *Shaking the Sleeping Beauty: Arousing the Church to
Its Mission.*[1] In our Western world the church is too often like a slumbering
giant, fast asleep while its energy and life are sorely needed. Kuyper's wrestling
with what it means to be the church is remarkable in its contemporary relevance and certainly a call to rouse the slumbering giant.[2]

From his conversion to the end of his life the church remained an issue
of major concern for Kuyper. As we saw in chapter one, God used Charlotte

---

[1]Michael Griffiths, *Cinderella with Amnesia: A Practical Discussion of the Relevance of the Church* (Leicester,
UK: Inter-Varsity Press, 1975); Griffiths, *Shaking the Sleeping Beauty: Arousing the Church to Its Mission*
(Leicester, UK: Inter-Varsity Press, 1980).
[2]G. C. Berkouwer, *The Church,* Studies in Dogmatics (Grand Rapids: Eerdmans, 1976), 334-38, has a
fascinating discussion of Kuyper's reflection on how it often goes well with the world but not with
the church.

Yonge's novel *The Heir of Redclyffe* to bring Kuyper to repentance. Yonge lived in the parish of Reverend John Keble, one of three founders of the Anglo-Catholic movement—namely, Keble, Pusey, and Newman. In order to spread their vision, they wrote a series of highly influential *Tracts for the Times,* and Yonge followed this model but in fiction rather than theology. Central to the Anglo-Catholic revival was the issue of the true church, the issue that would eventually move Newman into the Roman Catholic Church.[3]

In his "Confidentially" Kuyper notes how moved he was by the description of Guy de Morville's funeral in *The Heir of Redclyffe.*[4] Kuyper comments:

> That was what I wanted. Such a church I never saw or knew. Oh, to have such a church, a "mother who guides our steps from your youth!" . . . And so my ideal for churchly life came to me in this fleeting word. When I thumbed through this delightful book again, mindful of the care of the Church; when I realized how Guy had been touched by what we seem to have lost, by the lofty signifi-cance of the Sacrament, by the prescribed forms of private and public worship, by the impressive liturgy and the blessed "Prayerbook," which he bequeathed to Philip just before his death: at that moment the predilection for prescribed ritual, the high estimation of the Sacrament, the appreciation for the Liturgy became rooted in me for all time. From then on I have longed with all my soul for a sanctified Church wherein my soul and those of my loved ones can enjoy the quite refreshment of peace, far from all confusion, under its firm, lasting, and authoritative guidance.[5]

In his inaugural in the church in Amsterdam, Kuyper returns to this theme of the church as our mother: "'She is a mother'—to use Calvin's beautiful expression—'whose womb not only carried us, whose breast not only nursed us, but whose tender care leads us to the goal of faith. . . . Those to whom he is a Father, the Church must also be Mother, and apart from her motherly care no one grows to maturity.' The church is our mother!"[6]

---

[3]A perusal of the *Tracts for the Times* demonstrates this clearly. See Geoffrey Rowell, *The Vision Glorious: Themes and Personalities of the Catholic Revival in Anglicanism* (Oxford: Clarendon, 2003).

[4]See chapter one.

[5]*AK:CR,* 54-55. Kuyper is more critical of Anglicanism in his *Our Worship.*

[6]*R&G,* 15. Cf. Herman Dooyeweerd, *A New Critique of Theoretical Thought,* 4 vols. (Jordan Station, ON: Paideia, 1984), 3:535.

THE CHURCH AS OUR MOTHER

Kuyper's view of the church as our mother is noteworthy. Indeed, the language he uses has roots that go back way beyond Luther and Calvin.[7] The metaphor of the church as our mother, though found in Galatians 4:26—"But the Jerusalem that is above is free, and she is our mother"—was rarely used in the second century AD but became predominant in the third century, especially through the writings of Cyprian of Carthage (AD 200–258). Tertullian (c. 155–c. 240) refers to the church as our mother; and Cyprian famously wrote, "You cannot have God for your father if you have not the church as your mother."[8] The image of the church as our mother is more fully developed in Augustine. For example, at the end of his exposition of Psalm 89 he exhorts, "Let us love our Lord God; Let us love His Church: Him as a Father, her as a Mother. . . . Hold then, most beloved, hold all with one mind to God the Father, and the Church our Mother."[9] Elsewhere Augustine writes: "See the womb of Mother Church: see how she groans and is in travail to bring you to birth and make you reach the light of faith."[10] In his sermons on 1 John, Augustine asks,

> What is it to grow? To go onward by proficiency. What is it to decrease? To go backward by deficiency. Whoso knows that he is born, let him hear that he is an infant; let him eagerly cling to the breasts of his mother, and he grows apace. *Now his mother is the Church; and her breasts are the two Testaments of the Divine Scriptures.* Hence let him suck the milk of all the things that as signs of spiritual truths were done in time for our eternal salvation, that being nourished and strengthened, he may attain to the eating of solid meat, which is, "In the beginning was the Word, and the Word was with God, and the Word was God." Our milk is Christ in His humility; our meat, the self-same Christ equal with the Father. With milk He nourisheth thee, that He may feed thee with bread:

---

[7] In his *Large Catechism*, in *The Book of Concord*, ed. and trans. Theodore G. Tappert (Philadelphia: Fortress Press, 1959), 416, Luther writes that the Holy Spirit "has a unique community in the world. It is the mother that begets and bears every Christian through the Word of God."

[8] Tertullian, *Against Marcion* 5.4; Cyprian, "The Unity of the Catholic Church," 6, in S. L. Greenslade, ed., *Early Latin Theology: Selections from Tertullian, Cyprian, Ambrose, and Jerome*, Library of Christian Classics (Louisville: Westminster John Knox, 1956), 127-28. In context Cyprian is dealing with the fallout from Christians who had lapsed under the weight of persecution.

[9] Augustine, *Expositions on the Psalms*, trans. J. E. Tweed, in Nicene and Post-Nicene Fathers, First Series, vol. 8, ed. Philip Schaff (Buffalo, NY: Christian Literature Publishing, 1888), Psalm 89, paragraph 41. Revised and edited for New Advent by Kevin Knight, www.newadvent.org/fathers/1801089.htm.

[10] Quoted in Henri de Lubac, *The Christian Faith: An Essay on the Structure of the Apostles' Creed* (London: Geoffrey Chapman, 1986), 201.

for with the heart spiritually to touch Christ is to know that He is equal with the Father.[11]

The vision of the church that Kuyper received from Yonge's novel thus has an illustrious pedigree. However, this belief in "mother church" got derailed after the Reformation en route to modern Protestantism, with a growing emphasis on the individual. "Stress was placed on the religious personality, on the subjective experiences and feelings of the individual soul. Not much room was left for the church, neither for its creeds and confessions nor for its liturgical life and church offices."[12]

Thus once again we see just how contemporary are Kuyper's concerns. The Lutheran theologian Carl Braaten is, like Kuyper, concerned to retrieve the place of the church. He writes in the introduction to his important book *Mother Church*, "I write in the conviction that Protestants . . . need to rediscover the idea and experience of the church as mother. . . . It signifies life as we are born from her womb; it signifies identity as we are offspring of the bride of Christ; it signifies nourishment as from her hands we receive food and drink, the very body and blood of our Lord Jesus Christ."[13]

Apart from the individualism of modern Protestantism, Braaten foregrounds further concerns that Kuyper shared in his own context. Churches are characterized by the dilution of distinctively Christian beliefs, by accommodation to the *Zeitgeist*, by biblical illiteracy among the laity and a lack of faithfulness to Scripture among clergy and theologians. "The high toleration of heresy and apostasy causes heart failure in the Christian organism. . . . Uniting churches that have lost their way would be like the blind leading the blind."[14]

Kuyper would have said a hearty "Amen" to Braaten's definition of the church: "The church is Christ as his bodily presence in the world, prefiguring the future of the world in the kingdom of God." As we will see below, like Kuyper, Braaten is concerned to navigate between a dead orthodoxy and a

---

[11]Augustine, "Ten Homilies on the First Epistle of John," in P. Schaff, ed., *St. Augustine: Homilies on the Gospel of John, Homilies on the First Epistle of John, Soliloquies*, trans. H. Browne and J. H. Myers (New York: Christian Literature Company, 1888), 476, emphasis added.

[12]Carl E. Braaten, *Mother Church: Ecclesiology and Ecumenism* (Minneapolis: Fortress, 1998), 3. Cf. Gordon J. Spykman, *Reformational Theology: A New Paradigm for Doing Dogmatics* (Grand Rapids: Eerdmans, 1992), 433-35.

[13]Braaten, *Mother Church*, 2.

[14]Ibid., 4.

false liberalism. "The institutional level should be a sign and servant of what the Spirit of God is doing to build up the one body of which Christ is the head. Otherwise the organized institutional church can become a dying and empty shell, what Harnack called 'the aroma of an empty bottle' and worse, possibly an enemy of the kingdom of God in league with the anti-Christ."[15] *Unlike Kuyper, Braaten is concerned to breathe fresh life into the ecumenical movement, largely a movement that came after Kuyper's life, but one of which he would have been wary. Braaten's concern, nevertheless, will allow us to inquire critically into the capacity of Kuyper's ecclesiology to promote healthy Christian unity, as we will see below.*

KUYPER AND THE CHURCH

> Much of Kuyper's theology stemmed from his ecclesiology, from "thinking through his church ideal and his striving to realize it."...[16]
>
> Yet ecclesiology had central importance for Kuyper in its own right. It marked the crossroads where his twin passions of divine sovereignty and social formation intersected.[17]

James Bratt identifies three phases in Kuyper's evolving theology of the church.[18] From his graduate studies at Leiden until his pastorate in Amsterdam, Kuyper developed a theology of the church, moving from an emphasis on inner spirituality to an assertion of the fixed forms of Calvinism. From 1875 through to the Doleantie he emphasized soteriology over ecclesiology and focused on church law in particular. In the third phase he concentrated on Calvinism and on culture rather than church. As a theologian Kuyper began with the church and concluded with culture, with Calvinism as the glue

---

[15]Ibid., 7, 9.

[16]*AK*, 172.

[17]*AK*, 173.

[18]*AK*, 172-73. Kuyper never wrote a systematic theology, but "Locus de Ecclesias," in his *Dictaten Dogmatiek van Dr. A. Kuyper*, IV (Grand Rapids: J. B. Hulst, 1912), should also be taken into account. In terms of secondary literature on Kuyper and the church see P. A. Van Leeuwen, *Het Kerkbegrip in de Theologie van Abraham Kuyper* (Franeker, Netherlands: T. Wever, 1946); Henry Zwaanstra, "Abraham Kuyper's Conception of the Church," *CTJ* 9 (1974): 149-81; John H. Wood, *Going Dutch in the Modern Age: Abraham Kuyper's Struggle for a Free Church in the Nineteenth-Century Netherlands Century* (New York: Oxford University Press, 2013); Michael Wagenman, "A Critical Analysis of the Power of the Church in the Ecclesiology of Abraham Kuyper" (PhD diss., University of Bristol, 2014). G. C. Berkouwer repeatedly engages with Kuyper in his *Dogmatics*, and it is thus useful to consult his *The Church*, which I will reference in footnotes at appropriate points.

connecting the two. One must not forget that Kuyper's ecclesiology stands within his broader theology, one that was strongly trinitarian and God-centered, focused on redemption in Christ, emphasized personal and cosmic renewal or *palingenesis*, and celebrated the kingship of Christ.

Calvin and Laski. In chapter one we noted that Kuyper wrote a prize-winning essay on a comparison of Laski's and Calvin's views of the church. Jan Laski (1499–1560) was a Polish reformer who pastored churches at Emden (east Frisia, the northern border region between the Netherlands and Germany) and then, at the invitation of Archbishop Thomas Cranmer, pastored a church of Dutch refugees in London. The essay shows that even before his conversion Kuyper recognized the importance of the question of the church and was appalled at its current state. He argues that a Christian theologian must be driven by a desire to investigate the true concept of the church far better and then to embody it in his life. Kuyper is far more critical in this essay of Calvin than he was after his conversion back to Calvinism in Beesd. However, even after that rediscovery of Calvin, he continued to draw on themes we find in his work on Calvin and Laski.

In his essay Kuyper attends to the history of the theology of the church and argues that finally Schleiermacher has brought out into the open the truest notion of the church, showing the strength of the church in the mutual union and close cohesion in Christ of Christians.[19] Kuyper is at pains to inquire after the New Testament view of the church and notes that it is a spiritual brotherhood of God's children. He plays down any external form, foregrounding the church as a friendly association characterized by the pursuit of truth and virtue.

Kuyper finds Calvin and Laski both at fault in seeking a close bond between church and state. Overall, however, he finds Laski far closer to the essence of the church than Calvin. For Kuyper, Laski came much closer to the intention of the gospel in that he attended less to the consensus of church doctrine, but returns always to the gospel and proclaims Christ himself to the people rather than the received doctrine of Christ. Laski saw that the church would not be one because of unity in all doctrine but because, full of the Spirit and burning with the love of Christ, it loved one another in a holy way.

---

[19]Cf. Friedrich Schleiermacher, *On Religion: Speeches to Its Cultured Despisers*, 2nd ed., trans. Richard Crout, Cambridge Texts in the History of Philosophy (Cambridge: Cambridge University Press, 1988, 1996); *The Christian Faith* (London: T&T Clark, 1999).

Beesd. On August 9, 1863, Kuyper was officially installed as pastor, by his father, of the church in the Nederlandse Hervormde Kerk church at Beesd. By this time he had been converted, and in his early sermons at Beesd Kuyper articulated a view of the church with the following characteristics:[20]

1. The church is a free community of faithful believers,

2. voluntarily gathered through loyalty to Christ,

3. made alive by the work of the Spirit in the heart,

4. performs works of righteousness in the world, and

5. thus sows the seeds of the kingdom of God,

6. which is the distinctive teaching of Jesus.

Here we see continuity with the view argued for in his prize-winning essay. It was, for example, from Schleiermacher—and Laski—that Kuyper appropriated the ideal of the church as a free, voluntary community.[21] In this schema of the church external forms were secondary.

Utrecht. It was during his time at Beesd that Kuyper experienced his conversion to Calvinism. Kuyper's stay at Beesd was short, and on November 10, 1867, he was installed as pastor at the Domkerk in Utrecht. His recovery of Calvinism led Kuyper to an emphasis on the adherence to the confessions and forms of the church, and thus to a concern with the external forms of the church. This marked a shift, but continuity is found in his concern over the state of the national church and the urgent need for reform and purification. Even while at Beesd Kuyper was a vocal critic of the national church.

In his farewell sermon at Utrecht on July 31, 1870, "Conservatism and Orthodoxy: False and True Preservation," plus his first two sermons in Amsterdam, Kuyper attempted a full and definitive answer to the church question, an answer that was modern but orthodox, confessional but engaged, democratic and certainly disestablished. As Bratt observes, "Calvin would marry á Lasco."[22] For his farewell sermon Kuyper took as his text the second part of Revelation 3:11, "hold fast to what you have" (NRSV).

In this farewell sermon he recalls his first sermon at Utrecht, "The Incarnation of God: The Life-Principle of the Church," and notes, "As some of you

---

[20]*AK*, 173.
[21]*AK*, 174.
[22]*AK*, 56.

may remember it concerned the problem of the church. I spoke of that as being, in my opinion, the primary problem of the day." He reaffirms this as a great need of the day: "The absence of a church worthy of the name swelled the demand for its reconstruction."[23] He asks his congregation to imagine the reborn power of a free church. In this respect he argues that the Reformation did not go far enough in severing the bond of church and state, with the result that the Reformed church saw its life freeze over.

Kuyper asserts that in the culture of the Netherlands there is a new awareness of the influence of the church: "Now people on either side no longer deny the decisive weight that the church can bring to bear in the struggle over the schools, society, and the life of the people. Now people can more readily believe the truth that the problem of the church is none other than the problem of Christianity itself."[24] However, such a time of recognition is also a time of danger for the church. There is a great need to listen to Christ's exhortation to "hold fast to what you have."

"Hold fast" is not a call to a deadly conservatism. In chapter three we saw how for Kuyper a false conservatism is devoid of power. Kuyper provocatively calls this "sin" and maintains that a false conservatism seeks to maintain the sin-sick life as it is. "How . . . could Christianity refrain from fulminating against a conservatism . . . which seeks to dam up the stream of life, swears by the status quo, and resists the surgery needed to save the sick?"[25]

This sickness manifests itself in three forms: first, the desire to recall the old, to repristinate; second, the desire to retain only what is left of the Reformed legacy; and third, only to preserve what the enemy has left for us. None of these are acceptable to Kuyper: "But if your boundary has become uncertain, vague, even invisible, the fear of drawing your sword soon keeps your hand from the hilt." The result is that "the church of Christ has become a valley of dry bones rather than a field teeming with life."[26]

In contrast to false conservatism Kuyper argues for a healthy conservatism. "True conservatism seeks to preserve what is in terms of what it will become in Christ, that is, resurrected from the dead." The spirit of Christianity must

---

[23]*AK:CR*, 67.
[24]*AK:CR*, 69.
[25]*AK:CR*, 71.
[26]*AK:CR*, 77.

be retained at all cost: "That life which you have in Christ, that life in its uniqueness, in its sharply delineated principle, and in its eternal fullness—to have and to hold that life is our sacred calling. . . . For only that Christianity has in it the germ of life which can regenerate the world, and you are the ones called to bring that life to the world."[27] But the form in which this spirit is manifested as church must evolve with the times, and it is the responsibility of the church to search for new forms.[28]

Kuyper's view of the church is inseparable from his desire for God's people to play a formative role in their culture, a calling that is hindered by a false conservatism as it is by a capitulation to modernism. The Christian life is inherently both personal and social. Using a somewhat unusual metaphor Kuyper asserts, "The Christian spirit is . . . a caustic fluid that has to permeate every drop of your stream of life."[29] He insists,

> Christ does not tolerate our living a double life: our lives must be one, controlled by one principle, wherever it may express itself. Life forms in all its rich ramifications one high and holy temple in which the fragrance of the eternal must rise, and whoever wishes to serve at the altar of his soul but not at the altar of life's temple has perhaps been consecrated a priest by himself or others but certainly not by Christ.[30]

Amsterdam. Amsterdam would turn out to be Kuyper's last pastorate. There his conceptual framework reached maturity. Bratt notes of his first three sermons in Amsterdam that with these his conceptual framework was virtually complete, consisting of principial analysis, principial antithesis, principle developed into a worldview; and with the church emerging from the incarnation of Christ marked by its dual character of institute and organism, radiating out into every sphere of life.[31]

Modernism. Kuyper's farewell critique of a false conservatism at Utrecht was counterbalanced by his address "Modernism: A Fata Morgana in the Christian Domain," given the following year in Amsterdam. Kuyper treats modernism as a phenomenon in the church and theology but always as connected with the

---

[27] *AK:CR*, 80, 81.
[28] Cf. *AK*, 57.
[29] *AK:CR*, 82.
[30] *AK:CR*, 82-83.
[31] *AK*, 58-59.

spirit of the age. He begins by asserting that it is far more than a human conflict; draw back the curtain, and one will see that it is a conflict at the spirit level. "The collision of forces that really matter is occurring not here but up there, above us. In our struggles here below we experience only the after-shocks of that massive collision."[32] Such is the enormity of this conflict that one might see the French Revolution as a mere prelude to the current battles.

In such a context Kuyper sees resistance as a duty. "You cannot walk away from your own time but must take it as it is, and the times demand that we either accept the unsettling of our faith or enter the fray. Given this choice, the committed person does not hesitate."[33] Kuyper rightly notes that one must not belittle the enemy; indeed, it is his very appreciation for modernism that gives Kuyper grounds for opposing it.

Kuyper invokes the metaphor of the *fata morgana* to illustrate his critique of modernism. This is a strange but powerful metaphor from the legends of Italian peasantry. *Fata morgana* means the fairy Morgana, and it was believed that Morgana painted on Reggio's horizons a splendid vision.[34] This vision occurred at midday, akin to a mirage, though Kuyper is at pains to distinguish it from a mirage. At midday an extraordinary vision would appear, first of pillars, then colonnades, then magnificent palaces, towns, then of lush meadows, then of infantry and cavalry. It was a vision of fabulous beauty based on the fixed law of refraction since it mirrored the real.

However, it was a vision that vanished soon after it appeared. "Thus the Morgan-phenomenon was fabulously beautiful. It had to come. But it is devoid of all reality! That is why I called Modernism a Fata Morgana in the Christian domain."[35] Kuyper uses this intriguing vision to articulate three main characteristics of modernism.

First, it is beautiful. In the church virginal modernism wrapped itself in the old biblical dress, and it enchanted the best minds, who were tired of Sunday-school Christianity. It had about it a tragic sadness and was human to the core.

---

[32] *AK:CR*, 88.

[33] *AK:CR*, 89-90.

[34] *The Stanford Dictionary of Anglicised Words and Phrases* defines fata morgana as "a peculiar mirage occasionally seen on the straits of Messina, locally attributed to a Fay Morgana" (by C. A. M. Fennell [Cambridge: Cambridge University Press, 1892], 388, online at https://archive.org/stream/stanforddictiona 00fennuoft#page/388/mode/2up). Reggio Calabria is a city in northern Italy on the eastern side of the straits.

[35] *AK:CR*, 91.

Second, intriguingly, Kuyper argues that modernism had to appear, and it is no mistake that it summoned its apostles everywhere across Europe almost at the same time. It is a heresy, according to Kuyper, that "is but a necessary refraction of the beams of Christianity in the spiritual atmosphere of a given age." In every age one heresy finds an ideal breeding ground, and modernism manifests the same traits as other heresies, in line with the spirit of the particular context.[36] Kuyper asserts that major heresies always appear when knowledge resurfaces, and he highlights the fourth, ninth, and sixteenth centuries in this respect. The nineteenth century is another case in point. A resounding heresy was bound to surface since the light of knowledge had surfaced again, and modernism could only arise because there is a Christian church in our age, whose light it could refract.

Kuyper argues that the age is one of realism, a realism in reaction to the bankruptcy of philosophy, the impotence of revolution, expansion in the study of nature, and the somnolence of the church. He discerns strength and weakness in this realism. Negatively, there looms the fatal abyss of materialism, accompanied by a tendency toward the right of the most powerful, manifested not least in the dream of communism and the resort to violence.

Positively, modernism has tried to react against this and attempted to defend faith. Its strategy, however, was to try to mediate between the spirit of the age and faith, what we would nowadays in theology call correlation.[37] "How grandly that effort might have been rewarded if people had only let themselves be led to the realism of Scripture." Kuyper appeals to Franz von Baader's (1764–1841) statement that "corporeality is the end of the road of God."[38] Baader was a mystic-romantic theologian at the Catholic University of Munich. Kuyper found in Baader a theologian who could help defend the faith from both a false spiritualism and a false dualism.[39]

---

[36]*AK:CR*, 98.

[37]Cf. David Tracy, *Blessed Rage for Order: The New Pluralism in Theology* (Chicago: University of Chicago Press, 1975, 1996), 79-81.

[38]*AK:CR*, 102.

[39]In recent years von Bader and the relationship between von Baader and Kuyper have received renewed attention; see Leo Mietus, *Gunning en Kuyper in 1878: A. Kuypers Polemiek tegen het Leven van Jesus van J. H. Gunning Jr.*, Brochurereeks 28 (Velp, Netherlands: Bond van Vrije Evangelische Gemeenten in Nederland, 2009); Peter Koslowski, ed., *Die Philosophie, Theologie und Gnosis Franz von Baaders: Spekulatives Denken zwischen Aufklärung, Restauration und Romantik* (Vienna: Passagen Verlag, 1993); Peter Koslowski, *Philosophien der Offenbarung, Antiker Gnoticizmus, Franz von Baader, Schelling* (Vienna: Ferdinand Schöningh, 2001); J. G. Friesen, *Neo-Calvinism and Christian Theosophy: Franz von Baader, Abraham*

Modernism, however, had bowed before the majesty of our age and sought compromise with its spirit. Kuyper asserts that modernists have erased the boundary separating the sacred from the profane, a boundary that can never be crossed with impunity.[40] He notes that modernists like to claim the name "Protestants" for themselves, but by contrast they take human authority as their starting point, acting as though we were still in Eden.

Third and finally, Kuyper argues that, like the Fata Morgana, modernism is devoid of reality. He quotes the Romantic poet Bürger:

> Hurrah! The swift ride of the dead,
> But does it not fill you, my dear, with dread![41]

Modernism has built a beautiful temple that is meant to house all of life, but it is devoid of reality. Its God is an abstraction, a projection of desire as eternally beautiful love. The real test of a theology is its affirmation that God speaks, whereas modernism follows a god like Hamlet's ghost, who does not speak. Prayer is regarded merely as an outpouring of the soul; God is not someone one petitions and who answers prayer. The modernists deny divine government and do not take seriously the curse under which creation struggles. In their morality there is no knowledge of real sin. They speak of pursuing the ideal but, as Kuyper notes, it is not we who hound the ideal but the ideal that hounds us: "Bethlehem's cradle and that open sepulcher behind Golgotha are the holy realities in which alone that ideal can be known."[42]

Kuyper finds modernism wanting theologically. Modernism has an historical sense, but it presents Jesus of Nazareth to us in the image of a modern theologian.[43] The problem with modernism is its flawed lens, whereby it fancies itself to be objective. It professes to be very inclusive but is, in fact, stubbornly dogmatic.

As Bratt perceptively notes in a footnote, Kuyper's characterization of Modernism anticipates H. Richard Niebuhr's famous comment that liberals believed that a "God without wrath brought men without sin into a kingdom

---

Kuyper, Herman Dooyeweerd (Calgary: Aevum Books, 2015); Friesen, "The Mystical Dooyeweerd Once Again: Kuyper's Use of Franz von Baader," *Ars Disputandi* 3 (2003), www.tandfonline.com/doi/abs/10 .1080/15665399.2003.10819803.

[40]*AK:CR*, 104.

[41]*AK:CR*, 104.

[42]*AK:CR*, 113.

[43]*AK:CR*, 114.

without judgment through the ministrations of a Christ without a Cross."[44] As regards the church, for modernists it lacks every essential attribute, being characterized by free inquiry, which is said to equate with the spirit of the Reformation. Kuyper concludes,

> Wherever we threw out the plumbline, the bottom of reality sank away beneath us. No real God, no real prayer, no real divine government, the reality of human life under threat, no real sin, no real ideal, no genuine history, no true criticism, no dogma that could withstand scrutiny, nor a real church. We found the names and shadows of all these but no rootedness in real being.[45]

Kuyper nevertheless argues that modernism has been a blessing as well; it has saved orthodoxy, but only as cutting a cankerous root saves a plant.

Organism and institute. In his *Lectures on Calvinism* Kuyper says of Calvinism that its impulse was to adore God in the church and serve him in his world. "But it remained the special trait of Calvinism that it placed the believer before the face of God, not only in his church, but also in his personal, family, social, and political life."[46] The challenge for Kuyper was how to articulate this ecclesiologically. How does one relate the church as an institution to the life of the people of God as a whole in society? One way in which he responded to this challenge was with his theory of sphere sovereignty, as we saw in chapter six. The institutional church was a separate *sphere* in society, and this was by God's design. But how does the institutional church as a separate sphere relate to all the other spheres of life? To articulate this Kuyper came up with what some consider one of his most penetrating insights, though, as with worldview and sphere sovereignty, he does not articulate it with systematic precision.[47] Kuyper's solution is to argue that as the body of Christ the church is both institute and organism. Kuyper addressed this issue in his Amsterdam inaugural, titled *Rooted and Grounded*.

In the preface Kuyper poses the question of whether orthodoxy is fighting for a life principle or a few incidental consequences.[48] He argues that while we find the true principle in orthodoxy, insofar as the orthodox are not living

---

[44]*AK:CR*, 116n35. The quote is from H. Richard Niebuhr, *The Kingdom of God in America* (Chicago: Harper & Row, 1937), 193.

[45]*AK:CR*, 118.

[46]*LC*, 20-21, 57.

[47]Cf. Spykman, *Reformational Theology*, 429-80.

[48]*R&G*, xxiii.

by this principle they are impotent. Nonconservatives are influential in shaping public life, but this influence dissipates because it is not rooted and grounded in the true principle.[49]

The great need of the hour, according to Kuyper, is a church that is both organism *and* institution, two characteristics held together in a free church. The title, *Rooted and Grounded*, is taken from Ephesians 3:17. It is worth quoting the section in its totality:

> For this reason I kneel before the Father, from whom every family in heaven and on earth derives its name. I pray that out of his glorious riches he may strengthen you with power through his Spirit in your inner being, so that Christ may dwell in your hearts through faith. And I pray that you, *being rooted and established in love*, may have power, together with all the Lord's holy people, to grasp how wide and long and high and deep is the love of Christ, and to know this love that surpasses knowledge—that you may be filled to the measure of all the fullness of God.
>
> Now to him who is able to do immeasurably more than all we ask or imagine, according to his power that is at work within us, to him be glory in the church and in Christ Jesus throughout all generations, for ever and ever! Amen. (Eph 3:14-21)

In the Greek Ephesians 3:17 reads as follows: κατοικῆσαι τὸν Χριστὸν διὰ τῆς πίστεως ἐν ταῖς καρδίαις ὑμῶν, ἐν ἀγάπῃ ἐρριζωμένοι καὶ τεθεμελιωμένοι. The verb θεμελιόω can mean "to lay a foundation," and ῥιζόομαι can mean "to be rooted," so Kuyper is in line with the biblical text in his exegesis, although the development of the metaphors is his own. Kuyper understands rooted as an *organic* metaphor and grounded as one of building, that is, an *institutional* metaphor. Kuyper invokes other organic metaphors in the New Testament and especially that of the body for the life of the people of God. *Grounded* evokes for Kuyper the building of the church by human hands. The two must be held together: "By means of the person who sows and plants, the metaphor of vital growth overflows into that of the institution; by means of the living stone, the metaphor of the building flows over into that of the organism."[50]

The organic nature of the church fits with how God has created. Creation was fashioned by God, but humanity is called to develop the powers hidden

---

[49]*R&G*, xxv.
[50]*R&G*, 5.

in the creation. Without sin, however, there would have been no need for the church: "Had sin not come, Eden would have been cultivated, creation would gradually have been perfected, until finally it would have joined together with the life of heaven and transitioned into eternal glory."[51] The life that exists in Christ is a miracle of grace and does not proceed from sin-affected nature. Kuyper argues that today a double stream flows through the creation: the old life and a new stream, one that comes down from God's holy mountain. That new life needs a new form in a new institution, namely the church.

> The church is an organism because she bears a unique life within herself and self-consciously upholds the independence of that life over against the old life. The church is an organism because she lives according to her own rule and must follow her own vital law. The church is an organism, finally, because what will later unfold from her buds is fully supplied already within her seed.[52]

As institution, the church is the ordained means for feeding and expanding the organism. Kuyper invokes the image of the church as our mother, called to nurture believers: "To nurture means specifically to bring to the child the treasure that was acquired thus far, leading everyone along the pathway already cleared. The essence of nurture is to unleash, to feed, and to prune fully organic life, according to a fixed protocol chosen purposefully, according to an unswerving principle that governs the entire context."[53]

At Pentecost the Spirit created the church, but from then on the institution inevitably emerged, since Word and sacrament require human consciousness and participation. It is only through the institutional church sphere that we can be nourished on the life of the Spirit. Indeed, the life of the heart, the spiritual center of our existence, can only be awakened in the context of the nurturing atmosphere of the institutional church.[54]

In *Rooted and Grounded* Kuyper articulates the closest relationship between the institutional church and the other spheres of life:

> For that reason we have such an institution that is itself thoroughly formed, that works formatively upon the individual, structurally upon the family, directively upon society, and that chooses the Christian school as her vestibule. An

---

[51]*R&G*, 9; cf. 19-20.
[52]*R&G*, 11.
[53]*R&G*, 15, 16.
[54]*R&G*, 16-17.

institution that calls into being, from the roots of its own life, a unique science and art, that strives in its confession for a more correct expression of the eternal truth and for an ever purer worship of the Holy One.[55]

Kuyper distinguishes the visible church from the kingdom of God. He compares the visible church to scaffolding of a building that one day will fall away, and the glorious temple of the kingdom will be manifested.

If the role of the institutional church is to nurture believers, then it follows that the church is made up of believers. Kuyper argues that in this respect the church needs to be reformed to be the church.

> The marketplace of the world, not the church, is the arena where we wrestle for the prize, the racetrack where we wage the contest for the wreath. Far from being that battlefield itself, the church is rather like the army tent of the Lord where soldiers strengthen themselves before that battle, where they treat their wounds after the battle, and where one who has become "prisoner by the sword of the Word" is fed at the table of the Lord.[56]

Not surprisingly, therefore, Kuyper calls for freedom for the church to be the church. "We must *rebuild or relocate.*" The church must be free from the state, free from the control of money, and free from excessive control of the office of the minster. "One who holds office must be rooted in the priesthood of the church. Apart from that intimate relationship, the office becomes domineering."[57]

Kuyper concludes his *Rooted and Grounded* with a call for a Reformed church in which "God is her sovereign, eternal election is the heart blood of her life, and God's Word the foundation that cannot be dislodged, upon which she stands with both her feet." However, his vision of the Reformed church is one in which local autonomy is upheld: the "self-government and self-direction of the congregation." He envisages a close relationship between the church and the voluntary associations that have come into existence. The Reformed church must be open to development and cannot ignore the social issues of promiscuity and overpopulation, of labor and poverty. The church is called to support the rights of the poor: "Let whatever is oppressed have the church's support: may the poor find the church to be a place of refuge, and

---

[55]*R&G*, 17.
[56]*R&G*, 22.
[57]*R&G*, 25, 29.

may the church become for rich and poor together once again an Angel of peace who gently leads us from both the abuses and the utopias of our age back to the ordinance of God's Word."[58]

In 1875 Kuyper attended a holiness convention in Brighton in the United Kingdom. He was struck by the life and vitality of the movement but appalled when the leader was exposed for adultery. Shortly thereafter, Kuyper experienced his first nervous breakdown. Inter alia this caused him to think hard about the doctrine of the Holy Spirit, which became his major project of the 1880s and resulted in his well-known book *The Work of the Holy Spirit*. When he returned more than a year later, he chose to enter politics rather than stay on as pastor of the Amsterdam church.

DOLEANTIE

It will be apparent from our discussion thus far that Kuyper was deeply motivated to promote a pure and free church. Maneuverings toward a new denomination began in 1882. Kuyper used his position as an elder in the Amsterdam church council to step up the orthodox cause and began a series of lectures that became the *Tractate on the Reformation of the Churches*, published in 1883. Kuyper argued, as we have already seen, that the essence of the church is present fully in the local congregation, and any broader association such as synod or denomination is entirely voluntary. Synods and classes do not constitute the church; indeed, it is only by being freed from the synodical apparatus that the faithful can be reopened to the power of the Spirit.

A frustrating issue was the plight of the theological graduates of the Free University of Amsterdam, which the national church would not recognize for ministry. The village of Kootwijk, without a minister for eighteen years, was encouraged to call J. H. Houtzagers, who would be the first graduate of the Free University. Kootwijk issued him a call, but the classis refused to certify it. A number of pastors got together, examined him, and validated the call. The newly appointed (on February 7, 1886) Houtzagers was officially deposed, but the protest spread.

In Amsterdam the orthodox had the upper hand, and pairs of elders were delegated to shadow the three remaining modernist ministers. On the

---

[58]*R&G*, 31, 33.

recommendation of these elders the council refused to accept the credentials for membership of young people catechized under their tutelage. The modernists appealed successfully to the provincial synod, and the general synod upheld the decision. In the process the dispute became about church property. In December 1885 eighty members (75 percent) of the Amsterdam church council approved a revision in the bylaws so that church property would be awarded to those loyal to the confessions in the case of depositions or schism. They were suspended from office by the classis, and in the latter half of 1886 the suspension was upheld by the provincial synod and then the general synod. In the same month that the suspension was upheld by the provincial synod, Kuyper preached a sermon titled "It Shall Not Be So Among You."[59] It is a moving address, oscillating between clear denunciation of the national church hierarchy and an appeal to Kuyper's followers not to sin in their indignation. He is aware of the dangers and says to his fellow Christians: "If it cannot be said that there is more of Christ to be seen among us than among our oppressors, a blasting wind will blow through our ranks and our enthusiasm will go up in smoke."[60] Kuyper is wonderfully clear that

> all power in the church of Christ must forever be traced back to Christ. He and He alone is our King. To Him alone is given all power in heaven and on earth. And just as the sun has been set in the sky above as the greater light to rule the day, so the Son of righteousness shines out from above to exercise lordship over the church militant on earth. He is the Immanuel, beside Him there is no other. He is the rule in Israel, but only after letting Himself be trampled to give his life as a ransom for many.[61]

In January 1887 Kuyper convened a national church conference that essentially initiated a new denomination, the Nederduitsch Gereformeerde Kerk (the Doleantie). In some ways this turned out not to be Kuyper's finest hour. By the end of 1887 the Doleantie numbered only 150 out of the national church's 1,350 congregations. Kuyper's concern for a pure church was admirable, but his horror of hierarchy and bureaucracy left crucial questions of church government unanswered. He despised synods, at least the heterodox ones of the nineteenth century, but wanted the decisions of the Synod of

---

[59]AK:CR, 125-40.
[60]AK:CR, 139.
[61]AK:CR, 131.

Dordt to be binding. The split also divided Kuyper's supporters in church matters, many of whom remained in the national church. In 1892 the Doleantie merged with the Christelijke Gereformeerde Kerk to become the Gereformeerde Kerken in Nederland.

LITURGY

Although Kuyper's journey once he left the pastorate took him into many areas of life, he never relinquished his passion for the church. For example, some twenty-five years after he left the parsonage in Amsterdam, in 1874, he took up again the issue of liturgical reform in *De Heraut*, in a series of articles eventually published in 1911 as *Our Worship*.[62] Although *Our Worship* preceded the liturgical renewal of the twentieth century, and though some of the issues Kuyper addresses are now dated, there remains wonderfully rich material in this book.

If one needed evidence of the unique, indispensable role of the institutional church as one sphere among the many societal spheres, one finds it in *Our Worship*. Scripture uses *worship* for both the assembly of believers (Jn 4:24) and the life of God's people as a whole in response to what Christ has done for us (Rom 12:1). Both are good uses of *worship*, but the vital importance of the *assembly of believers*, as Kuyper repeatedly calls it, should not be blurred.[63] Kuyper is crystal clear that attendance at the worship service is indispensable for the believer: "For the congregation of the living God, this meeting with God together is not just advisable, desirable, and sanctifying, as it is for a household, a family, an institution, or a society, but it is in the most absolute sense *indispensable* and *essential*."[64]

Of course, Kuyper stresses that all of life is to be lived before and for God:

It is not, of course, that the practicing of worship consists exclusively in going to church. Rather, it must be the one, grand, royal action of our whole life, in all our thoughts, words and deeds. We are always God's priests, called to serve his holy purposes. In your family you must serve your God from early in the morning to late in the evening, and thus ceaselessly exercise the service of God,

---

[62]English ed., Abraham Kuyper, *Our Worship*, ed. Harry Boonstra (Grand Rapids: Eerdmans, 2009).

[63]See John Bolt's salient comments in his "All of Life Worship? Abraham Kuyper and the Neo-Kuyperians," in Kuyper, *Our Worship*, 321-29.

[64]Kuyper, *Our Worship*, 14.

and you and your family members gather around the Word and join in God's praise and adoration. In the same way, all members of the congregation must each according to their own calling serve God.[65]

However, says Kuyper, our service of God only comes to *full expression* when the assembly gathers for the express purpose of honoring God, praising him, and praying to him. He distinguishes between an *unmediated* and a *mediated* worship. Our daily life should be a mediated worship, whereas we assemble for unmediated worship, in which we pause in our daily lives, to focus intentionally on God together.[66]

The assembly is the appointed place for God's people to meet with God. "We must understand this clearly. God is alive. And we are dealing with this living God." Christ is central to the assembly: "thus emerges the crucial element of the worship service of the congregation—*the Christ*. The congregation assembles only as one in him."[67] The world and our daily lives divert us so easily from following God so that we need a counterbalance, a respite, a place to refocus, and this is provided by worship. John Bolt expresses this well: "Christian worship is distinguished from the daily life of service to God by the liturgy of God's called-out and assembled people in which they practice a storied communion with God that loosens their ties with and involvement in the world's counterstories."[68]

The worship service is the context in which God speaks to us, through the sermon and the reading of the Word:

> The custom to bare the head during the reading of the Word arose from that realization. And once this is clearly perceived, then all will feel at once the high significance to be accorded to the reading of Holy Scripture. For it is God himself speaking through and in his Word, without human addition, explanation, or application. . . . Now in the midst of the assembled people God communicates the Word as his Word.[69]

Kuyper is insightful too on the nature of preaching. The sermon is *not* a lecture but proclamation of the Word of God. It is more than instruction. The

---

[65]Ibid., 18.
[66]Ibid.
[67]Ibid., 126, 17.
[68]Bolt, "All of Life Worship?," 326.
[69]Kuyper, *Our Worship*, 162-63.

preacher does not perform for listeners but is present as an ambassador of the Lord; "he has to give the congregation something from God and in his name."[70]

For Kuyper, therefore, there is an integral relationship between our mediated and our unmediated worship. In his comments on the conclusion of the service, Kuyper notes that the congregation "should not feel as if by going home they are now leaving their God behind, who met them in the house of prayer. On the contrary, the service must prompt the congregation to feel near to God, also as they live their lives in the world."[71] Indeed, Kuyper suggests that the congregation should stand during the concluding song, to indicate that they are now ready to go out into the world!

Kuyper's *Our Worship* is comprehensive in its range of topics and surprisingly contemporary at many points. He rightly critiques the one-man ministry, stresses in a wonderful way the experiential aspect of worship, is somewhat open to the use of the church calendar, conceives of the liturgy as a whole, and is attentive to the aesthetics of church architecture even as he rightly acknowledges that the building is not essential to the assembly.[72] He delightfully suggests that we think of our church buildings as forecourts, since the temple is now in heaven, and rightly argues that church architecture must fit the purpose of the institutional church.[73] He asserts, "The building must also communicate something. There must be something alive in the whole of it. It should not be mute but it should speak to the receptive spirit. . . . And you desire that kind of lofty language from such a building not only when you take your place inside it, but also when you approach it from a distance."[74]

MISSION

In a real sense Kuyper's entire worldview and theology is mission on steroids. We will attend to the Kuyperian tradition and mission in chapter eight. For

---

[70]Ibid., 189.

[71]Ibid., 210.

[72]Ibid., 103, 15, 180. See Craig G. Bartholomew, "The Church and the World: The Power of Identity," in *Signposts of God's Liberating Kingdom: Perspectives for the Twenty-First Century* (Potchefstroom, South Africa: IRS, Potchefstroom University for CHE, 1998), 1:21-30.

[73]Kuyper, *Our Worship*, 66. I am grateful to Harry Van Dyke for pointing out to me that the octagonal church in Dordrecht tried to follow Kuyper's proposals on worship and church architecture. See Protestantse Wijkgemeente Wilhelminakerk-Petruskapel te Dordrecht, www.dewilhelminakerk.nl (accessed Aug. 16, 2016).

[74]Kuyper, *Our Worship*, 66.

now, it should be noted that Kuyper's mature reflections on mission are contained in his 1890 address. He treats mission mainly as evangelism,[75] and, as we will see in chapter eight, it is to J. H. Bavinck, Herman's nephew, that we need to look for seminal, mature work on a Kuyperian view of mission. However, there is an aspect of Kuyper's 1890 lecture that merits close attention.

Kuyper articulates *a trinitarian view of mission*: "All mission activity done through creatures is simply an adumbration, a reflection, or an instrument of the only principal mission, that of the Son through the Father." Kuyper is clear that "Christ is *the* Missionary. He conducts his mission."[76] Similarly, in his *The Work of the Holy Spirit*, Kuyper evocatively notes, "The Son does not distribute His treasures, but the Holy Spirit." Furthermore, Kuyper is closely attuned to the work of the Spirit in creation and the connection between this and his role in redemption and re-creation. He rejects the view that sees regeneration as the principal work of the Spirit and affirms, "the Holy Spirit remains in creation and re-creation the one omnipotent Worker of all life and quickening," thereby seeking to hold together the unity of the work of the Spirit in nature and grace.[77]

As we will see in chapter eight, missiology was revolutionized in the twentieth century through a rediscovery of mission as above all else the *missio Dei*. In the course of the centuries the integral link between mission and the trinitarian God had been lost sight of. David Bosch poignantly comments, "Unfortunately the relationship between the original and the modern meaning of *missio* has for a long time not been recognized. *Abraham Kuyper was one of the first theologians to point this out explicitly*."[78] Kuyper does not develop this insight and, as we have noted, confines mission to evangelism. It fell to later twentieth-century missiologists to work out this insight more fully, but the genius of Kuyper in drawing attention to this issue must be noted.[79]

---

[75]But see *AK*, 58, for Kuyper's critique of an evangelistic group for being too narrow in its focus.

[76]"Lecture by Prof. Dr. A. Kuyper Concerning 'Missions,' Mission Congress in Amsterdam, 28-30 January, 1890" (forthcoming), point 2. See also P. N. Holtrop, ed., *ZGKN100 Een bundel opstellen over de Zending van de Gereformeerde Kerken in Nederland ter gelegenheid van de honderjarige herdenking van de Synode van Middelburg 1896* (Kampen: WZOK, 1996).

[77]Abraham Kuyper, *The Work of the Holy Spirit*, trans. Henri de Vries (Grand Rapids: Eerdmans, 1900), 211, 47.

[78]David Bosch, *Witness to the World: The Christian Mission in Theological Perspective* (London: Marshall, Morgan and Scott, 1980), 240, emphasis added.

[79]Ibid., 239-48.

SPIRITUALITY

Both Kuyper and Bavinck were wary of Catholic mysticism, but both stressed the vital importance of a living faith in Christ that was nurtured above all in the assembly of believers but also in private and in family devotions. We will return to the issue of spirituality in chapter twelve. For now, it should be noted that a still largely untapped legacy of Kuyper's is his many meditations and books of devotional reflections.[80] Kuyper's concern in this regard is clearly expressed in his first devotional in *To Be Near unto God*:

> Thus for many years you may have had a general love for God and yet have never come to know God. This knowledge of God only comes when love for Him begins to take on a personal character; when on the pathway of life for the first time you have met Him; when the Lord has become a Personal Presence by the side of your own self; when God and you have entered into a conscious, vital, personal, particular relationship—He your Father, you His child.[81]

Kuyper, as we saw in chapter one, recognized the need for conversion, for entry into a personal relationship with God. He was well aware of the problem of the aridity of a barren intellectualism in the Reformed tradition:

> Intellectualism produces, as it were, beautifully shaped, finely cornered and dazzlingly transparent ice-crystals. But underneath that ice the stream of the living water so easily runs dry. . . . This is not necessary. The Fathers of the Church have set us an example. With them we find a virile gift of argument; but it is always permeated with ardent mysticism. . . . Only he who feels, perceives and knows that he stands in personal fellowship with the living God, and who continually tests his spiritual experience by the Word, is safe.[82]

Kuyper's points here are of great import. The vision he opens up in his thought is dazzling but full of challenges and dangers, as he himself discovered. In the absence of a deep spirituality, the Kuyperian tradition cannot be sustained without being distorted or collapsing in on itself. As we will see in

---

[80]See George Harinck, "'Met de telephoon onzen God oproepen.' Kuypers meditaties uit 1905 en 1906," in *Godsvrucht in geschiedenis. Bundel ter gelegenheid van het afscheid van prof. dr. F. Van der Pol als hoogleraar een de Theologische Universiteit Kampen*, ed. Erik A. de Boer and Harm J. Boiten (Heerenveen, 2015), 454-65.

[81]Abraham Kuyper, *To Be Near unto God*, trans. John H. de Vries, Kindle ed. (Vancouver: Regent, 2005), locs. 91-94.

[82]Ibid., locs. 58-68.

chapter twelve, the journey out into the world has to develop out of an ever-deeper journey into Christ.

HERMAN BAVINCK

Bavinck produced his *Reformed Dogmatics* before coming to the Free University of Amsterdam. He deals with the doctrine of the church in part two of the fourth volume of his *Reformed Dogmatics*. Bavinck's work is far more systematic than that of Kuyper on the church, though largely in agreement with him.

For Bavinck, "*A church is and remains the gathered company of true Christ-believers.*" Like Kuyper, he stresses that the church is a living organism and an institution. Bavinck is clearer in his articulation of the relationship between organism and institution than Kuyper, as befits a systematician. Organism and institution are for Bavinck *both* parts of the church *visible*. Organism refers to how "even when all these things [church offices and ministries] are removed from the screen of our mind, the church is still visible. For every believer manifests his or her faith in witness and walk in every sphere of life, and all believers together, with their faith and lives, distinguish themselves from the world." Bavinck grounds the visibility of the church in the incarnation.[83] The church "invisible" reminds us that behind the visible church is an invisible spiritual dimension.

As with Kuyper, so Bavinck is clear that we must not confuse the church as the people of God with the kingdom of God. The benefits of the kingdom are given to God's people on earth for the mission of God's people. The true church really only has one mark, namely that of the Word of God: "fellowship with Christ is bound to fellowship with the word of the apostles." In the real world the church has a shadow side and is marked by schism and apostasy. However, as does Kuyper, so Bavinck encourages us not to reject all diversity, since this characterizes God's creation. Indeed, after the Reformation, "uniformity forever gave way to multiformity."[84]

Like Kuyper, Bavinck uses the image of the church as our mother.[85] The attributes of the church are unity, holiness, catholicity, and apostolicity. Comparing the church with the state, Bavinck asserts, "while church and state are

---

[83]*RD* 4:274, 403-7, 285.
[84]*RD* 4:291, 297-98, 332.
[85]*RD* 4:326, 331, 332.

distinct from each other, the church also distributes its spiritual goods for the benefit of the whole of humanity and for every aspect of human life. This is Christianity's true Catholicity."[86] The gospel is good news not only for the individual but for humanity as a whole: for the family, for society, for the state, for art and academia, for the cosmos, for the entire groaning creation.[87]

As regards the government of the church Bavinck stresses, as does Kuyper, that Christ is the king of the church. If Kuyper stresses the church as a priesthood of believers, Bavinck uses the image of the church as a prophetess, in that all Christians are called to confess Christ. This does not detract from the particular office of the minister. Like Kuyper, Bavinck stresses the local church as a true manifestation of the church, but he has more time for synods than does Kuyper.[88]

EVALUATION

Renewing Mother Church. In the West we live in a day of Christianity lite and of church lite. Christians are now the most persecuted religious group in the world, but it is hard in the West to foreground this phenomenon, let alone to get governments to act on it. When radical Islam—literally—crashed into the West, many journalists were simply unprepared to know how to take religion seriously as a cultural phenomenon. Of course they were aware of Christianity, but the Christianity they encountered had largely succumbed to the privatization of religion characteristic of modernity and thus was of no major social concern.

Years ago, as we noted in our introduction to this chapter, Michael Griffiths spoke of the church as a slumbering giant, similar to Kuyper's critique of the somnolence of the church in his day. As in Kuyper's day, the issue of the church is perhaps *the issue for us today*. On the one hand we have mainstream churches falling over themselves to capitulate to the culture, as per the quote from Braaten at the outset of this chapter. Ernest Gellner contrasts Christianity with Islam in terms of resistance to modernity and sadly but truthfully comments, "Christian doctrine is bowdlerized by its own theologians, and

---

[86]*RD* 4:390.
[87]Herman Bavinck, "The Catholicity of Christianity and the Church," trans. John Bolt, *CTJ* 27 (1992): 220-51. This article is must reading! Cf. *RD* 4:437.
[88]*RD* 4:372-77, 418, 433.

deep literal conviction is not conspicuous by its presence."[89] On the other
hand we have orthodox churches springing up all over the place, but too often
without any nuanced sense of what it means to be the church as both institute
and organism, so that they too end up being a mirror—albeit a conservative
one—of the culture.

In this context Kuyper and Bavinck explode like a bomb. They rightly resist
the bowdlerization of which Gellner speaks, but so too do they forcefully
withstand the privatization of religion. As evangelicals have become more culturally attuned since Lausanne in 1974, as one major landmark, they have too
often lost their hold on doctrine and the church. Not so Kuyper and Bavinck.
For both, the institutional church is indispensable as a sphere within society
and as the place where we encounter God in Christ and hear his Word. Neither
would budge on the infallibility of Scripture, though neither was a fundamentalist. For both, Christ is king of his church and governs it by and through his
Word. Both exalted the office and practice of preaching. Both saw evangelism
as central to the life of the church. One is reminded of Lesslie Newbigin's
description of the local congregation as the "hermeneutic of the Gospel."[90]
Like Kuyper and Bavinck, Newbigin was passionately committed to the importance and relevance of the local congregation.

At the same time, through their masterful articulation of church as organism and institution, they articulate a vision of the church as truly catholic
in the sense of influencing all of life. Neither Kuyper nor Bavinck identify
mission as an attribute of the church, but it is implicit in Bavinck's notion of
catholicity and in both Bavinck's and Kuyper's view of the church as an organism. And it is a view of mission that is comprehensive, decidedly not one
restricted to evangelism. The whole of life is in view, and God's people are
called to give expression to his kingship in all areas of life.

The metaphor of the institutional church as mother evokes the importance
and possibilities of the local church. Just as mothers are indispensable to birth,
growth, nurture, and formation to maturity, so too is the church. Kuyper has
a big view of Christ, and he evokes a big view of the church. The image of
mother, however, also reminds us of the dangers of a dysfunctional church.
Mothers tend to be the primary caregivers in the home, and a range of deep

---

[89]Ernest Gellner, *Postmodernism, Reason and Religion* (London: Routledge, 1992), 6.
[90]Lesslie Newbigin, *The Gospel in a Pluralist Society* (Grand Rapids: Eerdmans, 1989).

psychological problems, such as narcissism, for example, are nowadays traced to an unhealthy mother-child relationship. One fears that too many churches today exercise their motherhood in dysfunctional ways. To take an obvious example, churches that are dualistic and embody a sacred/secular dichotomy will never produce disciples of Jesus who are salt and light in the world.

At its best the institutional church has indeed been a healthy mother through the ages. J. R. R. Tolkien's *Lord of the Rings* was voted "Book of the Century" in a large poll conducted by Waterstones in 1997. Worldwide sales are estimated to run between 150 and 200 million! Tolkien's father died in Bloemfontein, South Africa, when he was very young and while his mother, Mabel, and her two children had returned to England. His beloved mother died when he was twelve.

> The Tolkien biographer Humphrey Carpenter argues that after Mabel's death, the Church became Tolkien's new mother. Carpenter means this in the ordinary psychological sense, that the Church filled in for a missing parent, but it is true also in a deeper sense. . . . Throughout his life, Tolkien would draw comfort, courage, and artistic inspiration from this second mother, who, unlike Mabel, would never die ("Upon this rock I will build my church, and the gates of hell shall not prevail against it").[91]

Imagine what the world and the church would have lost if this had not been the case. We all need a healthy church mother, and few things would advance the case of Christ as much as a renewal in church life that nurtures and forms Christians to become what God intends for them.

A unified church? As we noted in our comparison of Braaten and Kuyper, an important question is whether Kuyper's ecclesiology is adequate to the need for church unity. Kuyper was aware of the need for church unity but celebrates the pluriformity of the church, and he was himself responsible for divisions among Dutch Christians with his formation of the Doleantie. Berkouwer points out that we should not equate Kuyper's concern for pluriformity with relativism or subjectivism, a criticism leveled falsely against Kuyper by Roman Catholic Th. F. Bensdorp in 1909. Kuyper was wrestling with a real problem that continues today. Berkouwer notes that both Kuyper and Roman

---

[91]Philip Zaleski and Carol Zaleski, *The Fellowship: The Literary Lives of the Inklings: J. R. R. Tolkien, C. S. Lewis, Owen Barfield, Charles Williams* (New York: Farrar, Straus and Giroux, 2015), 21.

Catholic theologian Karl Rahner see truth as one, and they connect with each other as regards the limited, and thus varied, understandings of the one truth. "From the nature of the case, there are profound problems here, both for Rahner in connection with the old tradition of the infallible confession of the Church and for Kuyper in connection with pluriformity in confessions."[92]

Berkouwer is deeply sensitive to the challenge of pluriformity, but he rightly, in my view, takes it in a different direction from Kuyper:

> Must the so greatly varied subjectivity inevitably lead to the pluriformity of the Church (in the sense of many concrete churches)? Convinced that this question must be answered in the negative, we want to point out that a different conclusion can be derived from the variations in subjectivity and the plural assimilation of new, modern information than the conclusion that Kuyper drew from history: precisely when plurality becomes more visible than ever before, the call to unity and fellowship gains more force![93]

For Kuyper attempts at church unity were doomed to failure and to be pitied. Unity would only be achieved in the eschaton. Berkouwer rejects this view as easily capitulating to defeatism, of allowing the eschaton to comfort us as we wash our hands of the problematic disunity of the church. Berkouwer insists that the eschaton resists such defeatism and calls us to wrestle with the challenge of unity.[94]

Ironically, it is precisely Kuyper's vision of cultural engagement that makes the unity of believing Christians a priority. The challenges, especially nowadays, are so huge that Christian cooperation, to say nothing of cooperation with cobelligerents from diverse worldviews on specific issues, is essential. This, for example, is what makes Evangelicals and Catholics Together such an important initiative. In practice Kuyper was somewhat contradictory in this respect. He was revolutionary in his recognition of the need for Protestants and Catholics to work together politically, but he comes close to espousing a sort of congregationalism ecclesiologically.

In my view ecumenicity needs to be taken seriously, albeit the sort proposed by theologians such as Lesslie Newbigin and Carl Braaten, and that takes Braaten's statement quoted as the epigraph of this chapter seriously.

---

[92]Berkouwer, Church, 60-61.
[93]Ibid., 62.
[94]Ibid., 35-36.

Braaten's "evangelical catholicism" is attractive, as is Newbigin's similar advocacy for an ecumenism centered on the gospel. Like Braaten, Newbigin is acutely aware of the demise within many mainline denominations of a firm commitment to the "question of the uniqueness, sufficiency and finality of Jesus Christ as the Lord and Saviour of the world." The result is that on the liberal side of Western Christianity we are left with an eviscerated "gospel" that aligns itself primarily with the left wing of our culture and is constitutionally unable "to face the negative as well as the positive implication of the confession of Jesus as Lord."[95] Within the evangelical world we too often retain a commitment to Jesus primarily as a personal savior so that we have little of consequence to say to a world in crisis.

In an important but neglected work, Newbigin points out that

> a proposal for a unity which includes both Christianity and other religions rests (openly or covertly) upon belief in some reality other than God's revelation in Christ. The experience of learning to listen to one another which the ecumenical movement has given us is certainly valid beyond the confines of Christendom. We have indeed to learn to enter into real conversation with men of other religions if they are to apprehend Jesus Christ as Saviour and if we are to learn the manifold wisdom of God which he set forth in Jesus. But the ecumenical movement remains missionary through and through because it is a movement not for any kind of unity, but for that unity which is God's creation through the lifting up of Jesus Christ upon the Cross and through the continuing work of his Spirit.[96]

The fault lines in Christianity between orthodoxy and heterodoxy now run through all the mainstream denominations, so that a new transdenominational ecumenism is called for. As the Kuyperian tradition becomes increasingly global, it would be wonderful if it could foster just such an ecumenism. In order to do so, it would need to attend closely to and discern the central truths of the faith as opposed to the adiaphora, rally Christians around the gospel of the kingdom with its creation-wide vision, and facilitate unity amid geographical and ecclesial particularity.[97]

---

[95]Lesslie Newbigin, *Trinitarian Doctrine for Today's World* (Eugene, OR: Wipf and Stock, 1988), 17-18.
[96]Ibid., 18-19.
[97]Cf. Berkouwer, *Church*, 280-89.

POLITICS, THE POOR,
AND PLURALISM

A born-again person is one whose new vitality has entirely penetrated his feelings and thought including the realm of politics. . . . The question is not if the candidate's heart is favorable to Christianity, but if he has Christ as his starting-point even for politics and will speak out for His Name!

ABRAHAM KUYPER, IN *DE STANDAARD*[1]

God has spoken.

There is a revelation of His will which we have in God's Word. On this basis we demand that the pronouncements of God's Word be obeyed in each clash of principles. Human inference or discretion is only to be decisive where God's Word is unclear.

Everyone agrees that human insight must yield to God's pronouncements. The disagreement begins because our opponents do not believe God Himself has spoken while we confess that He has spoken. The Gospel versus the Revolution! This is the conviction that we must be able to declare in order to awaken the proper type of belief. We only ask for this right, but this is what we are denied.

ABRAHAM KUYPER, IN *DE STANDAARD*, JUNE 7, 1873[2]

---

[1]Quoted in and translated by McKendree R. Langley, "Emancipation and Apologetics: The Formation of Abraham Kuyper's Anti-Revolutionary Party in the Netherlands, 1872–1880" (PhD diss., Westminster Theological Seminary, Philadelphia, 1995), 99.

[2]Quoted and translated by McKendree R. Langley, *The Practice of Political Spirituality: Episodes from the Public Career of Abraham Kuyper, 1879–1918* (Jordan Station, ON: Paideia Press, 1984), 12.

ISAIAH 60 IS A REMARKABLE PASSAGE, evoking in vivid imagery the future of Zion.[3] It is chock full of political and commercial—see the "ships of Tarshish" in Isaiah 60:9—imagery. Isaiah 60:11 envisages a time when Zion's gates will always be open, "so that people may bring you the wealth of the nations—their kings lead in triumphal procession."[4] Isaiah 60:16 speaks of a time when God's people will "drink the milk of nations and be nursed at royal breasts." There is no hint in this passage of politics being somehow alien to the reign of God.[5] Instead, the new city appears to provide the appropriate place for politics, not least through the maternal image of God's people being nursed at royal breasts! Kuyper, as we have seen, longed for the church to become a genuine mother to the faithful. Richard Mouw says of Isaiah 60:16, "Politics will become a force for the giving of life. King-mothers will feed the people of God."[6]

It is one thing to conceive of the church as our mother in the faith. It is a lot harder to think of government in maternal terms. One reason for this is that in the Protestant tradition government is generally thought of as a postfall institution, part of God's common grace for restraining evil and ensuring a measure of societal justice.[7] Personally, partly on the basis of passages like Isaiah 60, I am more persuaded by the Thomist view that government is given, potentially, with creation, so that even after the fall it has a far more positive role.

Either way, politics is a critical element in contemporary societies, and we neglect it at our peril. In our comfortable West, which has enjoyed decades of life with high rates of consumption and without war on its shores—though

---

[3]See Richard J. Mouw, *When the Kings Come Marching In: Isaiah and the New Jerusalem* (Grand Rapids: Eerdmans, 1983), for a delightful reflection on this chapter.

[4]There is some debate about the kings being led in procession. Brevard S. Childs, *Isaiah*, Old Testament Library (Louisville: Westminster John Knox, 2000), 497, notes that we do not need to see the kings as being led unwillingly.

[5]Alan Storkey, "The Bible's Politics," in *Witness to the World*, ed. David Peterson (Carlisle, UK: Paternoster, 1999), 65, asserts, "The biblical text is full of content relating to taxation, law, ethnic conflict, nation-states, justice, penal policy, labour wars, war, peace, treaties, particular governments or administrations, parties, political commentary, failure, empires, international trade, popular appeals and decisions, national decline and fragmentation, reform, political leaders, insurrection, occupation or whatever. This is precisely the content of every contemporary sense of politics. Biblical politics is far more like contemporary politics than the New Testament church is like the contemporary church. For the New Testament does not treat of denominations, liturgical forms, the priesthood, ecumenism or other contemporary matters, yet commentators have no problem in moving to what they see as the contemporary relevance of the text. Yet the biblical text is bang straightforward political, and the interpretation is not undertaken."

[6]Mouw, *When the Kings Come Marching In*, 36.

[7]Kuyper's view; *LC*, 67.

that is changing with terrorist attacks—it is sometimes hard to see just how important politics is. However, if we had stood watching five hundred or so bodies washing down a river each hour during the Rwandan genocide, or lived in southern Sudan during the first part of this century, it would not be difficult to see just how crucial is healthy politics.

Kuyper did not make that mistake. As the quotes at the outset of this chapter indicate, Kuyper believed that if God has spoken, it makes all the difference in the world to politics. Kuyper lived at a tumultuous time politically, when monarchies were being replaced and a variety of post-Enlightenment models for government were being theorized and instituted, and he saw the need for Christian thought and practice in politics, albeit in post-Christendom mode and in a way that allowed for genuine freedom for all major religious or confessional visions. Kuyper focused his attention and considerable energies on *Christian* political action, but it must not be overlooked that he always envisaged this in a pluralist context in which alternative visions competed in the public square.

It is one thing, of course, to see that God is relevant to politics, but quite another to work out what this means in theory and practice. Kuyper was not a political theorist, but when it came to politics he was certainly an organic intellectual.[8] Kuyper was deeply involved in politics even while a pastor, but after he returned from his breakdown in 1877, now nearly forty years old, he turned down the calls from many prominent churches and settled down into journalism and the organization of the antirevolutionary movement. Within three years he cofounded the Free University, established a political party (ARP), and facilitated the development of a nationwide network of Christian schools.[9]

---

[8]Langley, *Practice*, notes that Kuyper did not develop a political *theory* of the state. As with sphere sovereignty and the church, this might be true, but volume 5 of Kuyper's *Dictaten Dogmatiek*, "Locus De Magistratu," is too often ignored.

[9]It is important to note, as does Harry van Dyke, "Abraham Kuyper: Heir of an Anti-Revolutionary Tradition," in Steve Bishop and John H. Kok, eds., *On Kuyper: A Collection of Readings on the Life, Work and Legacy of Abraham Kuyper* (Sioux Center, IA: Dordt College Press, 2013), 7-26, that Kuyper did not achieve this by himself or de novo: "Kuyper steeped himself in a tradition that was nearly a century old. He reaped where many others had sown. He mobilized a people already armed, elaborated a worldview and a program of action already sketched, accelerated a movement already in motion. . . . Only against the backdrop of his historical context are we able to assess just how unique Abraham Kuyper really was" (26). Cf. Langley, "Emancipation and Apologetics," 1-80.

Founding a Political Party

Kuyper was determined to develop a political party, which he argued was "an urgent *confessional* necessity."[10] A turning point came in the June elections of 1877, when liberals received a 60 percent majority in the Lower House of the States General, thereby putting them in a position to pursue their liberal agenda. Kuyper quickly developed and circulated an eighteen-point party platform, which he published in *De Standaard* in early 1878 as the approved platform that members were to endorse. Kuyper discerned five requirements for a political party:

1. It must be defined by a common platform.

2. It must be composed of organized chapters in as many localities as possible.

3. Delegates from the chapters will gather at a national convention to nominate candidates for Parliament.

4. Endorsed candidates and sitting members of Parliament will be bound by the party platform.

5. A central committee will coordinate party operations.

To us these may seem obvious, but such organization was new in Kuyper's context.[11] Until this point Dutch politics had been the preserve of the elite, whereas Kuyper wanted to harness the energy of the "little people." Industrialization had spawned workers' grievances and movements across Europe, but generally without organizational leadership; this Kuyper was intent on providing.

If Kuyper's organizing needed a catalyst, it was provided by the liberals, when they successfully introduced a bill to modernize Dutch schools that, among other things, prohibited state aid to religious schools. "To that they [the liberals] brought a loud, dogmatic version of the earlier Liberal's quiet secularism. Religion, they insisted, especially religious education among young children, bred ignorance, superstition, and backwardness. It stunted the full development of the individual and of the nation." Johannes Kappeyne van de Coppello's school bill galvanized the opposition, with local committees springing up all over the country. A drive to secure signatures to a petition over several weeks in midsummer produced astonishing results among Protestants

---

[10]Quoted in *AK*, 113.
[11]*AK*, 114.

and Catholics,[12] and though the king signed the bill into existence, education became the Anti-Revolutionary Party's "catalyst and heart," and Kuyper now had his database. Despite accusations to the contrary, Kuyper's program was not a one-issue affair: it made freedom of conscience central to national culture, with education subject to conscience (i.e., religion) and the family, and made the family the first bulwark against the overweening state. Kuyper, along with many others of diverse convictions in Europe and America, regarded the future as revolving around the question of education.[13]

In January 1879 a national Union for the School with the Bible was established in Utrecht; in April the delegate assembly of the Anti-Revolutionary Party met and ratified the platform, the central committee, and the party structure, with Kuyper elected as party chairman. In August the formation of the Free University of Amsterdam was announced, and it opened its humble doors on October 20, 1880. Faculty pamphlets and study guides soon became regular materials for church discussion groups, and the annual meeting of the members of the union in midsummer achieved the ethos of a sort of holiday camp. The Free University of Amsterdam was entirely privately funded, and Kuyper celebrated the contributions of ordinary, uneducated folk toward the running of the university, asking, "Is this not a practical solution to the problem of connecting learning to life? Must not scholars who are supported by the people's money grow closer to the people and more averse to all that is dry and abstract?"[14]

Kuyper did extraordinary work in developing a political, informed, civic culture among his followers, with his journalism and the Free University as central prongs in his work. "As the university traced the thoughts of God across nature and society, the party would try to get the 'ordinances of the Lord' adopted by popular consent as the law of the land."[15] Kuyper wanted not just a mass movement but also an informed one, and so in March 1878 he began a series on the party platform in *De Standaard*. On completion, the seventy-three articles were published as *Our Program*, "a two-volume, 1,300-page open-university course in applied Calvinistic political philosophy, meant to be kept close at hand by the party faithful."[16] Bratt notes in this respect that

---

[12]The largest ever such petition up to this point, according to George Harinck, personal correspondence.
[13]*AK*, 115, 116, 117.
[14]Quoted in *AK*, 124.
[15]*AK*, 125.
[16]*AK*, 114. It should be noted that beginning in 1880, many of the appendices were dropped from reprint

Kuyper built a "thick sociology": a village baker could be a member of the local church council, an officer in the local council of the Anti-Revolutionary Party; his brother a member of the Christian school board, and his wife a volunteer for the Bible and missions society.[17]

Utterly central to Kuyper's political work was his doctrine of sphere sovereignty, which we explored in chapter five. At the end of *Our Program*, Kuyper delineates the three substantive principles that guide the Anti-Revolutionary Party's platform:[18]

1. sovereignty for each sphere of society;

2. the nation not an aggregate but an organism; and

3. no coercion but freedom for intellectual and spiritual formation and education.

Our Program explains that according to sphere sovereignty the right to execute authority is delegated only by the sovereign God. In opposition to such a view Kuyper sets popular sovereignty and state sovereignty.[19] In relation to the three points above, Kuyper observes intriguingly but hardly persuasively that "should someone protest that sphere-sovereignty cannot be separated from the organic viewpoint, and that this in turn presupposes the free working of the mind and spirit, then we may be allowed to ask whether this intersecting of the three rays, rather than cancelling the trinitarian character of our sketch, instead confirms it with an unmistakable hallmark."[20]

OUR PROGRAM

Kuyper recognized the need for an informed and active citizenry whose engagement would animate the spheres and keep them healthy.[21] In this context

---

editions, reducing the book to some five hundred pages. For an analysis of the series of articles that became *Our Program*, see Langley, "Emancipation and Apologetics."

[17]*AK*, 126-27.

[18]Abraham Kuyper, *Our Program: A Christian Political Manifesto*, trans. Harry Van Dyke, Collected Works in Public Theology (Bellingham, WA: Lexham, 2015), 380.

[19]Cf. *LC*, 69-70, 72. Cf. chapter five on this theme. For Kuyper, modern societies are in danger of absolutizing either the state or the will of the people.

[20]Kuyper, *Our Program*, 381. Langley, "Emancipation and Apologetics," 73, argues, "The organic element in his thinking can be traced back to Calvin, not to relativistic Romantic organicism." Cf. Langley, "Emancipation and Apologetics," 21-23, and chapter five above.

[21]Langley, "Emancipation and Apologetics," 82, calls this "integrated Reformed attitude to public affairs" "political spirituality." Cf. Langley, *Practice*.

Our Program is an extraordinary work. It set out the program of the Anti-Revolutionary Party with clarity and comprehensiveness and provided a standard of systematic commentary that Kuyper's rivals were compelled to match. The program consists of twenty-one articles, with the following headings:

- Our Movement
- Authority
- The Ordinances of God
- Government: No Secular State
- "By the Grace of God"

- Forms of Government
- Our Constitution[22]
- Popular Influence
- Budget Refusal
- Decentralization[23]
- Our States and Councils

- Education[24]
- The Justice System[25]
- Public Decency
- Public Hygiene
- Finances[26]
- National Defense[27]

---

[22]On this article and the following see Langley, "Emancipation and Apologetics," 150-52.

[23]On this article and how the Anti-Revolutionary Party and Kuyper worked for electoral reform see ibid., 132-35.

[24]On this article and how the Anti-Revolutionary Party and Kuyper worked it out in practice see ibid., 114-32.

[25]On this article and the following two see ibid., 147-49.

[26]On this article and Kuyper's approach to issues of national finances, tax, and economic policy see ibid., 143-45.

[27]See ibid., 145-47.

- Overseas Possessions[28]

- The Social Question[29]

- Church and State[30]

- Party Policy

As per the divisions provided above, there are three clusters in *Our Program*: generally speaking, the first deals with the law (ordinances) of God for government, the second with the structure of Dutch government, and the third with national policy, the attempt to put the divine ordinances into practice. Alternatively, to use the language that became common in the party, the first cluster deals with primary or first principles, and the second two clusters with applied principles.[31] Kuyper understandably asserted, "The other parties campaign for parliamentary seats, more or less. We campaign for our *principles*."[32]

While Kuyper recognizes that tyrannies sometimes have to be deposed he, following Groen van Prinsterer, strongly opposes "the revolution."[33] "We contend, after consulting our beliefs, examining our personal lives, and listening to the past, that there is no other cure to be found for Europe's malady than under the auspices of the Man of Sorrows." For Kuyper this means that history cannot be swept aside; instead, we must work constructively with the historical legacy we inherit. And for Kuyper the legacy the Anti-Revolutionary Party inherits is a very positive one. The party is heir to a political program once admired throughout Europe, and if this legacy is developed for the present, it has great promise for the future. However, political engagement by

---

[28]On this article and the Anti-Revolutionary Party's approach to colonialism, see ibid., 138-43. Ibid., 140, notes, "This eighteenth article contains Kuyper's entire colonial reform agenda in a nutshell. The practice of economic exploitation by either the state or by private firms should be replaced with an ethical guardianship policy over the colonies."

[29]On this article and how the Anti-Revolutionary Party and Kuyper approached it see ibid., 135-38.

[30]On articles 20 and 21 see ibid., 152-60. Kuyper's clearest discussion of the relationship between the standards of the Bible and the relative nature of a pluralist democracy is found in a series of articles written in 1874 titled "Is Error Punishable?" See ibid., 153-57.

[31]Cf. ibid., 85-112.

[32]Abraham Kuyper, in *De Standaard*, June 6, 1873, emphasis original. Quoted in and translated by Langley, "Emancipation and Apologetics," 99. Note the emphasis on "principles" in article 3.

[33]See Timothy Sherratt, "Rehabilitating the State in America: Abraham Kuyper's Overlooked Contribution," in Bishop and Kok, *On Kuyper*, 383-403, 391. For the struggle on the issue of resistance among neo-Calvinists see John W. Sap, *Paving the Way for the Revolution: Calvinism and the Struggle for a Democratic Constitutional State*, VU Studies on Protestant History 6 (Amsterdam: VU, 2001), 289-354.

Christians is not to aim at the restoration of Christendom or of an established church. "And, to put to rest once for all: we ourselves react more strongly than anyone to the idea of re-establishing a Reformed state church. On the contrary, we demand the strictest application of the principle that the state shall not itself promote 'the saving faith.'"[34]

In the first cluster Kuyper articulates a view of government within the vision of sphere sovereignty. God is the supreme sovereign, and *political* sovereignty is not therefore an isolated case but one link in the chain that causes the whole of the creation to cohere and to exist by the ordinances of God. Although the nation state is a modern invention, Kuyper affirms it as natural: "Moreover, when a country's political authority defines by law the boundaries where a different sovereign authority stops and its own begins, then this in no way restricts that sovereignty but merely indicates its natural limits."[35]

Kuyper argues that Scripture, and the study of creation and history, are the means by which a government discerns just law. When it comes to the question of justice, one has to choose for or against the true and living God. God alone has the right to determine what is just and unjust. Kuyper sees God's law as utterly comprehensive:

> If we may refer to these as "ordinances of God" then it follows that there are ordinances for soil and climate, for the products and resources of our country, and for the animals over which we were given dominion. But there are also ordinances of God for human life, for body and mind, for the development of our human capacities, for blood relations and kinship, for commerce and industry, for our calling and destiny as a nation. In short, there is a will, a command, an ordinance of the Lord for everything that people can have two opinions about. According to the firm principles that flow forth from God's holy Being, one will be commendable, the other unacceptable.[36]

The critical question, of course, is the epistemological one of how we know God's laws. Social questions are far more complex than natural ones, and then there is the additional effect of sin. Sin makes Scripture indispensable in our quest for God's norms for political life: "We have access to a 'Word of God' in a narrow sense that spreads considerable light on those eternal principles and

---

[34]Kuyper, *Our Program*, 4, 9.
[35]Ibid., 22.
[36]Ibid., 31.

indicates to a considerable degree those divine ordinances for human life."[37]

In this respect Kuyper articulates five propositions:

1. All law that is to pass for just law on earth must pass the test of justice.

2. God alone determines what is just, in accordance with his nature.

3. Insofar as human life is concerned, pure knowledge and the firmness of these divine ordinances were lost as a result of sin.

4. Natural theology and natural morality, however much to be appreciated, are therefore insufficient for getting to know the eternal principles.

5. The special, supernatural revelation of God's Word has spread important light on those principles, including principles relevant to civil life; and it is therefore our calling to confess, also in the political domain, the eternal principles revealed in that Word.

Having said this, Kuyper is careful to avoid biblicism. Scripture is not a repository of legal provisions ready at hand. Instead, it is the inspired record of God's revelation about life, covering several centuries. "Scripture contains God's ordinances—that is, his eternal and unchangeable principles—but mostly in mixed form, like nuggets in a gold mine."[38] Kuyper refers to Jules Michelet's (1798–1874) book on education *Nos fils* (Our Sons [1869]), in which Michelet, an ardent advocate of the Enlightenment, observes that whether or not we acknowledge sin represents the great divide in life. According to Michelet, "We must examine and penetrate the full meaning of the faith, for which we are combating. . . . There is no such thing as original sin. Every child is born innocent and is not marked beforehand by the sin of Adam."[39] Kuyper, of course, believed the exact opposite, and here we see his emphasis on sin and thus the antithesis. Scripture provides the lenses through which to read the world aright, and Kuyper is alert to the fact that we have to learn much from studying how politics works in reality. Kuyper notes the great role that legal scholars and political philosophers have in helping us to discern the mark of God's law in the political principles we develop. Hence the vital importance of the Free University of Amsterdam in Kuyper's scheme.

---

[37]Ibid., 32.

[38]Ibid., 34.

[39]Jules Michelet, *The People*, trans. C. Cocks (London: Longman, Brown, Green and Longmans, 1846).

Kuyper's view of how Christianity influences the conscience of government is interesting. He discerns a direct and an indirect influence. The direct influence is through members of government meditating on Scripture and carrying this into their vocations. Indirectly, influence is felt through the life of God's people in the country. He argues that the church should devote special care to its members who are in government, nurture theological studies to help the politician, and resist any view that sees civil society as of no concern for the Christian.

As a journalist, not surprisingly, Kuyper is aware of the role of the press in informing the conscience of government, for better or worse. He dreams of a context in which healthy, Christian journalism flourishes:

> But if daily newspapers appear that dare once more to base themselves on the Word of God, which recommend again the principles of that Word for the political domain and remind king and country of their duty toward the divine ordinances—then increasingly the conscience of the people in government will at first be shocked and provoked, and before long challenged, and the ordinances of God will gain in influence during their deliberations.[40]

Kuyper also notes briefly the influence of world opinion, which, in his view, is too often overlooked. Especially in a small country like the Netherlands, trends in the great centers of Europe profoundly influence public opinion. Kuyper laments the small indigenous contribution in this respect, as well as the fact that world opinion is often anti-Christian. He dreams of a day when Christian thought starts to influence the centers of world opinion.

As is typical of Kuyper's thought, he insists that the state is a dynamic moral organism arising in response to God's laws for creation. As such it is part of a living whole, one sphere among many. The role of the state in this living whole is to facilitate a social life in which citizens can deploy their latent strengths freely and to the fullest. Kuyper walks a fine line in his description of the Netherlands as a "Christian nation." It is Christian in that it is "not without God," and as such it is bound to

- remove from administration and legislation anything that impedes the free influence of the gospel on the nation;
- abstain from all direct meddling with the spiritual formation of the nation, being absolutely incompetent in this respect;

---

[40]Kuyper, *Our Program*, 39-40.

- treat all denominations or religious communities, and moreover all citizens, regardless of their views about things eternal, on a level of equality; and

- acknowledge in people's conscience, provided it does not lack the presumption of respectability, a limit to its power.[41]

Kuyper is crystal clear that no matter how much a government might sympathize with the gospel, it should never use its power against those who oppose the gospel. If a Jew takes exception to the Christian view of Jesus as the Messiah, or a Muslim to the Bible, or a scientific naturalist to the doctrine of creation, or a positivist against faith—they should all be free to do so. Even the rights of atheists—a small minority in Kuyper's context—should be protected.

Kuyper recognizes that Scripture does not prescribe one form of government over another, but he and the Anti-Revolutionary Party support the constitutional monarchy that has evolved in the Netherlands. Naturally, the party and Kuyper are concerned to reform the constitutional monarchy through legal avenues. For example, Kuyper argues for a new electoral system and an expansion of the electorate, a goal he achieved. He wished to replace provincial with functional representation in the Upper House (business, labor, universities, etc.), but this goal was never achieved. Not surprisingly, education features high in *Our Program*. Kuyper appeals for government to provide equal rights for all citizens in the sphere of education.

Our Program embodies a bold, courageous, contextual, and remarkable vision. In this context, it is important to remember that Kuyper was not just a theorist of politics, though he was certainly that, but also an active politician himself, a practitioner. Above we have concentrated on the program Kuyper set out for the Anti-Revolutionary Party as the movement got going. But, one might well ask, what did this look like in practice? Predictably, it was messy, amid many high points.[42] What must not be forgotten, as de Bruijn points out, is that "the ARP was not only the first modern political party in the Netherlands, but distinguished itself from the existing Liberal and Conservative factions by its specifically Christian foundations. Its establishment heralded the

---

[41]Ibid., 57.
[42]See *AK* for the history.

pillarization[43] of Dutch society, which was based on the 'antithesis' between confessional and non-confessional parties and organizations."[44]

Kuyper's involvement in politics yielded a rich literature that, certainly in English circles, remains to be fully excavated. John Stott spoke of the need for "ethical apologetics," and McKendree Langley describes Kuyper as a public apologist. This is an apt description. While theologically Kuyper was highly critical of piecemeal apologetics in the face of the onslaught of modernism, he recognized and was a master practitioner of ethical apologetics. The major evidence for this is in his journalism. Kuyper and his colleagues used *De Standaard* as the vehicle to engage with the issues of the day and to do so publicly, and especially for members of the Anti-Revolutionary Party.

And, of course, we must not forget that party members got elected to parliament so that an Anti-Revolutionary caucus developed there, eventually becoming the government of the day.[45] On my shelves I have four large volumes of Kuyper's *Parlementaire Redevoeringen* (Parliamentary Speeches).[46] They make for fascinating reading, and it is remarkable to see the range of topics they address. Topics include: the war in South Africa; conditions in the East Indies; revelation and reason; the "Sunday question"; the birth, position, and character of the cabinet; the injustice of Marxism; the social-democratic drift toward atheism; building of schools; teachers' pensions; work conditions; hospitals; the fight against tuberculosis; provincial taxes, and so on. Not only is the range remarkable, but so too is the way in which Christian thought is interspersed openly throughout the speeches.

It was Kuyper's practice of politics that also pushed him toward ecumenical cooperation. It might be hard nowadays for us to think of Catholic and Reformed cooperation as a problem, but in Kuyper's day this was certainly not the case. Bratt notes,

---

[43]*Pillarization* is a synonym for what we describe below as confessional pluralism.

[44]Jan de Bruijn, *Abraham Kuyper: A Pictorial Biography*, trans. Dagmare Houniet (Grand Rapids: Eerdmans, 2008, 2014), 91. For Barth's radical difference from Kuyper in this respect see Clifford Blake Anderson, "Jesus and the 'Christian Worldview': A Comparative Analysis of Abraham Kuyper and Karl Barth," *Cultural Encounters* 6, no. 1 (2006): 61-80.

[45]Langley, "Emancipation and Apologetics," 161-248, examines the oppositionist approach of the ARP during the five cabinets of Thorbecke III (1871–1872, liberal), De Vries (1872–1874, liberal), Heemskerk II (1874–1877, conservative), Kappeyne van de Coppello (1877–1879, liberal), and Van Lyden van Sandenburg (1879–1883, fusionist).

[46]Abraham Kuyper, *Parlementaire Redevoeringen* [Parliamentary Speeches] (Amsterdam: Van Holkema and Warendorf, 1908–1912).

Most startling of all was the transcendence of an ancient religious hostility. Kuyper helped arrange a meeting between Calvinist and Catholic leaders that forged a plan of comity whereby each side would support the other's candidate in the run-off phase of the general election. After three hundred years of fulminating against the pope and for a Protestant Netherlands, Kuyper's Calvinists now joined Roman Catholics to restore a Christian Netherlands.[47]

The effect was immediate. The expanded electorate of 1888 returned a 53–47 religious majority to the Lower House, and the first confessional cabinet was installed under the leadership of Baron Aeneas Mackay.

THE SOCIAL QUESTION AND THE POOR

The social question was a central and controversial issue in Kuyper's day, and he is keenly attentive to the changes that should be introduced to create more satisfactory relations between workers and employers.[48] Kuyper notes the ambiguous effects of industrialization: "The magical operation of iron machines has unfortunately led the capitalist to regard his employees as nothing but machines of flesh that can be retired or scrapped when they break down or have worn out."[49] He is alert to the multiple factors involved and not least to the loosening of the positive relationships that had previously bound worker and employer, relationships now reduced to impersonal contracts. Whereas Calvin stressed the need for face-to-face contact in business, Adam Smith argued that producers and buyers should not meet, and it is this impersonal dimension that Kuyper criticizes.[50] Kuyper is rightly concerned with the poor but again aware of the different types of poverty, including that of the healthy laborer who cannot find a permanent job and a living wage.[51]

Kuyper invokes in this regard Israel's laws in the Old Testament.[52] He refers to Israel's laws about usury, lending against collateral, creditors, day laborers,

---

[47]AK, 217.

[48]Cf. Jan L. van Zanden and Arthur van Riel, *The Strictures of Inheritance: The Dutch Economy in the Nineteenth Century*, trans. Ian Cressie (Princeton, NJ: Princeton University Press, 2004).

[49]Kuyper, *Our Program*, 333.

[50]Adam Smith, *The Wealth of the Nations* (Oxford: Oxford University Press, 1993).

[51]Cf. Herman Bavinck, *Essays on Religion, Science, and Society*, ed. John Bolt, trans. Harry Boonstra and Gerrit Sheeres (Grand Rapids: Baker Academic, 2008), chap. 7. Bavinck notes, "The gospel that he [Jesus] came to bring was therefore a gospel for the poor" (117).

[52]Cf. his comments in "Christ and the Needy," *Journal of Markets & Morality* 14, no. 2 (Fall 2011): 656: "The idea that someone could dispose absolutely over his property was unknown to Israel. All property gave only relative rights."

gleaning, the return of alienated fields, the tithe, the jubilee, and so on. These were given by God to ensure a system of social institutions that served to constrain the powerful and to protect the weak. "The dreadful gap between rich and poor never took root."[53] Society therefore requires laws for commerce and for labor, and Kuyper repeats his earlier call for a labor code, which might include such areas as: wage contracts; working hours, leisure hours, and holidays; suspension of a contract owing to sickness; disabled workers; workplace safety; on-site training; breaches of wage contracts; damages caused on the job; use of coercion against fellow workers; conspiring against employers; cooperative associations; the political rights of labor organizations; and so on.[54]

Kuyper is quite clear that *Our Program* is not a vision for a Calvinistic utopia but a sketch coming from the antirevolutionaries intended for the flourishing of the whole country. Remarkably, in the conclusion he argues that this is a trinitarian vision, and he ends with a quote from Proverbs about the fear of the Lord as the beginning of wisdom![55] As significant and robust as this is, nothing quite prepares one for the explosive force of Kuyper's "Christ and the Needy," a collection of articles published as a book in 1895.[56] This work reveals the depth of Kuyper as a biblical scholar and his willingness to allow Scripture to speak with all its unadulterated power to the social issues of his day.[57]

Kuyper asks why the strong social dimension in Jesus' ministry has been so neglected. He rightly notes that preachers are trapped "in the spiritual," so that they fail to proclaim the full Christ, whose gospel clearly manifests his intention and desire to impact social life. An extraordinary part of Kuyper's analysis is his investigation of the social context in which Jesus made his comments about the rich and the poor. Such an emphasis is relatively new in contemporary biblical studies. He concludes his analysis by arguing that the social conditions in which Jesus conducted his public ministry "were not unfavorable but much rather favorable when compared with present-day conditions."[58] Thus the radicality of Jesus' teaching in this area is enhanced and not reduced!

---

[53]Kuyper, *Our Program*, 333.

[54]For the full list see ibid., 349.

[55]See Herman Bavinck's approving comment in Herman Bavinck, "The Pros and Cons of a Dogmatic System," trans. Nelson D. Kloosterman, *The Bavinck Review* 5 (2014): 92.

[56]Cf. Abraham Kuyper, *The Problem of Poverty* (Sioux Center, IA: Dordt College Press, 2011), a translation of a speech Kuyper gave in 1891 at the First Christian Social Congress.

[57]Note the second quote at the outset of this chapter.

[58]Kuyper, "Christ and the Needy," 680, 657.

Kuyper rightly makes much of Jesus' social position as part of the lower classes. This is widely known, but its implications for the social question are too often not pursued. Kuyper attends closely to the teaching of the Gospels, and his work ranks with some of the best recent scholarship in this area. He draws attention to the fact that hunger is the first temptation; afterward, in the synagogue at Nazareth, Jesus opened and read from Isaiah 61:1, which says that Christ is anointed to preach the gospel to the poor; and that soon, in the Sermon on the Mount, the first Beatitude speaks of the blessedness of the poor. When Jesus provides evidence to John the Baptist that he is the Messiah, he alerts him that "the gospel was preached to the poor." Kuyper argues that in his public ministry Jesus by choice and by virtue of his calling turns first to the poor, among whom he seeks the main subjects for his kingdom.

Kuyper examines Calvin's and Godet's exegesis of the key Gospel texts and concludes that these texts cannot be used to support a spiritualization of Jesus' social teaching. He exclaims: "O, how different things would be in Christendom if Jesus' preaching on this point were also our preaching and if the basic principles of his Kingdom were not cut off and alienated from our society by over-spiritualization." For Kuyper, Jesus' teaching about Mammon is not peripheral to his vision but sets the tone for and governs all of his preaching. Jesus opposes Mammon the minute it tries to assert itself as a power not in the service of God.[59] Kuyper laments the obsession with wealth that he witnessed around him:

> Everything is measured by money. Whoever is rich is a celebrated and honored man. This is just what Jesus does not want. He sets himself diametrically against it. He proclaims that a world or a people who aim at it and pursue it corrupt themselves spiritually in the process. Storing up all kinds of treasures in order to heap fortune upon fortune, and imitating the financial barons on a small scale he regards as cursed.[60]

Kuyper recognizes that there is a legitimate desire for our basic provisions but insists that once we make our needs too great, we have succumbed to the enemy. John Stott appealed for Western Christians to adopt a simpler lifestyle, and Kuyper finds the same call in Jesus' teaching. We should free ourselves by controlling our desires, especially in relation to material things. "This is a basic

---

[59]Ibid., 665-66.
[60]Ibid., 666.

idea of Jesus, which is thus diametrically opposed to our century's propensity constantly to increase our income and surround ourselves with luxuries and so intensify the power and influence of gold on our hearts."[61]

Kuyper rejects the embrace of envy in relation to possessions; Jesus wants love to reign in this area of life. Such love should level inequality as much as is reasonably possible. Kuyper attends to texts such as someone asking for one's cloak and observes that, in reality, our situation is such that always two people stand side by side, one with two beds to sleep on, one with two garments, one with two portions of food, while the other does not have a bed to sleep on, or garments to cover his nakedness, or food to feed him. "This cries out to heaven."[62]

Kuyper is a realist and knows that inequality will always be with us this side of the new heavens and the new earth. What we should pursue is a certain equality in which the basic needs of all are met, such as shelter, clothing, and food. Kuyper invokes in this respect the language of the rights of the poor: "This is the right that the poor have, for Christ's sake, with respect to those possessing more. Those who possess more but fall short in this matter are not only unmerciful but commit an injustice, and for that injustice they will suffer the punishment of eternal judgment in eternal pain."[63] Kuyper refuses to disentangle Jesus' social concern from the gospel of the kingdom.

As scholars have noted about Luke's Gospel, Jesus mixes with rich and poor. The rich also receive Jesus' love and concern. Kuyper explores in this regard Jesus' visit to the home of the rich Zacchaeus. Zacchaeus gave half his wealth to the poor, and yet, Kuyper notes, he receives no special praise from Jesus for this act! Kuyper asserts,

> We respect the notables among Christians; we thank God that even among those of high social rank he has plucked a few out of the fire; we value highly the blessing they can bring us. Thus precisely for this reason the voice may not be stifled that tries to persuade them to follow in Jesus' footsteps also in the social field. Even in the midst of social unrest they can be a credit to their Savior, but only if, like Jesus, they stretch their hands toward the multitude and say with undivided heart, "These are my mother, and my brothers, and my sisters," and so keep them from greed and iniquity.[64]

---

[61]Ibid., 668.
[62]Ibid., 671.
[63]Ibid., 672.
[64]Ibid., 682-83.

Kuyper is unequivocal in making Jesus' social concern central to the Anti-Revolutionary Party. In 1918, in an address titled "What Next?" given to the meeting of deputies of the party, Kuyper argued that, in answer to this situation, after the education question has been dealt with, the next issue is the concerns of the working classes.[65] In "Christ and the Needy" he confesses that he has felt compelled to speak loudly and clearly against Mammon and "to choose the side of the little folk in the land."[66]

SECULARIZATION AND PLURALISM

There is so much to explore in Kuyper's thought on politics and society. In an important work John Bolt has explored the potential significance of Kuyper as a public, political theologian for the United States today.[67] Bolt types Kuyper as a "poet" and explores the intriguing comparisons between Kuyper and other key thinkers about America and public theology, namely Alexis de Tocqueville, Lord John Acton, Jonathan Edwards, Walter Rauschenbusch, and Pope Leo XIII.[68] Like Wolterstorff, Bolt opens up a critical dialogue between Kuyper and liberation theology.[69] Bolt argues, "Kuyper's rhetoric is in some respect formally similar to liberation theology, but his social metaphysic is quite different."[70]

Fortunately, Kuyper's political thought has been developed by a host of scholars, and the reader is referred to works by Jim Skillen, Richard Mouw, Paul Marshall, Jonathan Chaplin, and many others. Jim Skillen, for example, not only set up and directed the influential Center for Public Justice in Washington, DC, but over his career has produced a corpus of important works on politics in the Kuyperian tradition and continues to write and work in this area.[71]

Suffice it here to note that most of these thinkers have developed Kuyper's political thought on the back of Dooyeweerd's work in Christian philosophy.

---

[65]Utrecht, May 2, 1918.

[66]Kuyper, "Christ and the Needy," 682.

[67]See also Sherratt, "Rehabilitating the State in America."

[68]John Bolt, *A Free Church, A Holy Nation: Abraham Kuyper's Public Theology* (Grand Rapids: Eerdmans, 2001).

[69]Nicholas Wolterstorff, *Until Justice and Peace Embrace* (Grand Rapids: Eerdmans, 1983), 42-68.

[70]Bolt, *Free Church*, 301-2.

[71]Skillen's Center for Public Justice played a significant role in the Charitable Choice welfare reform in the United States. See James W. Skillen, "*E Pluribus Unum* and Faith-Based Welfare Reform: A Kuyperian Moment for the Church in God's World," in Bishop and Kok, *On Kuyper*, 405-18.

In the process two key elements of Kuyper's thought have been honed and consistently foregrounded, namely structural and confessional pluralism.[72] Structural pluralism is the more recent name for Kuyper's doctrine of sphere sovereignty, namely that it is normative for a society as it develops to open out into multiple spheres, each directly answerable to God.[73]

Confessional or directional pluralism furthermore argues that each societal structure or sphere is open to being directed in different ways. The idea is that in a genuinely free society each major religious or confessional vision should have the freedom to come to fruition in each sphere of life.[74] As we will see below, this social philosophy provides a major resource for some of our biggest contemporary challenges. Part of Kuyper's genius was his capacity to relate his Reformed tradition to the changing context in which he lived. His work is akin to casting a gospel net over our culture to see where it sticks, and this is the sort of strategy at which Kuyper was a master.[75] We can see this more clearly now, and not least through current discussions of secularism and religion.

In *The Many Altars of Modernity*, Peter Berger explains that secularization theory, which promotes the idea that modernity necessarily leads to a decline of religion, has until recently served as a paradigm for the study of religion. However, it can no longer stand up to the weight of the empirical evidence. Thus we need a new paradigm that takes into account the reality of religious pluralism, the fact of different worldviews and value systems in the same society.[76]

As Peter Berger has noted, globally we are living amid a resurgence of religion and a time of desecularization.[77] This resurgence has compelled scholars to reexamine secularism.[78]

---

[72]See, for example, Rockne McCarthy et al., *Society, State and School: A Case for Structural and Confessional Pluralism* (Grand Rapids: Eerdmans, 1981).

[73]Herman Dooyeweerd refers to this as the differentiation or—literally from the Dutch—"unlocking" process.

[74]See in particular the excellent book by Richard J. Mouw and Sander Griffioen, *Pluralisms and Horizons: An Essay in Christian Public Philosophy* (Grand Rapids: Eerdmans, 1993).

[75]I am indebted to Karen Harding for this metaphor.

[76]Peter Berger, *The Many Altars of Modernity: Towards a Paradigm for Religion in a Pluralist Age* (Berlin: de Gruyter, 2014).

[77]Peter Berger, ed., *The Desecularization of the World: Resurgent Religion and World Politics* (Grand Rapids: Eerdmans, 1999).

[78]The authors are many: see Charles Taylor, etc.

For our purposes a particularly insightful book is José Casanova's *Public Religions in the Modern World*.[79] Casanova argues that secularization is complex; what normally passes for a single theory is actually constituted by three different propositions. These three are[80]

1. secularization as differentiation of the secular spheres from religious institutions and norms;

2. secularization as decline of religious beliefs and practices; and

3. secularization as marginalization of religion to a privatized sphere.

Casanova argues that the first proposition remains the true insight of the theory of secularization. He refers to this as a "structural trend" and argues that this differentiation is one of the distinguishing characteristics of modern structures. The state and the economy, as well as other cultural and institutional spheres of society such as science, education, law, and art, each develop its own institutional autonomy and functional dynamics. Religion, for Casanova, is itself constrained to accept this modern principle of structural differentiation and to develop a differentiated, autonomous sphere of its own.[81]

For Casanova, the more religions resist modern differentiation, the more likely they are to decline in the long run. However, he is clear that there are other types of religions that work with differentiation, and these are not antimodern. Such religions take public life seriously and resist the privatization of religion—the third proposition above—but embrace differentiation. Such religions are not, according to Casanova, antimodern but

> immanent normative critiques of specific forms of institutionalization of modernity which presuppose precisely the acceptance of the validity of the fundamental values and principles of modernity, that is, individual freedoms and differentiated structures. In other words, they are immanent critiques of particular forms of modernity from a modern religious point of view.[82]

Casanova infers three requirements for a religion to flourish in our new situation: only those religions that by doctrine or tradition have a public, communal identity will want to assume public roles and resist the pressure of privatization. It is unlikely that religions weakened by secularization, and which have

---

[79]José Casanova, *Public Religions in the Modern World* (Chicago: University of Chicago Press, 1994).
[80]Ibid., 8.
[81]Ibid., 212.
[82]Ibid., 222.

declined as a result, will be able to survive. Amid globalization religions will tend to assume public roles when their identity as universal transsocial religions is reinforced by their actually being present and connected globally.

Casanova explores various examples of publically engaged churches and argues, "It was this combination of globalization, nationalization, secular involvement, and voluntary disestablishment that led to the change of orientation from state to society and permitted the church to play a key role in processes of democratization."[83] He describes this public engagement as deprivatization and identifies three such types. For our purposes his third one is most significant. Of this type he notes,

> By bringing publicity into the private moral sphere and by bringing into the public sphere issues of private morality, religions force modern societies to confront the task of reconstructing reflexively and collectively their own normative foundations. By doing so, they aid in the process of practical rationalization of the traditional lifeworld and of their own normative traditions.[84]

For Casanova we are in a situation in which religions are now challenging the secular spheres and foregrounding their ideologies, and, intriguingly, religion often supports human enlightenment.

In the process Casanova develops an intriguing account of the public square. Its norms cannot be presupposed but should be seen as the outcome of civil discourse and interaction.

The parallels with Kuyper are extraordinary. It was—Casanova helps us to see—Kuyper's genius to embrace the structural differentiation of modernity, while resisting tooth and nail the privatization of religion.[85] In the process he compelled the public square to become a place of interaction among different views, as was seen again and again in Kuyper's speeches and replies and questions in the Dutch parliament.

Conclusion

Kuyper's approach to and engagement in politics gives me hope that governments might promote the flourishing of all citizens. I find helpful and

---

[83]Ibid., 225.
[84]Ibid., 229.
[85]Cf. Jeanne H. Schindler, ed., *Christianity and Civil Society: Catholic and Neo-Calvinist Perspectives* (Lanham, MD: Lexington, 2008).

challenging his emphasis on the importance to society and government of a vital civil society. The connection between Kuyper's model of structural and directional pluralism with Casanova's theory of religion and secularization demonstrates just how perceptive Kuyper was in seeking a modern approach to politics from a Christian perspective. His emphasis on what has come to be called "a preferential option for the poor" is truly remarkable and resonates with the concerns of Pope Francis and of Bernie Sanders in the run-up to the 2016 US presidential election.

However, when it comes to Kuyper's thought on the social issues of his day, one cannot help but feel that Kuyperians have failed to hear this call. Prophetically, Kuyper saw consumerism emerging in the wake of industrialization, and in this respect he must be reckoned alongside Karl Marx. We live now amid the tsunami of global consumerism, with an apartheid-like economic divide between North and South. And most Western Christians seem quite content with this situation. In our situation reading Kuyper on "Christ and the Needy" feels like the prophet Amos is back and preaching in our churches. I doubt he would be very welcome. But he certainly is needed.[86]

I often ask my students whether the Kuyperian tradition could ever produce a Mother Teresa. Only, I think, if we really take Kuyper's "The Church and the Needy" to heart. Doubtless many different responses are called for to the multifaceted problem of poverty, but all will involve some form of "preferential option for the poor" if we are followers of Jesus—and true Kuyperians. Free-market ideology simply will not do. Indeed, in his Stoker lecture at the University of the Northwest in South Africa, Dutch economist Bob Goudzwaard wondered aloud whether sphere sovereignty remains relevant today when the borders of the nation-state are continually being blurred. One area he identifies of continuing relevance is economics. In our consumer world the economic sphere has overflowed its boundaries and is threatening to derail and control all the other spheres. To allude to a title of another work by Goudzwaard and de Lange, we are in desperate need of moving *Beyond Poverty and Affluence: Toward an Economy of Care*.[87]

---

[86]Cf. Gertrude Himmelfarb, *The Roads to Modernity: The British, French, and American Enlightenments* (New York: Vintage, 2004), 116-30, on Wesley and Methodism.

[87]Bob Goudzwaard and Harry de Lange, *Beyond Poverty and Affluence: Toward an Economy of Care*, trans. Mark R. Vander Vennen (Grand Rapids: Eerdmans, 1994). Absolutely essential reading.

MISSION

*He uttered a triumphant cry: IT IS ACCOMPLISHED! And
it was as though he had said: Everything has begun.*

Nikos Kazantzakis, *The Last Temptation*

*The Bible always includes all of the universe in God's
act of salvation through Jesus Christ.*

J. H. Bavinck, *The Church Between Temple and Mosque*

*Only in the perspective of the Kingdom of God do we really see the Church as God
has created it, and are set free to serve that Kingdom as members of that Church.*

D. T. Niles, *Upon the Earth*

All revelation is a calling and a mission.

Martin Buber, *I and Thou*

In Isaiah 61:1 the servant of the Lord speaks of being
"sent." Jesus appropriates this passage from Isaiah in the Nazareth manifesto in
Luke 4:16-21. In John's Gospel (Jn 20:21) Jesus says, "As the Father has sent
me, I am sending you." Mission—being sent—is the heartbeat of God's people,
and it is rare and wonderful to find such a comprehensive view of mission as
is embodied in Kuyper and in the Kuyperian tradition.

Lesslie Newbigin makes an important distinction between *missional dimension* and *missional intention*, which is helpful as we think of Kuyper in terms of mission.[1] This distinguishes "between mission as a dimension of the Church's whole life, and mission as the primary intention of certain activities. Because the Church is the mission there is a missionary dimension to everything that the Church does. But not everything the Church does has a missionary intention."[2]

Since the life of the church as a whole, both as a gathered community and as a scattered people throughout the world, is the major means by which the Spirit executes his mission in the world, the entire life of the church can be characterized from one aspect as witness or missional. However, not every activity is aimed at inviting people to repent and believe in Christ. All of Christian life has a missional *dimension*, but not all of it is characterized by a missional *intention*.

Kuyper did not use *mission* in this way, but he recognized as have few others the missional dimension of the life of the church, without for a moment neglecting the church's missional intention. Indeed, broadly speaking Kuyper's theology and worldview were *missional* through and through, as we have seen. As we noted in chapter six, when Kuyper did address the subject of *mission* he thought of mission mainly as evangelism and particularly as evangelism to Jews, Muslims, and pagans.[3] Using Newbigin's distinction, we can say that here he focused on *missional intention*. An important insight of his was the role of the local congregation in taking responsibility for such missional activity and of mission in this restricted sense as an extension of the institutional church.[4]

---

[1]Michael W. Goheen, *Introducing Christian Mission Today: Scripture, History and Issues* (Downers Grove, IL: IVP Academic, 2014), 82-83.

[2]Lesslie Newbigin, *One Body, One Gospel, One World: The Christian Mission Today* (London: International Missionary Council, 1958), 43-44.

[3]There are helpful insights in Kuyper's "Lecture by Prof. Dr. A. Kuyper Concerning 'Missions,' Mission Congress in Amsterdam, 28-30 January, 1890" (forthcoming). E.g., he emphasizes that mission proceeds from the sovereignty of God; Christ is *the* missionary, and he begins his mediatorial work immediately after the fall, but it comes into its own with the incarnation; Scripture is central to mission; preaching to the baptized is part of mission; etc. Intriguingly, Kuyper in proposition 3 addresses the mission of angels. Mission constitutes their existence, and they are sent out to serve those who inherit salvation. Cf. Abraham Kuyper, *De Engelen Gods* [The Angels of God] (Kampen: Kok, 1923).

[4]See proposition 20 in Kuyper, "Lecture by Prof. Dr. A. Kuyper Concerning 'Missions.'" Cf. here Lesslie Newbigin's view of the local congregation as the hermeneutic of the gospel in his *The Gospel in a Pluralist Society* (Grand Rapids: Eerdmans, 1989).

However, when it came to mission per se, Johan H. Bavinck (1895–1964), the nephew of Herman Bavinck, pioneered Kuyperian thought. Paul Visser notes that "Johan Herman Bavinck was the premier twentieth-century missiologist in the Dutch neo-Calvinist tradition. He extended the characteristic strengths of that tradition into new territories and a new era and did so compellingly enough that his thought reverberated in other schools of theology, and in nontheological disciplines as well."[5]

THE TWENTIETH CENTURY AND MISSION

J. H. Bavinck lived in the twentieth century, one of intense missional reflection and whose legacy continues to shape missiology today.[6] In Edinburgh in 1910 the world mission conference was held under the umbrella of the student movement's watchword of "the evangelisation of the world in this generation." Edinburgh is regarded as the symbolic starting point of the ecumenical movement. At Edinburgh, first steps were taken toward institutionalized cooperation between Protestant mission councils. Of the fourteen hundred participants, however, only seventeen came from the Global South.[7] Edinburgh gave rise to the journal *International Review of Mission* and to the committee that laid the groundwork for the International Missionary Council (IMC) in 1921. During Bavinck's lifetime, the IMC organized a series of international missionary conferences: at Jerusalem in 1928; Tambaram, India, in 1938; Whitby, Canada, in 1947; Willingen, Germany, in 1952; Achimota, Ghana, in 1958–1959; and Mexico City in 1963.

Whereas at Edinburgh mission remained largely connected with Western civilization, by Jerusalem in 1928 the mood had changed. World War I, fought by "Christian" countries, subverted the view of Western civilization as embodying the gospel. The Communist Revolution of 1917 brought a dose of realism to any dream of evangelizing the whole world in one generation. Two major questions emerged at Jerusalem, with no consensus: the relationship

---

[5]Paul Visser in John Bolt, ed., *The J. H. Bavinck Reader* (Grand Rapids: Eerdmans, 2013), 1.

[6]There are several good treatments of the history of mission in the twentieth century. For a brief overview, which I draw on, see "History," World Council of Churches website, www.oikoumene.org/en/what-we -do/cwme/history (accessed Aug. 27, 2016). See also, e.g., Timothy Yates, *Christian Mission in the Twentieth Century* (Cambridge: Cambridge University Press, 1994).

[7]The documents from Edinburgh are available online at Michigan Library Digital Collections, http://quod .lib.umich.edu. For a centennial assessment see David A. Kerr and Kenneth R. Ross, eds., *Edinburgh 2010: Mission Then and Now* (Oxford: Regnum, 2009).

between the gospel and other religions, and the role of Christian social and political involvement.

At Tambaram in 1938, just prior to WWII, discussions centered on the importance of the local church in mission, a major emphasis in Kuyper's and Newbigin's thought. Representatives of the "younger" churches became a majority. Tambaram defended the ultimate truth of the gospel in relation to other religions but emphasized the need to listen to and dialogue with them in the practice of mission.[8]

The IMC conference in Whitby, Canada, in 1947 reflected on the changed situation following WWII. Whitby's slogan was "Partnership in Obedience," with delegates abandoning the language of "Christian" and "non-Christian" countries, thereby opening the way to fresh new paths in missiology.

At Willingen, Germany, in 1952, after the Communist Revolution in China terminated traditional mission enterprise there, delegates rediscovered the dependence of mission on God's own activity. Mission was rediscovered as the action of the triune God. The idea of the *missio Dei* proved particularly fertile. The emphasis on the centrality of the church in mission was recontextualized within the larger frame of God's action, thus bringing world events into sharper focus. This important recontextualization of mission led Newbigin to his distinction between dimension and intent, as a way of retaining an emphasis on reaching the lost while embracing the comprehensive scope of mission.

In 1958, the IMC met in Achimota near Accra, Ghana, where it deliberated a proposal to unite with the World Council of Churches. The proposal was accepted. In 1961, the "integration" of church and mission, the IMC with the WCC, became operational in New Delhi. The IMC was affiliated with the Commission on World Mission and Evangelism of the WCC (CWME). From then on the world mission conferences were more truly "ecumenical," as a result of the involvement of more denominations, including Orthodox churches, and observers from the Roman Catholic Church.

In 1963 the first CWME met in Mexico City under the theme of "Mission in Six Continents." Pursuing the legacy of Willingen, the conference focused on witness in a world where God was already active, inviting churches to join

---

[8]Cf. J. H. Bavinck, *The Church Between Temple and Mosque* (Grand Rapids: Eerdmans, 1961), 117-18.

in God's mission. This was a time of a positive approach to secularization and of explanations of the Christian faith and action in nonreligious ways.

The conference went on after Bavinck's death. "Salvation Today," "Your Kingdom Come," and "Your Will be Done" were the respective themes of the CWME conferences in Bangkok (1972/73), Melbourne (1980), and San Antonio (1989). Bangkok explored the role of both spiritual and sociopolitical elements in the church's mission. At Melbourne the influence of liberation theology was felt, and the issue of the poor in mission moved front and center. San Antonio is noted for its exploration of the relationship between Christianity and other religions. It attempted to hold in tension that we can point to no other way of salvation than in Jesus Christ, but at the same time we cannot limit God's saving power. The 1996 conference in Salvador da Bahíl, Brazil, focused on the gospel and cultures, affirming the richness and ambiguity of cultural diversity. In 2005 the CWME met in Athens around the theme of "Come Holy Spirit, Heal and Reconcile." In 2010 a centenary conference was held in Edinburgh under the theme of "Witnessing to Christ Today," in which the CWME was fully involved.[9]

J. H. Bavinck died in 1964, the year after the first CWME met in Mexico City. Neither his work nor our evaluation of the Kuyperian tradition can be understood apart from this fertile discussion of mission, which spanned the twentieth century and continues today. The latter half of the twentieth century produced such luminaries as Lesslie Newbigin (1909–1998) and David Bosch (1929–1992), and contemporary Kuyperian missiologists such as Michael Goheen have brought the Kuyperian tradition into fertile dialogue with Newbigin's and Bosch's thought.[10] Before we turn to J. H. Bavinck's work, we will first attend to Kuyper and mission.

KUYPER AND MISSIOLOGY

> The Church of Christ is called to mission, and she falls short in obedience, if she delays in the fulfillment of this duty.[11]

---

[9]See Kirsteen Kim and Andrew Anderson, eds., *Edinburgh 2010: Mission Today and Tomorrow*, Regnum Edinburgh 2010 Series (Oxford: Regnum, 2011).

[10]See Michael W. Goheen, *"As the Father Has Sent Me, I Am Sending You": J. E. Lesslie Newbigin's Missional Ecclesiology* (Zoetermeer, Netherlands: Boekencentrum, 2000); *A Light to the Nations: The Missional Church and the Biblical Story* (Grand Rapids: Baker Academic, 2011); etc.

[11]Abraham Kuyper, *Encyclopaedie der heilige Godgeleerdheid*, 3 vols. (Kampen: Kok, 1909), 522.

When Kuyper gave his "Lecture... Concerning Missions," J. H. Bavinck was not yet born. In their *Gesprek over de onbekende Kuyper* (Conversation about the unknown Kuyper), G. Puchinger and N. Scheps discuss how to think of Kuyper. Scheps asserts that Kuyper represents the connection between the nineteenth century and the twentieth.[12] By comparison, Bavinck is clearly a twentieth-century figure, living amid all the major discussions of mission.

Nevertheless, Kuyper is certainly worth taking note of in terms of mission. Nowhere does he discuss it in detail, but in the third volume of his *Encyclopedia of Sacred Theology* he attends to mission as part of the theological encyclopedia. In my view, just to think in terms of the shape and contours of the encyclopedia of theology is right and useful.[13] Bavinck differed from Kuyper in some areas and developed a Reformed missiology in its own right. However, in the latter respect his work can and should be seen as a response to Kuyper's call for scriptural, foundational, and systematic work in this area.

Kuyper distinguishes four main areas in the encyclopedia of theology: the biblical, the ecclesial, the dogmatic, and the diaconological (practical theology).[14] *Diaconiological* is taken from the New Testament term διακονία, which Kuyper points out is the term used in the NT for "office without distinct function." The diaconal disciplines deal with "how the working of the Word of God, subject to his ordinances, *must be maintained.*"[15]

Kuyper discusses the diaconological group as such in the third volume of his encyclopedia.[16] He divides up this group as follows:

---

[12]G. Puchinger and N. Scheps, *Gesprek over de onbekende Kuyper* (Kampen: Kok, 1971), 10.

[13]Nowadays, in contrast, an "encyclopedia" of theology often refers to a dictionary of theology. Kuyper, *PST*, chap. 4, identifies three tasks for an encyclopedia of theology: it must establish the scientific character of theology; it must explain the relationship between theology and the other sciences; it must explain the different subdisciplines of theology and their interrelationship. Kuyper writes in the context of the modern European tradition, and he refers, among, others to J. F. Räbiger, *Theologik oder Encyklopädie der Theologie* (Leipzig: Fues Verlag, 1880), and also engages frequently with Schleiermacher. Cf. Friedrich Schleiermacher's *Brief Outline of the Study of Theology*, trans. William Farrer (Edinburgh: T&T Clark, 1850). Part 1 of Schleiermacher's *Brief Outline* is devoted to philosophical theology, and he develops a markedly different approach to Kuyper. See chapters nine and ten below. For a comparable work to Kuyper's around the same time see Alfred Cave, *An Introduction to Theology: Its Principles, Its Branches, Its Results, and Its Literature* (Edinburgh: T&T Clark, 1896).

[14]*PST*, 631. Readers should note that I have updated Kuyper's cumbersome terminology. It is significant that Kuyper assigns practical theology a place in theology as a science; he terms it "diaconology" and was followed in this by W. D. Jonker, *Leve de Kerk* (1969), and C. Trimp, *De volmacht tot bediening der verzoening* (1970).

[15]*PST*, 630, emphasis original.

[16]Abraham Kuyper, *Encyclopaedie der heilige Godgeleerdheid*, 3 vols. (Kampen: Kok, 1909).

1. the didactic (teaching) subjects

    a. homiletics

    b. catechism

    c. liturgics

    d. prosthetics

2. the presbyterial subjects

    a. cybernetics (communication)

    b. poemenics (pastoral theology)

3. the diaconal subjects

4. the laical (dealing with the laity) subjects (institutional laical and organic laical)

Kuyper argues for the term *prosthetics* for what we call missiology.[17] It deals with the investigation of the unbaptized who remain outside the church. He takes prosthetics from προστίθημι in Acts 2:41, 47; 5:14; 11:24, in which verses it has the meaning "to add to."

Kuyper's choice of vocabulary is admirable in its attempt to be biblical, but clearly such names would not work today. Kuyper argues that *prosthetics* avoids the danger of thinking of mission as the salvation of individual souls; mission is, by contrast, the expansion of the body of Christ and the responsibility of the church.[18] Prosthetics investigates the scriptural and most profitable way to evangelize those who still remain outside Christ. The work of prosthetics began on the day of Pentecost. In the first place, as a subject, prosthetics is bound to God's Word and the principles we find in it. Scripture must, however, not just be used to criticize missionary methods; instead, we need to build an architectonic theory of mission from Scripture. Ethnological, historical, and psychological study will be required, as well as detailed knowledge of other religions and of *elenctics*, the science concerned with persuasion and the conviction of sin.[19] Kuyper is clear that if the light of missions is to be

---

[17]Kuyper divides prosthetics into the following subdivisions: general theory of mission; particular theories of mission among Jews, Muslims, Buddhists, etc.; the history of mission.

[18]Kuyper, *Encyclopaedie* 3:519.

[19]J. H. Bavinck, *An Introduction to the Science of Missions*, trans. David H. Freeman (Phillipsburg, NJ: Presbyterian and Reformed, 1960), 221-23. Kuyper positions elenctics within dogmatics, but Bavinck, 232, positions it in missiology. In the history of Reformed theology cf. Francis Turretin, *Institutes of Elenctic Theology*, trans. George M. Giver, 3 vols. (Phillipsburg, NJ: P&R, 1997).

kindled, then the subject of mission will need to be taken up more fully and foundationally, that is, more Scripturally and systematically than had thus far been done.[20] Kuyper recognizes the need for what we call *contextualization* to be investigated. There is, in short, a great need for rigorous work in missiology, in Kuyper's view.[21]

Bavinck argues against *prosthetics* as missiology's name because in the verses Kuyper refers to προστίθημι is exclusively the work of God. Bavinck also rightly notes that placing missiology within the didactic group is too limiting: in the office of the missionary, the unity of offices is more clearly present than anywhere else. "Missions is surely concerned with the ministry of the Word, but on the mission field the Word operates in an intrinsic connection with the ministry of mercy and the government of the church."[22] Thus, Bavinck supports the idea of an "independent" missiology.

BAVINCK'S CAREER AND WRITINGS

J. H. Bavinck's career can be divided into distinct periods.[23] Initially, his interest in psychology led to a focus on the psychology of religion. His doctoral thesis dealt with the extent to which the affective, sensory dimension of human life influences the knowing process. In it he focused on the religious life of medieval mystic Heinrich von Suso (1295/1297–1366) as a case study. In his research Bavinck argued that human knowing is not autonomous but an extension of our intuitive grasp of reality. Later his ordination as a missionary to Java (1929) activated an interest in missiology. His fascination with Asian mysticism and his time as an instructor at the Theological School in Jogjakarta (1934–1938) drew his attention more clearly to theological issues. Prior to his appointment to teach mission at Kampen Seminary in 1938, Bavinck served two terms of missionary service in Indonesia, where he interacted closely with the great Dutch missiologist Hendrik Kraemer (1888–1965). After his return to the Netherlands as professor of missions at Kampen

---

[20]Kuyper, *Encyclopaedie* 3:523.

[21]Ibid., 3:524, refers to the work of Warneck, Buss, Plath, Petri, and Büttner as important sources to consult.

[22]Bavinck, *Introduction*, xx.

[23]The definitive work on J. H. Bavinck in English is by Paul Visser, *Heart for the Gospel, Heart for the World: The Life and Thought of a Reformed Pioneer Missiologist Johan Herman Bavinck (1895–1964)*, trans. Jerry Gort (Eugene, OR: Wipf and Stock, 2003); see also Visser's comprehensive introductory essay in Bolt, *J. H. Bavinck Reader*.

Theological Seminary and the Free University of Amsterdam (1939), and as professor of Practical Theology at the latter institution (1954), all these themes came together in his work. The high point of Bavinck's work to present the gospel contextually came with the publication of his book *Christus en de mystiek van het Oosten* (*Christ and the Mysticism of the East*) in 1934. Johannes Verkuyl considers this Bavinck's most significant work.[24]

Bavinck thus practiced mission as well as lived through and participated in some of the major twentieth-century conferences on mission, an opportunity that was not, of course, available to Kuyper. Bavinck's work demonstrates familiarity with the works of other leading Protestant and Roman Catholic missiologists.[25] Bavinck's work took place largely in the first half of the twentieth century, and thus he did not engage with later twentieth-century missiologists such as Lesslie Newbigin (1909–1998) and David Bosch (1929–1992).

Bavinck believed the church to be inherently ecumenical and supported his denomination, the Gereformeerde Kerken in Nederland (GKN), when in 1946 it joined the Dutch Missionary Council (DMC) and became affiliated with the IMC. In 1947 the GKN participated in the first meeting of the Reformed Ecumenical Synod (RES) in Grand Rapids, Michigan. Bavinck strongly supported the proposal to set up an international committee to study the implications of Reformed theology for mission. The second assembly of the RES, in Amsterdam in 1949, launched the International Reformed Missionary Council.

---

[24]Johannes Verkuyl, *Contemporary Missiology: An Introduction*, trans. Dale Cooper (Grand Rapids: Eerdmans, 1978), 39. Several chapters of this work by Bavinck are translated into English in Bolt, *J. H. Bavinck Reader*.

[25]Such as Dutch Johannes C. Hoekendijk (1912–1975), Albert C. Kruyt (1869–1949), and Barend M. Schuurman (1889–1945); German Gustaf Warneck (1834–1910), Walter Freytag (1899–1959), Bruno Gutmann (1876–1966), Karl Hartenstein (1894–1952), Walter Holsten (1908–1982), Christian Keysser (1875–1957), Julius Richter (1862–1940), Joseph Schmidlin (1876–1944), and Johannes Thauren (1892–1954); British William Carey (1761–1834), Roland Allen (1868–1947), G. E. Phillips, Stephen Neill (1900–1984), and M. A. C. Warren (1904–1977); Dutch-American Harry R. Boer (1913–1999); Indian Vengal Chakkarai (1880–1958); and Japanese Toyohiko Kagawa (1888–1960). See Paul Visser in Bolt, *J. H. Bavinck Reader*, 38-39. See Gerald Anderson, ed., *Biographical Dictionary of Christian Missions* (Grand Rapids: Eerdmans, 1999), for articles on all these fascinating figures. Also see Gerald Anderson et al., eds., *Mission Legacies: Biographical Studies of Leaders of the Modern Missionary Movement* (Maryknoll, NY: Orbis, 1994); Verkuyl, *Contemporary Missiology*, 26-88. In his encounter with Karl Barth, Hartenstein was the first to develop the *missio Dei* as an "inalienable indication of God's revelation," an emphasis that became central to Bavinck's missiology. Anderson, *Biographical Dictionary of Christian Missions*, 282.

The GKN was suspicious of the WCC from its inception in 1948, whereas Bavinck, like great British pastor and theologian John Stott, saw value in remaining in dialogue with the WCC. Bavinck died in 1964, ten years before the major evangelical conference in Lausanne in 1974, at which Stott emerged as the primary theologian and stood up to Billy Graham in insisting that mission not be reduced to evangelism.[26] Stott's *Christian Mission in the Modern World*, published shortly after Lausanne, remains a classic, and one can only wonder what role Bavinck might have played at Lausanne had he been alive then. Lausanne was a watershed conference for evangelicals in its approach to mission, followed up by a conference in Manila, and then in Cape Town. In his *Christian Mission in the Modern World* Stott engages positively, and critically, with Bavinck's thought.[27]

After World War II Bavinck moved in broader circles. In 1947 he traveled to the United States to lecture at Calvin College and Seminary. In 1952, 1953, and 1963, Bavinck lectured on missiology at Potchefstroom Theological Seminary in South Africa.

Bavinck's most important missiological works demonstrate a gradual deepening of insight, especially in terms of the relationship between the Christian faith and other religions. Early in WWII he published *De Boodschap van Christus en de niet-christelijke religies* (The message of Christ and non-Christian religions), which summarized the argument of Hendrik Kraemer's *The Christian Message in a Non-Christian World*—written for Tambaram—with supplementary notes engaging positively but critically with Kraemer's view of Christianity and the notion of "biblical realism." In *Alzoo wies het Woord* (And thus the Word grew and increased), Bavinck reflects on the methods of Paul for the missionary calling.[28] After WWII Bavinck published *Zending in een wereld in nood* (Mission in a world in need), an introduction to the principles of mission for church members. Bavinck's lectures at Calvin Theological Seminary in 1947 were published as *The Impact of Christianity on the Non-Christian World*, a reflection on missionary apologetics. In the foreword Clarence Bouma writes, "Though not as wide in scope, as to spirit and content, this

---

[26]Timothy Dudley-Smith, *John Stott: A Global Ministry* (Leicester, UK: Inter-Varsity Press, 2001), 220-24.
[27]John Stott, *Christian Mission in the Modern World* (Downers Grove, IL: InterVarsity Press, 2008), 42-43, 105-7.
[28]An allusion to Acts 19:20: "So mightily grew the word of God" (KJV).

work should be classed with Hendrik Kraemer's *The Christian Message in a Non-Christian World.*"[29]

In *Religieus besef en Christelijk geloof* (Religious consciousness and Christian faith), Bavinck elaborates on Kraemer's ideas but develops them according to his own approach. In relation to Romans 1, Bavinck explores the issues of general revelation, God's revelation of himself in Christ, and the origin and substance of religious consciousness. *Inleiding in de zendingswetenschap* (*Introduction to the Science of Missions*) served as a textbook, the first standard Reformed work in missiology published in the Netherlands. It was translated into English in 1960.[30] Finally, *The Church Between Temple and Mosque* was a posthumous publication of Bavinck's lectures in Chicago, dealing with the content of religious consciousness as it relates to Christian faith.

BAVINCK'S VIEW OF MISSION

Bavinck argued for the science of missions as an integral part of theology. In this he was influenced by Gustav Warneck (1834–1910), the German missiologist who "in every sense must be acknowledged as the man who first established Missiology as a comprehensive theological discipline."[31] Warneck's *Das Studium der Mission auf der Universität* (The study of mission at the university) was published in 1877 and argued for the academic recognition of missiology, both because of the importance of missions in the modern world and because "the idea of missions is an integral part of the saving revelation in Christ; it is such a fundamental idea of the gospel that whenever the latter is perceived in its innermost nature, the idea of missions necessarily emerges."[32]

Bavinck preferred the term *science* rather than *theology* of mission because he did not want to set knowledge and faith in opposition to one another.[33] From Bavinck's perspective, knowledge of God contains the highest possible

---

[29]J. H. Bavinck, *The Impact of Christianity on the Non-Christian World* (Grand Rapids: Eerdmans, 1948).

[30]J. H. Bavinck, *An Introduction to the Science of Missions*, trans. David H. Freeman (Phillipsburg, NJ: P&R, 1960).

[31]David Bosch, "Missiology," in I. H. Eybers, A. König, and J. A. Stoop, eds., *Introduction to Theology*, 3rd ed. (Pretoria, South Africa: NGKB, 1982), 263. For Warneck's influence on Bavinck, see Visser, *Heart for the Gospel*.

[32]Gustav Warneck, *Das Studium der Mission auf der Universität* (Gütersloh: C. Bertelsmann, 1877), 11. Quoted in Bavinck, *Introduction*, xviii.

[33]Readers should note that the Dutch *Wetenschap* has the same connotations as the German *Wissenschaft* and has the broader meaning of scholarship or academic analysis that *science* often does not have in English.

degree of objectivity. *Science* of missions also enables every aspect of mission to be brought into focus.

During his lifetime he developed four definitions of mission; the following is his most detailed and best one, in my opinion:[34]

> Mission is that activity of the church throughout the whole world—which in its deepest essence is an activity of Christ himself—through which it calls the nations in their diversity to faith in and obedience to Jesus Christ, demonstrates to them by the signs of [its] service and ministry how the salvation of Christ encompasses all of life, and at the same time teaches them to look forward to the perfection of the Kingdom, in which God will be all in all.[35]

Bavinck's earlier (1941) definition of mission focused on preaching the gospel and personal conversion. However, a key part of Bavinck's development was a growing concern with the central New Testament theme of the kingdom of God, and by 1947 he had clearly integrated in his view of mission the Kuyperian concept of the service of God in all areas of life, as is clear from the above definition.[36] Bavinck asserts,

> In our time we still struggle with the idea of the Kingdom of God. For a long time Christians have overemphasized the fact that the Christian faith is something that concerns man's innermost being and is the way to salvation, without paying enough attention to the fact that faith places man in the perspective of the Kingdom. . . . Something of the power of the new life in Jesus Christ must penetrate social and economic life, commerce and industry, science and art. We must not leave any sector of individual or social life to its own devices. God wants us to gather together right now all things in this world under one head, Christ.[37]

Among Kuyperian scholars, Bavinck anticipates the fertile work of Nicholas Wolterstorff in this respect with his fascination with the biblical concept of *shalom*.[38] He resists, of course, any notion of Christianization by

---

[34]Visser, *Heart for the Gospel*, 216-17.

[35]Bavinck, "Zendingsbegrip en zendingswerkelijkheid," 7-8. See Visser, *Heart for the Gospel*, 216.

[36]On the centrality of the kingdom of God in Bavinck's thought see Bavinck, *Church Between Temple and Mosque*, 131-37. E.g., Bavinck, 147, perceptively notes of Jesus' miracles that "by these miracles Jesus wanted to make clear that the whole cosmos will be redeemed, and that the curse which threatened the life of man through all the ages will be withdrawn. . . . All these miracles were signs that in Him the Kingdom of God was at hand. A new aeon had dawned, a new age, not only for man but for the whole universe."

[37]Bavinck, *Church Between Temple and Mosque*, 148.

[38]Ibid., 149; cf. Nicholas Wolterstorff, *Until Justice and Peace Embrace* (Grand Rapids: Eerdmans, 1983).

force and stressed with Kuyper that the struggle between the gospel and our cultures always presupposes diversity and pluriformity: one should not "force one's own culture on other nations" but should seek to give form to the rule of Christ in "living relationship to that which is central to the culture" of a given people.[39]

Bible and mission. Bavinck took as his point of departure the assumption that the Bible contains God's complete revelation, which is valid for all peoples and all times.[40] Indeed, one of the attractive characteristics of Bavinck's work, especially his more mature work, is always to develop his view of mission from Scripture and to take the whole narrative of the Bible into account. While Bavinck's interpretation of Romans 1:18-23 led him to disagree fundamentally with Barth on general revelation, Bavinck *was* positively influenced by Barth through Hendrik Kraemer, who introduced him to Barth's insistence on taking the Word of God as the only point of departure for theological reflection.

Bavinck had come to know the Reformed missionary theologian Hendrik Kraemer during their student days. However, it was in Solo, Indonesia, between 1930 and 1934 that Kraemer initiated Bavinck into the mysteries of Javanese literature and mysticism. Bavinck's 1934 publication *Christ and the Mysticism of the East* was at least in part a fruit of Kraemer's mentoring. At a later stage, Kraemer had a decisive influence on Bavinck's theology of religion. Kraemer's book *The Christian Message in a Non-Christian World*, written for the International Missionary Conference in Tambaram (1938), caused Bavinck to change his view of other religions from a psychological to a strongly theological approach. Comparably, Kraemer valued Bavinck's psychological insights in his reading of Romans 1:18-23.[41]

Bavinck rightly notes just how foundational the doctrine of *creation* is for mission.[42] Creation means that no one nation is higher or better than another

---

[39]J. H. Bavinck, "Zendingsbegrip en Zendingswerkelijkheid," *De Heerban* 2 (1949): 4-6. Quoted in Bolt, *J. H. Bavinck Reader*, 92.

[40]Paul Visser in *J. H. Bavinck Reader*, 121. Cf. Bavinck, *Church Between Temple and Mosque*, 129-37, for a wonderful chapter titled "The Bible Is Different." In *Introduction*, 239, Bavinck notes that "the philosophy of religion must, therefore, begin by listening to God's Word."

[41]Cf. Bavinck, *Church Between Temple and Mosque*, 117-27. His discussion of Rom 1 is well worth reading. On 120 he asserts, "The aerial of man's heart can no longer receive the wave length of God's voice, even though it surrounds him on all sides." Bavinck is keenly alert to the psychological insights of Rom 1:18-25, in relation to repression, exchange, and being given up.

[42]Bavinck, *Introduction*, 12.

before God, and God is sovereign over the whole creation, which is rightly his.[43] *Covenant* is also vital for mission, since it rejects a natural bond between Yahweh and Israel. Mission is only possible within such a framework: "If Jehovah is the God of Israel because he has made a covenant with Israel, it is conceivable that other nations will also some day be included in that covenant." Biblically, the motive for mission is the glory of Yahweh: "Israel is not primarily stirred to so deep a concern over the nations by compassion, but much more by the inner longing that it become clear to the whole world that only Jehovah is Lord, the true God."[44] Bavinck notes that texts like Psalms 47:1; 99:1 were most likely never heard by other nations; instead, they served to remind Israel that it lived before the entire world.

During the time of the prophets Israel increasingly found itself caught up in dealings with the emerging superpowers of the day. It faced a choice: either it would be absorbed into the world of its day, or it would become "a living power by means of which the nations would be drawn into the light of the salvation of Israel's God."[45] As the judgment of exile overshadows Israel, the figure of the Messiah appears more clearly in the preaching of the prophets.

As regards mission in the Old Testament, Bavinck rightly notes that one cannot really speak of the promise of missions within the Old Testament. For Bavinck, however, the vision is a more glorious one of the nations journeying to the God of Israel, drawn like a magnet. In this respect mission in the Old Testament is viewed *centripetally*, whereas in the New Testament it becomes far more *centrifugal*. This coming in the Old Testament is seen as eschatological, and it is utterly comprehensive, embracing life in its totality. Indeed, the entire creation will participate therein.[46]

The exile and the consequent emergence of the Jewish diaspora and the Septuagint translation of the Old Testament were providential, laying the foundations for the mission of the church after Pentecost.[47] As noted above, in Bavinck's work the kingdom of God moved to front and center. As the Gospels

---

[43]For Bavinck on creation order and kingdom see Bavinck, *Church Between Temple and Mosque*, 153-64, "The Law of the Kingdom." In this marvelous chapter he anticipates Oliver O'Donovan's *Resurrection and Moral Order* concept that resurrection reaffirms creation.

[44]Bavinck, *Introduction*, 14, 16.

[45]Ibid., 19.

[46]Ibid., 22, 23.

[47]Cf. Craig G. Bartholomew, *Introducing Biblical Hermeneutics: A Comprehensive Framework for Hearing God in Scripture* (Grand Rapids: Baker Academic, 2015), 163-64.

unfold, it becomes clear that the future will not unfold according to the expectations of the disciples and the crowds. "It is then that the intervening time comes to the fore, and with it also comes missions. Missions and the interim are inseparable."[48] Bavinck's recognition of mission as *the* characteristic of the time between *the already* and *the not-yet* of the coming of the kingdom is a seminal insight and fundamental for missiology.[49] Bavinck notes, "The gospel contains something of the glory of a king's commission. It must therefore end with a summons to proclaim the kingship of Christ over the whole world."[50]

God has committed to the church the ministry of reconciliation (2 Cor 5:18-19):

> We go into one land after the other throughout the entire world; we seek, and we preach, and all the time it is God who completes his work of reconciliation through us. For in his work of reconciliation God is concerned not only with individuals, but also with the "world," and in turning to the world, God takes us along. Missionary work is thus anchored in divine activity.[51]

For Bavinck, as for Paul in 2 Corinthians 5, *reconciliation* is a synonym for *salvation*. Salvation, like reconciliation, is thus all-inclusive: "There is nothing that lies outside of the gracious salvation that Christ gives those who love him."[52] Bavinck is clear that salvation includes personal and cosmic dimensions and asserts that the word *salvation* impinges on every aspect of human life.[53]

Theology and mission. Mission is quintessentially *God's work*. After his examination of the biblical data in *An Introduction*, Bavinck declares, "If we were to give a definition of missions there would be every reason to declare: Missions is the great work of Jesus Christ, through which after his completed work as mediator, he draws all peoples to his salvation and makes them to partake of the gifts which he has obtained for them."[54]

With regard to the *missio Dei*, Bavinck affirmed wholeheartedly the statement made at Willingen in 1952 that the trinitarian God is "a missionary

---

[48]Bavinck, *Introduction*, 34.

[49]For a critical response to such a view see John G. Flett, *The Witness of God: The Trinity, Missio Dei, Karl Barth, and the Nature of Christian Community* (Grand Rapids: Eerdmans, 2010), especially chap. 2.

[50]Bavinck, *Introduction*, 34.

[51]Ibid., 43.

[52]Ibid., 55.

[53]Bavinck, *Church Between Temple and Mosque*, 182.

[54]Bavinck, *Introduction*, 57-58.

God." "Out of the depths of His love for us, the Father has sent forth His own beloved Son to reconcile all things to Himself, that we and all men might, through the Spirit, be made one in Him with the Father in that perfect love which is the very nature of God."[55] Already at the GKN Synod of Middelburg in 1896, as Bavinck observed, the foundational importance of the doctrine of the Trinity had been foregrounded.[56]

After Willingen, in missionary theology under the influence of J. C. Hoek-endijk, the church came to be seen as a "function of the apostolate," and *missio ecclesiae* became defined in relation to the coming of God's kingdom rather than in relation to church planting. Many missiologists began to unpack the concept of *missio ecclesiae* within the eschatological framework of the already and not-yet of the kingdom of God. Significantly, from this time on, Bavinck's missiology bears traces of this emphasis. He uses the phrase "kingdom of God" more frequently (in *An Introduction to the Science of Missions*, published shortly after Willingen, he even included it in his definition of mission), and he noted positively that "the eschatological moment is being given a place of great importance in more recent thinking on mission."[57] However, Bavinck resisted defining the main thrust of the church in relation to the apostolate, arguing for worship and nurture as equally central tasks.[58]

Similarly, Bavinck welcomed the notion from the ecumenical movement of *missio ecclesiae*—the view that mission belongs to the essence of the church. God has entrusted to the church the ministry of reconciliation, which is at the heart of mission. He affirms the notion that it is to the *local church* in particular that mission is entrusted, and not just to the clergy: "The concept of missions can thus be developed as to leave a great deal of room for that which the ordinary church members can do in obedience to Christ's command, either as individuals or by means of societies or other organizations."[59]

The preaching of the Word is a prophetic witness that needs to be accompanied by the priestly witness of works of mercy. Mission is far more than

---

[55]Bolt, *J. H. Bavinck Reader*, 170. Note that here Bavinck follows Kuyper's seminal insight in grounding mission in the doctrine of the Trinity.

[56]Bavinck, *Introduction*, 65.

[57]Quoted in Bolt, *J. H. Bavinck Reader*, 40.

[58]This is a vital insight. Cf. Craig G. Bartholomew, "Theological Interpretation and a Missional Hermeneutic," in Michael W. Goheen, ed., *Reading the Bible Missionally*, The Gospel and Our Culture Series (Grand Rapids: Eerdmans, 2016), 68-85.

[59]Bavinck, *Introduction*, 61.

sending out missionaries: being a missionary involves representing Christ in our vocations and in all that we are involved in. There is thus room in mission for the most diverse activities. "Unity ought to be achieved, however, by knowing that God would disclose his salvation by our varied activity and would include us as his instruments in his inscrutable, divine work." Thus missionary activity occurs in all aspects of life.[60]

In dialogue with Kraemer, Bavinck poses the question of whether mission is the hallmark of the church. Kraemer writes, "the *raison d'être* for the church is to satisfy and to meet the need of the world."[61] Bavinck discerns three activities essential to the church:

1. The church exists to praise God; this is its *doxological* task, and contrary to Kraemer the church does not exist to satisfy the needs of the world but for God and his glory.

2. The church exists to bear the glory of the Word of God from generation to generation.

3. The church also exists to satisfy the needs of the world.

Despite his difference with Kraemer, Bavinck agrees that mission is part of the essence of the church.

In terms of the aims of mission Bavinck engages with Gisbertus Voetius's (1589–1676) view that mission has three aims: the conversion of the heathen, the establishment of the church, and the manifestation of God's grace. However, he asserts that these three aims are three aspects of a single purpose of God, namely the coming and growth of his kingdom. The kingdom is above all about God's glory; it includes the growth of the church throughout the earth; and it becomes concrete in the conversion of sinners. "These are not three separate purposes, but one great and exalted final purpose, that is disclosed to us in three blessings, of which the glorification of God is undoubtedly foremost, the establishment of the church second, and the conversion of the heathen third."[62] As noted above, Bavinck thus situates mission in the context of biblical eschatology and the kingdom of God: missionary activity is oriented

---

[60]Ibid., 67, 68.
[61]Quoted in ibid., 68.
[62]Ibid., 155-56.

toward God's purpose for the world, his eternal kingdom.[63] Mission in the interim looks toward that day when "all harsh, jarring notes of the terrifying drama we call world history will finally end in the exalted symphony of the kingdom of the most high."[64]

An important discussion in *An Introduction* is the relationship between mission to all nations and "the tribe." Bruno Gutmann (1876–1966), a German missionary in Tanzania, argued that the tribe is a given in creation order.[65] Bavinck is extremely cautious in this respect, noting the importance of the tribe, the importance for humankind of being in community, but resisting making the tribe the norm for human life. However, in true Kuyperian fashion Bavinck asserts,

> Although the church is an entirely different community than a nation or tribe, it is still never free of its important responsibility to society. By its whole attitude, by what it does within its own walls, it exercises an immeasurable influence upon the entire social order. And when the time is right the Church will sometimes need to testify forceably against certain national sins which distort the entire life of the society.[66]

As noted in chapter five, a debilitating aspect of Kuyper's thought was his view of the non-European peoples in southern Africa. Bavinck visited Potchefstroom Seminary in South Africa several times, and one suspects that his wariness here is partially informed by the absolutization of "the tribe" in South Africa.[67]

Mission and religious experience. Bavinck discusses the question of accommodation in relation to the gospel and a culture. He prefers to speak of "possession" rather than of accommodation or adaptation. Outside Christ,

---

[63]Cf. Johan A. Heyns, *The Church* (Pretoria, South Africa: N. G. Kerkboekhandel, 1980), for a similar ecclesiological approach.

[64]Bavinck, *Introduction*, 155, 156.

[65]Ibid., 161. For a brief introduction to Gutmann and further resources see Hans-Werner Gensichen, "Gutmann, Bruno," in *Biographical Dictionary of Christian Missions*, ed. Gerald H. Anderson (New York: Macmillan Reference USA, 1998), 271-72, available online at www.bu.edu/missiology/missionary-biography/g-h/gutmann-bruno-1876-1966. See also Flett, *Witness of God*, chap. 3; and David W. Congdon, *The Mission of Demythologizing: Rudolf Bultmann's Dialectical Theology* (Minneapolis: Fortress, 2015), 297-302.

[66]Bavinck, *Introduction*, 168-69.

[67]See Erica Meijers, "The End of the Colonial Mindset: Apartheid as Challenge for the Protestant Churches in the Netherlands," in *Globalisierung der Kirchen: Der Ökumenische Rat der Kirchen und die Entdeckung der Dritten Welt in den 1960er und 1970er Jahren*, ed. Katharina Kunter and Annegreth Schilling (Göttingen: Vandenhoeck and Ruprecht, 2014), 313-34.

practices and customs are misdirected in the service of idols. By *possession* Bavinck means that "Christ takes the life of a people in his hands, he renews and re-establishes the distorted and deteriorated; he fills each thing, each word, and each practice with a new meaning and gives it new direction."[68]

This brings us to the thorny issues of other religions, religious experience, general revelation, and elenctics.[69] Bavinck rightly notes that any serious missiology must engage in the development of a theology of religions because the church's assessment of and relationship to other religions is crucial in its missionary task. Bavinck disagrees with Kuyper when Kuyper argues that mission among Jews and Muslims must be connected with the *theologia naturalis* (natural theology).[70] For Bavinck, "The rational life of man is much too much bound up with his instinctive passions, with his emotional and volitional life, for rational argumentation to be able to bring about a real change."[71]

This is closely related to the question of general revelation. Bavinck rejected the meaning given to general revelation throughout much of the history of theology but rightly sees that Romans 1 teaches some form of general revelation. For him it was *not* a disclosure of divine truths discovered by reason but a person-oriented expression of God impinging on the life of humans:

> If we wish to use the expression "general revelation" we must not do so in the sense that one can logically conclude God's existence from it. This *may* be possible, but it only leads to a philosophical notion of God as the first cause. . . . When the Bible speaks of general revelation . . . it is divine concern for men collectively and individually. God's deity and eternal power are evident; they overwhelm man; they strike him suddenly in moments when he thought they were far away. They creep up on him; they do not let go of him, even though man does his best to escape them.[72]

Bavinck followed Calvin's view for a long time, based on the idea of God's voice reverberating throughout the creation and on God's ongoing providence

---

[68]Bavinck, *Introduction*, 179.

[69]The reader should note that this section covers much of what Bavinck calls *elenctics*. See his *Introduction*, 219-72.

[70]Cf. Abraham Kuyper, "The Natural Knowledge of God," trans. and annotated Harry Van Dyke, *The Bavinck Review* 6 (2015): 73-112.

[71]Bavinck, *Introduction*, 228.

[72]Bavinck, *Church Between Temple and Mosque*, 124.

and reign. However, in his posthumous *The Church Between the Temple and Mosque*, Bavinck develops this further into a christological foundation for general revelation:

> Christ now appears in a new form to him [man]. He was, of course, already present in this man's seeking; and because He did not leave Himself without a witness, Christ was wrestling to gain him, although he did not know it.... In the preaching of the gospel Christ once again appears to man, but much more concretely and in audible form. He awakes man from his long, disastrous dream.[73]

As regards the question of whether nonbelievers seek for God, Bavinck shifted his view by 1941:

> Earlier I referred now and again to the concept of *Suchen im Fliehen* [a searching for God while simultaneously fleeing from him]. Now I would like to express the matter differently. No one seeks God on his or her own, not even one (Rom 1: 11). If there is any kind of seeking anywhere, it exists by reason of the *horismos*, the divine purpose and guidance which does not relinquish its hold on a deeply sunken humankind.[74]

The relationship between religious experience and God's revelation in Christ is the theme governing the whole of Bavinck's missionary theology and career. Bavinck's understanding of religion evolved in two phases. Initially, he took his departure from the psychology of religion, which he then tried to support theologically. Later he reversed his approach: biblical-theological inquiry came first, and from that position he unpacked the psychological processes involved in religiosity. This shift resulted from Bavinck's reflection on Kraemer's *The Christian Message in a Non-Christian World*, a book that can be summarized in a single statement: God's revelation in Christ is not the fulfillment of all religious aspirations; instead it signifies God's judgment on these endeavors, and it catalyzes radical conversion.[75]

Bavinck is not persuaded by attempts to classify religions into groups and prefers to speak of "universal religious consciousness," which can only be examined indirectly.[76] Bavinck observes that the origin of religious consciousness

---

[73]Ibid., 127.

[74]Quoted in Bolt, *J. H. Bavinck Reader*, 51-52. Cf. Bavinck, *Introduction*, 62-65.

[75]Cf. Tim S. Perry, *Radical Difference: A Defence of Hendrik Kraemer's Theology of Religions* (Waterloo, ON: Wilfred Laurier University Press, 2001).

[76]Bavinck, *Church Between Temple and Mosque*, 29; cf. 2509.

is not firstly human but divine. From the human side, however, Bavinck notes several factors that play a role in religious life. First, he speaks of *the proto-word revelation*, an original revelation of God that took place before the fall and that remained in human memory. Second, he points to the possible flow of special revelation into different religions, to "the interesting datum . . . that the non-Christian religions are not truly religions that bloomed fully outside the sphere of special revelation, but that a certain measure of influx has to be regarded as a probability in several cases."[77] Bavinck thought this possibility existed in the modern period. Third, Bavinck calls attention to the role played by the demonic in all non-Christian religion.

Bavinck distinguished "a sort of framework within which the religious thought of humankind must move. . . . There appear to be certain intersections around which all sorts of ideas crystallize . . . so-called magnetic points to which the religious thinking of mankind is irresistibly attracted."[78] He identified these magnetic points or fundamental questions as[79]

1. the sense of belonging to the whole, the cosmos: *the relationship of I and the cosmos*;

2. the sense of transcendent norms: *the relationship of I and the norm*;

3. the sense that somehow our existence is governed: *the relationship of I and the riddle of my existence*;

4. the sense of a need for redemption: *the relationship of I and salvation*; and

5. the sense of our relatedness to a superior power: *the relationship of I and the supreme power*.

Bavinck notes the close interrelationship of all five points or questions; they are, in essence, one:

> But even if the answer is partial and uncertain, the fact remains that all questions force themselves upon man as one all-inclusive question: "Who am I, small mortal man, in the midst of all these powerful realities with which I am confronted and with which my life is most intimately related?" This very simple question reveals all the problems of religion in a nutshell.[80]

---

[77]Quoted in Bolt, *J. H. Bavinck Reader*, 56.

[78]J. H. Bavinck, *Religieus Besef en Christelijk Geloof* (Kampen: Kok, 1949), 103.

[79]Bavinck, *Church Between Temple and Mosque*, 32-34. Chapters 3–7 discuss each of these characteristics in turn.

[80]Ibid., 113.

Bavinck's view is thus to be located somewhere between Barth and Kuyper. He is clear that we can never use philosophical arguments to construct a bridge from a non-Christian religion to the Christian faith, for this would make conversion unnecessary and would thus make the call to repentance superfluous. In his view, this was a mistake made by the early church apologists. If they had not so anxiously grasped for the concept of the Logos, which we find, albeit transformed, in the Gospel of John, but had investigated John more closely, they would have seen that in John the strongest emphasis is laid on the religious nature of any arriving at truth.[81]

Unlike Barth, Bavinck saw in his magnetic points a place of connection for mission. This comes to the fore in Bavinck's approving quote of Kuyper with respect to the person of the missionary:

> As soon as you, as a man, encounter a person as a man, whether he be a pagan or a Mohammedan, you possess with him a common starting point, and this is first of all, the sin you both have committed, and secondly, the grace which saves you and which alone can save him when the light from Christ penetrates into the darkness, and the sinner is gripped by the mercy of God. Thus, there arises on the one hand a feeling of a common tie with the pagan, a common human heart, and in that heart, there is the same *sensus divinitatis*; that heart is disturbed by the same sin; you are by nature as heathen as he, the sole difference is the grace which has been given to you, and that he too can share in.[82]

Thus, Bavinck affirms a nuanced view of general revelation. However, he insists that humans are not seeking after the living God. In an insightful way Bavinck elaborates on the psychology of repression and exchange in Romans 1:18-25: "We can say that natural man is ever busy repressing or exchanging. But does he always succeed to the same degree? That depends on the strength with which God approaches him. . . . This shows that there are gradations in the history of religion."[83]

Bavinck notes that in some parts of the world the church finds itself between temple and mosque. In this context the first reaction the church encounters is fierce opposition to its message. "Is it not faced these days with an

---

[81]Bavinck, *Introduction*, 229, 226. Cf. Bavinck, *Church Between Temple and Mosque*, 26-27.

[82]Kuyper, *Encyclopedie* 3:449. Bavinck, *Introduction*, 229-30.

[83]Bavinck, *Church Between Temple and Mosque*, 125-26.

alarming crisis even in the countries where it is solidly rooted?" The second reaction is that all religions are equal, the challenge of syncretism. For Bavinck, it is possible that syncretism is more dangerous than outright opposition, since the syncretistic reception of Jesus can paralyze the preaching of the gospel. "It may work like a slow poison that sucks away the Church's strength. But whatever the Church may meet, it is clear that it has the duty to speak honestly and with dignity with the other religions."[84]

For Bavinck we find, somehow, in every religion, the silent work of the living God. However as Romans 1 reminds us, this is entwined with repression and substitution. The church confesses this because it brings itself under the judgment of this confession. Historically, the church itself has been guilty of repressing and substituting God's revelation, and its responsibility is greater! Indeed, it is only as it is characterized by such humility that the church can bear witness to other religions.[85]

History of missions. Bavinck is insightful in his quest to develop a peri-odization of mission based on how one defines mission. Goheen notes the importance for mission today of an historical perspective and that much hinges on how one defines *mission*. Defining mission as "missions" leads to a model of geographical expansion for the history of missions.[86] Goheen acknowledges the validity of such an approach but argues that we need a wider-angle lens that attends to the history of mission and not just missions. Goheen refers to Bavinck's approach as a pointer in this direction before moving on to discuss Andrew Walls's and Samuel Escobar's focus on the cultural diffusion of the gospel, and David Bosch's and Brant Myer's focus on different paradigms of mission through history. Bavinck discerns five pe-riods in the history of mission based on the principles the church used in its execution of its mission:

1. that of the early church;

2. the period when Christianity became the state religion;

3. when Pietism gained control in much of northern Europe;

---

[84]Ibid., 198, 199.

[85]Ibid., 200.

[86]Goheen, *Introducing Christian Mission Today*, chap. 3. Goheen refers to Stephen Neill and Kenneth S. Latourette as examples.

4. the nineteenth century, the so-called century of missions; and

5. the twentieth century, beginning with WWI.

He describes these periods as follows: "The first is that of *spontaneous extension*; the second, that of the *Christian empire and its expansion*; the third, is that of *a withdrawal to a shorter front*; the fourth period is a *probing for a new and totalitarian vision*; the fifth period is that of the *partnership of old and young churches in a feeling of mutual responsibility*."[87]

THE ENDURING LEGACY OF J. H. BAVINCK

It is really only since 1896, when Warneck became honorary professor of missiology at the University of Halle, that mission found a permanent place in theological faculties.[88] After 1896 faculty after faculty made appointments in mission, but since the 1950s many have abolished chairs in mission or changed them into chairs of a different sort. Bosch notes, "This trend is discernible especially in those institutions that are related to Churches affiliated to the World Council of Churches."[89] This reflects the growing problems in the WCC with holding on to anything like an orthodox view of mission in the years following Bavinck's death. Bosch notes that among evangelicals the reverse trend is true but that we need to remember that most evangelical missionary activity emerged fairly recently.

Mission and missiology are a crucial part of the church and theology, and what we need is an orthodox missiology that has dialogued with and learned deeply from twentieth-century missiology. This we find in Bavinck, which makes it extraordinary and unacceptable that his work is so little known today. It is greatly to the credit of John Bolt and Paul Visser that they have worked hard to revive interest in Bavinck's work. Bavinck did influence theologians such as Harvie Conn, and through him pastors such as Tim Keller. But there is nothing like the reception and development of Bavinck's work that it deserves. It was only in 1974 at Lausanne that evangelicals wrestled together with issues that Bavinck dealt with years before and often far more profoundly.

---

[87]Bavinck, *Introduction*, 305. By *totalitarian* here Bavinck means comprehensive, total.
[88]Bosch, "Missiology," 263-64.
[89]Ibid., 264.

What is it in Bavinck's work that merits renewed attention? There is so much, but let me highlight what I see as the major elements.

Mission is of the essence of the church. Bavinck rightly recognized that the church is missional through and through. We quoted Nikos Kazantzakis's insightful statement at the outset of this chapter: "He uttered a triumphant cry: IT IS ACCOMPLISHED! And it was as though he had said: Everything has begun." The church is a phenomenon of the interim period between the coming of the kingdom and its consummation, and this *is* the period of mission. Just as Jesus was sent, so too are his people, so that an *apostolic* church is not just one based on Scripture but also a *missional* people. At the same time Bavinck rightly refuses to reduce the church to mission, drawing attention also to its doxological (liturgical) and nurturing tasks.

Undoubtedly, parachurch organizations have their place, but Kuyper and Bavinck rightly drew attention to mission being the primary responsibility of the local church. Certainly churches should work in cooperation with one another, but, as Newbigin taught us, the local church is the hermeneutic of the gospel, explaining and embodying it before the world.

The emphasis on *missio Dei* is fecund. God is *the* missionary, and at its best the church can accompany him in his great work of redeeming his creation. Mission cannot therefore become our "messianic" activism but must be our discerning, dependent partnership with God in his work by his Spirit spreading the fragrance of Christ throughout the creation.

Evangelicals struggled in the twentieth century to know how to relate the different components of mission. Lausanne frames the debate in terms of the relationship between evangelism and sociopolitical involvement. In my view this sets up the problem with a false dichotomy, since evangelism is always by word *and* deed. Telling of Christ verbally and obeying him comprehensively can never be set against each other. Bavinck comes far closer to a healthy view, one we might describe as the people of God bearing comprehensive witness to the kingdom.

Scriptural. Both Kuyper and Bavinck see the need for mission to be built from the foundation of Scripture. Bavinck is, in my view, more consistent, but both saw the need for a rigorous missiology, and in his work Bavinck went a long way toward fulfilling Kuyper's call in this respect. Bavinck is exemplary in taking Scripture as *the* authority for mission. He draws on a range of other disciplines, but always it is back to Scripture. Indeed, like Karl Barth and Oliver O'Donovan, as his conceptual framework takes hold he returns again and again to Scripture.

Once he got there, it is remarkable how consistent Bavinck is in situating mission within the context of the story of the Bible and its central theme, especially in Jesus' ministry, of the kingdom of God. This is vital, as it positions mission within the eschatology and story line of Scripture, thus opening up its dynamism and comprehensiveness.

With his comprehensive view of the kingdom, Bavinck never lost sight of the exclusiveness of salvation in Christ, nor of the vital importance of personal conversion. Bavinck was an exclusivist, but it was a nuanced, thoughtful exclusivism akin to that of Newbigin. He took other religions with the utmost respect and spent years trying to understand them, as did Newbigin.[90]

Western baggage. Newbigin tells the story of sitting next to Indonesian General Simatoupong at the Bangkok conference on "Salvation Today." Newbigin heard him say under his breath, "Of course, the Number One question is, Can the West be converted?"[91] Newbigin spent his "retirement" in the United Kingdom doing some of his most fertile work as he sought to rouse the Western church from its slumber and not least to alert it to the dangers emerging from parts of the Muslim world.

Bavinck was acutely aware of the relationship between religion and culture, and he writes eloquently of the need for Western Christians to face up to the culture of which they are part:

> It is time for us to acknowledge frankly that our modern civilization, disintegrated though it may seem, is based upon certain presuppositions about man, his place in the world and his responsibility towards God, and that this implies a definite world view, and outlook upon the function of the individual in the community and upon the greatness and the misery of man. . . . Modern culture, too, is a religious phenomenon.[92]

Few scholars have been shouting from the rooftops about the importance of religion in the global world as has Philip Jenkins, and that significantly before

---

[90]For a sympathetic but critical approach to Bavinck on other religions see H. L. Richard, "The Missiological Vision of J. H. Bavinck: Religion, Reticence, and Contextual Theology," *International Journal of Frontier Mission* 31, no. 2 (2014): 75-84.

[91]Cf. Lesslie Newbigin, "Can the West Be Converted?," *Princeton Seminary Bulletin* 6, no. 1 (1985): 25-37.

[92]Bavinck, *Church Between Temple and Mosque*, 22-23.

9/11. He notes in the third edition of his classic *The Next Christendom* that

> For all their vast wealth, many churches in North America and Europe have far
> less interest or commitment in the global South than they once had. . . . For
> whatever reason, *Western involvement in missions has been cut back dramatically*
> *at just the point it is most desperately needed,* at the peak of the current surge in
> Christian numbers.[93]

For the sake of religion and politics, and perhaps the survival of the planet,
according to Jenkins, this needs to change. Western Christians need to become
intimately acquainted with the resurgent Christianity of the South. Western
myopia often prevents the phenomenal growth of Christianity from even
coming into focus, as does the fact that Christians are now the most persecuted
religion on the planet, predominantly in non-Western regions of the world.[94]

What are the major challenges that resurgent Christianity is facing? There
are many, but some of the major ones are:

1. Poverty: "A majority of global South Christians (an increasingly, of all
   Christians) really are the poor, the hungry, the persecuted, even the
   dehumanized."[95]

2. Persecution: A growing body of literature establishes the unprecedented
   persecution of Christians, especially in majority Muslim countries. Jenkins
   notes, "Christianity is flourishing wonderfully among the poor and persecuted, while it atrophies among the rich and secure."[96]

3. Relationship to Islam: Islam and Christianity are both growing apace, and
   the relationship between them is critical.

4. Societal involvement: Jenkins notes that Christians of the South are often
   politically and socially deeply involved in their contexts.[97]

5. Scripture: Jenkins notes how existentially and radically differently Southern
   Christians read their Bibles compared with Christians in the North.

---

[93]Philip Jenkins, *The Next Christendom: The Coming of Global Christianity*, 3rd ed. (Oxford: Oxford University Press, 2011), 267-68.

[94]Among many recent books see, e.g., Klaus Wivel, *The Last Supper: The Plight of Christians in Arab Lands*,
trans. Mark Kline (New York: New Vessel, 2016).

[95]Jenkins, *Next Christendom*, 272.

[96]Ibid., 275.

[97]Ibid., 171-200.

The emerging global church will require great wisdom as it negotiates its future. It will need a mission of wisdom and the wisdom of mission. Bankrupt Western theologies that have eviscerated the central tenets of Christian faith from their theologies in an attempt to gain acceptance in the West will be of little help. So too will evangelical theologies that have no comprehensive vision or insight into norms for societal and cultural development. So too will Western Christians who have no idea of the drain of real poverty or the challenge of other faiths on a daily basis. In short, we will need a missional church—and an abundance of missiologists—with a vision like that of Bavinck, resurrecting work like his and updating it and developing it for the challenges of today and tomorrow.

THE KUYPERIAN TRADITION AND CONTEMPORARY MISSIOLOGY

What might such work look like today? This is a large topic, and I can only make suggestive comments in this section. It would certainly need to be engaged with the best recent missiology, as was Bavinck in his day. Since Bavinck an immense amount of literature on mission has emerged, and our cultural contexts have changed significantly with globalization and its challenges. We have been privileged to have major missiologists such as David Bosch and Lesslie Newbigin in our midst. How might the Kuyperian tradition of Bavinck relate to their fertile work? Above I have indicated points of connection between Bavinck and contemporary missiology, demonstrating that his work provides a fertile node for engagement and further development. My colleague Michael Goheen has made much of his life's work an exploration of the interface between the Kuyperian tradition and contemporary missiology, and I am indebted to dialogue with him for these final reflections.

Both Kuyper and Bavinck rightly stress the biblical foundations for mission and the trinitarian God as the source of mission. Within the Kuyperian tradition, the redemptive-historical approach to Scripture, and the recognition of creation as foundational within Scripture and redemption as creation regained, along with the foregrounding of the kingdom of God as the major theme of Jesus' ministry, provide a fertile basis for a comprehensive view of mission. The redemptive-historical hermeneutic resonates with the best of recent narrative approaches to the Bible and connects well with Newbigin's emphasis on Scripture as the story we need to indwell, the story that tells the "universal truth" about the world and conflicts with alternative grand stories.[98]

All this is present in Bavinck, but too often followers of Kuyper in the Netherlands and in North America have failed to see the missional implications of Scripture taken as a whole. The clash of stories makes contextualization crucial in any context, allowing one to affirm and critique any culture at the same time. Goheen stresses in this context Hendrik Kraemer's fertile notion of contextualization as "subversive fulfillment," a notion almost identical to Bavinck's notion of *possessio*.[99]

A seminal contribution of David Bosch has been his close attention to Scripture, and nowadays this is being developed in all sorts of ways under the rubric of a missional hermeneutic.[100] Major work remains to be done on Scripture and mission, and not least on the relationship between a theological hermeneutic and a missional hermeneutic. In a recent essay I sought to tease out this relationship and found J. H. Bavinck and David Bosch insightful in this respect.[101]

Like Newbigin, Bavinck returned to teaching mission, albeit for a much shorter period abroad, in the West after missionary engagement in Asia. The parallel is telling, since both came to see the religious nature of the West and the missional challenge it represents. Newbigin, for example, was hugely significant in his insistence that the West was the major mission field of our day, an insight already found in Bavinck but never developed globally, as did Newbigin. Newbigin's work, however, Goheen thinks, lacks a firm grounding in a doctrine of creation so central to the Kuyperian tradition. It should be noted, furthermore, that amid our changing times, in which the West is being pushed into deeper engagement with Asian culture and religion, Bavinck's and Newbigin's profound enagment with Asian religions might turn out to be a significant fact in their legacy.[102]

---

[98]In our *The Drama of Scripture*, Goheen and I have sought to update the redemptive-historical approach in connection with narrative and literary readings of Scripture.

[99]Cf. Perry, *Radical Difference*, 63-68; Bavinck, *Introduction*, 155-90.

[100]See Goheen, *Reading the Bible Missionally*.

[101]Bartholomew, "Theological Interpretation and Missional Reading of Scripture."

[102]Long before 9/11, Newbigin was acutely aware of the growing challenge Islam represented to the West. See Lesslie Newbigin, Lamin Sanneh, and Jenny Taylor, *Faith and Power: Christianity and Islam in "Secular" Britain* (Eugene, OR: Wipf and Stock, 1998, 2005). Kuyper himself wrote about Islam, and one volume of the emerging Lexham Press series Abraham Kuyper Collected Works in Public Theology will be devoted to Islam.

CONCLUSION

Carl Braaten evocatively titled his theology of Christian mission *The Flaming Center*. He asserts, "The flaming center of the Christian message is Jesus, the Christ of God, the Savior of mankind and the Lord of history."[103] In every sense mission revoles around this center, and in this chapter we have argued that the Kuyperian tradition has significant resources for the church today in its attempts to promote the honor and glory of this flaming center. Positively, the Kuyperian tradition can help Christians, and evangelicals in particular, to overcome the pervasive individualism of too much Western mission, with its often-exclusive focus on sin and (individual) salvation, vital as these are. The Kuyperian tradition has resources for helping the church to recover the dimension of mission as utterly central to its life.

In following Bavinck's example, Kuyperian insights need to be honed and developed in ecumenical dialogue. For example, in terms of where the Kuyperian tradition needs help, Goheen rightly stresses the need for *far better communication of the tradition*, making its treasures available in dialogue with other views. Especially in North America the Kuyperian tradition has remained largely ethnic and, while understandable among immigrants, a danger has been the loss of the distinctive Christian elements of prayer, evangelism, the importance of local missional congregations, crosscultural missions, a passion for reaching the lost, and so on. The Kuyperian tradition can be corrected and enriched as Kuyperians listen to the pietistic tradition and its emphasis on these elements.

Indeed, a danger in the Reformed churches of North America that are the home of the Kuyperian tradition is that as they settle in to North American culture they forget the extraordinary resources in the Kuyperianism tradition for current life and thought. It is thus vital that the insights of the Kuyperian tradition be distinguished from Dutch culture, admirable as it is, so that the Kuyperian tradition can mature missionally in the North American and global context without losing its biblical roots.

---

[103]Carl E. Braaten, *The Flaming Center: A Theology of the Christian Mission* (Philadelphia: Fortress, 1977), 2.

PHILOSOPHY

NOWADAYS PHILOSOPHY IS AN AREA in which the achievements of the Kuyperian tradition are well known, with luminaries such as Alvin Plantinga, Nicholas Wolterstorff, and C. Stephen Evans, all of whom have drunk deeply at the wells of the Kuyperian tradition. However, philosophy was not an area to which Kuyper paid close attention.[1] He was well aware of the philosophies of his day and their importance, but he himself never attended to the project of a Christian philosophy. Nevertheless, especially in his *Encyclopedia of Sacred Theology*, he attends to the nature of "science" even as he defines the shape of the encyclopedia of *theology* and its distinctiveness as a science. In the process he attends to much of what we would nowadays call philosophy, and it is to this part of his work that we now turn our attention.

ABRAHAM KUYPER

It is important to remember that when Kuyper uses the word *science* he is using it as a synonym for what Germans call *Wissenschaft*. In English today we easily think of the *natural* sciences when we use the word *science*, but for Kuyper science includes all the academic disciplines. Kuyper approaches the issue of science through his great project on theology. As a science, theology is part of general science, but the problem is that the general concept of science is disputed and thus not clear. This necessitates Kuyper exploring the nature of

---

[1]Kuyper himself noted that he had contributed only something toward a foundation of a Christian philosophy. See George Puchinger, *Is de gereformeerde wereld veranderd?* (Delft, Netherlands: Meinema, 1966), 202. In vol. 2 of his *Encyclopaedie* Kuyper does discuss the relationship between theology and philosophy, and in *Encyclopaedie der heilige Godgeleerdheid* (Kampen: Kok, 1909), 569-77, he deals with philosophy of religion.

science and its major divisions, a central philosophical task. Strauss refers to philosophy as the discipline of the disciplines, and this is precisely where Kuyper focuses his attention.[2]

Kuyper defines *science* as follows: "*Science presents itself to us as a necessary and ever-continued impulse in the human mind to reflect within itself the cosmos, plastically as to its elements, and to think it through logically as to its relations; always with the understanding that the human mind is capable of this by reason of its organic affinity to its object.*"[3]

Kuyper teases out the relationship between knowledge and understanding, insisting that knowledge is more than understanding in its recognition that what one understands corresponds to existing reality. In modernity the relationship between subject and object in the process of knowing has received widespread attention, and Kuyper attends to this issue. The subject lies in human consciousness, the object in all existing things. Knowledge is not just about individual entities but about the interconnectedness of things. Kuyper argues that there is and must be an organic relation between subject and object: "Thus for all science a threefold organic relation between subject and object is necessary. There must be an organic relation between that object and our *nature*, between that object and our *consciousness*, and between that object and our *world of thought*." For true knowledge to be discovered, our consciousness must be fitted to take in what is signaled by the world. "There is, therefore, no perception or observation possible, unless there is a receptivity for the object in our human consciousness, which enables our consciousness to grasp it after its nature and form."[4]

Kuyper sees the human person as a microcosm of the macrocosm and thus fitted to know the macrocosm truly. He distinguishes between natural objects and spiritual objects; the latter are religious, ethical, intellectual, and aesthetic objects. He rightly notes that our consciousness or ego is more than thinking; thinking is but one form in which our consciousness operates. In terms of

---

[2]D. F. M. Strauss, *Philosophy: Discipline of the Disciplines* (Grand Rapids: Paideia, 2009).
[3]*PST*, 83, emphasis original.
[4]*PST*, 67-68, 71. Note the similarity to Alvin Plantinga's epistemology of warrant in his *Warranted Christian Belief*. This is also central to Plantinga's refutation of naturalistic evolution, since there is no reason our cognitive faculties should have evolved so as to provide true knowledge of the world. Dooyeweerd similarly develops a view of the human person that fits with the nature of the cosmos. Humans function in all fifteen modal aspects, as does every entity.

knowledge and science, it is through thinking that the objects of our knowledge are apprehended.

Our world not only consists of things but is also a world of relations. "The relations themselves are not only entirely immaterial, and therefore formless, but they are also void of entity in themselves. For this reason, they can be grasped by our thoughts alone, and all our thinking consists of the knowledge of these relations." Thinking carries an active power for Kuyper, since the setting for these relations is present in our consciousness. The logical germ of a world of thought is lodged in our thinking. "This identity of our thinking consciousness with the world of relations must be emphasized, however, in so far as these relations have no existence except for an original Subject, who has thought them out, and is able to let this product of his thoughts govern the whole cosmos." The original Subject, is, of course, God, and knowing is a process of thinking God's thoughts after him. Indeed, it is this sense that drives science, but "not in the sense that the cosmos exists *only* logically."[5]

Knowledge involves perception and comprehension. As we investigate more complex entities, these aspects are deeply interwoven.[6] However, the subject does not produce the object, nor vice versa; there is a power that binds the two that lies outside each. We are unable to explain the affinity between subject and object until, with Scripture, we see that humankind is made in the image of God.

Philosophy of language has become a major topic in our day, so much so that philosophers speak of the linguistic turn in the twentieth century. Kuyper addresses the role of language in knowing. Through language we retain and collect representations; furthermore, we make the content of our consciousness our property through language.

A central plank in Kuyper's view of science is the effect of sin. Apart from sin, our human consciousness would have entered more and more deeply into the entire cosmos so that "the cosmos would have been before us as an open book." The universality and necessity of science would not have clashed with our subjectivity; multiformity in knowledge would have been harmonious. Sin has, however, deeply affected the practice of science: "Truly the entire interpretation of science, applied to the cosmos as it presents itself to us now,

---

[5]*PST*, 76, 77, 78. Cf. *PR*, 59, 79.
[6]Note here the similarity to Dooyeweerd's concept of enkapsis.

and is studied by the subject 'man' as he now exists, is in an absolute sense governed by the question whether or no a disturbance has been brought about by sin either in the object or in the subject of science."[7]

Kuyper is alert to the differences in this respect between the natural and the "spiritual" sciences. The effect of sin is greater on the latter, but even in the natural sciences, when one moves to relations, the subjective side of knowing enters in and plays a significant role. Kuyper notes that everything material, what can be weighed, counted, measured, is subject to a universally compulsory certainty and bears an absolutely objective character. However, as soon as one moves to unify empirical data with broader thought, the subjective dimension enters in. The subjective dimension of knowing is profoundly affected by one's starting point: "This is most forcibly illustrated by Philosophy in the narrower sense, which, just because it tries logically to interpret, if not the cosmos itself, at least the image received of it by us, ever bears a strongly subjective character."[8]

Sin must therefore be taken seriously in science: "But of necessity we must accept this hard reality, and in every theory of knowledge which is not to deceive itself, the fact of sin must henceforth claim a more serious consideration." Kuyper is adamant that sin works its fatal effects *also in science* and is not restricted to the will. He outlines eight ways in which sin affects science and notes that it is especially the leading thought we have developed in the realm of life that most interests us that exercises a mighty dominion over the whole content of our consciousness, on one's worldview. "Everyone preaches for his own parish"![9]

Referring to Ephesians 4:17-18, Kuyper develops the theme of the darkening of the understanding. He argues that the structure of logic is not impaired by sin, but over against sin stands *love*, and love is indispensable for true knowledge:

> But, taken as a whole, standing over against the cosmos as its object, our mind feels itself isolated; the object lies outside of it, and the bond of love is wanting by which to enter into and learn to understand it. This fatal effect of sin must naturally find its deeper reason in the fact that the life harmony between us and

---

[7]*PST*, 90, 92.
[8]*PST*, 103-4.
[9]*PST*, 106-7, 110.

the object has been disturbed. What once existed organically, exists now consequently as foreign to each other, and this *estrangement* from the object of our knowledge is the greatest obstacle in the way to our knowledge of it.[10]

For Kuyper the effect of sin is clearly present in philosophy: "From which it follows at the same time that the knowledge of the cosmos as a whole, or, if you please, philosophy in a restricted sense, is equally bound to founder upon this obstruction wrought by sin." The answer to foundational questions, such as the origin and end of the whole, categories that govern the object, and the question of absolute being and the nature of nonbeing, require that one subjects the whole cosmos to oneself, but to do this one must have a place to stand (δῶς μοι πᾶ στῶ) from which to see the whole, and "this is altogether impossible as long as sin confines you with your consciousness to the cosmos." As Kuyper notes, "In this condition of affairs a holy interest is at stake in this struggle for *the truth*."[11]

Kuyper discusses the role of truth and falsehood in our epistemology, and he notes that science cannot decide the question between truth and falsehood. He explores wisdom and notes that unifying dimension of wisdom: "The leading characteristic of 'wisdom' is that it is *not* the result of discursive thought." Indeed, "only this antithetical conception of *foolishness* elucidates sufficiently the exact conception of *wisdom*."[12]

Kuyper argues that faith is a universal human function, which he defines as "that function of the soul (ψυχη) by which it obtains certainty directly and immediately, without the aid of discursive demonstration." In this universal sense faith "is necessary for the self-consciousness of the *ego*, for securing the axiomatic starting-point and for the forming of general conclusions."[13]

Two kinds of science. Kuyper's doctrine of two kinds of science sounds strange until one understands the nuance with which he develops it. He never denies that truth is one, nor that formally believer and nonbeliever engage in the same type of systematic attempts to understand what is. He insists, "There is but one logic, and not two." He acknowledges that there is a broad area of investigation in both natural and spiritual sciences in which the differences

---

[10]*PST*, 111.

[11]*PST*, 113, 115.

[12]*PST*, 119, 121.

[13]*PST*, 129, 139. Cf. the quote from von Hartmann in *PR*, 58.

between believer and nonbeliever exercise *no* influence. In both types of science, "a common realm presents itself."[14]

How, then, does he distinguish between two types of science? His answer lies in the antithesis, in that the difference between belief and unbelief is not a relative difference but an absolute one. The difference lies not within human consciousness but outside it. *Palingenesis* (regeneration) alters the human person in his or her depths and his or her orientation toward the world. And "since this fact exercises an absolutely dominating influence upon our view of science, it would be a culpable blindfolding of self if we passed it by in silence. This 'regeneration' breaks humanity in two, and repeals the unity of the human consciousness."[15] The believer and the nonbeliever

> face the cosmos from different points of view, and are impelled by different impulses. And the fact that there are two kinds of *people* occasions of necessity the fact of two kinds of human *life*, and of two kinds of *science*; for which reason the idea of the *unity of science*, taken in its absolute sense, implies the denial of the fact of palingenesis, and therefore from principle leads to the rejection of the Christian religion.[16]

The essential difference, for Kuyper, lies not in the world that impinges on the human consciousness but in the radically different starting points from which believer and nonbeliever engage the world. For the effect of this to become visible, development and time are required. We should not expect all believing scholarship to immediately agree.[17]

Christian scholarship is criticized because it is bound to revelation, its freedom is constrained by ecclesiastical approval, and its results are determined in advance. For Kuyper the new insights brought by revelation are to be welcomed! In relation to the institutional church, Kuyper appeals to sphere sovereignty and the freedom of scholarship in its own sphere. As regards the third criticism, Kuyper maintains that a sense of the conclusion is common to believer and nonbeliever. All science works with unproved assumptions.

Divisions of science. An important insight of Kuyper's is that the divisions of science emerge from practical life and the innate human inclination to

---

[14]*PST*, 159, 157, 158.
[15]*PST*, 152.
[16]*PST*, 154.
[17]*PST*, 178.

investigate. He compares this with a child's playful curiosity: "The needs of life add a nobler seriousness to this playful investigation and by its rule and continuity are imparted to the scientific task." However, "it is by no means asserted that the prosecution of science, and in connection with it the university life, should aim exclusively at a practical education. On the contrary, the pursuit of science for its own sake is the ideal which must never be abandoned."[18] However, the way to this ideal leads through practical life. Intriguingly, he notes how the struggle against evil in the body (medicine), in the soul (theology), and in society (juridical) led to the three great disciplines of medicine, theology, and law. Kuyper is attuned to the historical origin of the sciences and their historical development, on which we build.

He follows the tradition in identifying five faculties in the university: philological (linguistic, historical, and philosophical studies), medical, juridical, natural philosophy, and theology. In terms of philosophy, Kuyper identifies two tasks for it: first, to investigate the nature and laws of conscious life, and second, how the "World-Image" (worldview) has developed and how it manifests itself at present.

EVALUATION

Although Kuyper does not say he is doing philosophy in his discussion of science and the university, it is in fact what he is doing. And in my view he does it remarkably well, asking a host of the right questions, such as

- What is science?

- From where does the impulse to investigate emerge?

- How has science developed through history?

- How do we construe the subject-object relationship?

- What role do relations play in knowledge?

- How do the natural and "spiritual" sciences differ?

- How is language constitutive of knowledge?

- How does sin affect knowing?

---

[18]*PST*, 184, 188. Cf. *PR*, 81.

- Why and how is love so central to knowing?

- What is the shape of the encyclopedia of science?

Kuyper was not alone in his time in asking these sorts of questions, but his rigor, range, and Christian insight are nevertheless remarkable.[19] These are the foundational issues that *philosophy* addresses. Charles Taylor notes that in any discipline one can go deeper and deeper until one hits the really basic questions, and that is philosophy. Kuyper's genius is to recognize that if he is to deal with theology as a science, he first has to sort out the foundational issues, and remarkably he plunges right in. Later in this chapter we will explore the important insights contained in Kuyper's reflections that have been developed in subsequent Kuyperian philosophy. Implicitly, Kuyper practiced Christian philosophy; explicitly, Herman Bavinck recognized the need for a philosophy of revelation.

HERMAN BAVINCK: *THE PHILOSOPHY OF REVELATION*

Both Kuyper and Bavinck gave the Stone lectures at Princeton. Bavinck delivered his in the academic year 1908–1909. They are titled *The Philosophy of Revelation*.[20] Bavinck rightly notes that it is a mistake to collapse the Reformation into the revolution, as some are prone to do, thus seeing Kant as *the* Protestant philosopher. The Reformation was a recovery of God's Word, his written revelation, whereas the spirit of the revolution, and of Kant, is one of human autonomy. As Bavinck notes, if God does not exist, then religion is an illusion.

> But, built on the basis of revelation, theology undertakes a glorious task—the task of unfolding the science of the revelation of God and of our knowledge concerning him. It engages in this task when seeking to ascertain by means of exegesis the content of revelation, when endeavoring to reduce to unity of thought this ascertained content, when striving to maintain its truth whether by way of aggression or defence, or to commend it to the consciences of men.

---

[19]Cf. Thomas A. Howard, *Religion and the Rise of Historicism: W. M. L. de Wette, Jacob Burckhardt, and the Theological Origins of Nineteenth-Century Historical Consciousness* (Cambridge: Cambridge University Press, 2006).

[20]For the context in which Bavinck gave his Stone lectures see James D. Bratt, "The Context of Herman Bavinck's Stone Lectures: Culture and Politics in 1908," *The Bavinck Review* 1 (2010): 4-24. See also George Harinck, "Why Was Bavinck in Need of a Philosophy of Revelation?," in *The Kuyper Center Review*, ed. James Bowlin (Grand Rapids: Eerdmans, 2011), 2:27-42.

But side by side with all these branches there is room also for a *philosophy of revelation* which will trace the idea of revelation, both in its form and in its content, and correlate it with the rest of our knowledge and life.[21]

Bavinck's Stone lectures are devoted to this theme of a philosophy of revelation. He notes that theology has always felt the need for such a philosophy. Philosophy needs to take the real world seriously; neglect of this in rationalist philosophy led to the violence of speculative abstraction. A philosophy of revelation must not make the same mistake.

Bavinck points out that Christianity does not conflict with reason but has a content that transcends reason. Revelation discloses the mystery of God, providing us with insight that is available in no other way. Philosophy of revelation must make this revelation its starting point. "In the next place this philosophy of revelation seeks to correlate the wisdom which it finds in revelation with that which is furnished by the world at large."[22] Bavinck asserts,

> Revelation, while having its centre in the Person of Christ, in its periphery extends to the uttermost ends of creation. It does not stand isolated in nature and history, does not resemble an island in the ocean, nor a drop of oil upon water. With the whole of humanity, with the family and society, with science and art it is intimately connected.[23]

The world rests on revelation; indeed, the foundations of creation and redemption are the same. "The Logos who became flesh is the same by whom all things were made. The first-born from the dead is also the first-born of every creature." "General revelation leads to special, special revelation points back to general."[24]

Like Kuyper, Bavinck is conscious of the state of philosophy in his day and encouraged by the renewed interest in it. He notes that "modernism is in the air everywhere" and discerns two central characteristics in philosophy: the embrace of autonomy and the search for religion or a worldview. "Philosophy wishes itself to serve as religion, and from an attitude of contempt for all

---

[21]*PR*, 24.

[22]*PR*, 26.

[23]*PR*, 27.

[24]*PR*, 27, 28. Cf. Rob A. Nijhoff, *De logosfilosofie van Jan Woltjer (1849–1917): Logos en wijsbegeerte aan de vroege Vrije Universiteit* (Amsterdam: Buitjen & Schipperheijn, 2014).

theology has veered round to a profession of being itself at bottom a search after God." Philosophy often presents itself as new, but "the new roads in philosophy have all been travelled by the thinkers of ancient Greece."[25] Like J. H. Bavinck, Herman notes that the directions in which our thinking philosophically can go are limited. Every worldview revolves around the three poles of God, humankind, and the world, so that only three types of worldview are possible: theistic, humanist, and naturalist.

A genuine insight of idealism is that the mind is the basis and principle of knowledge; its mistake is to confuse the act with the content. The ego is no cold, lifeless point but "is rich in content, full of life and power and activity." The nature of the mind is such that at its root lies the sense of *dependence*, as befits the creature. By virtue of his creation, everyone believes in God. Atheism only developed at a later stage on the basis of philosophical reflection. Revelation alone accounts for the worship of "God" that characterizes humankind. "In self-consciousness God makes known to us man, the world, and himself. Hence this revelation is of the utmost importance, not only for religion, but also for philosophy, and particularly for epistemology."[26]

Bavinck is adamant that revelation has implications for all of life, including philosophy.[27] The dualism between faith and reason is unsustainable, since the human person cannot split himself into half. "The thinker and philosopher, as well as the common citizen and the day laborer, have to serve and glorify God in their work."[28] Philosophy seeks unity, but true unity, which protects difference and diversity, can only be found when the world is conceived of in terms of God's unfolding plan.

As with Kuyper, Bavinck's work is rich and insightful. However, he equates worldview with philosophy, and his work is more at the level of worldview studies than setting out the contours of a Christian philosophy. This was the task that Herman Dooyeweerd and Dirk Vollenhoven took on themselves at the Free University of Amsterdam.

---

[25]*PR*, 31, 32. H. Evan Runner developed this insight in his lectures, as did Vollenhoven.

[26]*PR*, 63, 79.

[27]At the Free University of Amsterdam Bavinck also taught ethics, and his *Reformed Ethics* is being translated into English at present. Cf. Dirk van Keulen, "Herman Bavinck's Reformed Ethics: Some Remarks About Unpublished Manuscripts in the Libraries of Amsterdam and Kampen," *The Bavinck Review* 1 (2010): 25-56.

[28]*PR*, 84.

PHILOSOPHY IN THE KUYPERIAN TRADITION

Kuyper and Bavinck engaged with the continental philosophical tradition in their forays into philosophy. Both were trained as theologians but conscious of the challenge of the post-Enlightenment philosophies of their day. Indeed, it is remarkable that Bavinck would give his Stone lectures on the *philosophy* of revelation, and it is a clear indication of the recognition for work in this area. Major work remained to be done in Christian philosophy.

The Kuyperian tradition has since been developed philosophically in exceptionally rich ways. Kuyper would doubtless not be surprised that it has been developed in a variety of ways; in his word its development is "multiform." In contemporary philosophy there are two major traditions: the continental and the analytic. Alvin Plantinga and Nicholas Wolterstorff are among the most prominent Christian philosophers today. Both have their roots in the Kuyperian tradition, but they have developed it along *analytic* lines. The vibrant and influential tradition that has developed out of their and their colleagues' labors is commonly known as Reformed epistemology. However, this is only one of at least two major philosophical developments in the neo-Calvinist tradition. The lesser known one is earlier, developed by Herman Dooyeweerd (1894–1977) and his brother-in-law Dirk Vollenhoven (1892–1978), particularly in Dooyeweerd's *A New Critique of Theoretical Thought*. Plantinga notes,

> The main positive development in Christian philosophy during the first half of our century [twentieth] must surely be the work of the man whose 100th birthday we are presently celebrating. Dooyeweerd's work was comprehensive, insightful, profound, courageous, and quite properly influential. . . . Let us simply note the sheer size of Dooyeweerd's accomplishment, remembering that it took place in a context going back to Abraham Kuyper and indeed back all the way to Bonaventura, Augustine and Tertullian.[29]

Philosophy in Dooyeweerd's and Vollenhoven's line is commonly known as Reformational philosophy.

DOOYEWEERD AND VOLLENHOVEN: REFORMATIONAL PHILOSOPHY

Kuyper's influence thoroughly permeated the life of Herman Dooyeweerd.[30]

---

[29]James F. Sennett, ed., *The Analytic Theist: An Alvin Plantinga Reader* (Grand Rapids: Eerdmans, 1998), 329.

[30]See Marcel E. Verburg, *Herman Dooyeweerd: The Life and Work of a Christian Philosopher*, trans. Herbert D. Morton and Harry Van Dyke (Jordan Station, ON: Paideia, 2009).

Dooyeweerd grew up in Amsterdam in a Kuyperian home, attended a Kuyperian classical high school, studied at the Free University of Amsterdam
(earning his PhD in 1917), worked for some years as director of the Kuyper
Institute in The Hague, and then returned to the Free University as professor.
Dooyeweerd's philosophical work is simply inconceivable without the foundation of Kuyper's work.

Of course the insights of Kuyper need to be personally appropriated, as we
noted in our chapter on worldview. Dooyeweerd's describes his epiphany in
this respect as follows:

> Originally I was strongly under the influence first of the Neo-Kantian phi-
> losophy, later on of Husserl's phenomenology. The great turning point in my
> thought was marked by the discovery of the religious root of thought itself,
> whereby a new light was shed on the failure of all attempts, including my own,
> to bring about an inner synthesis between the Christian faith and a philosophy
> which is rooted in the self-sufficiency of human reason. . . . From a Christian
> point of view, the whole attitude of philosophical thought which proclaims the
> self-sufficiency of the latter, turns out to be unacceptable, because it withdraws
> human thought from the divine revelation in Christ Jesus.[31]

This insight is implicit in Kuyper but became the explicit foundation for
Dooyeweerd's philosophy of the law-idea (de wetsidee). Like Kuyper, Dooyeweerd traces this insight back to Calvin and argues therefore that an integral
Christian philosophy could only develop in the tradition of John Calvin, with
his religious starting point.[32] Indeed, central to Dooyeweerd's philosophy is
his view of the human person. Especially in Old Testament Wisdom literature,
we find the concept of the heart as the center of the person, and this emphasis
is closely related to Dooyeweerd's turning point. For Dooyeweerd the heart is
the religious center of the person, and it is always religiously directed, either
toward the true God or an idol. The heart and its religious direction influence
the whole of the person, including theoretical thought and thus philosophy.

Even from this brief introduction it is obvious how deeply Dooyeweerd
draws on Kuyper. In his examination of "The Intellectual Milieu of Herman
Dooyeweerd," Wolters draws attention to the numerous ways in which Dooyeweerd is indebted to Kuyper.

---

[31]Herman Dooyeweerd, A New Critique of Theoretical Thought, 4 vols. (Jordan Station, ON: Paideia, 1984), 1:v.
[32]Ibid., 1:515-18.

First, there is the poignant Kuyperian insight that grace restores nature, the subject of chapter two, which is central to Dooyeweerd's theory of ground motives and which Dooyeweerd used to get at the religious dimension of all philosophic thought and indeed of cultural development. Dooyeweerd argues that beneath the cultural and spiritual development of the West one can identify deep driving forces, and he calls these ground motives:

> In every religion one can point to a ground-motive having such a force. It is a force that acts as a spiritual mainspring in human society. It is an absolutely central driving force because, from the religious center of life, it governs temporal expressions and points towards the real or supposed origin of all existence. In the profoundest sense it determines a society's entire life- and world-view. It puts its indelible stamp on the culture, science and the social structure of a given period. This applies so long as a leading cultural power can be identified as giving clear direction to the historical development of society. If such ceases to be the case, then a real crisis emerges at the foundations of that society's culture. Such a crisis is always accompanied by spiritual uprootedness.[33]

Ground motives are communal and can govern the life of an individual even when the individual is unconscious of it.[34] Dooyeweerd identifies four major ground motives in the history of Western philosophy/culture. It is important to note that the emergence of a new ground motive does not displace the former ones; the former ones continue in tension with the new one.

1. *The form-matter ground motive.* Dooyeweerd discerns this as the basic ground motive in Greek and Roman thought. Central to Dooyeweerd's analysis is that once an aspect of the creation is absolutized, it causes its opposite pole to emerge, with the two in irreconcilable dialectical tension and thought oscillating between the poles in an attempt to close down the tension. For Dooyeweerd the Greek thinkers move back and forward between matter and form, with the sophists opting for matter, Aristotle for a harmony between the two, and so on.

2. *The nature-grace ground motive.* This ground motive was dominant in the high and later Middle Ages and thus follows the Christian ground motive of creation-fall-redemption, which we will discuss below. Dooyeweerd's prime

---

[33]Herman Dooyeweerd, *Roots of Western Culture: Pagan, Secular, and Christian Options*, trans. John Kraay (Toronto: Wedge, 1979), 8-9.

[34]Ibid., 9. James Sire points out that a worldview can be held unconsciously. See chapter four.

example of this ground motive at work is in the scholastic thought of Thomas Aquinas. Through his appropriation of Aristotle, Aquinas embraced the Greek dualistic understanding of nature and sought to synthesize this with the gospel (grace). For Dooyeweerd the result is an unsustainable synthesis of conflicting ground motives and would inevitably lead to trouble. Nature became separated from grace in the Renaissance and Enlightenment, with the upper storey of grace being more and more marginalized until it was denied altogether.

3. *The nature-freedom ground motive.* The fruits of modern science are undeniable and seemed to affirm a mechanistic view of the world, dominated by natural, scientific laws. However, this creates problems for any view of humankind as free, and thus the emphasis on nature calls forth the freedom pole. One finds, for example, science championed by Comte and freedom by the Romantics. Dooyeweerd refers to this ground motive as humanism. It pushed Roman Catholicism and Protestantism onto the defensive for nearly three centuries.

4. *Creation-fall-redemption.* This ground motive comes second historically, and is the true ground motive, which escapes the dialectical tensions of the other three. Dooyeweerd is adamant that this ground motive does not arise from *theological* reflection. It arises solely from the work of the Spirit in the hearts of believers. In my view Reformational philosophy rightly stresses that the gospel is the power of God that brings salvation (Rom 1:16) and that it alone has the capacity to redirect the heart toward the living, true God. Implicit in the faith that results from such transformation will be the concepts of creation-fall-redemption, but the sort of reflection on this ground motive found in Dooyeweerd's philosophy does indeed involve reflection and analysis, at least of a worldviewish sort. Much depends on how we define theology, but it cannot be dispensed with so easily. Creation-fall-redemption is itself an abstraction from the biblical story and as such includes a view of God, his work in Christ, and the work of the Holy Spirit.

The important point to note is that Dooyeweerd's understanding of the biblical ground motive draws deeply from the Kuyperian view of the relationship between nature and grace. As Wolters rightly says, "It is not too much to say that this central understanding of creation, fall, and redemption is the key to Dooyeweerd's philosophy and to the entire intellectual project to which he devoted his life."[35]

---

[35]Albert M. Wolters, "The Intellectual Milieu of Herman Dooyeweerd," in Carl T. McIntire, ed., *The Legacy of Herman Dooyeweerd: Reflections on Critical Philosophy in the Christian Tradition* (Lanham, MD: University Press of America, 1985), 1-19, on 5.

Second, there is Kuyper's emphasis on creational law and creational diversity. Kuyper celebrates both God's ordinances for all of creation and the incredible diversity built into the creation. In terms of society, we explored Kuyper's fertile concept of sphere sovereignty in chapter five. In comparison with Groen van Prinsterer, Kuyper grounded sphere sovereignty in creation, an insight central to Dooyeweerd's philosophy. Wolters asserts, "It is not too much to say that Dooyeweerd first began to elaborate his systematic philosophy in an attempt to provide a more general ontological foundation for Kuyper's principle of sphere sovereignty."[36] Dooyeweerd expanded sphere sovereignty into a general theory of ontological irreducibility.

Third, there is Kuyper's emphasis on the development of the potentials of creation in history.[37] Dooyeweerd develops this in his concept of the differentiation process, a concept that Calvin Seerveld describes as his most poignant insight.[38] Primitive societies are relatively undifferentiated; they contain no distinct spheres of the school, the government, and so on. There is nothing bad about such undifferentiation, but Dooyeweerd argues that it is normative for a society to become differentiated into a variety of spheres over time. Thus it is normative for schools and universities to develop and for parents to hand over the substance of their children's education to such institutions. It is normative for government to become a separate sphere in society and for the institutional church to develop as the place where formal worship takes place.

Fourth, there is Kuyper's concept of the antithesis, according to which a vast spiritual battle is going on amid human affairs. This is central to Dooyeweerd's philosophy, who saw with keen insight that the antithesis runs through theoretical thought as much as in any other area of life. Hence the need for an integrally Christian philosophy.

And so we could continue. Wolters concludes, "Indeed, the whole infrastructure of Dooyeweerd's philosophy, the operative assumptions which are often not explicitly discussed, derives directly from the commonly accepted worldview of neo-Calvinism."[39]

---

[36]Ibid., 7.

[37]See *LC*, 22-28. Kuyper's view of development is often jarring to a twenty-first-century reader, but the principle is surely right.

[38]Calvin Seerveld, "Dooyeweerd's Idea of 'Historical Development': Christian Respect for Cultural Diversity," *Westminster Theological Journal* 58, no. 1 (1996): 41-61.

[39]Wolters, "Intellectual Milieu," 10.

Living when Dooyeweerd did, it is not hard to imagine the radicality of his view and the difficulty of gaining an audience for it. Nowadays, with the onset of so-called postmodernism and the global revival of religion, it is far easier to get religion on philosophical agendas. Dooyeweerd lived in a very different context, and a result is that he first needed to clear the ground by demonstrating that all theoretical thought is irretrievably rooted in religion before proceeding to develop a systematic Christian philosophy. The former he does under the title of his transcendental critique. Dooyeweerd takes over the word *transcendental* from Kant, with the connotation of *the conditions that make thought possible*. Dooyeweerd expresses this as follows: "By this we understand a critical inquiry . . . into the *universally valid conditions which alone make theoretical thought possible, and which are required by the immanent structure of this thought itself*."[40] Through an examination of the conditions for thought to function, Dooyeweerd endeavors to show that all thinking is rooted in religion, that is, in the central selfhood of the knower. Not surprisingly, therefore, he often referred to the transcendental critique as the "entrance" to his philosophy. However, for Dooyeweerd there is a significant difference between ordinary, everyday thinking and logical, theoretical thought of the sort that characterizes the disciplines of the university; hence his emphasis on "theoretical thought" in the quote above. Thus an important distinction arises between worldview as *pretheoretical* and philosophy as *theoretical*, a distinction we do not find in Kuyper and Bavinck.

I cannot here expand on the contours of Dooyewerd's philosophy or explore the similarities and differences between his and Vollenhoven's fertile work.[41] Suffice it to note that in his construction of an integrally Christian philosophy Dooyeweerd draws deeply on neo-Kantianism and phenomenology. As Wolters notes, "The underlying worldview of Dooyeweerd's thought stands in essential continuity with the vision of neo-Calvinism, while the philosophical elaboration of that vision is basically constructed with conceptual tools drawn from German philosophy—chiefly neo-Kantianism, secondarily phenomenology." In Wolters's judgment, "the significance of Dooyeweerd and his

---

[40]Dooyeweerd, *New Critique*, 1:37.

[41]See Craig G. Bartholomew and Michael W. Goheen, *Christian Philosophy: A Systematic and Narrative Introduction* (Grand Rapids: Baker Academic, 2013), chap. 15, for an outline of Dooyeweerd's and Vollenhoven's philosophies.

legacy resides more in the impact of the worldview component on his philosophy than in the systematic categories which depend on neo-Kantianism and phenomenology."[42]

An important point to note is that Dooyeweerd and Vollenhoven worked in the Continental tradition in their construction of a Christian philosophy. The great influences on Dooyeweerd were neo-Kantianism, Martin Heidegger, and Edmund Husserl, and though his philosophy has a definite place for logic, it is not nearly as central as it is in Reformed epistemology.[43] René van Woudenberg observes,

> The philosophical tradition behind analytic epistemology is, broadly speaking, Anglo-American empiricism and rationalism. . . . The philosophical tradition behind Dooyeweerd, however, is German transcendental idealism, with its towering figures, Kant, the neokantians . . . and Husserl. The differences between these traditions are enormous: there are differences in style, differences as to the role the history of philosophy is assigned in the actual doing of philosophy, differences as to the methods of philosophy, and differences as to the conceptuality in which philosophical problems are couched.[44]

We need to bear this in mind as we come to the second major branch of Kuyperian philosophy, namely Reformed epistemology. To conclude our brief foray into Reformational philosophy, it should be noted that this tradition of Kuyperian philosophy has been developed by a range of scholars in a whole variety of areas. For example,

- in philosophy of language and metaphor (M. Elaine Botha)
- in philosophy of religion (Roy Clouser)
- in political philosophy (Jim Skillen, David Koyzis, Paul Marshall, Jonathan Chaplin)
- in aesthetics (Hans Rookmaaker, Calvin Seerveld)
- in economics (Bob Goudzwaard, Alan Storkey)
- in theology (Gordon Spykman)

---

[42]Wolters, "Intellectual Milieu," 16.

[43]See ibid., 1-19.

[44]René van Woudenberg, "Two Very Different Analyses of Knowledge," in John H. Kok, ed., *Ways of Knowing in Concert* (Sioux Center, IA: Dordt College Press, 2005), 101-23, on 103.

- in ethics (Andre Troost)
- in history (Meyer Smit)

And so on. There are rich resources here for further development.

REFORMED EPISTEMOLOGY

In 1980 *Time* magazine reported that in a

> quiet revolution in thought and arguments that hardly anyone could have
> foreseen only two decades ago, God is making a comeback. Most intriguingly,
> this is happening not among theologians or ordinary believers . . . but in the
> crisp, intellectual circles of academic philosophers, where the consensus had
> long banished the Almighty from fruitful discourse.[45]

Time identified Alvin Plantinga, professor of philosophy at Calvin College, as
a leader in this revolution and described him as the "world's leading Protestant
philosopher of God." The approach to knowing that Plantinga, Wolterstorff,
and others have developed is known as Reformed epistemology. *Faith and
Rationality*, edited by Plantinga and Wolterstorff, was the first comprehensive
account of this project.

Wolterstorff points out the benefit of the emergence of metaepistemology,
the practice of surveying the various epistemologies at work in scholarship. He
explains this as follows: "Rather than just plunging ahead and developing epistemological theories, philosophers have stood back and reflected seriously on
the structural options available to them in their construction of such theories."[46]

The result of such reflection is revealing: one theory, namely classical foundationalism (CF), has long been dominant. Classical foundationalism is "a
picture or total way of looking at faith, knowledge, justified belief, rationality,
and allied topics. This picture has been enormously popular in Western
thought; and despite a substantial opposing groundswell, I think it remains
the dominant way of thinking about these topics."[47]

---

[45]"Modernizing the Case for God," *Time*, April 7, 1980.

[46]See here Nicholas Wolterstorff, "Introduction," in Plantinga and Wolterstorff, eds., *Faith and Rationality: Reason and Belief in God* (Notre Dame, IN: University of Notre Dame Press, 1983), 1-15.

[47]Plantinga in Sennett, ed., *Analytic Theist*, 129. Diagrams below are modeled on those in Kelly James Clark, *Return to Reason: A Critique of Enlightenment Evidentialism, and a Defense of Reason and Belief in God* (Grand Rapids: Eerdmans, 1990), 134, 137.

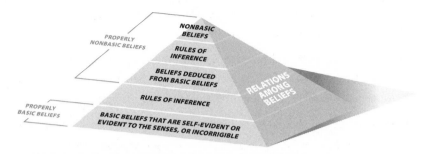

Figure 2. Classical Foundationalism

It is important to distinguish foundationalism from CF. CF is a variant of foundationalism. Both view the acquisition of knowledge as akin to building a house and stress the need for a solid foundation, on which the house of theory can be built. Foundationalism has been the dominant epistemology since the high Middle Ages.

Figure 3. Foundationalism

For foundationalism, the foundation of the house of knowledge contains a set of basic beliefs that one is justified in believing *without* the support of other beliefs, that is, they are properly basic. If the foundation is solid, then one can build upper-level beliefs upon it, using the appropriate methods (rules of inference). Rational assent moves upward as warrant for beliefs is transferred from the lower levels to the higher levels by the rules of inference. The crucial question is *which beliefs* are properly basic, that is, which beliefs may legitimately occupy the foundation?

CF is foundationalist in its assertion that our basic beliefs are of two sorts:

1. Those that are foundational; these do not require arguments or evidence for them to be held rationally. In this sense they are *basic*.

2. Those that are not foundational but are believed on the basis of other beliefs that are foundational.

Basic beliefs do not require evidence, while nonbasic beliefs do. Where CF develops foundationalism is in its specifying which beliefs are properly basic. According to classical foundationalists, the following are *basic beliefs*:

1. Self-evident beliefs; that is, beliefs that are seen to be true simply by understanding them. 2+1 = 3 is an example of a self-evident belief; one only has to understand it to see that it is true.

2. Incorrigible beliefs; that is, beliefs that one could not be mistaken in holding.

3. Some CFs have held that beliefs formed on the basis of sense experience are basic.

CF has been very bad news for Christian scholarship. W. K. Clifford, for example, states that "it is wrong always, everywhere, and for anyone to believe anything upon insufficient evidence." When asked what he would say if he arrived in heaven to discover that Christianity was true, Bertrand Russell replied: "I'd say, 'Not enough evidence, God. Not enough evidence!'"[48] This sounds persuasive until one realizes that Clifford and Russell are operating within a CF framework that defines in a very narrow way what can and cannot be counted as evidence. For CF, it is illegitimate to take belief in God as properly basic, and thus one would only be justified in believing in God if his existence can be inferred from properly basic foundational beliefs.

The challenge this presents to belief in God is known as *evidentialism*; belief in God is only warranted on the basis of adequate "evidence." Some evangelicals have sought to demonstrate that Christian belief is up to such a challenge. Examples are Norman Geisler, Henry Morris, R. C. Sproul, and John Gerstner. In his evaluation of this approach Kelly James Clark demonstrates its failure and notes, "The failure of evangelical evidentialism is its uncritical commitment to Enlightenment evidentialism. . . . They . . . are unduly wedded to modern thought in their commitment to classical natural theology and its assumption of Enlightenment evidentialism. . . . They fall short of their own standards."[49]

---

[48]Plantinga in Sennett, *Analytical Theist*, 104.
[49]Clark, *Return to Reason*, 46-53.

Indeed, "most philosophers who have seen clearly the structure of this particular option [CF] have rejected it. On close scrutiny they have found classical foundationalism untenable."[50] Plantinga and Wolterstorff have played a major role in the critique and demise of CF. However, if this is the wrong way to envisage the acquisition of reliable knowledge, what is the right way? Both Plantinga and Wolterstorff, and other Christian philosophers such as William Alston, have developed constructive alternative models of epistemology.

In 1976, for example, Wolterstorff published his *Reason Within the Bounds of Religion*, a turning on its head of Kant's *Religion Within the Limits of Reason*. Early church father Tertullian provocatively posed the question, What does Jerusalem have to do with Athens? with the implied answer "Nothing whatsoever!"[51] Few contemporary Christian scholars would follow Tertullian in this respect, but his way of framing the question remains influential. Wolterstorff notes, "Without a doubt a person can simply live in the two different communities, doing as the Athenians do when in Athens and as the Jerusalemites when in Jerusalem. But if one who is a scholar as well as a Christian wants coherence in life . . . he cannot help asking, how does my membership in these two communities fit together?"[52]

In *Reason Within the Bounds of Religion* Wolterstorff attends to the role of Christian commitment in the practice of scholarship. At the heart of Reformed epistemology is the Kuyperian insight that one can be thoroughly rational in taking belief in God as properly basic in one's scholarship. Plantinga is perhaps best known for his development of this insight in his three-volume work on epistemology, and especially in the third volume, *Warranted Christian Belief*.[53] As with Dooyeweerd, Plantinga and Wolterstorff have followed Kuyper's example in attending to the philosophical foundations of knowledge, brilliantly clearing the ground for a Christian perspective, and then have gone on to develop this in a range of areas such as art, science and evolution, education, liturgy, justice, biblical interpretation, and so on.

---

[50]Ibid., 4.

[51]Tertullian, *Prescription Against Heretics* 7.

[52]Wolterstorff, *Faith and Rationality*, 21.

[53]Alvin Plantinga, *Warranted Christian Belief* (New York: Oxford University Press, 2000).

BACK TO KUYPER

Wolters begins his chapter "The Intellectual Milieu of Herman Dooyeweerd" by noting correctly that "more than most philosophers of international stature, Herman Dooyeweerd's thought stands in need of explanation outside his home country because of widespread ignorance of the intellectual milieu in which he developed his philosophy."[54] For a variety of reasons, even those who are familiar with Reformational philosophy in the non-Dutch world often know little of Kuyper and Bavinck. This, in my view, is a major mistake. If Wolters is right, and I suspect he is, in stating that "Dooyeweerd's *philosophical* significance is strictly proportionate to his success in carrying out Kuyper's program of a Christian reformation of scholarship,"[55] then the Kuyperian—and biblical—foundations are of fundamental importance and need to be revisited regularly.

Wolters himself has unpacked these foundations in his classic *Creation Regained: Biblical Basics for A Reformational Worldview*. Wolters wrote this book as an introduction to Reformational philosophy, and every part of the title is significant. "Creation Regained" evokes the Kuyperian view of the relationship between nature and grace, particularly as articulated by Herman Bavinck. "Worldview" speaks for itself, and "Reformational" alerts the reader that the book is oriented toward the Reformational philosophical tradition. "Biblical Basics" is crucial, since it serves as a reminder that for Kuyper and Bavinck Scripture is normative for all of life and that the foundations of Christian scholarship in the Bible need to be taken with utmost seriousness. Neither biblicism nor dualism will do, but in an appropriate way the authority of Scripture for all of life, including philosophy, must be taken seriously. Major work remains to be done in this area.

To a large degree Dooyeweerd and Vollenhoven *assumed* the Kuyperian ethos and foundations, but the same cannot be said of some of their followers. There has been a tendency in North America for Reformational philosophy to take on a life of its own, thereby obscuring the Kuyperian foundations. While we should never absolutize Kuyper or Bavinck and should continually reform their work in the light of Scripture, it is important that such reform be done consciously so that we can see what is at stake in the moves that are made.

---

[54]Wolters, "Intellectual Milieu," 1. But see the biography by M. Verburg.
[55]Ibid., 17.

In its structure Reformed epistemology is very different from Reformational philosophy, just as Continental philosophy is to analytic. In recent decades we have, however, witnessed something of a rapprochement between analytic and continental philosophy, and it is important to note that now, as we look back at the achievements of Reformed epistemology and Reformational philosophy, it is possible to see important areas of agreement between them.

When Plantinga and Wolterstorff were philosophy majors at Calvin College, there was acrimony between the more analytical style of W. Harry Jellema and Henry Stob and the overtly Reformational philosophy of H. Evan Runner. As the years have gone by, tensions have diminished, and Reformed epistemology has emerged as a major player on the international philosophical stage. One can see how both streams are deeply Kuyperian, and both have crucial insights to offer for the practice of Christian philosophy today. An advantage of the passing of the years is that we can now see more clearly the major areas of overlap between the two streams as well as the differences.

The crucial Kuyperian insight that Reformational philosophy and Reformed epistemology have foregrounded is the legitimacy—indeed imperative—of a Christian starting point for philosophy. With Kuyper, Dooyeweerd, and Vollenhoven, Plantinga and Wolterstorff have effectively taken on the myth of religious neutrality.[56] Missionally, this cuts to the heart of the contemporary challenge of modernity *and* of postmodernism, without for a moment dismissing their insights. Both types of Reformed philosophy have in their own ways recovered this biblical insight and have laid the basis for continuing to do Christian philosophy in the context of the biblical story and Christian worldview.

My preference is for the more Continental Reformational philosophy, but one cannot doubt that Reformed epistemology has been far more effective in communicating its message. In our *Christian Philosophy*, Mike Goheen and I argue that Christian philosophy is inherently missional, and Reformed epistemology has been more astute in this respect than Reformational philosophy, in attending to the epistemological foundations of philosophy in a major dialogue with the philosophical mainstream.

---

[56]See the important book by Roy Clouser, *The Myth of Religious Neutrality: An Essay on the Hidden Role of Religious Beliefs in Theories*, 2nd ed. (Notre Dame, IN: University of Notre Dame Press, 2005).

Reading Kuyper and Bavinck, I continue to think that untapped resources remain in their work for philosophy. The questions Kuyper poses about the nature of scholarship and the shape of the disciplines remain as relevant today as when he posed them. Several colleagues and I think that the project of *integration* at most Christian colleges and universities has not worked so that disciplines remain separate and fragmented. Kuyper's work offers a fertile node from which to revisit these issues.

I do not know, for example, of any Kuyperian scholar who has developed Kuyper's poignant insight into the role of love in scholarship.[57] Over against sin, says Kuyper, stands love, and it is essential for scholarship. I am reminded of a liturgical refrain in *Common Prayer: A Liturgy for Ordinary Radicals*: "Bury us in wonder, Lord: and raise us to sing your praise."[58] Love for God and wonder at his creativity are fundamental to Christian scholarship, and the Kuyperian tradition would do well to revive and develop this emphasis, reminding us as it does that Christian spirituality is an essential component of Christian scholarship.

With Kuyper, many of his followers have also recognized the need for separate Christian institutions, for the space in which Christian scholarship and Christian philosophy can flourish. I affirm this desire and need, but only if such a withdrawal is made in order to reengage the culture out of love more vigorously. Within our secular universities, knowledge is notoriously fragmented, and sadly it is not always that different in Christian universities. Recovery of a vibrant Christian philosophy in dialogue with theology working at first-order (ontology, epistemology, anthropology) and second-order (philosophy of . . .) philosophy would make a major contribution to contemporary Western culture and beyond.

A major insight of Kuyper's is that scholarship and theory develop out of practical life, or what I would call lived experience. The same insight, couched in different vocabulary, is found in Dooyeweerd, with his notion of naive experience. In his *Reason Within the Bounds of Religion* Wolterstorff opens up the important discussion of the extent to which Christian scholarship should be oriented toward praxis. Where this issue needs to be developed, in my view, is

---

[57]But see James K. A. Smith, *You Are What You Love: The Spiritual Power of Habit* (Grand Rapids: Brazos, 2016).

[58]Shane Claiborne, Jonathan Wilson-Hartgrove, and Enuma Okoro, *Common Prayer: A Liturgy for Ordinary Radicals* (Grand Rapids: Zondervan, 2010), 458.

on the relationship between theory and lived experience.[59] Not only does theory emerge out of lived experience, but a test of theory's validity is what it does when it returns to lived experience. Good scholarship should deepen lived experience and not become an alternative royal route to truth, as has so often happened in modernity.

Kuyper's philosophical work was done primarily in relation to the foundations for *theology* as a science. In chapter ten we will examine Kuyper and theology in some detail. For now, it should be noted that neither the Reformational tradition nor that of Reformed epistemology have generated major work in theology. Indeed, Dooyeweerd manifests something of an antitheological tendency, which is a mistake. Among Reformational thinkers there is, furthermore, a wide variety of views about the relationship between philosophy and theology, with Reformed theology too often neglected or treated simply as one among the many special sciences. Kuyper attends in detail to the unique aspects of theology, and his work in this area warrants reinvestigation.

Much is at stake in the endeavor of Christian philosophy. I learned from the Kuyperians in South Africa, and from Elaine Botha in particular, that if I wanted to do Christian scholarship I needed a grounding in Christian philosophy. That led me on a journey to Canada and eventually to occupying the H. Evan Runner Chair in philosophy at Redeemer University College. Every day of my scholarly life, I remain grateful for the insights gained from Christian philosophy. In an interview with Richard Kearney, Jacques Derrida rightly identifies the foundational role of philosophy:

> In all the other disciplines you mention, there is philosophy. To say to oneself that one is going to study something that is not philosophy is to deceive oneself. It is not difficult to show that in political economy, for example, there is a philosophical discourse in operation. And the same applies to mathematics and the other sciences. Philosophy, as logocentrism, is present in every scientific discipline and the only justification for transforming philosophy into a specialized discipline is the necessity to render explicit and thematic the philosophical subtext in every discourse. The principal function which the teaching of philosophy serves is to enable people to become "conscious," to become aware of what exactly they are saying, what kind of discourse they are engaged in when

---

[59]See Craig G. Bartholomew, *Where Mortals Dwell: A Christian View of Place for Today* (Grand Rapids: Baker Academic, 2011).

they do mathematics, physics, political economy, and so on. There is no system of teaching or transmitting knowledge which can retain its coherence without, at one moment or another, interrogating itself philosophically, that is, without acknowledging its subtextual premises; and this may even include an interrogation of unspoken political interests or traditional values.[60]

As Christian scholars we either go our merry ways, ignorant of the philosophical foundations at work in our disciplines, or we explore them and bring them into obedience to Christ, as best we are able. In so doing my hunch is that we will need the Kuyperian tradition. To quote Kuyper once again: "In this condition of affairs a holy interest is at stake in this struggle for *the truth*."[61]

---

[60]Richard Kearney, "Jacques Derrida," in Kearney, *Dialogues with Contemporary Thinkers. The Phenomenological Heritage* (Manchester, UK: Manchester University Press, 1984), 105-26, on 114-15.
[61]*PST*, 115.

THEOLOGY

Christian doctrine is a grand house, with foundation, building blocks, girders, roof, and windows. Many doors give entrance from the front, the back, and the sides, and open upon every room in the house. Above the main entryway to this house of Christian theology is the password: Life is religion. The "welcome" mat is out. Come on in!

GORDON J. SPYKMAN, *CHRISTIAN FAITH IN FOCUS*

The Trinity is the foundational principle of a theology pro ecclesia.

CARL BRAATEN, *MOTHER CHURCH: ECCLESIOLOGY AND ECUMENISM*

ACADEMICALLY, KUYPER WAS FIRST AND FOREMOST a theologian. However, because he was involved in so many areas of life, his public work has often received far more attention than his work as a theologian. In recent years the Kuyperian tradition has been developed in philosophy and politics, but far less so in theology.[1] This is a mistake. The theology of Kuyper, Bavinck, and Berkouwer, to mention the three major figures, is exceptionally rich and needs to be retrieved and updated for today.[2]

Several factors have contributed to its neglect. First, there is the liberalization of theology at the Free University of Amsterdam. Harry M. Kuitert's

---

[1] The only major recent English Kuyperian theology is Gordon Spykman's excellent *Reformational Theology: A New Paradigm for Doing Dogmatics* (Grand Rapids: Eerdmans, 1992). Under Craig Bartholomew's editorship a new Kuyperian dogmatics is under way with IVP Academic.

[2] There are many other figures to mention. Note should be made of Klaas Schilder (1890–1952). See Richard J. Mouw, "Klaas Schilder as Public Theologian," *CTJ* 38 (2003): 281-98; George Harinck, ed., *Alles of nites: Opstellen over K. Schilder* (Barneveld: De Vuurbaak, 2003).

controversial work, for example, is a far cry from Kuyper and Bavinck, and his mentor Berkouwer.[3] In his book *Jesus: The Legacy of Christianity*, for example, Kuitert asserts, "Jesus supported the Jewish view of God, so he never saw himself as God on earth. He is not a Second God, nor the Second Person of the Holy Trinity," adopting a Unitarian stance on the doctrine of the Trinity.[4]

Hendrikus Berkhof (1914–1995), a professor at Leiden and not at the Free University, was an influential Dutch theologian in the Reformed tradition.[5] His work is always stimulating and full of insight, and certainly more orthodox than Kuitert. However, in his *Two Hundred Years of Theology*, an examination of theology through the lens of the relationship between the gospel and modern thought, he largely leaves aside confessional theology and keeps the focus on liberal theology. He argues that "liberal theologians, in virtue of their liberalism, have done much more with the theme that occupies me than their orthodox colleagues, who aimed more at the exposition of the given content of Scripture or the treasures of tradition."[6]

Berkhof labels both Kuyper and Bavinck as scholastic. He asserts that Bavinck chose submission to Scripture principles over faith as an encounter with God and embraced neo-Thomism philosophically. Berkhof argues,

> Hence Bavinck remained more strongly burdened than he wished by the legacy
> of the Reformed scholasticism of the seventeenth century and gave up intel-
> lectual tools he could not well do without in the continuing confrontation with
> the modern spirit. It is not surprising, therefore, that in the first three or four
> decades of the twentieth century Reformed theology fell back on the tradi-
> tional scholastic elements of Bavinck. This tendency was furthered by the pre-
> dominance of Kuyper, who in his dogmatics was much closer to the old scho-
> lasticism than Bavinck. Not until after World War II did Gerrit Cornelis
> Berkouwer, Bavinck's second successor, consciously go back to the original,

---

[3]See Hendrikus Berkhof, *Two Hundred Years of Theology: Report of a Personal Journey*, trans. John Vriend (Grand Rapids: Eerdmans, 1989), 208-28. Berkhof notes, "Barth's insight that one who does not start with God will never get to him seems to be confirmed by Kuitert, positively, by outright affirmation, and nega-tively, by the failure of his alternative method" (223). Kuitert is emeritus professor of ethics and dogmat-ics at the Free University of Amsterdam.

[4]Harry M. Kuitert, *Jesus: The Legacy of Christianity*, trans. John Bowden (London: SCM Press, 1999). See, for example, p. 275: "He [Jesus] isn't a second God, or the second person of the Holy Trinity, who took flesh from the Virgin Mary."

[5]See E. P. Meijering, *Hendrikus Berkhof (1914–1995): Een Theologische Biografie* (Kampen: Kok, 1997).

[6]Berkhof, *Two Hundred Years*, xiv.

antischolastic lines of Bavinck's thought, while in the 1960s historical research again uncovered his numerous (forgotten) links with "ethical theology."[7]

With H. Berkhof there has been a tendency to label Kuyper's and Bavinck's work as *scholastic*, a label that too often enables us to ignore them and move on to more "creative" fields without closely exploring their work in theology. As we explore Kuyper's view of theology and to a lesser extent Bavinck's and Berkouwer's, we will assess this critique. At this point the heroic attempt of Kuyper (and Bavinck) to engage constructively and critically with modernism should be noted, and to me it seems extraordinary that one could argue that, in a book on modern thought and theology, liberalism deserves the main attention![8]

Second, there was considerable conflict at the Free University between the theologians and the philosophers, and Dooyeweerd's work was controversial among some of the theologians at the university.[9] In his philosophy theology becomes one of the special sciences and thus dependent for its foundations on (Dooyeweerd's) Christian philosophy. Third, there were the ongoing church conflicts that absorbed a great deal of time and energy and left far less time for constructive theology. And fourth, there was the profound impact of two world wars on Europe.

In this chapter we will focus mainly on Kuyper and then take Bavinck and Berkouwer into account. Both Bavinck and Kuyper wrote prolegomena to theology; Berkouwer, like Karl Barth, did not. In conclusion we will assess the work that needs to be done to retrieve, renew, and develop the Kuyperian *theological* tradition for today.

KUYPER AND THEOLOGY

Kuyper's concern to explore the shape of the encyclopedia of theology has always struck me as penetratingly insightful—indeed exhilarating—so that one can see how theology and its subdisciplines form an ecology, or the sort of house referred to by Spykman in the quote at the outset of this chapter. Kuyper recognized that if we want to talk about theology as a science, which

---

[7]Ibid., 114.

[8]Berkouwer's work is noticeably different from H. Berkhof's. He always engages with Kuyper and Bavinck. A useful comparison with Berkhof's *Two Hundred Years* is G. C. Berkouwer, *A Half Century of Theology*, trans. Lewis B. Smedes (Grand Rapids: Eerdmans, 1977).

[9]See Marcel E. Verburg, *Herman Dooyeweerd: The Life and Work of a Christian Philosopher*, trans. Herbert D. Morton and Harry Van Dyke (Jordan Station, ON: Paideia, 2009), 229-59.

he does, then we first need to work out just what science is. In chapter nine, on philosophy, we explored Kuyper's view of science or scholarship. That is indispensable background for his view of theology as a science.

The need for a science of theology. Kuyper regularly notes how the sciences emerge out of our lived and historical experience. Lived experience alerts us to inner and outward existence, personal and social, human life and the life of nature. Is there not, he asks, also a need for a science of our relationship to God? His answer is yes, but we need to attend closely to how we define theology. Kuyper rejects the understanding of theology as the science of religion: "Nothing is to be gained, on the other hand, by the notion that Theology has religious feeling, subjective religion, the phenomena of piety, etc., for its object, and that for this reason it is not to be taken as Theology, but as Science of Religion."[10]

Religious feeling is very important, but it belongs to humankind's psychical life and would not therefore be the object of study for theology. Kuyper rejects a trichotomous view of the human person and affirms a dichotomy: "But the antithesis should be between *body* and *soul*, and within that soul the distinction between psychical and the pneumatical should be sought."[11] In relation to the human person, theology is particularly concerned with the pneumatical part of the person.

Theology as a particular science. Kuyper never denies that all sciences should be studied from a Christian perspective or out of a Christian worldview. He says of palingenesis that it "is a universal conception which dominates your whole person, and all of life about you; moreover, palingenesis exerts an influence not merely in your religious life, but equally in your ethical, aesthetical, and intellectual life."[12] However, Kuyper is keenly attentive to the difference between theology and other sciences.[13] In other sciences the thinking subject stands above the object, but this can never be the case with God: "Thinking man, taken as *subject* over against God as *object* is a logical contradiction in terms."[14]

---

[10]*PST*, 213. Cf. *RD* 1:50-54.

[11]*PST*, 214. Reformational philosophy has argued for a much more unified, holistic view of the human person. In broader circles the question of anthropology continues to be widely debated. Within the Reformed tradition see the important book by John Cooper, *Body, Soul, and Life Everlasting: Biblical Anthropology and the Monism-Dualism Debate*, 2nd ed. (Grand Rapids: Eerdmans, 2000).

[12]*PST*, 225.

[13]Cf. *RD* 1:40.

[14]*PST*, 214.

In relation to the knowledge of God, which, for Kuyper, is the object of theology, natural theology is of little consequence.[15] In his discussion of the influence of palingenesis on theology, Kuyper notes, "This applies to all faculties, but becomes more important in proportion as the part of the object which a given faculty is to investigate stands higher."[16] Thus we would expect regeneration to have a major effect on theology, and this, for Kuyper, rules out any possibility of a natural theology, proceeding as though the fall had never happened:

> This whole matter assumes an entirely different phase, however, when palingenesis is taken as the starting-point. For then it ceases to be a problem whether there is a God; that the knowledge of God can be obtained is certain; and in the revelation which corresponds to this palingenesis there is presented of itself an *objectum sui generis*, which cannot be subserved under any of the other faculties; this impels the human mind to a very serious scientific investigation, which is of the utmost importance to practical life.[17]

Kuyper is well aware of the mutual relations between academic disciplines and their regular need to borrow from one another. He thinks, however, that theology alone studies palingenesis and that in this regard other disciplines must lean on theology's insights.

Kuyper distinguishes between God's knowledge of himself, which he refers to as *archetypal knowledge*, and the knowledge of God revealed by God to humankind, which he refers to as *ectypal knowledge*. Theology finds its object in the revealed, ectypal knowledge of God. God alone knows himself, and, as with persons, but to a much greater extent, unless he reveals himself to us we have no hope of knowing him. And he needs to reveal himself in a form that is knowable by humans, hence the distinction between archetypal and ectypal. We cannot know God in his essence, but we can know him truly, as he reveals himself to us. Theology, unlike the other sciences, does not deal with created things but illumines our minds about God as creator and redeemer, about the origin and telos of all things, and thus it follows that theological knowledge must come to us in a different way in comparison to the other sciences. Theology is human knowledge, but it is human knowledge *of*

---

[15]Cf. *RD* 1:38: "Dogmatics is, and can only exist as, the scientific system of the knowledge of God."
[16]*PST*, 220.
[17]*PST*, 223. Cf. *RD* 1:37-38.

God: "The idea of Theology can be none other than the *knowledge of God*, and all activity impelled by Theology must in the last instance be bent upon the *knowledge of God*."[18]

But how are we to learn about God? This question alerts us to the dependent character of theology; it is utterly dependent on the good pleasure of God:

> This is true in an absolute sense of the Theologian over against his God. He *cannot* investigate God. There is nothing to analyze. There are no phenomena from which to draw conclusions. Only when that wondrous God will speak, can he listen. And thus the Theologian is absolutely *dependent* upon the pleasure of God, either to impart or not to impart knowledge of Himself.[19]

The theologian stands not above but beneath the "object" he investigates: "We of ourselves . . . can never enter into the holy place of the Lord, to examine it and gather knowledge concerning it, but that it behooves us to take our stand on this side of the veil, and to wait for what God Himself will communicate to us from this holy place and from behind this veil."[20] Kuyper rejects a theology of the *analogia entis*; it is only once God has revealed himself that we see signs of him everywhere.

A fierce debate raged in the twentieth century between Karl Barth and Emil Brunner about whether the gospel finds points of contact within the creation.[21] Kuyper comes down on the side of Brunner in this regard. "The ectype does not arise unless there is a material that can receive the impression of the archetype."[22] Throughout his *PST* Kuyper is alert to the context of creation and that special revelation presupposes creation, and in relation to ectypal revelation he rightly notes that the *imago Dei* provides the appropriate receptacle for God's revelation of himself.

A major and rich insight of Kuyper's is that God reveals himself for his own sake and not first for humankind's sake, as is apparent in creation.[23] "With a

---

[18]*PST*, 242.

[19]*PST*, 251.

[20]*PST*, 252.

[21]Brunner's "Nature and Grace" and Barth's reply, "No," both appeared in 1934. They are published together in *Natural Theology*, trans. Peter Fraenkel (Eugene, OR: Wipf and Stock, 1946, 2002).

[22]*PST*, 257.

[23]Cf. *RD*, 1: "Finally, the purpose and goal of special revelation is God's own trinitarian glory, his delight in himself."

little thought one readily sees that Revelation is not merely founded in Creation, but that all creation is revelation." "Creation neither can nor may be conceived as anything but a sovereign act of God, for His own glorification."[24]

Revelation assumes a creature capable of transposing this revelation into subjective knowledge of God: "Hence, without every giving themselves to intellectualism, the Holy Scriptures always put this *knowledge of God* in the foreground."[25] Like Justin Martyr and many other theologians, Kuyper makes much of the logos in the human person in relation to the Logos through which God made the world. It is by the human's logos that one appropriates revelation.[26] Kuyper evocatively argues, "If the cosmos is the theatre of revelation, in this theatre man is both actor and spectator."[27] He does not add to God's revelation but is the "richest instrument by which and in which God reveals Himself."[28]

The human capacity for *faith* is not lost but misdirected by the fall. Regeneration and faith are thus not alien to human beings but restorative to what God intended us to be. Faith must never be reduced to being intellectualistic. "Only when your God and you have met each other and associate and walk together, does religion *live* in your heart."[29] Theology emerges out of a living relationship with God.

Special revelation has to take sin into account. In this respect Kuyper is fascinating in his anti-individualist view of revelation.[30] Revelation is for all humanity and the whole of the creation, not just the solitary individual. It thus has a social and historical dimension. Whereas prefall God could appear directly to the human person, now his self-manifestation must start in the outer world, as it does preeminently in the incarnation. Whereas originally revelation began inwardly, with a view to developing into the general possession

---

[24]*PST*, 259-60.

[25]*PST*, 263.

[26]Cf. *RD* 1:208: "The human intellect also has the capacity to abstract general and universal judgments from particular events. . . . The theological explanation for this is the conviction that it is the same Logos who created both the reality outside of us and the laws of thought within us."

[27]*PST*, 264.

[28]*PST*, 264.

[29]*PST*, 268. Cf. *RD* 1:235-36: "Biblical religion is in the first place a matter of the heart. . . . True religion embraces the whole person in relation to God."

[30]And in his—and Herman Bavinck's—view of the image of God. This point is helpfully appropriated by Anthony B. Bradley, *Black Scholars in White Space: New Vistas in African American Studies from the Christian Academy* (Eugene, OR: Pickwick, 2015), 136-37.

of humankind, now it begins outwardly, with a view to becoming inward again. "Revelation goes out to *humanity* taken as a whole. Since humanity unfolds itself *historically*, this Revelation also bears an *historic* character. Since this humanity exists organically, having a centrum of action, this Revelation also has to be *organic*, with a centrum of its own."[31]

The essential ego of restored humanity is Christ. He is our prophet and able to be such because he is the Logos and the human logos images him as *the* Logos. This is not to reduce the Christ event to thought, but it is to insist that Christ reveals God in being *and* in thought. Christ is the head of his body, and knowledge of God descends from him to individual believers.

However, Kuyper *never* makes the mistake of equating Scripture with propositional theology. In contemporary language we would say that he is alert to the different types of *speech acts* in the Bible and in the science of theology: "Christ does not argue, he *declares*; he does not demonstrate, he *shows* and *illustrates*; he does not analyze, but with enrapturing symbolism *unveils* the truth." The apostolic revelation of the New Testament is not scientific theology, "But in their writings the lines are indicated along which the logical activity of the so-called scientific Theology must conduct itself through all ages."[32]

Kuyper is also quite clear that Scripture is God's revelation to the communion of saints and thus theology cannot just be an individual pursuit. He is also crystal clear that Scripture requires the accompanying, illuminating work of the Spirit for us to hear God's address through it. The Spirit interprets the content of revelation to the church. Kuyper evocatively describes the Spirit as the *Doctor ecclesiae*!

Theology as science. Kuyper is clear that for theology the regulative principle is Scripture: "The material principium is *the self-revelation of God to the sinner*. From which principium the data have come forth in the Holy Scriptures, from which theology must be built up." Scripture emerged during a set period and as a given whole. The idea of theology is contained in the knowledge God has revealed to us, but he has not given us a theology textbook. "The Holy Bible is, therefore, neither a law-book nor a catechism, but the documentation of a part of *human life*, and in that human life of a *divine process*." God has

---

[31]*PST*, 282-83.
[32]*PST*, 287, 289.

revealed himself to us in a veiled form that is relevant to all ages: "God the Lord has spread one table for His entire Church, has given one organically connected revelation for all, and it is from this one revelation designed for all, and which neither repeats nor continues itself, lies for us in Holy Scripture."[33]

Kuyper rejects completely a dictation theory of inspiration and notes that the Heidelberg Catechism requires no theory of Scripture but merely asks that one believe. He uses the analogy of a telephone for the Bible: God is transcendent, but in Scripture he addresses you as if he were standing right next to you![34] The relationship between Scripture and our consciousness is immediate. God's action does not cease with the finalization of Scripture as canon; rather, this is where the great work of mission begins!

Whereas Dooyeweerd classifies theology as a special science and carefully—and largely insightfully—distinguishes between theory (science) and naive (lived) experience, Kuyper, rightly in my view, is aware that there are different levels in articulating the content of God's revelation, from basic confessional statements in Scripture, to creeds, to confessions, to systematic theology per se. Wisdom is given in Christ, but this is different from the understanding characteristic of theology. Theology "is that science which has the revealed knowledge of God as the object of its investigation, and raises it to 'understanding.'" Theology provides scientific insight into the revealed knowledge of God. "And *science* is called in, to introduce this knowledge of God, thus revealed, into our human thought."[35] Theology must not intellectualize living faith, and neither does it add certainty to faith.[36] However, its systematic reflection is of great benefit to the church:

> The Church, therefore, has not hesitated to profit by it; and though there is no single pearl in her confession which she owes theology as such, since all her pearls are gathered from the depths of spiritual life, it is equally certain that she would not have been able to string these pearls so beautifully in her confession, had not the light of theology illuminated her spiritual labor.[37]

---

[33]*PST*, 360.

[34]*PST*, 363-64.

[35]*PST*, 295-96, 299, 327.

[36]Cf. *RD* 1:60: "The knowledge of God given in revelation is not abstract and impersonal but the vital and personal knowledge of faith"; *RD* 1:562: "The certainty of faith is as firm as that of knowledge, though it is more intense, unshakable, and ineradicable." Again, cf. *RD* 1:601, "The certainty of faith rests in the Word of God and does not require theological science."

[37]*PST*, 329. Cf. *RD* 1:602: "Theology deepens and broadens this faith-knowledge but remains inextricably

Theology must be theological: "It must be strictly *theological*, so that from the beginning to the end of its epic God Himself is the *hero*."[38] And if God is the real hero, then theology must be catholic in the sense of being universal. Kuyper notes that after the canon was stabilized, "Then there arose that universal circle among all nations, that circle of confessors in their general human character, who live by this special principium."[39]

Holy Scripture. Intriguingly, Kuyper is adamant that Scripture as revelation is written for the whole human race. It was essential that God's special revelation be *written* because writing perpetuates and disperses the Word through its fixedness and purity. Writing is *catholic* in that it overcomes the limits of the local: "The Divine revelation, in order to reach immediately those who were called to life, *had* to assume the form of writing, and that only by *printed* writing could it enter upon its fullest mission of power."[40]

I like to think of Scripture as the deposit of God's work with Israel, culminating in the Christ event, and Kuyper thinks similarly: "Revelation did not merely make its appearance intellectually, but in life itself, and therefore dramatically, the inspiration, which only at the end of this drama could complete its action, was *eo ipso* linked to that process of time which was necessary for this drama."[41]

In terms of the authority and inspiration of the Bible, Kuyper has lengthy discussions of the different modes of revelation and inspiration narrated in Scripture.[42] He establishes the authority of the Old Testament on the basis of Christ's view of it: of the two great symbols of the Judaism of his day, the temple and the Bible, Jesus let go of the temple but retained the Bible![43] He anchors the New Testament in apostolic eyewitness testimony. He makes

---

connected to it.... Faith preserves theology from secularization; theology preserves faith from separatism."

[38]*PST*, 331. Cf. *RD* 1:61: "Theology is about God and should reflect a doxological tone that glorifies him."

[39]*PST*, 391. Cf. 393 for Kuyper's rejection of individualistic interpretation of Scripture.

[40]*PST*, 408, 412. Cf. *RD* 1:354: "For divine revelation to fully enter the life of humankind, it assumed the servant form of written language."

[41]*PST*, 419. Cf. *RD* 1:324: "God's self-revelation to us does not come in bits and pieces; it is an organic whole, a grand narrative from creation to consummation.... This revelation is historical and progresses over the course of many centuries, reaching its culmination in Jesus Christ. From this history we discover that revelation is not exclusively addressed to the human intellect. In Christ, God himself comes to us in saving power. At the same time we must not make the opposite error and deny that revelation communicates truth and doctrine."

[42]Cf. *RD* 1:387-448. See Dirk van Keulen, *Bijbel en dogmatiek: Schriftbeschouwing en schriftgebruik in het dogmatisch werk van A. Kuyper, H. Bavinck en G. C. Berkouwer* (Kampen: Kok, 2003).

[43]*PST*, 441.

much of the fact that Scripture is authoritative and inspired in its totality, what we today call *tota Scriptura.*

Kuyper is alert to the diversity of Scripture but rightly gives primacy to its unity: "He who believes in God cannot represent it otherwise than that there must be a *Word* of God, one coherent utterance of His Divine thought." His view of Scripture is wonderfully christocentric: "Christ is the whole Scripture, and the Scripture brings the *TÓ esse* of the Christ to our consciousness."[44]

> To this unity faith stretches forth it hands. From this unity of conception flows the Divine authority, to which the child of God gives itself captive. How this unity hides in that wondrous book remains a mystery which refuses all expla-nation. Only when you stand before it, and with the faith-eye of the connoisseur you gaze upon its multiplicity of tints and lines, the full image discovers itself stereoscopically to you. Then you see it. Then you can no longer *not* see it. The eye of your soul has caught it. In all its glory, it speaks to you.[45]

Kuyper distinguishes between the primary author and the secondary au-thors of Scripture, and he says that we must study its diversity but always return to the unity. In terms of the nature of inspiration, Kuyper avoids any-thing mechanical but argues for a view whereby God supervises the pro-duction of Scripture through human instruments. "Inspiration rests upon the antithesis between the Spirit of God and the spirit of man, and indicates that the Spirit of God enlists into His service the spirit of man, disposes of it, and uses it as His conscious or unconscious organ."[46]

The hermeneutics of theology. Although he does not use the word *herme-neutics*—Hans-Georg Gadamer, the father of modern hermeneutics, was only nine years old when Kuyper published his *Encyclopaedie!*—Kuyper is aware that there is a hermeneutics of doctrine.[47] He is quite clear that Scripture is not a code, and while Scripture contains an extended series of definite and positive utterances that we might call propositions, he strongly rejects any type of proof-texting scholasticism as a "grotesque representation of Scripture."[48] Indeed, "The task imposed on us is much more difficult and intricate; and so

---

[44]*PST*, 476, 477.
[45]*PST*, 478.
[46]*PST*, 506. Cf. *RD* 1:44: "God's thoughts cannot be opposed to one another and thus necessarily form an organic unity."
[47]Cf. Anthony C. Thiselton, *The Hermeneutics of Doctrine* (Grand Rapids: Eerdmans, 2007).
[48]*PST*, 565. Cf. *RD* 1:60 for Bavinck's critique of Charles Hodge's approach.

far from consisting of a mechanical quotation with the help of a concordance, the production of what the Scripture contains demands gigantic labor."[49]

Scripture, in terms of theology, simply does not provide us with bread that is already baked and cut up, ready-made for theological systematization. Kuyper even notes that we cannot reduce Scripture to authorial intention. He is alert to the multiple genres of texts and language we encounter in Scripture, all of which must be *interpreted*. Indeed, "To realize this purpose our thinking consciousness must descend into this gold mine, and dig out from its treasure, and then assimilate that treasure thus obtained; and not leave it as something apart from the other content of our consciousness, but systematize it with all the rest into one whole."[50]

The theologian's task is threefold: to determine, to assimilate, and to reproduce the contents of Scripture.[51] Kuyper is well aware of the difficulties and dangers in this process. He notes of the second stage of assimilation, "This is the more exceedingly difficult because an analysis made too hastily so readily destroys the mystical element, and thus leads to rationalism, while, on the other hand, the synthesis must be able to enter into *our* thinking."[52] We have to expel from our consciousness all that is untrue according to God's revelation and weave God's revelation together with what remains so that the unity of our worldview remains intact.

Kuyper is conscious of the holy calling of theology but never makes it the royal route to appropriating Scripture. Scripture offers us the grain of wheat, and we must not rest until the golden ears are seen in the field. However, "this can be done spiritually by piety of mind, practically by deeds of faith, aesthetically in hymns, parenetically in exhortation, but must also be done by scientific exposition and description."[53]

Theology takes *tradition* seriously.[54] Kuyper rejects the sort of ahistorical approach that tries to go directly back to the era of the apostles. Rather, theology is

---

[49]*PST*, 567.

[50]*PST*, 568, 567.

[51]Cf. *RD* 1:41, where Bavinck is clear that "then that knowledge of God also lies spread out before us objectively in his revelation and can be absorbed and thought through by us in faith."

[52]*PST*, 569. Cf. *RD* 1:45.

[53]*PST*, 570.

[54]Cf. *RD* 1:451: "For religions of the Book, the need for tradition as an interpretive guide is essential. . . . Radical groups that deliberately set aside all intervening tradition to return, in a primitivist way, to the letter of the Bible alone doom themselves to extinction unless they adapt to a new age."

the work of centuries. Kuyper begins at this point to expand his view of theology into its different subdisciplines. Church history, for example, is an essential part of theology because, "After it was finished, the Holy Scripture was not hidden in some sacred grotto, to wait for the theologian to read and to make scientific exhibition of its content; no, it was carried into the world, by reading and recitation, by teaching and by preaching, in apologetic and in polemic writings."[55]

In chapter nine, on philosophy, we set out how Kuyper ends up dividing theology into multiple subdisciplines. In chapter five, on sphere sovereignty, we noted the tensions between Kampen Seminary and the Free University of Amsterdam as to whether a seminary was part of the academic sphere or the ecclesial.[56] Kuyper recognizes the important place of church seminaries but also argues strongly for a university theology with appropriate academic freedom[57]—but never at the expense of a vital spirituality nurtured by the institutional church: "But however strenuously we emphasize this intellectual development, unless a spiritual development be its guide, it degenerates of necessity into intellectualism, and becomes cold, barren and unfruitful."[58]

Theology and philosophy. In a way that anticipates Alasdair MacIntyre's fertile work on tradition, Kuyper recognizes the important place of logic in theology, but this operates in theology—and philosophy—within one's worldview.[59] For Kuyper, *philosophy*, in the narrow sense, focuses on the human person's psychical life and the way in which the cosmos holds together and, as such, complements theology. "Philosophy ... is called to construct the human knowledge, which has been brought to light by all the other sciences, into one architectonic whole, and to show how this building arises from one basis. ... To say that a Christian is less in need of philosophy is only the exhibition of spiritual sloth and lack of understanding."[60]

---

[55]*PST*, 572.

[56]On Herman Bavinck and the tensions between the seminary in Kampen and the Free University, see Ron Gleason, *Herman Bavinck: Pastor, Churchman, Statesman, and Theologian* (Phillipsburg, NJ: P&R, 2010), chaps. 5, 7, 10. For differences between Bavinck and Kuyper on sphere sovereignty and education see Timothy S. Price, "Abraham Kuyper and Herman Bavinck on the Subject of Education as Seen in Two Public Addresses," *The Bavinck Review* 2 (2011): 59-70.

[57]Cf. *RD* 1:601-2, where Bavinck notes that theology is a fruit of the church as organism rather than institute. Church and theological schools ought to remain in solidarity with each other.

[58]*PST*, 583. Cf. *RD* 1:60: "The best-equipped theologian carries out the task by living in the full communion of faith with the church of Christ." Cf. Abraham Kuyper, *Band aan het woord. Antwoord op de vraag: Hoe is eene universiteit aan het woord van God te binden?* (Amsterdam: Höveker & Wormser, 1899).

[59]Alasdair MacIntyre, *Whose Justice? Which Rationality?* (Notre Dame, IN: University of Notre Dame Press, 1980).

[60]*PST*, 614.

Christian philosophy, whose theistic point of departure is fixed, is able to lead to a comprehensive unity of interpretation *within the circle of regeneration*: "A Christian philosopher knows his own soul . . . and views the ethical life differently from the philosopher who stands outside of regeneration. The antithesis, therefore, does not consist in the fact that theology offers a Christian ethics and philosophy a neutral one."[61] Kuyper perceptively notes that what theology provides is not a *Christian* ethics but a *theological* one!

KUYPER, BAVINCK, AND BERKOUWER

It will be obvious from our discussion above what a rich prolegomena to theology Kuyper provides. Herman Bavinck also wrote a prolegomena as the first volume of his extensive dogmatics, and in footnotes above I have included locations in Bavinck's *Prolegomena* and quotes from it where he deals with the same subjects as Kuyper.[62] Bavinck is more systematic than Kuyper, but the agreement between them is remarkable. The similarities between Bavinck and Kuyper will be obvious from Bavinck's definition of theology:

> But, built on the basis of revelation, theology undertakes a glorious task—the task of unfolding the science of the revelation of God and of our knowledge concerning him. It engages in this task when seeking to ascertain by means of exegesis the content of revelation, when endeavoring to reduce to unity of thought this ascertained content, when striving to maintain its truth whether by way of aggression or defence, or to commend it to the consciences of men. But side by side with all these branches there is room also for a *philosophy of revelation* which will trace the idea of revelation, both in its form and in its content, and correlate it with the rest of our knowledge and life.[63]

Kuyper's lecture notes on the different loci of theology are published as his *Dictaten Dogmatiek*. His major work on a particular doctrine is, however, *The Work of the Holy Spirit*. This is a penetrating work that bears close attention. Others have written about Kuyper's doctrine of the Holy Spirit, and I will not explore it further here, other than encouraging readers to read it.[64] Note

---

[61]*PST*, 613.

[62]*RD* 1. Cf. Herman Bavinck, "The Pros and Cons of a Dogmatic System," trans. Nelson D. Kloosterman, *The Bavinck Review* 5 (2014): 90-103.

[63]*PR*, 24. Cf. *RD* 1:26 and the discussion following.

[64]See, e.g., Vincent E. Bacote, *The Spirit in Public Theology: Appropriating the Legacy of Abraham Kuyper* (Grand Rapids: Baker Academic, 2005); W. H. Velema, *De leer van de Heilige Geest by Abraham Kuyper* (The Hague: Van Keulen, 1957).

should also be taken of Kuyper's multivolume *E Voto*, a commentary on the Heidelberg Catechism.

In 1884, in a lecture on the theology of Daniel Chantepie de la Saussaye to the Reformed Minister's Conference, Bavinck aligns himself with Kuyper's approach of "isolation" rather than a Christian-culture synthesis and concludes by expressing the hope, "It could be that thus a beautiful day might still dawn upon the horizon for a church and theology in our fatherland!"[65] After Kuyper and Bavinck, the major Dutch theologian in the Kuyperian tradition is Gerrit C. Berkouwer (1903–1996), whose *Studies in Dogmatics* are well-known to English speakers. Berkouwer continually engages with Kuyper and Bavinck in his twenty-volume *Dogmatics*. In the English language mention should also be made of the fine work of Gordon Spykman, namely his *Reformational Theology: A New Paradigm for Doing Dogmatics*.[66] While, as will be noted below, I disagree with his definition of theology, his work is rich and deeply Kuyperian, albeit in Dooyeweerdian mode, at least in terms of his theory of science and theology.[67]

The significance of the twentieth century for the Kuyperian tradition must be borne in mind, and not least for theology.[68] Kuyper died shortly after World War I. At this time liberal theology and historical criticism expanded their influence, and Karl Barth's theology began to attract attention. We noted at the outset of this chapter how H. Berkhof sets confessional theology aside in his engagement with the gospel and modern culture over the last one hundred years. Berkouwer, however, takes Barth with utmost seriousness as his major dialogue partner.[69] The experience of two world wars in short succession changed Europe forever and provided theology with new and unforeseen challenges.[70] Biblical studies and theology tended to be dominated

---

[65]Quoted in Berkhof, *Two Hundred Years*, 111. *Isolation* is a term of Groen van Prinsterer's that he took from da Costa.

[66]Spykman, *Reformation Theology*, includes brief evaluations of Berkouwer (51-52), Berkhof (52-55), and Kuitert (55-58).

[67]In Dutch mention should be made of theologians such as Cornelis van der Kooi and Willem Ouweneel, both of whom have published major theologies in recent years.

[68]For an overview see Heinz Zahrnt, *The Question of God: Protestant Theology in the Twentieth Century*, trans. R. A. Wilson (London: Collins, 1969).

[69]See Gerrit C. Berkouwer, *The Triumph of Grace in the Theology of Karl Barth*, trans. Harry R. Boer (Grand Rapids: Eerdmans, 1956); *Half Century of Theology*, 39-74.

[70]See Gerrit C. Berkouwer, "World War and Theology," an address at the Free University of Amsterdam in October 1945.

by Germany, and this is reflected in Dutch theology too. The great theologians of the day were Karl Barth, Emil Brunner, Dietrich Bonhoeffer, Helmut Thielicke, Wolfhart Pannenberg, and Jürgen Moltmann, and biblical studies inevitably responded in one way or another to German historical criticism. In this context Berkouwer's work stands out in the Dutch context, and in his *A Half Century of Theology* he reflects on the developments since Kuyper and Bavinck and on the challenges facing the churches.

Bavinck's successor was Valentine Hepp, who sought a renewed emphasis on apologetics if theology was to retain its intellectual credibility. Hepp was overshadowed by Barth, who was more radical than either Kuyper or Bavinck in terms of being wary of natural theology and thus of apologetics. One gets the sense that it was a confusing time at the Free University of Amsterdam for a young theological student like Berkouwer. Berkouwer identifies the following areas as flashpoints of controversy and concern in roughly the first half of the twentieth century:

1. scripture, and in particular the challenge of historical criticism;[71]

2. the role of faith in the modern world, in particular the relationship between faith and reason;[72]

3. a new emphasis on eschatology;

4. uncertainty about the fundamental doctrines of the Trinity and Christology; and[73]

5. in Reformed circles, an uncertainty and doubt about the centrality of election.[74]

The debate about election was a debate within Reformed circles, but the other challenges indicate how world issues pressed in on Dutch theology. It could hardly be otherwise amid such tumultuous times, and Berkouwer notes that beneath all these issues lay the foundational issue of "the question of the living God, the reality of his revelation within our world."[75] Gordon Spykman

---

[71]See Gerrit C. Berkouwer, *Het probleem der Schriftkritiek* (Kampen: Kok, 1938); *Half Century of Theology*, 107-43.

[72]Berkouwer, *Half Century of Theology*, 179-264.

[73]Ibid., 215-64.

[74]Ibid., 75-106.

[75]Ibid., 76-77.

observes, "Western Christianity is being literally swamped by the tidal wave of modern secularism," and this wave gathered strength as the twentieth century developed.[76] In the twentieth century modernity revealed its powers as never before, powers that were brought into question again and again during a brutal century, so that by the end of the century some thought that modernity was close to death. Certainly much of its ideology/ies had been severely challenged, so that as one looks back now on twentieth-century theology one gains a longer view and feels less threatened or put on the defense by the "scientism" of modern thought.

In the remainder of this chapter we will revisit Kuyper and Bavinck's approach to theology with a view to asking whether it can and should be renewed in our day.

EVALUATION

First, and in defense of Kuyper and Bavinck, it is far too easy to write them off as "scholastic." Bavinck, for example, consciously distances himself from the scholasticism of seventeenth- and eighteenth-century theology.[77] He rejects, as does Kuyper, any sense that in Scripture the data for theology is ready-made and merely needs to be collated and ordered systematically.

Both Kuyper and Bavinck are wary of a theologized faith that becomes purely intellectual, but both see an important, albeit limited, role for theology as an academic analysis of the content of faith given to us in Scripture for today. Here Dooyeweerd begs to differ. He refers to the Scriptures as a *"temporal manifestation of the Word-revelation."*[78] By *temporal* he means a manifestation in time, in history. It is only by faith that we experience Scripture as the Word of God. For Dooyeweerd the principle of unity of the Bible is its central theme of creation, fall, and redemption. Remarkably, however, for Dooyeweerd, "this theme cannot become the theoretical object of theological thought, since it is the very starting point for such thought, at least if theology is to be truly biblical."[79] For Dooyeweerd theology can never reflect directly on the Word-

---

[76]Spykman, *Reformational Theology*, 3-4.
[77]Cf. *RD* 1:180-83.
[78]Herman Dooyeweerd, *In the Twilight of Western Thought: Studies in the Pretended Autonomy of Philosophical Thought* (Lewiston, NY: Edwin Mellen, 1999), 99.
[79]Ibid., 99-100.

revelation but only on the faith modality or aspect of human experience.[80] Thus he notes that "dogmatic theology can doubtless engage in a theoretical reflection on creation, fall into sin, and redemption, insofar as their revelation is related to the faith aspect of our temporal experience and forms the contents of articles of Christian belief." Again: "All theological problems such as the significance of the imago Dei before and after the fall, the relation between creation and sin and that of particular grace to common grace, that of the union of the two natures in Jesus Christ, etc., can only arise in the theoretical opposition of the faith-aspect to the logical aspect of our thought."[81]

Dooyeweerd's unusual view is tied in to the shape of his philosophy as a whole and not least to his epistemology. Epistemologically, he developed his *gegenstand* theory, whereby a science is thought to set the logical mode opposite one of the other fifteen modes of human experience.[82] This is a part of his philosophy that many of his followers do not agree with, and in my view it simply does not represent what theologians down through the centuries have done, namely reflect systematically out of a living faith on God's Word. Dooyeweerd himself also assumes *theological* insights in his philosophy, assumptions such as the Trinity, which certainly does not leave his philosophy without theological input. Finally, to make theology's focus the faith aspect of human life sounds to me far too much like Schleiermacher's approach to theology, which makes religious experience the focus of theology.[83]

Thus Kuyper and Bavinck's articulation of the limited but important task of theology seems correct, indeed, very insightful. Dooyeweerd would see their approaches as scholastic, but this is an unfair critique. Furthermore, even though Bavinck himself carefully distances himself from "Protestant scholasticism," in recent years Richard Muller has done herculean work in retrieving

---

[80]Spykman, *Reformational Theology*, 97, similarly says that "theology explores in depth a community's faith-life and confessional expressions." However, if one looks at what Spykman actually does in his rich work, Scripture is constantly taken as the norm, and he reflects continually on it, just as do Kuyper and Bavinck.

[81]Dooyeweerd, *Twilight*, 100, 101.

[82]For the contours of Dooyeweerd's philosophy see Craig G. Bartholomew and Michael W. Goheen, *Christian Philosophy: A Systematic and Narrative Introduction* (Grand Rapids: Baker Academic, 2013).

[83]Theodore Vial, *Schleiermacher: A Guide for the Perplexed*, Guides for the Perplexed (London: Bloomsbury, 2013), 83, notes that for Schleiermacher, "religion in essence is an experience of the infinite. For Christians, religion is the experience of redemption found in the Christian community. That is the key thing for Schleiermacher. Theology is an attempt to express this experience in as adequate a language as possible."

and reassessing post-Reformation theology, and it has become clear in the light of his work that it cannot simply be written off as scholastic.

Contra H. Berkhof, Kuyper and Bavinck *did not* choose an intellectual view of Scripture over encounter with God.[84] As will be obvious from our discussion in the first part of this chapter, they resolutely refused to drive a wedge between encounter and cognitive knowledge of God, insisting that one without the other would be totally inadequate and that Scripture is given to us first to bring us into a relationship with God.

Kuyper could certainly be faulted for his theology of the logos in both God and the human person. This, if not nuanced, has a rationalist tendency, but I do not think Kuyper uses it this way, and in Bavinck's *RD* we find a more nuanced use of it. Helmut Thielicke helpfully comments, "Christ can be defined in terms of the logos concept but also himself determines the content of the concept."[85]

Enough in defense of Kuyper and Bavinck. What are key elements in the sacred calling of theology that we can learn from them?

First, both of them build their theologies with a sure certainty that *God has spoken* and done so preeminently in Christ and in Scripture, which is God's infallible Word. This, of course, changes everything and is utterly fundamental to the practice of theology. As Bavinck notes of too much theology, "The weakness of dogmatics consists precisely in the fact that this discipline itself has so little faith in this 'God has spoken.'"[86] Kuyper and Bavinck presuppose and celebrate this reality so that their theologies are fundamentally and beautifully constructive. And both of them do theology with full engagement with Scripture, a practice that has become far too rare in contemporary theology. Theologians such as Barth and O'Donovan are, alas, the exception in that as their theological frameworks take hold they do more and not less exegesis! The same is true of Kuyper, Bavinck, and Berkouwer. Of course, in many areas biblical studies has advanced since Kuyper and Bavinck;

---

[84]In his *Drie Kleine Vossen* [Three Small Foxes] (Kampen: Kok, 1901), the title of which is taken from Song of Songs 2:15, in which reference is made to the little foxes that ruin the vineyards, Kuyper identifies intellectualism, mysticism, and excessive activity as such foxes when it comes to the Christian life. He notes that "three dimensions in us must work in harmony, three dimensions, the symbol of which is provided by the head, the heart, and the hand. The head is the symbol of the work of understanding, the heart of the feeling of mysticism, and the hand of Christian action" (1).

[85]*RD* 1:586-87; Helmut Thielicke, *The Evangelical Faith*, vol. 2, *The Doctrine of God and of Christ*, trans. Geoffrey W. Bromiley (Grand Rapids: Eerdmans, 1977), 103.

[86]Cf. *RD* 1:46.

indeed, they recognized the need for it to do so. Some of their contemporaries and followers at the Free University of Amsterdam and Kampen did rich biblical work, and this too needs to be recovered. But, as Spykman recognizes, there is rich contemporary work in biblical theology and exegesis for theologians to draw on today, and we urgently need a creative relationship between theologians and biblical scholars. Indeed, we are seeing something of this emerge in the renascent theological interpretation of our time.[87]

Second, both of them, but Kuyper in more detail, see theology as one discipline among many, all of which are called to operate out of a Christian worldview. Each science is unique in its own way, and they articulate the uniqueness of theology in its focus on the knowledge of God contained in Scripture. Both nuance this approach carefully, and neither elevates theology to lord it over faith or over the other disciplines.

Third, and this is one of the great things about the Reformed tradition, they insist that the sovereign God must be the "hero" of theology. From him, through him, and to him are all things! As Bavinck notes,

> Dogmatics shows us how God, who is all-sufficient in himself, nevertheless glorifies himself in his creation, which, even when it is torn apart by sin, is gathered up again in Christ (Eph. 1:10). It describes for us God, always God, from beginning to end—God in his being, God in his creation, God against sin, God in Christ, God breaking down all resistance through the Holy Spirit and guiding the whole of creation back to the objective he decreed for it: the glory of his name. Dogmatics, therefore, is not a dull and arid science. It is a theodicy, a doxology to all God's virtues and perfections, a hymn of adoration and thanksgiving, a "glory to God in the highest" (Luke 2:14).[88]

Their theologies are theocentric and christocentric, and thus trinitarian. When I was at Oxford a lecturer mentioned that on Trinity Sunday he would go to different college chapels to hear what Oxford theologians and chaplains had to say. In general, they ignored the Trinity. However, this represented the modernity that Berkouwer refers to in *Half a Century*. In the second half of the twentieth century we witnessed a surprising flourishing of trinitarian theology developing out of Barth's theology and articulated by major theologians such

---

[87]Cf. Craig G. Bartholomew and Heath A. Thomas, eds., *A Manifesto for Theological Interpretation* (Grand Rapids: Baker Academic, 2016).
[88]*RD* 1:112.

as Jürgen Moltmann, Colin Gunton, John Zizioulas, and so on, in which Bavinck's elevation of the doctrine of the Trinity as absolutely central to theology fits perfectly. In this and so many other ways, there is a sense in which a century later Kuyper and Bavinck's time has come!

Fourth, as modernity unraveled in the twentieth century and as a radical secularism took hold, not least in postmodernism, confessional theology has made something of a comeback, so that Kuyper and Bavinck look far more relevant and contemporary than they must have done in the half-century that Berkouwer writes about. However, as both would remind us, we cannot allow ourselves to be dictated to by the fashions of the day. Yes, we need to engage them, but they cannot finally set our agenda.

Fifth, as we noted with Kuyper, and the same can be said of Bavinck, he was way ahead of his time in identifying the key elements in a hermeneutics of theology. To me, Kuyper is simply a genius in asking the right questions and pursuing them so rigorously. This is a far cry from so-called scholasticism and provides fertile ground for renewing theology in our day.

Sixth, both Kuyper and Bavinck did theology that had the whole of creation in view. Their theology is inherently public theology, and in this, once again, they anticipate a need in our day to develop a theology of the world. They did this remarkably well, and unlike so much contemporary theology, they were well aware that Christian witness required equally rigorous Christian scholarship in all disciplines.

Seventh, both Kuyper and Bavinck were aware of the diversity in Scripture and wrestled with the challenge of biblical criticism. Indeed, the views they express on critical issues are generally far from fundamentalist and fit well with the best contemporary evangelical work. However, they never succumbed to the fragmenting effect of biblical criticism and were always conscious of the underlying philosophies informing biblical criticism as it emerged. Both gave priority to the unity of Scripture, and so should we!

Eighth, as Brannon Ellis of Lexham Press commented to me, if Kuyper and Bavinck had written in English, their work would be far more influential than it has been thus far. Fortunately, we are now close to all their major works being available in English, so that we are presented with a marvelous feast, inviting us to tuck in. This is not to absolutize Kuyper or Bavinck. They would be the first to remind us of the Reformed principle of *semper reformanda*, but one has to have something solid, rigorous, and creative to work with, and they have provided us with that in spades.

It is too easy to nitpick at details of Kuyper and Bavinck's work. Such detailed work is essential, but we need, especially today, to distinguish the forest from the trees. And the forest is deeply impressive and invites us to inhabit it and to develop it further. Perhaps Bavinck's vision of a beautiful day for theology will still dawn. Much will depend on what we do with his and Kuyper's fertile work.

EDUCATION

*Is education to be a "passport to privilege" or is it something like
a monastic vow, a sacred obligation to serve the people?*

E. F. SCHUMACHER, *SMALL IS BEAUTIFUL*

IN 2003 GERALD GRAFF PUBLISHED *Clueless in Academe: How
Schooling Obscures the Life of the Mind*. Graff describes how in the 1950s he
took courses in Romantic literature and introductory sociology back to back.
He was bounced back and forth between incommensurate paradigms, but as
he notes, "What was striking about my experience . . . was how little *cognitive
dissonance* there actually was. Since the perspectives of the literature and sociology courses never came together to be compared and contrasted, they remained in separate mental compartments, leaving my exposure to divergent
viewpoints incomplete and unconsummated."[1]

In a chapter titled "The Mixed-Message Curriculum," Graff has sections
with headings such as "The Student as Volleyball," "Contradiction and Com-
partmentalization," and "Redundancy Lost." As part of the solution and in
hope of developing intellectual community and intellectuals, Graff asserts,
"Clearly, it is crucial to begin providing students with a *more connected view of
the academic intellectual universe, one that lets them recognize and enter the conversation that makes that universe cohere and relates it to the wider world.*"[2]

---

[1]Gerald Graff, *Clueless in Academe: How Schooling Obscures the Life of the Mind* (New Haven, CT: Yale
University Press, 2003), 65.
[2]Ibid., 77, emphasis added.

Kuyper completely rejects this sort of volleyball education. He asserts, "Now then, pedagogically speaking, an education that calls a lie in Tuesday's lecture what was recommended in Monday's lecture as the truth mocks the primordial demands of a formative education."[3]

It is intriguing that already in the fifties Graff experienced the fragmentation in the university that we associate with postmodernism. Certainly the problem has gotten worse and not better. Catholic philosopher and ethicist Alasdair MacIntyre compares the contemporary ethical landscape to one in which shards are scattered around; ethicists try to connect these shards, but they have no understanding of the traditions in which they are embedded.[4] Similarly, Oliver O'Donovan imagines our time ethically as one in which icebergs are to be seen all over the place but we have no idea what holds them together.[5] In this context the question of how to provide a more connected view of the academic intellectual universe for students becomes a poignant one indeed.

The crisis in education is widely acknowledged today.[6] Two of my favorite authors in this respect are both non-Christians: Neil Postman and Robert Carroll. Both of them have an uncanny ability for foregrounding the crucial issues in contemporary culture and education. Postman, for example, begins his *End of Education* with a chapter titled "The Necessity of Gods." Postman rightly points out that the surest way to kill education is for us to be unclear on the goal, the "end" of education. A mechanical, technological approach will not do, and nor will the consumer answer of getting educated in order to get a good job. Education requires some sort of grand narrative within which it can find its purpose. As Postman says, "My intention here is neither to bury nor to praise any gods, but *to claim that we cannot do without them*, that whatever else we may call ourselves, we are the god-making species."[7]

Carroll makes similar claims, but neither Postman nor Carroll think the Christian metanarrative is up to the challenge. As we will see below, Kuyper's lifelong advocacy for distinctively Christian education inevitably involves

---

[3]Abraham Kuyper, *Scholarship: Two Convocation Addresses on University Life*, trans. Harry van Dyke (Grand Rapids: Christian's Library Press, 2014), 43.

[4]Alasdair MacIntyre, *After Virtue* (Notre Dame, IN: University of Notre Dame Press, 1980).

[5]Oliver O'Donovan, *The Ways of Judgment* (Grand Rapids: Eerdmans, 2005), xi, xiii.

[6]The literature is extensive. Titles include Bill Readings, *The University in Ruins* (Cambridge, MA: Harvard University Press, 1996).

[7]Neil Postman, *The End of Education: Redefining the Value of School* (New York: Knopf, 1996), 6. Emphasis added.

cultural pluralism, but for Postman this is dangerous. He lumps what he calls "multiculturalism" with the false gods of economic utility, consumership, and technology, and he argues that a pluralist approach to education is positively dangerous: "This path not only leads to the privatization of schooling but to a privatizing of the mind, and it makes the creation of a public mind quite impossible. The theme of schooling would then be divisiveness, not sameness, and would inevitably lead to hate."[8]

Little wonder that when George Marsden published his book on Christian scholarship he titled it *The Outrageous Idea of Christian Scholarship!*[9] Despite the fact that historically, most Western scholarship was for centuries done from a Christian perspective, we are now in a context in which the very idea is outrageous, even for so perceptive a commentator as Postman. The quote from Postman above is illuminating. Clearly, in his view, public education must produce a *public mind*, a mind characterized in his word by "sameness." Pluralism in education *must* lead to hate; Postman appeals to the effect of a talk by Minister Louis Farrakhan in December 1993 in this respect.[10] Apparently, it cannot be otherwise! In the earlier quote from Postman he also reveals his position; we are "the god-making species." Here we see Ludwig Feuerbach revived.[11] The "gods" are our projections on the universe in order to provide the grand narratives so that we can indwell them and thus find meaning in life and purpose for education. Would it not, one wonders, be more honest to acknowledge such projections for what they are and embrace the nihilism that results, as some encourage us to do?

Postman is right; neither we nor our education can do without "gods"—but in all the major religions the "gods" are not of our making; we are of their making! The whole point of a religion is that it aims to tell the true story of the world and this yields an inevitable pluralism.

For those of us who are religious—the vast majority of the world, but generally not the secular elite of the West—inventing a narrative because we need one simply will not do. The question is, rather, What is the true story of the world, and how does education look within that context? And for Christians

---

[8]Ibid., 57.
[9]George Marsden, *The Outrageous Idea of Christian Scholarship* (New York: Oxford University Press, 1997).
[10]Postman, *End of Education*, 58.
[11]Feuerbach argued that religion is a human projection on the universe.

what does that mean in a secular, pluralist culture? These are the questions with which Kuyper grappled even as post-Enlightenment thought gained traction in Dutch culture.

KUYPER AND EDUCATION

With growing secularization in the Netherlands Kuyper was not the first to become concerned about its influence on the schools.[12] Led by Groen van Prinsterer, the Réveil political wing had argued from the start that the interpretation of the formula whereby public schools were to train their pupils in "Christian and social virtues" but to give no offense to the consciences of any pupils or parents was not viable. Groen van Prinsterer's solution was to divide the system along Protestant and Catholic lines, allowing each side to educate on the basis of their convictions. The Réveil's traditionalists, however, were reluctant to concede the residual Protestant control over public education, while liberals wanted to promote the secularization of education. Despite Groen van Prinsterer's objections, in 1857 a compromise was proposed for a state-funded "neutral" system, with subsidies provided for private religious schools. The bill was passed by the States General, but the subsidies were dropped. In disgust Groen van Prinsterer resigned from Parliament and concentrated his attention on developing a national network that would assist private Christian schools and eventually provide the pressure for a change in the law.

In May 1869 Kuyper gave the keynote address, "Het Beroep op het Volksgeweten" [An Appeal to the National Conscience], at the annual convention of the Union for Christian National Education.[13] This address also marked Kuyper's debut into national civic life.[14] Kuyper used the opportunity to expose the fault line in the union's vision and to argue for a genuine pluralism in education. The changes in the Netherlands needed to be faced; it was now a nation in which Calvinists were in a minority. Consequently,

---

[12]See the essays on education in J. L. van Essen and H. D. Morton, *Guillaume Groen van Prinsterer: Selected Studies* (Jordan Station, ON: Wedge, 2000). Herman Bavinck was also very influential through his reflections on education. See Herman Bavinck, *Essays on Religion, Science, and Society*, ed. John Bolt, trans. Harry Boonstra and Gerrit Sheeres (Grand Rapids: Baker Academic, 2008), chaps. 12 and 13; Cornelius R. Jaarsma, *The Educational Philosophy of Herman Bavinck: A Textbook in Education* (Grand Rapids: Eerdmans, 1935).

[13]Amsterdam, May 18, 1869.

[14]*AK*, 68-69.

In a land such as ours is today, the state school must be pluralistic, and therefore must either intentionally reject religion or become a nursery of religion, which chooses the minimum positive confession in the land as its own maximum confession. Either it must be religionless or it must feature a Christianity that transcends differences of confession. That is the dilemma.[15]

Kuyper points out the inadequacy of a diluted form of Christianity that all can agree to and notes how a religionless education ignores the formative role of Christianity in the history of the Netherlands. A neutral public education is, according to Kuyper, "moral suicide." In terms of sphere sovereignty, Kuyper appeals to the primary responsibility of the parents for the education of their children and the danger of inappropriate state interference in education. He confesses that he too is a father and that he would find it painful if he had to hand over his two sons to an education he sees as damaging.[16]

Kuyper lists five characteristics that should shape one's view of education and concludes that

devotion, prizing our national history, the flourishing of family life, the "self-government" of the citizenry, and respect for the freedom of conscience—this is the set of five characteristics that, in our view, are inscribed too deeply upon the visage of our nation finally to be able to be misunderstood. A set of five demands upon our national life that the State school cannot satisfy, and to which justice can be done only when the constraints of the State school are dissolved, the discredited protection system is chased out of the land, and the unrestrained, complete freedom of instruction is acknowledged.[17]

A noteworthy element in Kuyper's speech is his concern for the poor, who do not have the money to send their children to private schools. Kuyper's speech sparked a fierce debate, and in subsequent years the school question became central to Kuyper's political work and was a central plank in the establishment of the Anti-Revolutionary Party, whose delegate assembly met shortly after the establishment of a national Union for the School with the Bible in January 1879. In the same year the establishment of the Free University of Amsterdam was announced, and it opened on October 20, 1880.

---

[15]Lexham, forthcoming education anthology.
[16]Ibid.
[17]Ibid.

By 1887 Dutch politics was at an impasse, with liberals badly divided. In a remarkable move for his time, Kuyper organized a meeting between Calvinist and Catholic leaders that resulted in an agreement to support each other's candidates in the runoff phase of the general election. The expanded electorate of 1888 returned a 53–47 religious majority to the Lower House, and within a year a bill was passed providing state subsidies for teachers' salaries at religious schools. Full parity was achieved in 1917.

Kuyper continued to write and speak on the school issue, and in 1899 he gave his "As Sheep Among Wolves" address. He invokes the example of Jesus and his disciples. In order to form his disciples, Jesus did not send them to the academy of the Pharisees or Sadducees! Yes, they needed to be sent out into the world, but only once they were properly formed and ready. It is the same with children and education. Children are called to fight the good fight of faith, and one cannot do that if one remains isolated from the culture. But it is essential that one be properly prepared first.[18]

And so Kuyper argues, "So this is the secret of Christian education. Keep your children in the company of Jesus and educate them under the shadow of his wings until they are ready. And when they are ready, send them out into the world, among the wolves, but as sheep—as young people *whose shield is the Lord*."[19]

Sphere sovereignty is a fascinating issue in relation to the school, because the family, the school, and the government all connect in the sphere of the school. Kuyper addresses this directly and argues,

> If we now try to put the above in an organic relationship and ask how the right and the duty to operate schools should be regulated if each of the four participants (father, church, teacher, and government) is to be capable of fulfilling its task within its own sphere, then it is obvious that on the main point the decision lies with the *father*.
>
> The father, after all, has authority over the child. The father is responsible for the child. The father is obligated to pay for its nurture and education. And the father has agreed to certain conditions set by the church.[20]

---

[18]Ibid.

[19]Ibid.

[20]Abraham Kuyper, *Our Program: A Christian Political Manifesto*, trans. Harry Van Dyke, Abraham Kuyper Collected Works in Public Theology (Bellingham, WA: Lexham Press, 2015), 202-3.

For Kuyper, parents decide on the spirit in which their children will be educated; the church decides on the principle by which that spirit can be preserved in the school; the government decides on the level to which public education will rise; and teachers decide on the manner in which children will be taught. "*Formally* they have to decide this in accordance with the science of pedagogy. *Materially* they decide this depending on the formative power of the various disciplines, the time a child needs to learn about their basic results, and the benefits they offer for life."[21]

Kuyper thus articulates a sevenfold view of Christian schooling:[22]

1. Parents hold primary responsibility for the education of their children.

2. The church has a right and the responsibility to see performed what has been promised at the time of a child's baptism.

3. Teachers must be able to make their own decisions about matters of pedagogy.

4. Nurture and education are inseparable.

5. Voluntary donations to support schools are better than compulsory taxation.

6. Free initiatives by citizens ennoble a nation, whereas state meddling debases it.

7. A school that makes it difficult for the intellect to submit to God's ordinances and so sets itself against the Christian religion must be deemed a curse and not a blessing for the nation.

At a tertiary level, Kuyper worked hard for the certification of private university degrees, and this was passed in March 1904 in the Second Chamber and in May 1905 in the First Chamber.

THE UNIVERSITY AND CHRISTIAN SCHOLARSHIP

The establishment of the Free University of Amsterdam was a project close to Kuyper's heart, and he served there as rector and as a professor. His two convocation addresses, published as *Scholarship: Two Convocation Addresses on University Life*, make for wonderful and inspiring reading. Both would be inspiring if simply read at a university convocation today.

Kuyper speaks evocatively of "the holy grail of scholarship." Academic work is a sacred calling, and he says to the students at the Free University of

---

[21]Ibid., 349.
[22]Ibid., 207.

Amsterdam that God "ordained you a priest of learning and anointed you with consecrated oil for the holy priesthood." Kuyper speaks of the world of scholarship as "the *res publica litterarum*, the entire republic of letters, that distinctive sphere in society which indeed centers on the university yet pervades the country with young men who thirst after knowledge and with men of learning who illumine our towns and villages like bright stars."[23]

For Kuyper, God made us logical beings, so we should trace his reason in the creation, his Logos, study it, publish it, wonder at it, and spread that wonder to others. Scholarship also proclaims the glory of God's name.[24] Scholarship is thus about far more than just accumulating facts or getting a degree to get a job. The purpose of scholarship is threefold: to bring to light the hidden things of God, to give us joy in digging up the gold hidden in the creation, and to contribute to the well-being of human life.

Scholarship requires *humility*: "Genius of genuine gold, as Fichte put it so beautifully, does not know its own beauty. Real talent has the fragrance of a flower without being aware of it." It also requires *faith*: "And scholars, far from being able to do without that faith, must begin by being rich in that faith if they are ever able to feel their heart stir with the holy impulse that drives them to engage in true scholarship." Kuyper appeals for scholarship done out of prayer and before the face of God.[25]

Kuyper is keenly alert to the secularization scholarship was undergoing in his day but stresses that even this "derailed science brings gain" and argues that secularization is no excuse for Christians to abandon the world of scholarship. Instead, it provides an imperative to get this gift of God back on its tracks and to refute the lie that faith is antithetical to science. Simultaneously, we should not despise the academic work of others but work with them in the scholarly task given to humankind, provided we—and they—can do so in our own confessional institutions.[26]

Kuyper stresses dedicated work but also rest and relaxation, and he notes that scholarship takes time to mature. Intriguingly, he stresses the aesthetic, literary dimension of scholarship: "Form and design are the hydraulic drills

---

[23]Kuyper, *Scholarship*, 6, 9, 3.
[24]Ibid., 8.
[25]Ibid., 11, 12-13.
[26]Ibid., 10.

with which you penetrate the public with what you have to say."[27] Kuyper had particular literary gifts, but his point is well taken; one is only too familiar with scholarship that is of the highest standard, but the prose works against the insight and not along with it.

Kuyper acknowledges the delight in seeking for knowledge but is clear that the aim is *to find* and to find *truth*. Indeed, for Kuyper scholarship should always be *to serve*—not to rule—and to serve by searching for the truth:

> Seeking should be in the service of finding. The ultimate purpose of seeking is finding. Only from this lofty goal does seeking derive its reason for existence. The shepherd who had lost his sheep did not rejoice in searching for it but in finding it; it was then that he called together his friends and neighbors and exclaimed: "Rejoice with me, for I have found my sheep." . . . Delight in searching is priceless, and without it you won't get there; but finding must be the goal and motive and therefore the main thing, above all for science that seeks truth.[28]

This is not for a moment to forgo rigor. Kuyper urges his students toward the utmost rigor, provided it is in the service of the truth.[29]

Kuyper urges on his students a deep sense of history and advises against being fashionable for the sake of gaining attention and promotion. Scholarship should never lose what was not lost to begin with; Christian scholarship takes common sense seriously. "And what is never legitimate is that we imagine that we ourselves have to prove being itself and that we willfully discard what we know immediately in order to regain it as the product of our own thinking."[30]

Kuyper finds Descartes's doubting everything only to find solid ground in his *cogito* (I think) absurd. Yes, with Kant we should examine thoroughly the thinking self, but no, we should not think we have to start again de novo. He imagines such individualistic scholarship as hurling a ring into a vortex only in order to spend all one's energy trying to find it again: "That is the just punishment for people who cause to be lost what they already possessed by

---

[27]Ibid., 19-20.
[28]Ibid., 28-29. Kuyper quotes Lessing as an example of a philosopher for whom seeking was more important than finding.
[29]Ibid., 44.
[30]Ibid., 32.

casting it into the vortex and who then dive into that vortex in vain hopes of recovering it. As real children of Pilate, they are left with not one fixed starting point for their thinking, not a single pillar in their temple of justice, not one firm rule for their moral code."[31]

It is hard to imagine a more penetrating critique of postmodernism! Postmodernism is well known for its celebration of play, and intriguingly Kuyper says of critical individualism that "it speaks of the play enjoyed by people who delight in the search, but not of the earnest desire for humanity to advance to ever clearer light of knowledge."[32]

Kuyper unashamedly acknowledges the reformed common starting point of the Free University: "We inhabit the Reformed house bequeathed to us by our forebears and that is where we carry on our lives. If that is called unscientific, then notice how those who label us with that stigma factually do the same thing, only on less solid grounds."[33]

Kuyper is right to stress the fact that he openly acknowledges this, whereas in mainstream scholarship to this day the worldview informing it is often unacknowledged or unconscious. And, like Alvin Plantinga, Kuyper finds it absurd that we would do scholarship without the truth revealed to us, if indeed we really believe it to be the truth. He advises us to stop seeking if God reveals to us what we were seeking: "To continue searching when someone else brings you what you are looking for is contrary to everything that is reasonable, and what is unreasonable should not be called scientific."[34] The questions and answers Kuyper has in mind here are the basic worldviewish questions such as the nature of prime reality, what is wrong with the world, who rules this world, and so on. This is not to say that Kuyper thinks scholarship should avoid such questions; on the contrary, he urges us to critically examine our most foundational beliefs. Take Scripture, for example:

> Here too it is an altogether false idea that Scripture offers a ready confession and a cut-and-dried catechism for life. What Scripture reveals can only be established after thorough study. And although belief in the truth of Scripture is

---

[31]Ibid., 33.
[32]Ibid., 34.
[33]Ibid., 35.
[34]Ibid., 36.

a fruit of the *testimonium Spiritus Sancti*, which is surer than anything else, knowledge of Scripture and its contents can only be the fruit of study and research. So much so, in fact, that there is no book in any language that has been subjected to more thoroughgoing, comprehensive, and unremitting study than Holy Scripture.[35]

Kuyper recognizes the need for apologetics in relation to opponents of Christian thought; indeed, he himself keeps making the case for Christian scholarship in a context wary of it. He argues, however, that as long as our resources are limited we should concentrate on the constructive, systematic investigation of our own principles. At the same time, he stresses that engagement with non-Christian scholars and scholarship is essential. Scholarship is a common human endeavor, and "he who shuts himself up within his own circle without ever 'having it out' with those who think otherwise leaves the refreshing stream and ends up in a stagnant bog."[36]

There are so many acute insights in Kuyper's speeches that one is tempted to discuss all of them! Suffice it to confine myself to two rich insights. First, he is keenly alert to the community of scholarship and alerts students to the fact that they are the future. Second, he is conscious always that Christian scholarship not only serves the church but the entire country.[37]

ENGAGING WITH KUYPER

If one concedes with Kuyper, as I do, that a worldview is formative on the learning and knowing process, that the post-Enlightenment worldview/s is not neutral, and that parents take primary responsibility for the education of their children, then it is hard to deny his case for Christian schools and universities. Since Kuyper's day secularization has continued apace with postmodernism, on the whole, providing a toxic form of the same even as it sawed away at many of the foundational beliefs of modernity, but without providing a constructive alternative, let alone a retrieval of orthodox Christianity. In John Carroll's view, "it is within the walls of the academy that the slow and sharp corrosions of the Death of God and radical liberalism have etched most deeply into the steel of inherited belief. Indeed, the steps in the advance of

---

[35]Ibid., 40.
[36]Ibid., 41.
[37]Ibid., 24.

nihilistic high culture are most clearly to be observed in the history of changes to the university."[38]

An example of what Carroll is talking about is in Roy Brassier's *Nihil Unbound*. Brassier notes that two contentions underlie his book:

1. The disenchantment of the world whereby the Enlightenment shattered the great chain of being and "defaced the 'book of the world' is a necessary consequence of the coruscating potency of reason, and hence an invigorating vector of intellectual discovery, rather than a calamitous diminishment."[39] The disenchantment of the world should be celebrated as an achievement!

2. Nihilism is to be welcomed and embraced. "Philosophers would do well to desist from issuing any further injunction about the need to re-establish the meaningfulness of existence, the purposefulness of life, or mend the shattered concord between man and nature."[40]

Christian parents do well to reflect on whom they are granting the privilege of forming the minds of their children as they send them off to school each day and then on to college.

A fascinating contemporary of Kuyper's was John Henry Newman, who wrote *The Idea of a University*, which remains a classic. However, Carroll, rightly in my view, notes, "The tone of *The Idea of a University*, read today, lacks gravity, religious or other. Its mood is buoyant with Victorian upper-class optimism."[41] By the end of World War I this optimism was gone, and Max Weber, for example, scrutinized the very rationale of the university in his honest and disturbing "Science as a Vocation."[42] Weber denies that science teaches us anything about the meaning of the world, or leads to happiness, or provides an answer to the question of how then shall we live. He discerns three functions for science: advancing knowledge, teaching methods of thinking, and imposing on students clarity of thought. However, that it does these and is thus worth being known cannot be proven.

---

[38]John Carroll, *Ego and Soul: The Modern West in Search of Meaning* (Berkeley, CA: Counterpoint, 2008), 143.

[39]Roy Brassier, *Nihil Unbound: Enlightenment and Extinction* (New York: Palgrave Macmillan, 2007), xi.

[40]Ibid.

[41]Carroll, *Ego and Soul*, 145.

[42]Max Weber, "Wissenschaft als Beruf," in *Gesammlte Aufsaetze zur Wissenschaftslehre* (Munich: Duncker & Humblodt, 1919), 524-55. Translation online at www.wisdom.weizmann.ac.il/~oded/X/Weber ScienceVocation.pdf.

Nietzsche's work, which Weber invokes, undermined any naive confidence in the humanist tradition, and it is Nietzsche who lies behind much of postmodernism. Carroll traces the journey of the modern university via Weber, F. R. Leavis, Michael Oakeshott, Nietzsche, and Phillip Rieff.[43] Rieff's work is particularly important.[44] He agreed with Leavis that the maintenance of culture is the primary task of the university but argues that culture is interdictory; it commands and translates sacred order into social order so that a "vertical in authority" ("v i a") is essential to its health.

Carroll agrees with Graff: "The university requires a unifying vision." But where is it to be found? Carroll despairs of the church: "The humanist university has run down. The Christian university, founded in medieval form, is too culturally alien to the contemporary West to be revived. Likewise the church, the one institution that could replace the university as the master teacher of eternal truths, is in a state of hopeless despair."[45]

Carroll thinks that Rieff cannot help us here because the crisis in the West is one of culture and not morality. For Carroll we have to find the resources for a unifying vision in how we live now. He argues,

> Central to this idea of the university is a retelling of the human story as a kind of epic, with gravity and dignity, following the diverse ways it plays out its fateful tragedies. This requires interpretations of the story which reveal that life is more than an egoistic performance governed by biological necessity. Today's students crave just this sort of education.[46]

Carroll is critical of Newman's optimism, but his vision seems to me even more unrealistic. We need a unifying vision, but . . . it has to come from us, out of the tissue of our everyday life. This is humanism reincarnated, and the crisis of the West, which Carroll diagnoses so acutely, makes such optimism almost laughable—were it not so tragic—in such a context. However, Carroll's analysis should make us take a closer look at the viability of Kuyper's vision. Kuyper never sought to revive the medieval university but sought to work with the development of modernity in casting an alternative Christian vision.

---

[43]Carroll refers to Philip Rieff's unusual book, *Fellow Teachers* (New York: Delta, 1972, 1973).
[44]See Bob Goudzwaard and Craig G. Bartholomew, *Beyond the Modern Age* (Downers Grove, IL: IVP Academic, 2017).
[45]Carroll, *Ego and Soul*, 154, 155.
[46]Ibid., 158.

Kuyper rightly saw that education is profoundly formative and that it is never neutral. Too many Christian parents have discovered this to their cost as they have relinquished such formation to the public schools and universities of our day only to have their children lose whatever faith they once had. In our context the provision of really good Christian education is a greater rather than a lesser need, at least in the West. Globally, however, religion, and especially Christianity and Islam, is booming, so that the context in the developing world and parts of Asia is different from that of the largely post-Christian West.

As the West increasingly has to take Islam into account, it will also have to come to grips with the fact that Islam is a worldview and decidedly not a privatized religion like too much Western Christianity. Islam is committed to Islamic education, and as the West faces this, and as Islam faces the fact that freedom of religion really means *freedom of religion*, Kuyper's vision of cultural pluralism—in which different worldviews are allowed to come to fruition, not least in education—might be seen for the powerful model it in fact is. Indeed, this is an area in which moderate, mainstream Islam could work with Christians against the imposition of monolithic, post-Enlightenment thought in "public" education. Perhaps then it will start to become clearer that the West's celebrated "freedom of religion" is important, but too often only a freedom for a privatized form of religion.

I cannot here explore the implications of Kuyper's thought in detail for schools *and* the university. Kuyper himself alerted his followers to the fact that once they won the right to religious schools without financial penalty, the real challenge of producing outstanding Christian education had just begun.[47] As Kuyperians moved to the United States and Canada, they developed remarkable networks of Christian schools. There is much to be said about this achievement and the possibility of its ongoing renewal in our day.

In what remains of this chapter, my focus will be on Kuyper's legacy and the university today. Before we get to that, it is worth remembering Kuyper's concern for the poor and the education of the children of the poor. In South Africa, which we mentioned in the introduction, the poor are those most likely to receive a horribly insufficient education and thus remain locked into

---

[47]Christians in the Netherlands had the right to religious schools since the Constitution of 1848.

poverty. Ironically, many—perhaps most—are Christian. One thing should be clear about Christian education: it cannot be allowed to remain a middle-class entity but should have a preferential option for the poor, not least when most of the poor are Christian. It would be an extraordinary gift and witness if first-rate Christian schools were to emerge in South Africa specifically for the poorest of the poor. Kuyper would, I like to think, approve!

As we move on to an assessment of Kuyper's view of the university and its relevance today, a word or two of comment is needed. The discussion below might seem to focus on the foundations rather than moving beyond them. If so, this is deliberate. Although Marsden rightly speaks of the triumph or near-triumph of the Kuyperian worldview in American evangelicalism, this is mainly at the level of the lordship of Christ over all of life and generally not in much more detail. Furthermore, the Christian college's philosophy of "integration" does not seem to be working as well as it might, with Christian colleges often practicing their own version of educational volleyball, dangerously concealed under religion. There is therefore a great need for exploring the basics of Kuyper's vision for today.

The need for intellectual coherence. Graff, as we noted above, asserts that education needs to start providing "students with a more connected view of the academic intellectual universe, one that lets them recognize and enter the conversation that makes that universe cohere." This is something that is at the heart of the Kuyperian vision and thus of the Christian school and especially of the university, whose raison d'être is to be continually opening up the connectedness in Christ of the disciplines that make up the university. Indeed, it is worth pausing to note how significant it is that we have Christian universities in North America. In the United Kingdom they are virtually unknown. The growing number of Christian universities spread across North America is a wonderful sign of "Christ as the clue to all that is" being taken seriously.

However, even as we rightly celebrate this, we ought to reflect on just how successful Christian universities are in providing students with a connected view of the universe. In his *The Idea of a Christian Society*, T. S. Eliot has much to say about education. He rightly notes,

> Any apologetic which presents the Christian faith as a preferable alternative to secular philosophy, which fights secularism on its own ground, is making a concession which is preparation for defeat. . . . Should we not first try *to apprehend*

the meaning of Christianity as a whole, leading the mind to contemplate first the
great gulf between the Christian mind and the secular habits of thought and
feeling into which, so far as we fail to watch and pray, we all tend to fall?[48]

In Reformed language we would say that Eliot here touches on what Kuyper
calls the antithesis, that rift that runs through the creation between the
kingdom of light and the kingdom of darkness. A sense of the antithesis means
that we need *to start* our reflections on education from an intentionally
Christian perspective; only in this way is there hope of achieving a *uni-versity*
as opposed to the *multi-versity* that Graff critiques.

And in fact, as Kuyper saw, we have no choice as to whether we start from
a faith commitment; the only question ultimately is *which* faith commitment?
Weber himself acknowledges that he cannot prove his vision for the university;
it too has to be taken on faith. Lesslie Newbigin notes that much discussion
of epistemology has rested on the visual sense. Michael Polanyi, by comparison, approaches epistemology through the tactile sense. Polanyi invokes
the example of a surgeon using a probe—the surgeon gradually learns to *indwell* the probe. Thus Newbigin says,

> All knowing, therefore, involves the acritical acceptance of a language of con-
> cepts, of ideas and images, that we indwell and through which we seek to probe
> the world around us. This acritical acceptance is at first not a matter of choice.
> . . . In due course, if we lead a normal life of active intercourse with others, this
> "fiduciary framework" or faith-based outlook will be called into question by
> those who inhabit a different framework. From that point onwards, my per-
> sonal choice is involved: I can step outside the framework and look at it criti-
> cally from within another. And I can be so impressed by the clarity and the
> coherence of the view obtained from within that other framework that I am
> drawn into it. In other words I am converted.[49]

Newbigin encourages Christians to indwell the biblical story as the true
story of the world. He asserts, as we earlier noted, "Christ is the clue to all that
is."[50] This helpfully avoids the simplistic "Jesus is the answer" while holding

---

[48]T. S. Eliot, *The Idea of A Christian Society* (New York: Harcourt, Brace, 1940), 190, 191. Cf. Michael J.
   Buckley, *At the Origins of Modern Atheism* (New Haven, CT: Yale University Press, 1990).
[49]Lesslie Newbigin, *A Word in Season: Perspectives on Christian World Missions* (Grand Rapids: Eerdmans,
   1994), 107-8.
[50]Lesslie Newbigin, *The Gospel in a Pluralist Society* (Grand Rapids: Eerdmans, 1989), 103-15.

fast to the conviction that Christ is indeed *the* clue to the whole of reality. It also alerts us, as does the wisdom motif that the fear of the Lord is the *beginning* of wisdom, that faith in Christ opens up the quest for knowledge rather than closing it down, as has often happened in evangelical circles. The clue is there, and it is *the* clue, but as such it needs to be pursued with all the rigor that we can muster.

What does this mean for the university today, with its particular focus on intellectual knowledge and development?

It means that we need to know the biblical story intimately if we are to indwell it. It is a sheer delight to see how Kuyper continually returns to Scripture. Our time is one of rampant biblical illiteracy, and we need to note that we have no hope of pursuing the clue that is Christ if we are not continually digging in the field of Scripture to find again and again and again that pearl of great price. The early church fathers were immersed in Scripture, and it was through such immersion that they shaped a language, a vocabulary, a worldview for relating to the culture of their day.[51]

Within the Reformed tradition today, one sometimes gets the impression that one starts with Scripture, from which one develops a Christian worldview, and then a Christian philosophy, and then does Christian scholarship. There is truth to this, but if we are not careful we find ourselves left with an empty, abstract scholarship that is disconnected from Scripture. Indeed, it is not uncommon to meet students and scholars who know the Kuyperian worldview but have little idea how it is authorized by Scripture.

It is not so with the great thinkers of the church: Augustine, Aquinas, Calvin, Barth, O'Donovan, and so on. One could talk at length about Augustine, Aquinas, and Calvin, but Barth and O'Donovan are more contemporary examples of what Calvin aimed at with his *Institutes*. It is commonly assumed that the *Institutes* emerged from reading Scripture, and while this is true, it is instructive that Calvin wrote the *Institutes* in order to help his readers become better readers of Scripture! And in Barth's and O'Donovan's work what is so attractive is that, as their conceptual frameworks take hold, they do more and not less biblical exegesis. One suspects that this pattern is rare in Christian universities nowadays, but it ought not to be so. Scripture is our

---

[51]See Robert L. Wilken, *The Spirit of Early Christian Thought: Seeking the Face of God* (New Haven, CT: Yale University Press, 2005).

foundational text and infallible authority, and without falling prey to biblicism or dualism we ought, I think, to find exegesis popping up all over the place in the Christian university.

It means that we have to attend closely to how Scripture functions authoritatively in the Christian university. H. Evan Runner published an important book called *The Relation of the Bible to Learning*, a topic that bears renewed scrutiny today.[52] It is not a topic on which there is much expertise available. Academic work requires conceptual frameworks, and I think O'Donovan is right that these need to be authorized by Scripture, but how?[53]

One of the things postmodernism has been helpful with is in enabling us to see just how right Karl Popper was to reject the image of knowledge acquisition as akin to collecting facts in a bucket and then arranging the collected facts in logical order. Popper's alternative image is that of a torchlight, which shines on what we seek to know and has a significant impact on what we see.[54] Every discipline in the university operates with a conceptual framework, which influences the process of acquiring knowledge. Such a framework is unavoidable; the only question is *which* framework we are working with. And it should not be assumed that the sort of student volleyball Graff refers to is avoided in the Christian university; if anything, it might be more concealed because of our declared intention to provide a Christian education.

Students and faculty need to become attuned to the conceptual frameworks at work in their studies; differences need to be foregrounded, discussed, and debated. This is particularly important because conceptual frameworks often function *implicitly* rather than explicitly.

The big question, of course, is how one moves from Scripture to a conceptual framework. This is a complex issue; suffice it here to note that in *Living at the Crossroads* Mike Goheen and I suggest that an important start is to develop a Christian worldview by identifying the key building blocks in the biblical story and articulating their interrelationship. But scholarship requires more than this; it requires a *conceptual* framework—a task in which Christian

---

[52]H. Evan Runner, *The Relation of the Bible to Learning* (Toronto: Wedge, 1974).

[53]See Oliver O'Donovan, *The Desire of the Nations: Rediscovering the Roots of Political Theology* (Cambridge: Cambridge University Press, 1996).

[54]Karl R. Popper, "The Bucket and the Searchlight: Two Theories of Knowledge," in David R. Keller and Frank B. Golley, eds., *The Philosophy of Ecology: From Science to Synthesis* (Athens: University of Georgia Press, 2000), 141-46.

philosophy and theology have a particularly important role to play. I trust that it goes without saying that this is not a call to impose philosophy and theology on other disciplines but rather a call for dialogue between philosophy and theology and other disciplines.

It is obvious that taking intellectual coherence seriously is no easy task. But why should it be? The clue has to be pursued! However, if we are serious about the potential of the Christian university to provide the sort of education that Graff identifies as a great need of our day and which Kuyper gave his life to, then the hard work will have to be done.

The need for plausibility. It is intriguing and important to note that Bosch juxtaposes "plausibility structures" with "worldview" in his diagnosis of what the church needs to offer Western culture today and asserts that these need to be "demonstrated."[55] A Christian worldview is not merely an academic construct, but it is regularly in danger of being so perceived, not least in the Reformed tradition. A plausibility structure is clearly *not* just an academic construct. The concept of a plausibility structure is particularly associated with sociologist Peter Berger.[56] In his *The Sacred Canopy* Berger defines a plausibility structure as follows. He points out that the maintenance of the world we inhabit "depends upon *specific* social processes, namely those processes that ongoingly reconstruct and maintain the particular worlds in question. . . . Thus each world requires a social 'base' for its continuing existence as a world that is real to actual human beings. This 'base' may be called its plausibility structure."

A plausibility structure thus refers to that network of practices, habits, and social intercourse that supports and makes credible a particular set of beliefs, a particular way of viewing the world. In his discussion of the legitimation of a plausibility structure, Berger is clear that

> it would be a serious mistake to identify legitimation with theoretical ideation. "Ideas," to be sure, can be important for purposes of legitimation. However, what passes for "knowledge" in a society is by no means identical with the body

---

[55]See the introduction. On plausibility structures see Peter L. Berger, *The Sacred Canopy* (Garden City, NY: Doubleday, 1967); Clifford Geertz, "Religion as a Cultural System," in *Anthropological Approaches to the Study of Religion*, ed. M. Banton (London: Tavistock, 1966), 1-46; F. Musgrove, *Margins of the Mind* (London: Methuen, 1977); D. Snow, "On the Presumed Fragility of Unconventional Beliefs," *Journal for the Scientific Study of Religion* 21 (1982): 15-26.

[56]Berger, *Sacred Canopy*, 192, relates his use of the concept to that of Marx, Mead, and Schutz.

of "ideas" existing in the society. There have always been some people with an interest in "ideas," but they have never yet constituted more than a rather small minority. . . . Most legitimation, consequently, is pretheoretical in character.[57]

Again he notes, "The need for legitimation arises in the course of activity. . . . Most men in history have felt the need for religious legitimation—only very few have been interested in the development of religious 'ideas.'"[58]

Think of the Amish, for example. We might disagree with them, but in our consumer culture it is hard not to be impressed by the prophetic nature of their worldview. Why? Not just because of their beliefs but because their beliefs are made *plausible* by a lifestyle that is visible and in stark contrast to that of contemporary Western culture.

Modernity, as well as the pluralism and consumerism of postmodernism, has wreaked havoc on the possibility of a Christian plausibility structure.[59] Neo-Calvinism critiques the Amish as withdrawing from culture; instead, we are those who remain involved in order to transform culture. But how successful are we? The great danger of the Kuyperian is accommodation to the culture of the day, and I fear that this is well under way, at least in North America.

For the Christian university to achieve its intention, it will need to attend to an appropriate plausibility structure as part of its mission. As Berger notes,

> The reality of the Christian world depends upon the presence of social structures within which this reality is taken for granted and within which successive generations of individuals are socialized in such a way that this world will be real *to them*. When this plausibility structure loses its intactness or continuity, the Christian world begins to totter and its reality ceases to impose itself as self-evident truth.[60]

Clearly this cannot be the sole responsibility of the university—it is something Christians from different spheres of society will need to attend to together. However, one has to start somewhere, and why not start with the Christian university? It will be obvious from what I have said above that the *content* of what is taught in the classroom is crucial, but so too is the way we *structure* the Christian university, the habits and practices we adopt and

---

[57]Ibid., 45, 30.
[58]Ibid., 41.
[59]A major theme of ibid.
[60]Ibid., 46.

develop. There is a Zulu proverb that says, "Your life speaks so loudly that I cannot hear what you are saying!" To relate this to the Christian university, it means that we need to attend not only to what is being taught but to the structures of the university. We need to attend to questions such as

1. Does the built environment of the Christian university embody the Christian ethos or shout out against it? Are classrooms, the library, and public spaces conducive to pursuing that clue that is Christ, or do they quietly militate against it?

2. How do we structure the university year and why? Historically, the church has sought to indwell the biblical story through the church calendar: Advent through to Easter, Pentecost, Ascension, ordinary time, and on again to Advent. If the Christian university took this story seriously, what effect would it have on the shape of the academic year?

Jesus lived with his disciples for three years—an interesting model of formation if you want to transform the world. Nowadays, one never has the same group of students for more than one course in one semester. Why? Is this the best way to educate? In my university education, courses were generally a year long, with the same professor. At Oxford we had one-on-one tutorials with professors, and lectures were downplayed.

3. What rituals shape the university year? Is commencement experienced as the welcome and induction of a new year of students into the extraordinary task and opportunity of together pursuing that clue that is Christ in whatever disciplines we study? Do our convocation addresses bear any resemblance to those of Kuyper?

4. How does the administration of the Christian university work?

5. How do food and celebration function in the Christian university?

The need to be for the world. One might think that all this smacks too much of the Amish spirit of withdrawal or of a sort of monasticism. Again David Bosch is helpful here: Bosch rejects the Christendom model of mission but equally warns against a withdrawal from public life. "It belongs," he says,

> to our missionary mandate to ask questions about the use of power in our societies, to unmask those that destroy life, to show concern for the victims of society while at the same time calling to repentance those who have turned them into

victims, and to articulate God's active wrath against all that exploits, squanders, and disfigures the world for selfishness, greed and self-centered power.[61]

Not least is this important for mission in relation to the Majority World, in whose poverty the West is complicit—more than a fifth of the world lives in complete poverty, and it is vital that the church in the West embrace a world-formative understanding of the gospel.[62]

The vital point to note is that a Christian worldview needs to be rooted in and to embody a plausibility structure as part of its witness to the world and as the basis from which it can exercise a credible witness. Monasticism is instructive in this respect. We tend to think of monasticism as radical withdrawal from the world, and indeed it has sometimes been so. But as Bosch notes in his *Transforming Mission*, it was the monks in the monasteries who transformed Europe and helped it to recover from the fall of the Roman Empire.[63] Lewis Mumford notes how the medieval city is fashioned on the model of the monastery, with revolutionary consequences.[64]

The Romans were an extraordinary city-building people, and by the Augustinian period they had built hundreds of new towns, laid out simply and in human proportion. The cities of the Roman Empire were characterized by the wall, the forum (public spaces), and the bath: "The one supreme god they really worshipped was the body." However, the empire came to be centered more and more on rites of extermination: "Even before Rome had changed from Republic to Empire, that city had become a vast collective torture chamber." Rome's decadence and overextension led to its demise. Amid the urban decay of Rome, the seed of slow, fresh life was, however, already sprouting in the form of the medieval city. "The new religious vision that made this life possible gave a positive value to all the negations and defeats that the Romanized people had experienced: it converted physical illness into spiritual health, the pressure of starvation into the voluntary act of fasting, the loss of worldly goods into increased prospects for heavenly salvation."[65]

---

[61]David Bosch, *Believing in the Future: Toward a Missiology of Western Culture* (Valley Forge, PA: Trinity Press International, 1995), 34.

[62]Cf. Nicholas Wolterstorff, *Until Justice and Peace Embrace* (Grand Rapids: Eerdmans, 1983).

[63]David Bosch, *Transforming Mission: Paradigm Shifts in Theology of Mission*, 20th anniversary ed. (Maryknoll, NY: Orbis, 2011), 237-40.

[64]Lewis Mumford, *The City in History: Its Origins, Its Transformations, and Its Prospects* (New York: Harcourt, Brace and World, 1961).

[65]Ibid., 226, 230, 243.

The monastery was central to the emergence of the medieval city:

> If it was in the royal palace that the secular instruments of urban civilization first took shape, it was in the monastery that the ideal purposes of the city were sorted out, kept alive, and eventually renewed. It was here, too, that the practical value of restraint, order, regularity, honesty, inner discipline was established, before these qualities were passed over to the medieval town and post-medieval capitalism, in the form of inventions[66] and business practices: the clock, the account book, the ordered day.[67]

Indeed, "the medieval city in Europe may be described as a collective structure whose main purpose was the living of a Christian life." Within this Christian ethos hospitals and almshouses sprang up throughout cities. The Christian ethos dignified work, as is apparent in the guilds, which were religious associations based on the Benedictine principle of *ora et labora*. "A city that could boast that the majority of its members were free citizens, working side by side on a parity, without an underlayer of slaves was, I repeat, a new fact in urban history."[68]

As a missional institution the Christian university can never exist *for itself*. It exists for Christ and thus for his world. The relationship of the Christian university to its culture is multifaceted. It is to be a sign of the winsome reign of Christ in a consumer culture gone mad. In this respect it has a critical function of continually holding up a different way. But we must never forget that the Spirit remains at work in his world, and so we need to be open to learn from the world and non-Christian academia.

Our pursuance of that clue that is Christ must lead us into dialogue with academics of all types—we have much to offer and much to learn. In responding to scholarship from very different perspectives to my own, I have found Al Wolters's advice very helpful. First you need to spot the idolatry in the scholarship, but second you need to note that it is precisely at the point of idolatry that the poignant insights are to be found. Thus begins the hard task of extracting the insights without dragging the ideological baggage along, of bringing every thought captive to Christ.

---

[66]See ibid., 258, 259.
[67]Ibid., 247.
[68]Ibid., 267, 271.

THE NEED FOR
SPIRITUAL FORMATION

Follow my example, as I follow the example of Christ.

1 Corinthians 11:1

AND SO WE COME TO THE END OF OUR JOURNEY through the land-marks of the Kuyperian tradition. It is a rollercoaster of a ride and one that I find extraordinarily stimulating. Readers should be aware that there is more, far more, to be learned about Kuyper and about his predecessors and followers. More of Kuyper's writings than ever before are now available in English, but I estimate—it is only a guess—that this is less than 50 percent of his extensive corpus. And then there are luminaries such as Isaac da Costa, Guillaume Groen van Prinsterer, Herman Bavinck, J. H. Bavinck, and so on. A rich and extensive feast awaits the readers who are inspired to plunge in and to learn more. And as I have tried to argue throughout, it is an important feast *for today*. As I say in the preface, in my view Kuyper's time has arrived.

If you are as enamored with Kuyper as I am, there is a danger we must avoid, namely that of absolutizing him. We do not want to become like some of the Corinthian Christians: "What I mean is this: One of you says, 'I follow Paul,' another, 'I follow Apollos,' another, 'I follow Cephas,' still another, 'I follow Christ'" (1 Cor 1:12). And still another, "I follow Kuyper!"

The Kuyperian tradition is valuable insofar, and *only* insofar, as it is biblical and an authentic expression of the Christian faith. Scripture remains God's infallible Word, never Kuyper, and we need constantly to test what we learn from Kuyper against Scripture and the Christian tradition, of which Kuyper is a part.

THREE LITTLE FOXES

Kuyper himself, as we saw in his *Drie Kleine Vossen* [*Three Little Foxes*], was keenly alert to the dangers of intellectualism and activism.[1] In my *personal* opinion, Kuyperians have not been nearly careful enough in chasing these foxes out of their vineyards. Such is the power of the Kuyperian vision that it easily becomes cerebral in an unhelpful way. So too, it sometimes manifests as a kind of messianic activism and triumphalism, anticipating that we will shortly usher in the kingdom of God. This kind of hubris is very damaging and to be avoided at all costs. At their best, the Reformed and the Kuyperian traditions have a wonderful sense of God's sovereignty, which places our limited and broken-at-best efforts in a healthy, creaturely perspective.

The fox that we have least been in danger of entertaining is mysticism. Everything hinges here, of course, on what we mean by *mysticism*. I prefer, positively, to refer to *Christian spirituality*, which I see as *the* great need of the Kuyperian tradition if it is to be retrieved today and to begin to fulfill its potential. However, I am well aware that for some readers the word *spirituality* will raise a red flag. Sometimes there are good reasons for this. A friend told me that some say that evangelicals are recovering spirituality but in the process losing the Bible. If this is the case, then we are indeed on dangerous ground. In my own experience, having a spiritual director for some eight years, I was always reminded and aware that prayer and the Word are to be held inseparably together. Reading the Word will lead to prayer, and prayer leads us back into the Word, and so on and so forth.

The problem is that neither the Reformed nor the evangelical nor the Kuyperian tradition has deep resources for the ongoing *practice* of prayer. I have in mind here the sort of practices that over years profoundly form the individual into the likeness of Christ. There is, however, a significant recovery of such practices among evangelicals today, which I welcome.

Many of my friends and I discovered the importance of spirituality through an important book by Elizabeth O'Connor, titled *Journey Inward, Journey*

---

[1]Abraham Kuyper, *Drie Kleine Vossen* (Kampen: Kok, 1901). Forthcoming in English.

Outward, a book that captures the early philosophy and practice of Church of the Savior in Washington, DC.[2] The journey in involves committed participation in a local church, deep engagement with Scripture, small group community, and engagement with oneself. A crucial point of O'Connor's book is that the journey out into the world—which the Kuyperian tradition evokes so powerfully—*only* emerges out of and is sustained by the journey in, as Kuyper stresses in his meditations.[3]

HERMAN BAVINCK: IMITATING JESUS

What we urgently need is a theology of spirituality and a tradition of practices grounded in that theology. As I have noted in this book, there *are* important resources in Kuyper, and in Herman Bavinck,[4] for Christian spirituality, but generally neither they nor appropriate practices have been prominent in the tradition as it has developed.[5] A notable exception, theologically, is John Bolt's fine work on the theme of the imitation of Christ in the writings of Herman Bavinck.[6]

One of the most famous works of spirituality is Thomas à Kempis's *The Imitation of Christ*. Alas, right at the outset, à Kempis's work is shaped unhelpfully by Jerome's *contemptus mundi* reading of Ecclesiastes so that "this is the greatest wisdom—to seek the kingdom of heaven through contempt of the world."[7] Thus, even as we draw from the deep wells of Catholic spiritual thought and practice, there is a great need to rethink the theology underlying such classics. And this precisely is what Bavinck does.

---

[2]Elizabeth O'Connor, *Journey Inward, Journey Outward* (New York: Harper & Row, 1968).

[3]Ad de Bruijne, "Midden in de wereld verliefd op God. Kuypers aanzet tot een neocalvinistische spiritualiteit," in *Godsvrucht in geschiedenis. Bundel ter gelegenheid van het afscheid van prof. dr. F. Van der Pol als hoogleraar een de Theologische Universiteit Kampen*, ed. Erik A. de Boer and Harm J. Boiten (Heerenveen: Groen, 2015), 441-53.

[4]George Harinck, "'Something That Must Remain if the Truth Is to Be Sweet and Precious to Us': The Reformed Spirituality of Herman Bavinck," *CTJ* 38 (2003): 248-62, on 250, observes, "If, in Dutch Reformed circles, Abraham Kuyper was the man who loved pomp and circumstance, then Bavinck was the man of quiet contemplation and encounter."

[5]Cf. "Verschalingsrapport," the 1959 report to the Synod of the GKN about the status of spiritual life among its members, which addresses the decline in personal Bible reading and prayer.

[6]John Bolt, *A Theological Analysis of Herman Bavinck's Two Essays on the* Imitatio Christi: *Between Pietism and Modernism* (Lewiston, NY: Edwin Mellen, 2013); *Bavinck and the Christian Life: Following Jesus in Faithful Service* (Wheaton, IL: Crossway, 2015), 103-20. Translations of Bavinck's two essays on the imitation of Christ are found in Bolt, *Theological Analysis*, 372-440.

[7]Thomas à Kempis, *The Imitation of Christ* (Peabody, MA: Hendrickson, 2004), 3.

Bavinck argues that the imitation of Christ is "the heart of spiritual life."[8] In his first foray into this theme, Bavinck surveys the history of "imitation spirituality" from the postapostolic period to the modern era, and through such analysis he discerns four types: the martyr, the monk, the mystic, and the modern rationalist.[9] In recent decades in biblical studies scholars have come to see the importance of reception history, and it is wonderful to see Bavinck modeling such an approach in his exploration of the motif of imitating Christ.[10] He is evenhanded in his critique of all four models and argues for an understanding of this motif in which the mediatorial work of Christ and union with Christ are central. Furthermore, "This primary spiritual fellowship with Jesus Christ must also find concrete expression in the realm of the ethical."[11] In this way Bavinck is able to hold together deep, christocentric spirituality with cultural engagement, just as Kuyper does with palingenesis. True imitation, for Bavinck, involves being conformed to the image of Christ.

Retrieval and Renewal

This sort of spiritual theology needs to be retrieved, as Bolt has done, appropriated, and developed. Have you ever wondered why, for example, after God's covenant with Abraham in Genesis, we have some thirty-eight chapters dealing with the endlessly strange behavior of the patriarchs? The reason is that, having received the promises of the covenant, they have to be formed to become like the promises and worthy of bearing such promises in God's world. In theological language, we need to retrieve the doctrine of sanctification. If we are going to serve Christ in his world, then we need to be on a journey toward becoming like Christ, being conformed to his image. Eugene Peterson perceptively asks, "How can I lead people into the quiet place beside the still waters if I am in perpetual motion?"[12] Unformed persons do immense damage to the Kuyperian tradition, shouting about sovereignty and grace while failing to manifest grace and humility in their lives.

---

[8]Bolt, *Bavinck and the Christian Life*, 103.

[9]Bavinck in Bolt, *Theological Analysis*, 372-401. The modern rationalist sees Jesus as a mere example to follow.

[10]See Craig G. Bartholomew, *Introducing Biblical Hermeneutics: A Comprehensive Framework for Hearing God in Scripture* (Grand Rapids: Baker Academic, 2015), 113-21.

[11]Bavinck, quoted in Bolt, *Bavinck and the Christian Life*, 111.

[12]Eugene Peterson, *The Contemplative Pastor* (Grand Rapids: Eerdmans, 1993), 5.

Within the Reformed tradition, no one has done more to promote a recovery of biblical spirituality than Eugene Peterson, and I commend his entire corpus of writings. What we must not do, however, is to make the mistake of *thinking* that if we read his and other books, we have now "got" spirituality. Spirituality is a practice, a "long obedience in the same direction," and it is normally passed on as an oral tradition. It involves depth transformation over a lifetime, and its practices, rightly, generally remain hidden.

I am all for a type of sphere universality that opens a university class with prayer, has regular college chapels on campus, and so on. But these are at the surface level, whereas spirituality is about daily, ongoing, hidden practices that create the space for the Spirit to change and transform us from the inside out, so that more and more we become like the Christ-light that we seek to shine into a dark and needy world.

It is in this critical area that Kuyperians will need to learn from those outside the Kuyperian tradition. Below I conclude this book with examples of non-Kuyperians from whom we need to learn.

EDUCATION REVISITED

Max Weber distinguished three types of education in history: education for culture, specialist education, and charismatic education.[13] According to Karl Mannheim (1893–1947), charismatic education is "dominant in the magical period or in periods in which religion reaches its highest point. In the first case it wants to arouse hidden powers latent in man, in the second to awaken religious intuition and the inner readiness for transcendental experience."[14] T. S. Eliot perceptively notes that Christian education most closely approximates charismatic education. And this is important because

> our tendency has been to identify wisdom with knowledge, saintliness with natural goodness, to minimize not only the operation of grace but self-training, to divorce holiness from education. Education has come to mean education of the mind only; and an education which is only of the mind . . . can lead to scholarship, to efficiency, to worldly achievement and to power, but not to wisdom.[15]

---

[13]T. S. Eliot, *The Idea of A Christian Society* (New York: Harcourt, Brace, 1940), 142.
[14]Quoted in ibid., 143.
[15]Ibid.

For Eliot, the values that we most ignore in education are wisdom and holiness.

In his *Lessons of the Masters* George Steiner alerts us to what is at stake in education: "To teach seriously is to lay hands on what is most vital in a human being." He provocatively argues that antiteaching is close to being the norm and that schools are full of "amiable gravediggers" who "labor to diminish their students to their own level of indifferent fatigue. They do not 'open Delphi' but close it." In contrast, Steiner describes his experience of his doctoral seminar in Geneva, which continued more or less unbroken for twenty-five years: "Those Thursday mornings were as near as an ordinary, secular spirit can come to Pentecost."[16]

Charismatic education, Pentecostal education, education drenched in the Spirit and thus Christ. What will prevent Christian education from succumbing to "that most corrosive of acids, boredom, the marsh gas of ennui"?[17] What will prevent Kuyperian thought and practice from selling out to the spirits of the age? The only ultimate answer is *Jesus himself*. How do we bring wisdom and holiness into education, for example? Only by living ever more deeply into Christ.

THE DIFFERENCE JESUS MAKES

What distinguishes Mother Teresa's Sisters of Charity from social workers? What makes L'Arche and Jean Vanier's work different from other groups that work with the disabled? And what enables them to sustain and nurture this difference?[18]

In his journal *The Road to Daybreak*, Henri Nouwen describes the heart of Trosly, the mother house of L'Arche, as follows:

> L'Oratoire is a prayer room where the Blessed Sacrament is exposed all day long and where people are always present in silent adoration. The room itself is a large, rather dark space with small kneelers and little mats. The space is divided by a thick stone wall built of heavy grey stone. . . . On both sides of the wall people kneel, sit, or lie down in prayer.
>
> In many ways L'Oratoire is the heart of L'Arche. The unceasing silent prayer in the presence of the hidden God who gives himself completely to us in unlimited

---

[16]George Steiner, *Lessons of the Masters* (Cambridge, MA: Harvard University Press, 2003), 18, 19.
[17]Ibid., 18.
[18]Readers should note that this is not to argue that there is only one correct way to work among the poor and disabled.

love is the breath that makes L'Arche possible. Every time I enter L'Oratoire I feel a deep rest coming over me, and even if it is hard for me to pray I feel held there. It is as if the room prays for me. I know of few places where the presence of prayer is so tangible. If I can't pray, I go there so that I can at least breathe air rich with prayer. In L'Oratoire I meet the poverty of God, the God who became flesh and even our food and drink, the God who does not hold back any of his love and who says, "Eat of me, drink of me," the God who is so deeply hidden that he can be recognized only by the eye of faith.[19]

It is this deep centeredness in Jesus that sustains the work of Mother Teresa and Jean Vanier. Sometimes in the name of sphere sovereignty Kuyperians have delegated spirituality to the church while we focus on the tasks of the other spheres, and there is of course truth in this; we should not turn the university, the family, or the school into a church. But what of sphere universality? And we cannot demand of the church that it focus on the specific spirituality appropriate to and needed by the other spheres. Yes, we need to be deeply involved in local churches, but yes, too, we need to make spirituality integral to our lives in all the spheres we are involved in.

Of his return to Kentucky Wendell Berry says,

> That return made me finally an exile from the ornamental Europeanism that still passes for culture with most Americans. . . . It occurred to me that there was another measure for my life than the amount or even the quality of the writing I did; a man, I thought, *must be judged by how willingly and fully he can be present where he is*, by how fully he can make himself at home in his part of the world. I began to want desperately to learn to belong to my place.[20]

When you meet people like Jean Vanier it is their presence to the moment that is most striking, and it is this I suspect that would most invigorate the Kuyperian tradition and Christian organizations and empower them to be distinctive in a truly Christian sense.

We should not underestimate the challenge such a vision sets before us. In her delightful book *Finding Calcutta*, Mary Poplin tells of her two months with Mother Teresa and her sisters as part of Poplin's sabbatical from university teaching.[21] The time in India affected her profoundly. Strangely, when she

---

[19]Henri J. M. Nouwen, *The Road to Daybreak: A Spiritual Journey* (New York: Doubleday, 1988), 28.
[20]Wendell Berry, *The Hidden Wound*, 2nd ed. (Berkeley, CA: Counterpoint, 2010), 13, emphasis added.
[21]Mary Poplin, *Finding Calcutta: What Mother Teresa Taught Me About Meaningful Work and Service*

returned to her secular university, she found herself crying every time she was in her study getting ready to teach. Resolution came when she realized the disconnect between her inner journey and her teaching, and this led her to the importance of a Christian worldview and university!

For most of us Kuyperians the journey required is the other way around—we are convinced of the need for Christian worldview and action, but . . . are we on an inner journey ever deeper into Jesus that will nourish and sustain our active lives? Nouwen tells of his encounter with Father George Strohmeyer, cofounder of a L'Arche community:

> As he told his story, it became clear that Jesus is the center of his life. . . . When he pronounces the name of Jesus you know that he speaks from a deep, intimate encounter. His life has become simpler, more hidden, more rooted, more trusting, more open, more evangelical, and more peaceful. . . . I now know for sure that there is a long, hard journey ahead of me. It is the journey of leaving everything behind for Jesus' sake. I now know that there is a way of living, praying, being with people, caring, eating, drinking, sleeping, reading, and writing in which Jesus is truly the center.[22]

Stanley Hauerwas, in a recent dialogue with Jean Vanier, notes that one of the great gifts of L'Arche and the disabled is that they slow us down—the disabled cannot be rushed. "This is what I think L'Arche has to say to the church today: slow down. Just slow down. L'Arche embodies the patience that is absolutely crucial if we are to learn to be faithful people in our world. . . . We live by slowing down and saying with our lives that the world cannot be saved by frantic activity."[23]

Kuyperian organizations committed to pursuing that clue that is Christ will also need to be slow. They will need to have public spaces and reflective spaces, perhaps even chapels. They will need to be patient as the Spirit shapes us and molds us into the image of Christ. The biblical narrative, the institutional narrative, and participants' narratives will need to be rehearsed again and again so that they weave an organic, living whole. We need time and space to live deeply into Christ and to journey in his name into all of life.

(Downers Grove, IL: InterVarsity Press, 2011).

[22]Nouwen, *Road to Daybreak*, 7.

[23]Stanley Hauerwas, "Finding God in Strange Places," in Hauerwas and Jean Vanier, *Living Gently in a Violent World: The Prophetic Witness of Weakness* (Downers Grove, IL: InterVarsity Press, 2008), 45.

It is a vision of what we might call incarnate obedience. In his acute comparison of the classical with the biblical worldview Newbigin notes, "Because ultimate reality is personal, God's address to us is a word conveying his purpose and promise, a word which may be heard or ignored, obeyed or disobeyed. Faith comes by hearing and unbelief is disobedience."[24] Kuyperian thought and practice have to emerge *from* and take place *in* the context of obedience, the very word Paul uses for the appropriate response to the gospel, what he calls the "obedience of faith." And this obedience is of course comprehensive—it involves every square inch of life: food, pots and pans, what we do with our genitals, the TV we watch, the houses we build, the way we shape classrooms, and so on. But it is not only comprehensive; it is also very deep, and such depth is not easily acquired. As Mary Rose O'Reilley notes, a few people seem to have rhythm and integrality built into their DNA; for the rest of us it is practice, practice, practice.[25] To allude to Richard Foster, what the Kuyperian tradition most urgently needs is not more students, more professors, more programs, more books, but a few saints.

THE JOURNEY IN; THE JOURNEY OUT

Dick Staub notes,

> In this intellectually and aesthetically impoverished age of Christianity-Lite, it is heartening to remember that for centuries, Christians were known for their intellectual, artistic, and spiritual contributions to society. Bach, Mendelssohn, Dante, Dostoevsky, Newton, Pascal, and Rembrandt are but a few who personified the rich tradition of faith, producing the highest and best work, motivated by a desire to glorify God and offered in service of others for the enrichment of our common environment: culture. These were culturally savvy Christians—serious about the centrality of faith in their lives, savvy about both faith and culture, and skilled in relating the two.[26]

The Kuyperian tradition has the resources to produce culturally savvy Christians today. My hope is that this book has demonstrated this beyond

---

[24]Lesslie Newbigin, *Proper Confidence: Faith, Doubt, and Certainty in Christian Discipleship* (London: SPCK, 1995) 14.

[25]Mary Rose O'Reilley, *The Love of Impermanent Things: A Threshold Ecology* (Minneapolis: Milkweed Editions, 2006).

[26]Dick Staub, *The Culturally Savvy Christian: A Manifesto for Deepening Faith and Enriching Popular Culture in an Age of Christianity-Lite* (San Francisco: Jossey-Bass, 2008), ix.

doubt. It is a rich and fecund tradition crying out for renewal and development. But this is only if it learns to take formation seriously. It is a dismal experience to encounter Kuyperians with well-developed minds and Calvinistic work ethics, only to discover that they are unformed as whole people.

In this respect I find the language of the journey in and the journey out most helpful. You cannot have the one without the other; the candle needs to burn at both ends. The call to journey out itself emerges from a deep encounter with Christ, the journey in, and can only be sustained in the same way. If the messianic and cerebral temptations of the Kuyperian vision are to be avoided, this is only possible by living ever more deeply into Christ. The missional vision of the Kuyperian tradition is creation-wide, and so too will be the suffering that accompanies it. Where will we find the resource to carry such crosses? Only by living ever more deeply into Christ. We do not have great role models in this respect and will need to learn from such luminaries as Thomas Merton, Mother Teresa, and Jean Vanier, among many others.

One thing they will all teach us is that amid our journey out into the world, we will constantly need to recenter ourselves in Christ, *even as* we journey out. As we seek to spread the fragrance of Christ in his world, we will need to be formed to be like Christ. As we suffer we will, like Christ, need to take up our cross again and again, knowing that it leads to Golgotha. Only in this way will we be able to embody the Kuyperian tradition in the biblical style of washing one another's feet, of offering a glass of cold water, of serving as our Master served.

One of the things I love about the Reformed tradition, and about Kuyper in particular, is that we are always brought back to God, the King. At the end of the day it is all about him and not about us. We are called to live *coram deo* and *pro Rege*. We are called to be faithful, not successful. Insofar as the Kuyperian tradition helps us to do this, it needs to be revived, embodied, developed, and, like the body of Christ, broken again and again to feed a hungry world.

POSTSCRIPT

Resources for Studying the Kuyperian Tradition

GOOD NEWS FOR ENGLISH SPEAKERS is that more and more Dutch works in the Kuyperian tradition are being translated into English, and more and more Dutch (and English) sources are available online.

Readers should note that I have concentrated below on primary sources, apart from biographies. In my research for this book it has become ever clearer to me just how important it is to read the primary sources.

ABRAHAM KUYPER

For Abraham Kuyper's extensive corpus the indispensable guide is Tjitza Kuipers, *Abraham Kuyper: An Annotated Bibliography 1857–2010*, Brill's Series in Church History (Leiden: Brill, 2011).

Several biographies of Abraham Kuyper are available in English, but the definitive, academic one is James D. Bratt, *Abraham Kuyper: Modern Calvinist, Christian Democrat*, Library of Christian Biography (Grand Rapids: Eerdmans, 2013).

At a more popular level Jan De Bruijn, *Abraham Kuyper: A Pictorial Biography* (Grand Rapids: Eerdmans, 2008, 2014), is very useful.

Some of Abraham Kuyper's works have long been available in English, namely his *Lectures on Calvinism* (from several publishers), *Principles of Sacred Theology* (from several publishers, also under the title of *Encyclopedia of Sacred Theology*), *The Work of the Holy Spirit* (from several publishers), and various collections of Kuyper's devotionals.

Kuyper's *Lectures on Calvinism* is essential reading and easily available.

James D. Bratt, ed., *Abraham Kuyper: A Centennial Reader* (Grand Rapids: Eerdmans, 1998), is an invaluable resource.

Kuyper's *Principles of Sacred Theology* is a translation of part of Kuyper's three-volume *Encyclopedia of Sacred Theology*, a monumental work that demonstrates Kuyper's rigor and creativity as a theologian. Kuyper's academic training was as a theologian, and for those interested in this aspect of his legacy *Principles* is must reading. For an example of his theological work applied to a particular doctrine, *The Work of the Holy Spirit* is the obvious example. It originally appeared, as did so many of Kuyper's books, in a series in installments, in this case in *De Heraut*.

Kuyper's five-volume *Dictaten Dogmatiek* (Dictated dogmatics) is not nearly as well-known as it should be. Plans are under way to translate and publish this work.

Kuyper continually engages with Scripture in his writings, and his *The Revelation of St. John* (Eugene, OR: Wipf and Stock, 1999) provides an example of his interpretive work—again, originally a series of installments.

Kuyper is best known in North America as a public theologian and activist. A massive Kuyper translation project has been under way, and the results are steadily appearing in a series of handsome volumes under the title Abraham Kuyper, Collected Works in Public Theology (Bellingham, WA: Lexham Press). This series will cover most of the major areas of public life addressed by Kuyper and is an indispensable addition to the library of anyone interested in Kuyper and the Kuyperian tradition.

In North America the major collection of Kuyper's works and significant online resources are available at The Kuyper Center, Princeton Theological Seminary.

HERMAN BAVINCK

In relation to Herman Bavinck's corpus, Eric Bristley's small work is very useful: Eric D. Bristley, *Guide to the Writings of Herman Bavinck* (Grand Rapids: Reformation Heritage Books, 2008).

Ron Gleason, *Herman Bavinck: Pastor, Churchman, Statesman, and Theologian* (Phillipsburg, NJ: P&R, 2010), is a useful introduction to Bavinck's life and thought.

Herman Bavinck was above all else a theologian. Parts of his *Reformed Dogmatics* have long been available in English, as have other smaller works of his. A major achievement in recent years has been the publication of his complete *Reformed Dogmatics* in four volumes (Grand Rapids: Baker Academic, 2008).

An important work of his that has been available but needs renewed attention and is still in print is his *Our Reasonable Faith* (Grand Rapids: Eerdmans, 1956).

Frustratingly, Kuyper and Bavinck do not regularly reference each other! An obvious point of comparison is Kuyper's *Work of the Holy Spirit* with Bavinck's *Saved by Grace: The Holy Spirit's Work in Calling and Regeneration*, edited by J. Mark Beach (Grand Rapids: Reformation Heritage Books, 2008).

Bavinck's *Essays on Religion, Science and Society*, edited by John Bolt, have been published by Baker Academic, 2008, and plans are under way to publish his *Ethics*.

The Bavinck Institute, https://bavinckinstitute.org, contains a multitude of useful resources.

J. H. Bavinck

In English J. H. Bavinck's best-known (and still in print) book is his *An Introduction to the Science of Missions*, translated by David H. Freeman (Phillipsburg, NJ: P&R, 1960).

Two recent works have done much to alert us to the fertile work of J. H. Bavinck, namely Paul Visser, *Heart for the Gospel, Heart for the World: The Life and Thought of a Reformed Pioneer Missiologist Johan Herman Bavinck (1895–1964)*, translated by Jerry Gort (Eugene, OR: Wipf & Stock, 2003), and *The J. H. Bavinck Reader*, edited by John Bolt (Grand Rapids: Eerdmans, 2013).

Older translations include *The Church Between Temple and Mosque* (Grand Rapids: Eerdmans, 1961). Encouragingly, Eerdmans has recently published two new translations of J. H. Bavinck's work, namely *Between the Beginning and the End: A Radical Kingdom Vision* (Grand Rapids: Eerdmans, 2014) and *The Riddle of Life* (Grand Rapids: Eerdmans, 2016).

Then and Now

So much is now available in English that English speakers have no excuse for not reading the primary sources of the tradition. A feast awaits!

At the same time, it must be noted that there is far more to the tradition than Abraham Kuyper and Herman Bavinck, colossal figures that they are. Prior to Kuyper, during his lifetime, and after his death a plethora of influential figures and their writings remain important. Some of this material is available in English (e.g., Guillaume Groen van Prinsterer, *Lectures on Unbelief and Revolution*; Berkouwer's *Studies in Dogmatics*), but much remains in Dutch. Amid this Kuyperian moment, we need a group of young scholars who will become fluent in Dutch and continue to excavate the Kuyperian tradition for us, working, of course, with contemporary Dutch scholars and those in the many other countries where there is a growing interest in the Kuyperian tradition. This is particularly true of biblical studies and the theological disciplines, where rich resources wait.

It is also important to note that there has been an ongoing reception of the Kuyperian tradition in the Netherlands, Great Britain, the United States, South Africa, and many, many other countries. Substantial work has been and continues to be done in philosophy, politics, economics, art, and many other areas. Furthermore, the Kuyperian tradition has never been just about theory for theory's sake. As with Groen van Prinsterer and Kuyper, it has been deeply committed to practice, and this dimension of its life needs to be taken into account as well.

BIBLIOGRAPHY

à Kempis, Thomas. *The Imitation of Christ*. Peabody, MA: Hendrickson, 2004.

Aalders, G Ch. *Het verbond Gods*. Kampen: Kok, 1939.

Allen, Diogenes. *Spiritual Theology: The Theology of Yesterday for Spiritual Help Today*. Cambridge, MA: Cowley, 1997.

Allen, John L. *The Global War on Christians: Dispatches from the Front Lines of Anti-Christian Persecution*. New York: Image, 2013.

Althusius, Johannes. *Politica*. Abridged. Edited and translated with introduction by Frederick S. Carney. Indianapolis: Liberty Fund, 1995.

Anderson, Clifford B. "Jesus and the 'Christian Worldview': A Comparative Analysis of Abraham Kuyper and Karl Barth." *Cultural Encounters* 6, no. 1 (2006): 61-80.

Anderson, Gerald, ed. *Biographical Dictionary of Christian Missions*. Grand Rapids: Eerdmans, 1999.

Anderson, Gerald, Robert T. Coote, James M. Phillips, and Norman A. Horner, eds. *Mission Legacies: Biographical Studies of Leaders of the Modern Missionary Movement*. Maryknoll, NY: Orbis, 1994.

Anderson, Owen. *Reason and Worldviews: Warfield, Kuyper, Van Til and Plantinga on the Clarity of General Revelation and the Function of Apologetics*. Lanham, MD: University Press of America, 2008.

Aquinas, Thomas. *Commentary on the Gospel of St. John*. Part 1: Chapters 1–7. Translated by James A. Weisheipl. New York: Magi, 1998.

———. *Summa Theologiae: Questions on God*. Cambridge Texts in the History of Philosophy. Edited by Brian Davies and Brian Leftow. Cambridge: Cambridge University Press, 2006.

———. *Thomas Aquinas: Selected Writings*. Edited and translated by Ralph McInerny. New York: Penguin, 1998.

Assad, Talal. *Formations of the Secular: Christianity, Islam, Modernity*. Stanford, CA: Stanford University Press, 2003.

Augustine. *Expositions on the Psalms*. Translated by J. E. Tweed. In Nicene and Post-Nicene Fathers, First Series, vol. 8. Edited by Philip Schaff. Buffalo, NY: Christian Literature Publishing, 1888.

———. "Ten Homilies on the First Epistle of John." In P. Schaff, ed., *St. Augustine: Homilies on the Gospel of John, Homilies on the First Epistle of John, Soliloquies*. Translated by H. Browne and J. H. Myers. New York: Christian Literature Company, 1888.

Bacote, Vincent E. *The Spirit in Public Theology: Appropriating the Legacy of Abraham Kuyper*. Grand Rapids: Baker Academic, 2005.

Barth, Karl. *Church Dogmatics*. Edited by G. W. Bromiley and T. F. Torrance. 14 vols. Edinburgh: T&T Clark, 1957–1975.

Bartholomew, Craig G. "The Challenge of Islam in Africa." *Journal of Interdisciplinary Studies* 6 (1994): 129-46.

———. *Church and Society*. Pinetown, South Africa: CESA, 1988.

———. "The Church and the World: The Power of Identity." In *Signposts of God's Liberating Kingdom. Perspectives for the Twenty-First Century*, 1:21-30. Potchefstroom, South Africa: IRS, Potchefstroom University for CHE, 1998.

———. "Covenant and Creation: Covenantal Overload or Covenantal Deconstruction." *CTJ* 30, no. 1 (April 1995): 11-33.

———. *Ecclesiastes*. Grand Rapids: Baker Academic, 2009.

———. *Introducing Biblical Hermeneutics: A Comprehensive Framework for Hearing God in Scripture*. Grand Rapids: Baker Academic, 2015.

———. "Not So Common." Introductory essay for Abraham Kuyper, *Common Grace* II. Bellingham, WA: Lexham Press, forthcoming.

———. "Theological Interpretation and a Missional Hermeneutic." In Michael W. Goheen, ed., *Reading the Bible Missionally*, 68-85. The Gospel and Our Culture Series. Grand Rapids: Eerdmans, 2016.

———. *Where Mortals Dwell: A Christian View of Place for Today*. Grand Rapids: Baker Academic, 2011.

———. "Wisdom and Atonement." Forthcoming.

Bartholomew, Craig G., and Michael W. Goheen. *Christian Philosophy: A Systematic and Narrative Introduction*. Grand Rapids: Baker Academic, 2013.

———. *The Drama of Scripture: Finding Our Place in the Biblical Story*. 2nd ed. Grand Rapids: Baker Academic, 2014.

Bartholomew, Craig G., and Thorston Moritz, eds. *Christ and Consumerism: A Critical Analysis of the Spirit of the Age*. Carlisle, UK: Paternoster, 2000.

Bartholomew, Craig G., and Heath A. Thomas, eds. *A Manifesto for Theological Interpretation*. Grand Rapids: Baker Academic, 2016.

Bavinck, Herman. "The Catholicity of Christianity and the Church." Translated by John Bolt. *CTJ* 27 (1992): 220-51.

———. *The Certainty of Faith*. Translated by Harry der Nederlanden. St. Catherines, ON: Paideia, 1980.

———. *Christilijke Wereldbeschouwing*. Kampen: Kok, 1913.

———. *Essays on Religion, Science, and Society*. Translated by Harry Boonstra and Gerrit Sheeres. Edited by John Bolt. Grand Rapids: Baker Academic, 2008.

———. "Herman Bavinck's 'Common Grace.'" Translated by Raymond van Leeuwen. *CTJ* 24, no. 1 (1989): 35-65.

———. "John Calvin: A Lecture on the Occasion of His 400th Birthday, July 10, 1509–1909." Translated by John Bolt. *The Bavinck Review* 1 (2010): 57-85.

———. "The Kingdom of God, The Highest Good." Translated by Nelson D. Kloosterman. *The Bavinck Review* 2 (2011): 133-70.

———. *The Philosophy of Revelation*. Grand Rapids: Baker, 1909.

———. "The Pros and Cons of a Dogmatic System." Translated by Nelson D. Kloosterman. *The Bavinck Review* 5 (2014): 90-103.

———. "Recent Dogmatic Thought in the Netherlands." *Presbyterian and Reformed Review* 10 (April 1892): 209-28.

———. *Reformed Dogmatics*. 4 vols. Grand Rapids: Baker Academic, 2008.

———. "The Theology of Albrecht Ritschl." Translated by John Bolt. *The Bavinck Review* 3 (2012): 123-63.

Bavinck, J. H. *The Church Between Temple and Mosque: A Study of the Relationship Between the Christian Faith and Other Religions*. Grand Rapids: Eerdmans, 1961.

———. *The Impact of Christianity on the Non-Christian World*. Grand Rapids: Eerdmans, 1948.

———. *An Introduction to the Science of Missions*. Translated by David H. Freeman. Phillipsburg, NJ: Presbyterian and Reformed, 1960.

———. *Religieus Besef en Christelijk Geloof*. Kampen: J. H. Kok, 1949.

Bayer, Oswald. *Freedom in Response. Lutheran Ethics: Sources and Controversies*. Oxford: Oxford University Press, 2007.

Beauchamp, Paul. *Création et Séparation: étude exégétique du chapitre premier de la Genèse*. Paris: Aubier Montaigne-Éditions du Cerf, 1969.

Benne, Robert. *Good and Bad Ways to Think About Politics*. Grand Rapids: Eerdmans, 2010.

———. "A Lutheran Vision of Christian Humanism." In Angus J. L. Menuge, ed., *Christ and Culture in Dialogue*, 314-32. Saint Louis, MO: Concordia Academic Press, 1999.

————. *A Paradoxical Vision: A Public Theology for the Twenty-First Century*. Minneapolis: Augsburg Fortress, 1995.

————. *Quality with Soul: How Six Premier Colleges and Universities Keep Faith with Their Religious Traditions*. Grand Rapids: Eerdmans, 2010.

Berger, Peter L., ed. *The Desecularization of the World: Resurgent Religion and World Politics*. Grand Rapids: Eerdmans, 1999.

————. *The Many Altars of Modernity: Towards a Paradigm for Religion in a Pluralist Age*. Berlin: de Gruyter, 2014.

————. *The Sacred Canopy*. Garden City, NY: Doubleday, 1967.

Berkhof, Hendrikus. *Two Hundred Years of Theology: Report of a Personal Journey*. Translated by John Vriend. Grand Rapids: Eerdmans, 1989.

Berkouwer, Gerrit C. *The Church*. Studies in Dogmatics. Grand Rapids: Eerdmans, 1976.

————. *General Revelation*. Studies in Dogmatics. Grand Rapids: Eerdmans, 1955.

————. *A Half Century of Theology*. Translated by Lewis B. Smedes. Grand Rapids: Eerdmans, 1977.

————. *Het probleem der Schriftkritiek*. Kampen: Kok, 1938.

————. *The Triumph of Grace in the Theology of Karl Barth*. Translated by Harry R. Boer. Grand Rapids: Eerdmans, 1956.

————. "World War and Theology." Speech given at the Free University of Amsterdam. October 1945.

Berry, Wendell. *The Hidden Wound*. 2nd ed. Berkeley, CA: Counterpoint, 2010.

————. *The Mad Farmer Poems*. Berkeley, CA: Counterpoint, 2008.

————. *What Are People For?* New York: North Point, 1990.

Betz, John R. *After Enlightenment: The Post-Secular Vision of J. G. Hamann*. Malden, MA: Wiley-Blackwell, 2008.

Blair, Kirstie, ed. *John Keble in Context*. London: Anthem, 2004.

Böhl, E. *Zwölf messianische Psalmen: Nebst einer grundlegenden christologischen Einleitung*. Basel, 1862.

Bolt, John. "All of Life Is Worship? Abraham Kuyper and the Neo-Kuyperians." In *Abraham Kuyper, Our Worship*, 321-29. Grand Rapids: Eerdmans, 2009.

————. *Bavinck and the Christian Life: Following Jesus in Faithful Service*. Wheaton, IL: Crossway, 2015.

————, ed. *Five Studies in the Thought of Herman Bavinck, A Creator of Modern Dutch Theology*. Lewiston, NY: Edwin Mellen, 2011.

————. *A Free Church, a Holy Nation: Abraham Kuyper's American Public Theology*. Grand Rapids: Eerdmans, 2001.

———. "Herman Bavinck and Islam." *The Bavinck Review* 2 (2011): 171-73.

———, ed. *The J. H. Bavinck Reader.* Grand Rapids: Eerdmans, 2013.

———. *A Theological Analysis of Herman Bavinck's Two Essays on the* Imitatio Christi: *Between Pietism and Modernism.* Lewiston, NY: Edwin Mellen, 2013.

Bonhoeffer, Dietrich. *Ethics.* London: SCM Press, 1955.

Boraine, Alex. *What's Gone Wrong? On the Brink of a Failed State.* Johannesburg: Jonathan Ball, 2014.

Bosch, David. *Believing in the Future: Toward a Missiology of Western Culture.* Valley Forge, PA: Trinity Press International, 1995.

———. "Missiology." In I. H. Eybers, A. König, and J. A. Stoop, eds., *Introduction to Theology,* 263-86. 3rd ed. Pretoria, South Africa: NGKB, 1982.

———. *Transforming Mission: Paradigm Shifts in Theology of Mission.* 20th anniversary edition. Maryknoll, NY: Orbis, 1991, 2011.

———. *Witness to the World: The Christian Mission in Theological Perspective.* London: Marshall, Morgan and Scott, 1980.

Bossenbroek, Martin. *The Boer War.* Translated by Yvette Rosenberg. Auckland Park, South Africa: Jacana, 2015.

Braaten, Carl E. *The Flaming Center: A Theology of the Christian Mission.* Philadelphia: Fortress, 1977.

———. "Foreword." In Angus J. L. Menuge, ed., *Christ and Culture in Dialogue,* 7-13. Saint Louis, MO: Concordia Academic Press, 1999.

———. *Mother Church: Ecclesiology and Ecumenism.* Minneapolis: Fortress, 1998.

———. "Natural Law in Theology and Ethics." In Carl E. Braaten and Robert W. Jenson, eds., *The Two Cities of God: The Church's Responsibility for the Earthly City,* 42-58. Grand Rapids: Eerdmans, 1997.

Bradley, Anthony B. *Black Scholars in White Space: New Vistas in African American Studies from the Christian Academy.* Eugene, OR: Pickwick, 2015.

Brassier, Roy. *Nihil Unbound: Enlightenment and Extinction.* New York: Palgrave Macmillan, 2007.

Bratt, James D., ed. *Abraham Kuyper: A Centennial Reader.* Grand Rapids, Eerdmans, 1998.

———. *Abraham Kuyper: Modern Calvinist, Christian Democrat.* Library of Christian Biography. Grand Rapids: Eerdmans, 2013.

———. "The Context of Herman Bavinck's Stone Lectures: Culture and Politics in 1908." *The Bavinck Review* 1 (2010): 4-24.

Britz, Dolf. "Politics and Social Life." In *The Calvin Handbook,* ed. Herman J. Selderhuis, 437-48. Grand Rapids: Eerdmans, 2009.

Brown, R. "Translating the Whole Concept of the Kingdom." *Notes on Translation* 14, no. 2 (2000): 1-48.

Bruijn, Jan de. *Abraham Kuyper: A Pictorial Biography*. Translated by Dagmare Houniet. Grand Rapids: Eerdmans, 2008, 2014.

Bruner, Frederick D. *Matthew, A Commentary: The Christbook, Matthew 1–12*. Grand Rapids: Eerdmans, 2004.

Brunner, Emil, and Karl Barth. *Natural Theology*. Translated by Peter Fraenkel. Eugene, OR: Wipf and Stock, 1946, 2002.

Buber, Martin. *I and Thou*. Translated by Walter Kaufmann. Edinburgh: T&T Clark, 1970.

———. *Kingship of God*. 3rd ed. Atlantic Highlands, NJ: Humanities Press International, 1990.

Buckley, Michael J. *At the Origins of Modern Atheism*. New Haven, CT: Yale University Press, 1990.

Bull, Malcolm. "Who Was the First to Make a Pact with the Devil?" *London Review of Books* 14 (May 1992): 22-23.

Bultmann, Rudolf. *What Is Theology?* Translated by Roy A. Harrisville. Fortress Texts in Modern Theology. Minneapolis: Fortress, 1997.

Burke, Edmund. *Reflections on the Revolution in France*. New York: Bobbs Merrill, 1955.

Caird, George B. *New Testament Theology*. Completed and edited by L. D. Hurst. Oxford: Clarendon, 1994.

Calvin, John. *Institutes of the Christian Religion*. Edited by John T. McNeill. Translated by Ford Lewis Battles. Vol. 1. Philadelphia: Westminster, 1960.

Carroll, John. *Ego and Soul: The Modern West in Search of Meaning*. Berkeley, CA: Counterpoint, 2008.

Casanova, José. *Public Religions in the Modern World*. Chicago: University of Chicago Press, 1994.

Cave, Alfred. *An Introduction to Theology: Its Principles, Its Branches, Its Results, and Its Literature*. Edinburgh: T&T Clark, 1896.

Chantepie de la Saussaye, Daniël. *Verzameld werk. Een keuze uit het werk van Daniël Chantepie de la Saussaye*. Selected and annotated by F. G. M. Broeyer, H. W. de Knijff, and H. Veldhuis. 3 vols. Zoetermeer, Netherlands: Boekencentrum, 1997–2003.

Chaplin, Jonathan. *Herman Dooyeweerd: Christian Philosopher of State and Civil Society*. Notre Dame, IN: University of Notre Dame Press, 2011.

Childs, Brevard S. *Isaiah*. Old Testament Library. Louisville: Westminster John Knox, 2000.

Claiborne, Shane, Jonathan Wilson-Hartgrove, and Enuma Okoro. *Common Prayer: A Liturgy for Ordinary Radicals*. Grand Rapids: Zondervan, 2010.

Clark, Kelly James. *Return to Reason: A Critique of Enlightenment Evidentialism, and a Defense of Reason and Belief in God*. Grand Rapids: Eerdmans, 1990.

Clouser, Roy. *The Myth of Religious Neutrality: An Essay on the Hidden Role of Religious Beliefs in Theories.* Notre Dame, IN: University of Notre Dame Press, 1991.

Colson, Charles, and Nancy Pearcey. *How Now Shall We Live.* Wheaton, IL: Tyndale, 1999.

Congdon, David W. *The Mission of Demythologizing: Rudolf Bultmann's Dialectical Theology.* Minneapolis: Fortress, 2015.

―――. *Rudolph Bultmann: A Companion to His Theology.* Cascade Companions. Eugene, OR: Cascade Books, 2015.

Conradie, Ernst M., ed. *Creation and Salvation: Dialogue on Abraham Kuyper's Legacy for Contemporary Ecotheology.* Leiden: Brill, 2011.

Cooper, John. *Body, Soul, and Life Everlasting: Biblical Anthropology and the Monism-Dualism Debate.* 2nd ed. Grand Rapids: Eerdmans, 2000.

Costa, Isaac da. *De Heraut.* 1857.

De Blij, Harm. *The Power of Place: Geography, Destiny, and Globalization's Rough Landscape.* Oxford: Oxford University Press, 2009.

De Klerk, Willem A. *The Puritans in Africa: A Story of Afrikanerdom.* Middlesex, UK: Penguin, 1975.

De Vries, Simon J. "Hexateuchal Criticism of Abraham Kuenen." *Journal of Biblical Literature* 82, no. 1 (1963): 31-57.

Dengerink, Jan D. *Critisch-Historisch Onderzoek Naar de Sociologische Ontwikkeling van het Beginsel der "Sovereiniteit in Eigen Kring" in de 19e en 20e Eeuw.* Kampen: Kok, 1948.

Dilthey, Wilhelm. *Selected Writings.* Translated by H. P. Rickman. Cambridge: Cambridge University Press, 1976.

Dirksen, Peter W., and Aad W. Van Der Kooij, eds. *Abraham Kuenen (1828-1891): His Major Contributions to the Study of the Old Testament: A Collection of Old Testament Studies Published on the Occasion of the Centenary of Abraham Kuenen's Death (10 December 1991).* Oudtestamentlische Studiën 29. Leiden: Brill, 1993.

Dooyeweerd, Herman. *In the Twilight of Western Thought: Studies in the Pretended Autonomy of Philosophical Thought.* Lewiston, NY: Edwin Mellen, 1999.

―――. *A New Critique of Theoretical Thought.* 4 vols. Translated by David H. Freeman and William S. Young. Jordan Station, ON: Paideia, 1984.

―――. *Roots of Western Culture: Pagan, Secular, and Christian Options.* Translated by John Kraay. Toronto: Wedge, 1979.

Du Bois, W. E. B. *The Souls of Black Folk.* Edited by David W. Blight and Robert Gooding-Williams. Bedford Series in History and Culture. Boston and New York: Bedford Books, 1997.

Du Preez, Max. *A Rumour of Spring: South Africa After 20 Years of Democracy*. Cape Town: Zebra Press, 2013.

Duchnow, Ulrich, ed. *Lutheran Churches—Salt or Mirror of Society*. Geneva: Lutheran World Federation, 1977.

Dudley-Smith, Timothy. *John Stott: A Global Ministry*. Leicester, UK: Inter-Varsity Press, 2001.

Dumbrell, William. *Covenant and Creation: An Old Testament Covenantal Theology*. Exeter, UK: Paternoster, 1984.

Dyck, Cornelius J. "The Anabaptist Understanding of Good News." In Shenk, ed., *Anabaptism and Mission*, 24-39. Scottdale, PA: Herald Press, 1984.

Dyrness, William A. *Reformed Theology and Visual Culture: The Protestant Imagination from Calvin to Edwards*. Cambridge: Cambridge University Press, 2004.

Eglinton, James, and George Harinck, eds. *Neo-Calvinism and the French Revolution*. London: Bloomsbury, 2014.

Eliot, T. S. *The Idea of a Christian Society*. Boston: Houghton Mifflin Harcourt, 2014.

Ellis, Stephen. *External Mission: The ANC in Exile, 1960–1990*. Oxford: Oxford University Press, 2013.

Elrod, John W. *Kierkegaard and Christendom*. Princeton, NJ: Princeton University Press, 1981.

Essen, J. L. van, and H. D. Morton. *Guillaume Groen van Prinsterer: Selected Studies*. Jordan Station, ON: Wedge, 2000.

Faber, Jelle. *Essays in Reformed Doctrine*. Neerlandia, Canada: Inheritance Publications, 1990.

Fennell, C. A. M. *The Stanford Dictionary of Anglicised Words and Phrases*. Cambridge: Cambridge University Press, 1892.

Finger, Thomas N. *A Contemporary Anabaptist Theology: Biblical, Historical, Constructive*. Downers Grove, IL: IVP Academic, 2004.

Flett, John G. *The Witness of God: The Trinity, Missio Dei, Karl Barth, and the Nature of Christian Community*. Grand Rapids: Eerdmans, 2010.

Follis, Bryan A. *Truth with Love: The Apologetics of Francis Schaeffer*. Wheaton, IL: Crossway, 2006.

Fretheim, Terence E. *God and World in the Old Testament: A Relational Theology of Creation*. Nashville: Abingdon, 2005.

Friesen, Duane K. *Christian Peacemaking and International Conflict*. Scottdale, PA: Herald, 1986.

Friesen, J. G. "The Mystical Dooyeweerd Once Again: Kuyper's Use of Franz von Baader." *Ars Disputandi* 3 (2003). www.arsdisputandi.org/publish/articles/000088/index.html.

———. *Neo-Calvinism and Christian Theosophy: Franz von Baader, Abraham Kuyper, Herman Dooyeweerd*. Calgary: Aevum Books, 2015.

Gäbler, Ulrich. "Eduard Böhls Auseinandersetzung mit dem Holländer Abraham Kuenen über die rechte Auslegung des Alten Testaments, 1864." In *Jahrbuch für die Geschichte des Protestantismus in Österreich* 96, parts 1-3, 101-16. Vienna: Verlag des Evangelischen Presseverbandes in Österreich, 1980.

Gadamer, Hans-Georg. *Truth and Method*. London: Bloomsbury, 2013.

Gaffin, Richard B., Jr. *God's Word in Servant Form: Abraham Kuyper and Herman Bavinck on the Doctrine of Scripture*. Jackson, MS: Reformed Academic Press, 2008.

Geertz, Clifford. "Religion as a Cultural System." In Michael Banton, ed., *Anthropological Approaches to the Study of Religion*, 1-46. London: Tavistock, 1966.

Gellner, Ernest. *Postmodernism, Reason and Religion*. London: Routledge, 1992.

Gensichen, Hans-Werner. "Gutmann, Bruno." In *Biographical Dictionary of Christian Missions*, ed. Gerald H. Anderson, 271-72. New York: Macmillan Reference USA, 1998.

Gleason, Ron. *Herman Bavinck: Pastor, Churchman, Statesman, and Theologian*. Phillipsburg, NJ: P&R, 2010.

Goheen, Michael W. *"As the Father Has Sent Me, I Am Sending You": J. E. Lesslie Newbigin's Missional Ecclesiology*. Zoetermeer, Netherlands: Boekencentrum, 2000.

———. *Introducing Christian Mission Today: Scripture, History and Issues*. Downers Grove, IL: IVP Academic, 2014.

———. *A Light to the Nations: The Missional Church and the Biblical Story*. Grand Rapids: Baker Academic, 2011.

Goheen, Michael W., and Craig G. Bartholomew. *Living at the Crossroads: An Introduction to Christian Worldview*. Grand Rapids: Baker Academic, 2008.

Goheen, Michael W., and Erin G. Glanville, eds. *The Gospel and Globalization: Exploring the Religious Roots of a Globalized World*. Vancouver: Regent, 2009.

Goudzwaard, Bob. *Capitalism and Progress: A Diagnosis of Western Society*. Carlisle, UK: Paternoster, 1997.

Goudzwaard, Bob, and Craig G. Bartholomew. *Beyond the Modern Age: An Archaeology of Contemporary Culture*. Downers Grove, IL: IVP Academic, 2017.

Goudzwaard, Bob, and Harry de Lange. *Beyond Poverty and Affluence: Toward an Economy of Care with a Twelve-Step Program for Economic Recovery*. Translated by Mark R. Vander Vennen. Grand Rapids: Eerdmans, 1995.

Graff, Gerald. *Clueless in Academe: How Schooling Obscures the Life of the Mind*. New Haven, CT: Yale University Press, 2003.

Greenslade, S. L., ed. *Early Latin Theology: Selections from Tertullian, Cyprian, Ambrose, and Jerome*. Library of Christian Classics. Louisville: Westminster John Knox, 1956.

Greidanus, Sidney. *Sola Scriptura: Problems and Principles in Preaching Historical Texts.* Toronto: Wedge, 1970.

Griffith, Michael. *Cinderella with Amnesia: A Practical Discussion of the Relevance of the Church.* Leicester, UK: Inter-Varsity Press, 1975.

———. *Shaking the Sleeping Beauty: Arousing the Church to Its Mission.* Leicester, UK: Inter-Varsity Press, 1980.

Grim, Brian J., and Roger Finke. *The Price of Freedom Denied: Religious Persecution and Conflict in the Twenty-First Century.* Cambridge: Cambridge University Press, 2011.

Groen van Prinsterer, Guillaume. *Groen van Prinsterer's Lectures on Unbelief and Revolution.* Edited by Harry Van Dyke. Toronto: Wedge, 1989.

Gross, Leonard. "Sixteenth Century Hutterian Mission." In Shenk, ed., *Anabaptism and Mission*, 97-118. Scottdale, PA: Herald Press, 1984.

Gunning, J. H., Jr., and A. de Lange. *J. H. Gunning Jr.: Brochures En Brieven Uit Zijn Leidse Tijd (1889–1899).* Kampen: Kok, 1984.

Harinck, George. "Abraham Kuyper, South Africa, and Apartheid." In Steve Bishop and John H. Kok, eds., *On Kuyper: A Collection of Readings on the Life, Work, and Legacy of Abraham Kuyper*, 419-22. Sioux Center, IA: Dordt College Press, 2013.

———, ed. *Alles of nites: Opstellen over K. Schilder.* Barneveld: De Vuurbaak, 2003.

———. "Gerhardus Vos as Introducer of Kuyper in America." In Hans Krabbendam and Larry J. Wagenaar, eds., *The Dutch-American Experience: Essays in Honor of Robert P. Swieringa*, 242-62. Amsterdam: VU, 2000.

———, ed. *Holwerda Herdacht: Bijdragen over leven en werk van Benne Holwerda (1909–1952).* Barneveld, Netherlands: De Vuurbaak, 2005.

———. "'Met de telephoon onzen God oproepen.' Kuypers meditaties uit 1905 en 1906." In *Godsvrucht in geschiedenis. Bundel ter gelegenheid van het afscheid van prof. dr. F. Van der Pol als hoogleraar een de Theologische Universiteit Kampen*, ed. Erik A. de Boer and Harm J. Boiten, 454-65. Heerenveen, 2015.

———. "'Something That Must Remain if the Truth Is to Be Sweet and Precious to Us': The Reformed Spirituality of Herman Bavinck." *CTJ* 38 (2003): 248-62.

———. "Twin Sisters with a Changing Character: How Neo-Calvinists Dealt with the Modern Discrepancy Between the Bible and Modern Science." In Jitse M. van der Meer and Scott Mandelbrote, eds., *Nature and Scripture in the Abrahamic Religions*, 1:317-70. Leiden: Brill, 2008.

———. "Why Was Bavinck in Need of a Philosophy of Revelation?" In *The Kuyper Center Review*, ed. James Bowlin, 2:27-42. Grand Rapids: Eerdmans, 2011.

Hauerwas, Stanley. "Finding God in Strange Places: Why L'Arche Needs the Church." In Hauerwas and Jean Vanier, *Living Gently in a Violent World: The Prophetic Witness of Weakness*, 43-58. Downers Grove, IL: InterVarsity Press, 2008.

Heidegger, Martin. *The Basic Problems of Phenomenology.* Bloomington: Indiana University Press, 1982.

Heideman, E. P. *The Relation of Revelation and Reason in E. Brunner and H. Bavinck.* Assen, Netherlands: Van Gorcum, 1959.

Henderson, R. D. *Illuminating Law: The Construction of Herman Dooyeweerd's Philosophy 1918–1928.* Amsterdam: Buijten and Schipperheij, 1994.

Henry, Carl F. H. *God, Revelation and Authority.* Vol. 5, *God Who Stands and Stays,* part 1. Waco, TX: Word, 1982.

Henry, Matthew. *Letterlijke en Practicale Verklaring van het N.T.* With Introduction by Herman Bavinck. Kampen: Kok, 1909.

Herms, Eilert. ">>Weltanschauung<< bei F. Schleiermacher and A. Ritschl." In *Theorie für die Praxis,* 121-43. München: Chr. Kaiser Verlag, 1982.

Hertz, Karl H., ed. *Two Kingdoms and the World.* Minneapolis: Augsburg, 1976.

Heslam, Peter S. *Creating a Christian Worldview: Abraham Kuyper's Lectures on Calvinism.* Grand Rapids: Eerdmans, 1998.

Heyns, Johan A. *The Church.* Pretoria, South Africa: N. G. Kerkboekhandel, 1980.

Hiltner, Seward. *Preface to Pastoral Theology.* Nashville: Abingdon, 1958.

Himmelfarb, Gertrude. *The Roads to Modernity: The British, French, and American Enlightenments.* New York: Vintage Books, 2004.

Hinlicky, Paul. *Beloved Community: Critical Dogmatics After Christendom.* Grand Rapids: Eerdmans, 2015.

Hobson, George. *The Episcopal Church, Homosexuality, and the Context of Technology.* Eugene, OR: Wipf and Stock, 2013.

Hoitenga, Dewey J. *Faith and Reason from Plato to Plantinga: An Introduction to Reformed Epistemology.* New York: SUNY Press, 1991.

Holtrop, P. N., ed. *ZGKN100 Een bundel opstellen over de Zending van de Gereformeerde Kerken in Nederland ter gelegenheid van de honderjarige herdenking van de Synode van Middelburg 1896.* Kampen: WZOK, 1996.

Holwerda, B. *" . . . Begonnen Hebbende van Mozes . . ."* Terneuzen: D. H. Littooij, 1953.

Houtman, Cornelius. "Abraham Kuenen and William Robertson Smith: Their Correspondence." *Nederlands Archief voor Kerkgeschiedenis* 80, no. 2 (2000): 221-40.

———. "Die Wirkung der Arbeit Kuenens in den Niederlanden." In Dirksen and van der Kooij, eds., *Abraham Kuenen,* 29-48. Leiden: Brill, 1993.

Howard, Thomas A. *Religion and the Rise of Historicism: W. M. L. De Wette, Jacob Burckhardt, and the Theological Origins of Nineteenth-Century Historical Consciousness.* Cambridge: Cambridge University Press, 2006.

Hueglin, Thomas O. *Early Modern Concepts for a Late Modern World: Althusius on*

Communalism and Federalism. Waterloo, ON: Wilfred Laurier University Press, 1999.

Hughes, Heather. *First President: A Life of John L. Dubbe, Founding President of the ANC.* Auckland Park, South Africa: Jacana, 2011.

Jaarsma, Cornelius R. *The Educational Philosophy of Herman Bavinck: A Textbook in Education.* Grand Rapids: Eerdmans, 1935.

Jannssen, Heinrich. *Die Bibel als Grundlage der Politischen Theorie des Johannes Althusius.* Frankfurt: Peter Lang, 1992.

Jenkins, Philip. *God's Continent: Christianity, Islam, and Europe's Religious Crisis.* Oxford: Oxford University Press, 2007.

———. *The New Faces of Christianity: Believing the Bible in the Global South.* Oxford: Oxford University Press, 2006.

———. *The Next Christendom: The Coming of Global Christianity.* 3rd ed. Oxford: Oxford University Press, 2011.

Johnson, R. W. *How Long Will South Africa Survive? The Looming Crisis.* Johannesburg: Jonathan Ball, 2015.

Jonker, W. D. *Leve de Kerk.* Nijkerk: Callenbach, 1969.

Jordan, Ellen, Charlotte Mitchell, and Helen Schinske. "'A Handmaid to the Church': How John Keble Shaped the Career of Charlotte Yonge, the 'Novelist of the Oxford Movement.'" In *John Keble in Context,* edited by Kirstie Blair, 175-91. London: Anthem, 2004.

Jürgens, Henning P. *Johannes a Lasco in Ostfriesland: der Werdegang eines europäischen Reformators.* Tübingen: Mohr Siebeck, 2000.

Kass, Leon R. *The Beginnings of Wisdom: Reading Genesis.* Chicago: University of Chicago Press, 2003.

———. *The Hungry Soul: Eating and the Perfecting of Our Nature.* New York: Free Press, 1994.

Kearney, Richard. *Dialogues with Contemporary Thinkers. The Phenomenological Heritage.* Manchester, UK: Manchester University Press, 1984.

Keet, B. B. *Whither South Africa?* Translated by N. J. Marquard. Stellenbosch and Grahamstown, South Africa: University Publishers and Booksellers, 1956.

Kerr, David A., and Kenneth R. Ross, eds. *Edinburgh 2010: Mission Then and Now.* Oxford: Regnum, 2009.

Keulen, Dirk van. *Bijbel en dogmatiek: Schriftbeschouwing en schriftgebruik in het dogmatisch werk van A. Kuyper, H. Bavinck, en G.C. Berkouwer.* Kampen: Kok, 2003.

———. "Herman Bavinck's Reformed Ethics: Some Remarks About Unpublished Manuscripts in the Libraries of Amsterdam and Kampen." *The Bavinck Review* 1 (2010): 25-56.

———. "The Internal Tension in Kuyper's Doctrine of Organic Inspiration of

Scripture." In Cornelis van der Kooi and Jan de Bruijn, eds., *Kuyper Reconsidered: Aspects of His Life and Work,* 123-30. VU Studies on Protestant History. Amsterdam: Vrije Universiteit Amsterdam, 1999.

Kierkegaard, Søren. *Journals and Papers.* Translated by Howard V. Hong and Edna H. Hong, and assisted by Gregor Malantschuk. Bloomington: Indiana University Press, 1967.

Kim, Kirsteen, and Andrew Anderson, eds. *Edinburgh 2010: Mission Today and Tomorrow.* Regnum Edinburgh 2010 Series. Oxford: Regnum, 2011.

Koslowski, Peter, ed. *Die Philosophie, Theologie und Gnosis Franz von Baaders: Spekulatives Denken zwischen Aufklärung, Restauration und Romantik.* Vienna: Passagen Verlag, 1993.

———. *Philosophien der Offenbarung, Antiker Gnoticizmus, Franz von Baader, Schelling.* Vienna: Ferdinand Schöningh, 2001.

Kuehn, Heinz R. "Introduction." In Romano Guardini, *The Essential Guardini: An Anthology of the Writings of Romano Guardini,* 1-12. Chicago: Liturgy Training Publications, 1997.

Kuenen, Abraham. *De Godsdienst tot den ondergang van den Joodschen staat.* English translation, 1874–1875.

———. *De profeten en de profetie onder Israël.* English translation, 1877.

———. *Historisch-Kritisch Onderzoek naar het ontstaan en de verzameling van de Boeken des Ouden Verbonds.* 3 vols. 1861–1865. 2nd ed., 1885–1893.

———. *Levensbericht van J. Henricus Scholten.* 1885.

Kuipers, Tjitza. *Abraham Kuyper: An Annotated Bibliography 1857–2010.* Brill's Series in Church History. Leiden: Brill, 2011.

Kuitert, Harry M. *Jesus: The Legacy of Christianity.* London: SCM Press, 1999.

Küng, Hans. *Great Christian Thinkers.* New York: Continuum, 1995.

Kuyper, Abraham. *Abraham Kuyper: A Centennial Reader.* Edited by James D. Bratt. Grand Rapids: Eerdmans, 1998.

———. *Band aan het woord. Antwoord op de vraag: Hoe is eene universiteit aan het woord van God te binden?* Amsterdam: Höveker & Wormser, 1899.

———. "The Biblical Criticism of the Present Day." Translated by J. Hendrik de Vries. *Bibliothecra Sacra* LXI, no. 243 (1904): 410-42, 666-88.

———. "Christ and the Needy." *Journal of Markets & Morality* 14, no. 2 (Fall 2011): 647-83.

———. *Christianity and the Class Struggle.* Translated by Dirk Jellema. Grand Rapids: Piet Hein, 1950.

———. *Common Grace: God's Gifts for a Fallen World.* Vol. 1. Translated by Nelson D.

Kloosterman. Edited by M. van der Maas. Abraham Kuyper Collected Works in Public Theology. Bellingham, WA: Lexham Press, 2015.

———. *De Engelen Gods*. Kampen: Kok, 1923.

———. *De vastigheid des verbond*. Masterdam: Kirchener, 1908.

———. *Dictaten Dogmatiek van Dr. A. Kuyper*. Grand Rapids: J. B. Hulst, 1910–1913.

———. *Drie Kleine Vossen*. Kampen: Kok, 1901.

———. *Encyclopaedie der heilige Godgeleerdheid*. 3 vols. Kampen: Kok, 1909.

———. *Het Rassenvraagstuk: Probleem van Wereldformaat*. Kampen: Kok, 1956.

———. "Lecture by Prof. Dr. A. Kuyper Concerning 'Missions,' Mission Congress in Amsterdam, 28-30 January, 1890." Forthcoming.

———. *Lectures on Calvinism*. Peabody, MA: Hendrickson, 2008.

———. "The Natural Knowledge of God." Translated by Harry Van Dyke. *The Bavinck Review* 6 (2015): 73-112.

———. *Our Program: A Christian Political Manifesto*. Translated by Harry Van Dyke. Abraham Kuyper Collected Works in Public Theology. Bellingham, WA: Lexham Press, 2015.

———. *Our Worship*. Translated by Harry Boonstra. Grand Rapids: Eerdmans, 2009.

———. *Parlementaire Redevoeringen*. Amsterdam: Van Holkema and Warendorf, 1908–1912.

———. *Principles of Sacred Theology*. Translated by Hendrik J. De Vries. Grand Rapids: Baker Book House, 1980.

———. *The Problem of Poverty*. Sioux Center, IA: Dordt College Press, 2011.

———. *The Revelation of St. John*. Eugene, OR: Wipf and Stock, 1999.

———. *Rooted and Grounded: The Church as Organism and Institution*. Translated by Nelson D. Kloosterman. Grand Rapids: Christian's Library Press, 2013.

———. *Scholarship: Two Convocation Addresses on University Life*. Translated by Harry van Dyke. Grand Rapids: Christian's Library Press, 2014.

———. *The South-African Crisis*. 4th ed. Translated by A. E. Fletcher. London: Stop the War Committee, 1900.

———. *To Be Near unto God*. Translated by John H. de Vries. Vancouver: Regent, 2005.

———. *Two Convocation Adresses on University Life*. Translated by Harry van Dyke. Grand Rapids: Christian's Library Press, 2014.

———. *Van de voleinding*. 4 vols. Kampen: Kok, 1929–1931.

———. *The Work of the Holy Spirit*. Translated by Henri de Vries. Grand Rapids: Eerdmans, 1900.

Lane, Tony. *The Lion Concise Book of Christian Thought*. Herts, UK: Lion, 1984.

Langley, McKendree R. "Emancipation and Apologetics: The Formation of Abraham Kuyper's Anti-Revolutionary Party in the Netherlands, 1872–1880." PhD diss. Westminster Theological Seminary, Philadelphia, 1995.

———. *The Practice of Political Spirituality: Episodes from the Public Career of Abraham Kuyper, 1879–1918.* Jordan Station, ON: Paideia, 1984.

Leeuwen, P. A. van. *Het Kerkbegrip in de Theologie van Abraham Kuyper.* Franeker, Netherlands: T. Wever, 1946.

Levenson, Jon D. *The Hebrew Bible, the Old Testament, and Historical Criticism: Jews and Christians in Biblical Studies.* Louisville: Westminster John Knox, 1993.

Lilla, Mark. *The Stillborn God: Religion, Politics, and the Modern West.* New York: Vintage, 2007, 2008.

Lubac, Henri de. *A Brief Catechism on Nature and Grace.* Translated by Br. Richard Arnandez. San Francisco: Ignatius, 1984.

———. *The Christian Faith: An Essay on the Structure of the Apostles' Creed.* London: Geoffrey Chapman, 1986.

Luther, Martin. *Large Catechism.* In *The Book of Concord*, ed. and trans. Theodore G. Tappert. Philadelphia: Fortress Press, 1959.

———. *Luther's Works.* 55 vols. St. Louis: Concordia, 1955–1986.

MacIntyre, Alasdair. *After Virtue.* Notre Dame, IN: University of Notre Dame Press, 1980.

———. *Whose Justice? Which Rationality?* Notre Dame, IN: University of Notre Dame Press, 1988.

Maier, Bernhard. *William Robertson Smith: His Life, His Work and His Times.* Tübingen: Mohr Siebek, 2009.

Marsden, George. "The Collapse of American Evangelical Academia." In *Faith and Rationality*, edited by Alvin Plantinga and Nicholas Wolterstorff, 219-64. Notre Dame, IN: University of Notre Dame Press, 1983.

———. *The Outrageous Idea of Christian Scholarship.* New York: Oxford University Press, 1997.

———. "The State of Evangelical Christian Scholarship." *Reformed Journal* 37 (1987): 12-16.

Marshall, Paul, and Nina Shea. *Silence: How Apostasy and Blasphemy Codes Are Choking Freedom Worldwide.* Oxford: Oxford University Press, 2011.

Mattson, Brian G. *Restored to Our Destiny: Eschatology and the Image of God in Herman Bavinck's Reformed Dogmatics.* Studies in Reformed Theology. Leiden: Brill, 2012.

McCarthy, Rockne, Donald Oppewal, Walfred Peterson, and Gordon Spykrnan. *Society, State and School: A Case for Structural and Confessional Pluralism.* Grand Rapids: Eerdmans, 1981.

McGrath, Alister. *C. S. Lewis—A Life: Eccentric Genius, Reluctant Prophet.* Carol Stream, IL: Tyndale House, 2013.

McIntire, C. T. "Dooyeweerd's Philosophy of History." In *The Legacy of Herman Dooyeweerd: Reflections on Critical Philosophy in the Christian Tradition*, edited by C. T.

McIntire, 81-117. Lanham, MD: University Press of America, 1985.

Meijering, E. P. *Hendrikus Berkhof (1914–1995): Een Theologische Biografie*. Kampen: Kok, 1997.

Meijers, Erica. "The End of the Colonial Mindset: Apartheid as Challenge for the Protestant Churches in the Netherlands." In *Globalisierung der Kirchen: Der Ökumenische Rat der Kirchen und die Entdeckung der Dritten Welt in den 1960er und 1970er Jahren*, edited by Katharina Kunter and Annegreth Schilling, 313-34. Göttingen: Vandenhoeck and Ruprecht, 2014.

Menuge, Angus J. L., ed. *Christ and Culture in Dialogue: Constructive Themes and Practical Applications*. St. Louis: Concordia Academic Press, 1999.

Merton, Thomas. *Contemplative Prayer*. London: DLT, 1969.

Michelet, Jules. *Nos Fils*. Librairie Internationale: 1869.

———. *The People*. Translated by C. Cocks. London: Longman, Brown, Green and Longmans, 1846.

Mietus, Leo. *Gunning en Kuyper in 1878: A. Kuypers Polemiek tegen het Leven van Jesus van J. H. Gunning Jr.* Brochurereeks nr. 28. Velp: Bond van Vrije Evangelische Gemeenten in Nederland, 2009.

Milbank, John. *The Suspended Middle: Henri de Lubac and the Debate Concerning the Supernatural*. Grand Rapids: Eerdmans, 2005.

"Modernizing the Case for God." *Time Magazine*. April 7, 1980. http://content.time .com/time/magazine/article/0,9171,921990,00.html.

Mouw, Richard J. *He Shines in All That's Fair: Culture and Common Grace*. Grand Rapids: Eerdmans, 2001.

———. "Klaas Schilder as Public Theologian." *CTJ* 38 (2003): 281-98.

———. *Political Evangelism*. Grand Rapids: Eerdmans, 1973.

———. *When the Kings Come Marching In: Isaiah and the New Jerusalem*. Grand Rapids: Eerdmans, 1983.

Mouw, Richard J., and Sander Griffioen. *Pluralisms and Horizons: An Essay in Christian Public Philosophy*. Grand Rapids: Eerdmans, 1993.

Mouw, Richard J., and Douglas A. Sweeney. *The Suffering and Victorious Christ: Toward a More Compassionate Christology*. Grand Rapids: Baker Academic, 2013.

Mumford, Lewis. *The City in History: Its Origins, Its Transformations, and Its Prospects*. San Diego: Harcourt Brace, 1989.

Musgrove, F. *Margins of the Mind*. London: Methuen, 1977.

Naugle, David. *Worldview: The History of a Concept*. Grand Rapids: Eerdmans, 2002.

Newbigin, Lesslie. "Can the West Be Converted?" *Princeton Seminary Bulletin* 6, no. 1 (1985): 25-37.

———. *Foolishness to the Greeks: The Gospel and Western Culture.* London: SPCK, 1986.

———. *The Gospel in a Pluralist Society.* Grand Rapids: Eerdmans, 1989.

———. *One Body, One Gospel, One World: The Christian Mission Today.* London: International Missionary Council, 1958.

———. *Proper Confidence: Faith, Doubt, and Certainty in Christian Discipleship.* London: SPCK, 1995.

———. *Sign of the Kingdom.* Grand Rapids: Eerdmans, 1981.

———. *Trinitarian Doctrine for Today's World.* Eugene, OR: Wipf and Stock, 1988.

———. *A Word in Season: Perspectives on Christian World Missions.* Grand Rapids: Eerdmans, 1994.

Newbigin, Lesslie, Lamin Sanneh, and Jenny Taylor. *Faith and Power: Christianity and Islam in "Secular" Britain.* Eugene, OR: Wipf and Stock, 1998, 2005.

Nicholson, Ernest. *The Pentateuch in the Twentieth Century: The Legacy of Julius Wellhausen.* Oxford: Clarendon, 1998.

Niebuhr, H. R. *Christ and Culture.* New York: Harper & Row, 1951.

———. *The Kingdom of God in America.* Chicago: Harper Torchbooks, 1937.

Nijhoff, Rob A. *De logosfilosofie van Jan Woltjer (1849–1917): Logos en wijsbegeerte aan de vroege Vrije Universiteit.* Amsterdam: Buitjen & Schipperheijn, 2014.

Niles, D. T. *Upon the Earth.* New York: McGraw-Hill, 1962.

Noll, Mark. *The Scandal of the Evangelical Mind.* Grand Rapids: Eerdmans, 1994.

Noll, Mark, and James Turner. *The Future of Christian Learning: An Evangelical and Catholic Dialogue.* Edited by Thomas A. Howard. Grand Rapids: Brazos, 2008.

Nouwen, Henri. *The Road to Daybreak: A Spiritual Journey.* New York: Doubleday, 1988.

O'Connor, Elizabeth. *Journey Inward, Journey Outward.* New York: Harper & Row, 1968.

Odendaal, André. *The Founders: The Origins of the ANC and the Struggle for Democracy in South Africa.* Auckland Park, South Africa: Jacana, 2012.

O'Donovan, Oliver. *The Desire of the Nations: Rediscovering the Roots of Political Theology.* Cambridge: Cambridge University Press, 1996.

———. *Resurrection and Moral Order: An Outline for Evangelical Ethics.* Grand Rapids: Eerdmans, 1986, 1994.

———. *The Ways of Judgment.* Grand Rapids: Eerdmans, 2005.

Oort, Henricus, Isaäc Hooykaas, and Abraham Kuenen. *The Old Testament for Learners.* Boston: Little, Brown, 1900.

O'Reilley, Mary Rose. *The Love of Impermanent Things: A Threshold Ecology.* Minneapolis: Milkweed Editions, 2006.

Orr, James. *The Christian View of God and the World*. 2nd ed. Edinburgh: Andrew Elliot, 1893.

Parler, Branson L. *Things Hold Together: John Howard Yoder's Trinitarian Theology of Culture*. Scottdale, PA: Herald, 2012.

Paton, Alan. *Cry, The Beloved Country*. New York: Scribner, 1948, 2003.

———. *Hofmeyr*. Oxford: Oxford University Press, 1964.

———. *Hope for South Africa*. London: Pall Mall Press, 1958.

———. *Towards the Mountain: An Autobiography*. London: Penguin, 1986.

Pearcey, Nancy. *Total Truth: Liberating Christianity from Its Cultural Captivity*. Wheaton, IL: Crossway, 2004.

Pennington, Jonathan T. *Heaven and Earth in the Gospel of Matthew*. Grand Rapids: Baker Academic, 2009.

Perry, Tim S. *Radical Difference: A Defence of Hendrik Kraemer's Theology of Religions*. Waterloo, ON: Wilfred Laurier University Press, 2001.

Peterson, Eugene H. *Answering God: The Psalms as Tools for Prayer*. New York: HarperCollins, 1989.

———. *The Contemplative Pastor*. Grand Rapids: Eerdmans, 1993.

———. *Leap over a Wall: Earthly Spirituality for Everyday Christians*. New York: HarperCollins, 1997.

———. *Working the Angles: The Shape of Pastoral Integrity*. Grand Rapids: Eerdmans, 1993.

Pflanze, Otto. *Bismarck and the Development of Germany: The Period of Unification 1815–1871*. Princeton, NJ: Princeton University Press, 1968.

Pieper, Josef. *Guide to Thomas Aquinas*. San Francisco: Ignatius, 1991.

Plantinga, Alvin. *Warranted Christian Belief*. New York: Oxford University Press, 2000.

Plantinga, Alvin, and Nicholas Wolterstorff, eds. *Faith and Rationality: Reason and Belief in God*. Notre Dame, IN: University of Notre Dame Press, 1983.

Plaut, Martin. *Promise and Despair: The First Struggle for a Non-Racial South Africa*. Auckland Park, South Africa: Jacana, 2016.

Polanyi, Michael. *Personal Knowledge: Towards a Post-Critical Philosophy*. Chicago: University of Chicago Press, 1958.

Poplin, Mary. *Finding Calcutta: What Mother Teresa Taught Me About Meaningful Work and Service*. Downers Grove, IL: InterVarsity Press, 2011.

Popper, Karl R. "The Bucket and the Searchlight: Two Theories of Knowledge." In David R. Keller and Frank B. Golley, eds., *The Philosophy of Ecology: From Science to Synthesis*, 141-46. Athens: University of Georgia Press, 2000.

Postman, Neil. *The End of Education: Redefining the Value of School*. New York: Knopf, 1996.

Price, Timothy S. "Abraham Kuyper and Herman Bavinck on the Subject of Education as Seen in Two Public Addresses." *The Bavinck Review* 2 (2011): 59-70.

Puchinger, George. *Abraham Kuyper: De Jonge Kuyper (1837–1867)*. Franeker, Netherlands: T. Wever, 1987.

———. *Abraham Kuyper: His Early Journey of Faith*. Edited by George Harinck. Amsterdam: VU University Press, 1988.

———. *Is de gereformeerde wereld veranderd?* Delft, Netherlands: W. D. Meinema N. V., 1966.

———. "Newman en Kuyper." In *Ontmoetingen met theologen*, 94-105. Zutphen, Netherlands: Terra, 1980.

Puchinger, George, and N. Scheps. *Gesprek over de onbekende Kuyper*. Kampen: Kok, 1971.

Räbiger, J. F. *Theologik oder Encyklopädie der Theologie*. Leipzig: Fues Verlag, 1880.

Readings, Bill. *The University in Ruins*. Cambridge, MA: Harvard University Press, 1996.

Rees, Wyn, ed. *Colenso: Letters from Natal*. Pietermaritzburg, South Africa: Shuter and Shooter, 1958.

Richard, H. L. "The Missiological Vision of J. H. Bavinck: Religion, Reticence, and Contextual Theology." *International Journal of Frontier Mission* 31, no. 2 (2014): 75-84.

Ricoeur, Paul, and Andre LaCocque. *Thinking Biblically: Exegetical and Hermeneutical Studies*. Translated by David Pellauer. Chicago: The University of Chicago Press, 1998.

Ridderbos, Herman N. *The Coming of the Kingdom*. Jordan, ON: Paideia, 1979.

———. *When the Time Had Fully Come: Studies in New Testament Theology*. Grand Rapids: Eerdmans, 1957.

Ridderbos, Simon J. "De theologische cultuurbeschouwing van Abraham Kuyper." PhD, Vrije Universiteit Amsterdam, 1947.

Rieff, Philip. *Fellow Teachers*. New York: Delta, 1972, 1973.

Rogerson, John W. "J. W. Colenso's Correspondence with Abraham Kuenen, 1863–1878." In *The Bible, the Reformation and the Church: Essays in Honour of James Atkinson*, edited by W. P. Stephens, 190-223. Journal for the Study of the New Testament Supplement 105. Sheffield: Sheffield Academic Press, 1995.

———. *Old Testament Criticism in the Nineteenth Century: England and Germany*. London: SPCK, 1984.

Rowell, Geoffrey. *The Vision Glorious: Themes and Personalities of the Catholic Revival in Anglicanism*. Oxford: Clarendon, 2003.

Runner, H. Evan. *Christian Perspectives 1961*. Hamilton, ON: Guardian Publishing, 1961.

———. *The Relation of the Bible to Learning*. Toronto: Wedge, 1974.

Santmire, H. Paul. *Before Nature: A Christian Spirituality*. Minneapolis: Fortress, 2014.

———. *Nature Reborn: The Ecological and Cosmic Promise of Christian Theology*. Minneapolis: Fortress, 2000.

———. *The Travail of Nature*. Minneapolis: Fortress, 1985.

Sap, John W. *Paving the Way for Revolution: Calvinism and the Struggle for a Democratic Constitutional State*. VU Studies on Protestant History 6. Amsterdam: Vrije Universiteit Amsterdam, 2001.

Schaeffer, Edith. *The Tapestry: The Life and Times of Francis and Edith Schaeffer*. Waco, TX: Word, 1985.

Schaff, Philip, and Henry Wace. *Early Church Fathers: Second Series: Nicene and Post Nicene Fathers*. Edited by Alexander Roberts and James Donaldson. Peabody, MA: Hendrickson, 1994.

Schelling, Friedrich. *System of Transcendental Idealism*. 1800. Translated by Peter Heath. Charlottesville: University of Virginia Press, 1978.

Schilder, Klaas. *Christus in zijn lijden*. English trans., *Christ in His Suffering*. 3 vols. Translated by Henry Zylstra. Grand Rapids: Eerdmans, 1954.

———. *Wat is de Hemel?* Kampen: Kok, 1935.

Schindler, Jeanne H., ed. *Christianity and Civil Society: Catholic and Neo-Calvinist Perspectives*. Lanham, MD: Lexington Books, 2008.

Schleiermacher, Friedrich. *Brief Outline of the Study of Theology*. Translated by William Farrer. Edinburgh: T&T Clark, 1850.

———. *The Christian Faith*. London: T&T Clark, 1999.

———. *On Religion: Speeches to Its Cultured Despisers*. 2nd ed. Translated by Richard Crout. Cambridge Texts in the History of Philosophy. Cambridge: Cambridge University Press, 1988, 1996.

Schmemann, Alexander. *For the Life of the World: Sacraments and Orthodoxy*. 2nd ed. Crestwood, NY: St. Vladimir's Seminary Press, 1973.

Scholten, J. H. *Afscheidsrede bij het Neerleggen van het Hoogleeraarsambt*. 1881.

———. *Het Evangelie naar Johannes: kritisch, historisch onderzoek*. Leiden: P. Engels, 1864.

———. *Principles of the Theology of the Reformed Church*. 2 vols., 1848–1850. 4th ed., 1861–1862.

Schumacher, E. F. *Small Is Beautiful*. London: Abacus, 1973.

Schutte, Gerrit. *A Family Feud: Afrikaner Nationalism and Dutch Neo-Calvinism*. Amsterdam: Rozenberg, 2010.

Seerveld, Calvin. "Dooyeweerd's Idea of 'Historical Development': Christian Respect for Cultural Diversity." *Westerminster Theological Journal* 58, no. 1 (1996): 41-61.

Sennet, James F., ed. *The Analytic Theist: An Alvin Plantinga Reader.* Grand Rapids: Eerdmans, 1998.

Shenk, Wilbert R., ed. *Anabaptism and Mission.* Scottdale, PA: Herald, 1984.

Sherratt, Timothy. "Rehabilitating the State in America: Abraham Kuyper's Over-looked Contribution." In *On Kuyper: A Collection of Readings on the Life, Work and Legacy of Abraham Kuyper,* edited by Steve Bishop and John H. Kok, 383-403. Sioux Center, IA: Dordt College Press, 2013.

Simon-Netto, Uwe. *The Fabricated Luther: Refuting Nazi Connections and Other Modern Myths.* 2nd ed. St. Louis: Concordia, 1995, 2007.

Sire, James. *How to Read Slowly: Reading for Comprehension.* Downers Grove, IL: InterVarsity Press, 1978.

———. *Naming the Elephant: Worldview as a Concept.* Downers Grove, IL: InterVarsity Press, 2004.

———. *The Universe Next Door.* 4th ed. Downers Grove, IL: InterVarsity Press, 2004.

Skillen, James W. "The Development of Calvinistic Political Theory in the Nether-lands, with Special Reference to the Thought of Herman Dooyeweerd." PhD diss., Duke University, 1993.

———. "*E Pluribus Unum* and Faith-Based Welfare Reform: A Kuyperian Moment for the Church in God's World." In *On Kuyper: A Collection of Readings on the Life, Work and Legacy of Abraham Kuyper,* edited by Steve Bishop and John H. Kok, 405-18. Sioux Center, IA: Dordt College Press, 2013.

Smend, Rudolph. "Kuenen and Wellhausen." In Peter W. Dirksen and Aard W. van der Kooij, eds., *Abraham Kuenen (1828–1891): His Major Contributions to the Study of the Old Testament: A Collection of Old Testament Studies Published on the Occasion of the Centenary of Abraham Kuenen's Death (10 December 1991),* 113-27. Oudtes-tamentische Studiën 29. Leiden: Brill, 1993.

———. "The Work of Abraham Kuenen and Julius Wellhausen." In Magne Sæbø, ed., *Hebrew Bible / Old Testament. III/1 The Nineteenth Century,* 424-53. Göttingen: Vandenhoeck & Ruprecht, 2013.

Smith, Adam. *The Wealth of the Nations.* Oxford: Oxford University Press, 1993.

Smith, David W. *Transforming the World? The Social Impact of British Evangelicalism.* Carlisle, UK: Paternoster, 1998.

Smith, James K. A. *You Are What You Love: The Spiritual Power of Habit.* Grand Rapids: Brazos, 2016.

Snow, D. "On the Presumed Fragility of Unconventional Beliefs." *Journal for the Scien-tific Study of Religion* 21 (1982): 15-26.

Sparks, Allister. *First Drafts: South African History in the Making.* Johannesburg and Cape Town: Jonathan Ball, 2009.

————. *Tomorrow Is Another Country: The Inside Story of South Africa's Negotiated Revolution.* Wynberg, Cape Town, Struik: 1994.

Springer, Michael S. *Restoring Christ's Church: John a Lasco and the Forma ac ratio.* Aldershot, UK: Ashgate, 2007.

Spykman, Gordon J. *Christian Faith in Focus.* Jordan Station, ON: Paideia, 1992.

————. *Reformational Theology: A New Paradigm for Doing Dogmatics.* Grand Rapids: Eerdmans, 1992.

Stahl, Friedrich Julius. *The Philosophy of Law.* Translated by Ruben Alvarado. Aalten, Netherlands: Wordbridge, 2007.

Staub, Dick. *The Culturally Savvy Christian: A Manifesto for Deepening Faith and Enriching Popular Culture in an Age of Christianity-Lite.* San Francisco, CA: Jossey-Bass, 2008.

Steiner, George. *Lessons of the Masters.* Cambridge, MA: Harvard University Press, 2003.

Steinmetz, David. *Luther in Context.* 2nd ed. Grand Rapids: Baker Academic, 1995, 2002.

Stephens, W. P., ed. *The Bible, the Reformation and the Church: Essays in Honour of James Atkinson.* Journal for the Study of the New Testatment Supplement 105. Sheffield: Sheffield Academic Press, 1995.

Stiglitz, Joseph E. *Making Globalization Work.* New York: Norton, 2006.

Storkey, Alan. "The Bible's Politics." In *Witness to the World,* edited by David Peterson. Carlisle, UK: Paternoster, 1999.

————. *Jesus and Politics: Confronting the Powers.* Grand Rapids: Baker Academic, 2005.

Stott, John. *Christian Mission in the Modern World.* Downers Grove, IL: InterVarsity Press, 2008.

————. *The Contemporary Christian: An Urgent Plea for Double Listening.* Leicester, UK: Inter-Varsity Press, 1992.

Strauss, D. F. M. *Philosophy: Discipline of the Disciplines.* Grand Rapids: Paideia, 2009.

Swenson, R. A. *Margin.* Colorado Springs: NavPress, 1992.

Tenzythoff, Gerrit J. *Sources of Secession: The Netherlands Hervormde Kerk on the Eve of the Dutch Immigration to the Midwest.* Historical Series of the Reformed Church in America 17. Grand Rapids: Eerdmans, 1987.

Thielicke, Helmut. *The Evangelical Faith.* Vol. 2, *The Doctrine of God and of Christ.* Translated by Geoffrey W. Bromiley. Grand Rapids: Eerdmans, 1977.

Thiselton, Anthony C. *The Hermeneutics of Doctrine.* Grand Rapids: Eerdmans, 2007.

Tracy, David. *Blessed Rage for Order: The New Pluralism in Theology.* Chicago: University of Chicago Press, 1975, 1996.

Trimp, C. *De Volmacht Tot Bedieniug Der Verzoening.* 2nd ed. Groningen: De Vuurbaak, 1970.

Troelstch, Ernst. *Social Teaching of the Christian Churches*. Louisville: Westminister John Knox, 1992.

Turretin, Francis. *Institutes of Elenctic Theology*. Translated by George M. Giver. 3 vols. Phillipsburg, NJ: P&R, 1997.

VanDrunen, David. *Living in God's Two Kingdoms*. Wheaton, IL: Crossway, 2010.

———. *Natural Law and the Two Kingdoms: A Study in the Development of Reformed Social Thought*. Emory University Studies in Law and Tradition. Grand Rapids: Eerdmans, 2010.

Van Dyke, Harry. "Abraham Kuyper: Heir of an Anti-Revolutionary Tradition." In *On Kuyper: A Collection of Readings on the Life, Work and Legacy of Abraham Kuyper*, edited by Steve Bishop and John H. Kok, 7-26. Sioux Center, IA: Dordt College Press, 2013.

Veenhof, Jan. *Nature and Grace in Herman Bavinck*. Translated by Al Wolters. Sioux Center, IA: Dordt College Press, 2006.

Veith, Gene. "Two Kingdoms Under One King: Towards a Lutheran Approach to Culture." In Menuge, *Christ and Culture in Dialogue*, 129-44.

Velema, W. H. *De leer van de Heilige Geest by Abraham Kuyper*. The Hague: Van Keulen, 1957.

Verburg, Marcel E. *Herman Dooyeweerd: The Life and Work of a Christian Philosopher*. Translated by Harry Van Dyke. Grand Rapids: Paideia, 2009.

Verkuyl, Johannes. *Break Down the Walls: A Christian Cry for Racial Justice*. Translated by Lewis B. Smedes. Grand Rapids: Eerdmans, 1973.

———. *Contemporary Missiology: An Introduction*. Translated by Dale Cooper. Grand Rapids: Eerdmans, 1978.

Vial, Theodore. *Schleiermacher: A Guide for the Perplexed*. Guides for the Perplexed. London: Bloomsbury, 2013.

Visser, Paul. *Heart for the Gospel, Heart for the World: The Life and Thought of a Reformed Pioneer Missiologist Johan Herman Bavinck (1895–1964)*. Translated by Jerry Gort. Eugene, OR: Wipf & Stock, 2003.

Vree, Jasper. *Abraham Kuyper's "Commentatio" (1860): The Young Kuyper About Calvin, a Lasco, and the Church*. 2 vols. Leiden: Brill, 2005.

Wagenman, Michael. "A Critical Analysis of the Power of the Church in the Ecclesiology of Abraham Kuyper." PhD diss., University of Bristol, 2014.

Wagner, Tamara S., ed. *Charlotte Yonge: Reading Domestic Religious Fiction*. Abingdon, Oxford: Routledge, 2012.

Walker, Andrew. *Telling the Story: Gospel, Mission, Culture*. London: SPCK, 1996.

Walsh, Brian J., and J. Richard Middleton. *The Transforming Vision: Shaping a Christian*

Worldview. Downers Grove, IL: InterVarsity Press, 1984.

Wannenwetsch, Berndt. "Luther's Moral Theology." In Donald K. McKim, ed., *The Cambridge Companion to Martin Luther*, 120-35. Cambridge: Cambridge University Press, 2003.

Warneck, Gustaf. *Das Studium der Mission auf der Universität*. Gütersloh: C. Bertelsmann, 1877.

Warren, Max. *I Believe in the Great Commission*. Grand Rapids: Eerdmans, 1976.

Webber, Robert. *The Church in the World: Opposition, Tension, or Transformation?* Grand Rapids: Zondervan, 1994.

Weber, Max. *The Vocation Lectures*. Translated by Rodney Livingstone. Edited by David Owen. New York: Hackett, 2004.

———. "Wissenschaft als Beruf." In *Gesammlte Aufsaetze zur Wissenschaftslehre*, 524-55. Munich: Duncker & Humblodt, 1919. Translation online at www.wisdom .weizmann.ac.il/~oded/X/WeberScienceVocation.pdf.

Weigel, George. *The End and the Beginning: Pope John Paul II—The Victory of Freedom, The Last Years, The Legacy*. New York: Image, 2010.

Welsh, David. *The Rise and Fall of Apartheid*. Johannesburg and Cape Town: Jonathan Ball, 2009.

Wentsel, B. *Natuur en Genade: Een introductie in en confrontatie met de jongste onwikkelingen in de Rooms-Katholieke theologie inzake dit thema*. Kampen: Kok, 1970.

Westermann, Claus. *Blessing in the Bible and the Life of the Church*. Minneapolis: Fortress, 1978.

———. *Genesis 1–11: A Commentary*. Translated by John J. Scullion. Minneapolis: Augsburg, 1984.

Wilder, A. N. "Preface." In *The Kingdom of God in 20th Century Interpretation*, vii-x. Peabody, MA: Hendrickson, 1987.

Wilken, Robert L. *The Spirit of Early Christian Thought: Seeking the Face of God*. New Haven, CT: Yale University Press, 2003.

Witte, John, Jr. *God's Joust, God's Justice*. Grand Rapids: Eerdmans, 2006.

Wivel, Klaus. *The Last Supper: The Plight of Christians in Arab Lands*. Translated by Mark Kline. New York: New Vessel Press, 2016.

Wolters, Albert M. *Creation Regained: Biblical Basics for a Reformational Worldview*. 2nd ed. Grand Rapids: Eerdmans, 2005.

———. "Dutch Neo-Calvinism: Worldview, Philosophy and Rationality." In H. Hart, J. van der Hoeven, and Nicholas Wolterstorff, eds., *Rationality in the Calvinian Tradition*, 113-31. Toronto: University Press of America, 1983.

———. "Glossary." In L. Kalsbeek, *Contours of a Christian Philosophy: An Introduction to Herman Dooyeweerd's Thought*, 346-54. Amsterdam: Buijten and Schipperheijn, 1975.

———. "The Intellectual Milieu of Herman Dooyeweerd." In *The Legacy of Herman Dooyeweerd: Reflections on Critical Philosophy in the Christian Tradition*, edited by Carl T. McIntire, 1-20. Lanham, MD: University Press of America, 1985.

———. "Nature and Grace in the Interpretation of Proverbs 31:10-31." *CTJ* 19 (1984): 153-66.

———. "The Nature of Fundamentalism." *Pro Rege*, September 1986, 2-9.

Wolterstorff, Nicholas. "Introduction." In Plantinga and Wolterstorff, eds., *Faith and Rationality: Reason and Belief in God*, 1-15. Notre Dame, IN: University of Notre Dame Press, 1983.

———. *Reason Within the Bounds of Religion*. Grand Rapids: Eerdmans, 1976.

———. *Until Justice and Peace Embrace*. Grand Rapids: Eerdmans, 1983.

Wood, John H. *Going Dutch in the Modern Age: Abraham Kuyper's Struggle for a Free Church in the Nineteenth-Century Netherlands Century*. New York: Oxford University Press, 2013.

Woudenberg, René van. "Two Very Different Analyses of Knowledge." In John H. Kok, ed., *Ways of Knowing in Concert*, 101-23. Sioux Center, IA: Dordt College Press, 2005.

Wright, Christopher J. H. *The Mission of God: Unlocking the Bible's Grand Narrative*. Downers Grove, IL: InterVarsity Press, 2006.

Wright, N. T. *The Climax of the Covenant: Christ and the Law in Pauline Theology*. Edinburgh: T&T Clark, 1991.

———. *Jesus and the Victory of God*. Christian Origins and the Question of God 2. Minneapolis: Fortress, 1996.

———. *The New Testament and the People of God*. Christian Origins and the Question of God 1. Minneapolis: Fortress, 1992.

Wright, N. T., and Marcus Borg. *The Meaning of Jesus*. London: SPCK: 1999.

Wright, William J. *Martin Luther's Understanding of God's Two Kingdoms: A Response to the Challenge of Skepticism*. Texts and Studies in Reformation and Post-Reformation Thought. Grand Rapids: Baker Academic, 2010.

Yates, Timothy. *Christian Mission in the Twentieth Century*. Cambridge: Cambridge University Press, 1994.

Yinger, Kent L. *The New Perspective on Paul: An Introduction*. Eugene, OR: Cascade Books, 2011.

Yonge, Charlotte M. "Authorship." *The Monthly Packet* (September 1892). Available at http://community.dur.ac.uk/c.e.schultze/index.html.

———. *The Heir of Redclyffe*. Wordsworth Classics. Ware, UK: Wordsworth Editions, 1998.

———. *John Keble's Parishes: A History of Hursley and Otterbourne*. 1898.

Zahrnt, Heinz. *The Question of God: Protestant Theology in the Twentieth Century*. Translated by R. A. Wilson. London: Collins, 1969.

Zaleski, Philip, and Carol Zaleski. *The Fellowship: The Literary Lives of the Inklings: J. R. R. Tolkien, C. S. Lewis, Owen Barfield, Charles Williams*. New York: Farrar, Straus and Giroux, 2015.

Zanden, Jan L. van, and Arthur van Riel. *The Strictures of Inheritance: The Dutch Economy in the Nineteenth Century*. Translated by Ian Cressie. Princeton, NJ: Princeton University Press, 2004.

Zuidema, S. U. *Communication and Confrontation*. Toronto: Wedge, 1972.

Zulu, Paulus. *A Nation in Crisis: An Appeal for Morality*. Cape Town: Tafelberg, 2013.

Zwaanstra, Henry. "Abraham Kuyper's Conception of the Church." *CTJ* 9 (1974): 149-81.

Zylstra, Bernard. "Preface to Runner." In H. Evan Runner, *The Relation of the Bible to Learning*. Jordan Station, ON: Paideia, 1982.

AUTHOR INDEX

SUBJECT INDEX

Finding the Textbook You Need

The IVP Academic Textbook Selector
is an online tool for instantly finding the IVP books
suitable for over 250 courses across 24 disciplines.

ivpacademic.com